LEGACIES OF THE PORTUGUESE COLONIAL EMPIRE

LEGACIES OF THE PORTUGUESE COLONIAL EMPIRE

Nationalism Citizenship and Popular Culture

Edited by
Elsa Peralta and Nuno Domingos

BLOOMSBURY ACADEMIC
LONDON • NEW YORK • OXFORD • NEW DELHI • SYDNEY

BLOOMSBURY ACADEMIC
Bloomsbury Publishing Plc
50 Bedford Square, London, WC1B 3DP, UK
1385 Broadway, New York, NY 10018, USA
29 Earlsfort Terrace, Dublin 2, Ireland

BLOOMSBURY, BLOOMSBURY ACADEMIC and the Diana logo are trademarks of
Bloomsbury Publishing Plc

First published in Great Britain 2023
This paperback edition published 2025

Copyright © Elsa Peralta and Nuno Domingos, 2023

Elsa Peralta and Nuno Domingos have asserted their right under the Copyright, Designs
and Patents Act, 1988, to be identified as Editors of this work.

This book was financed by Portuguese national funds through FCT – Foundation for Science
and Technology, I.P., under Projects PTDC/CPC-CMP/2661/2014 and UIDB/00509/2020.

Cover image: © Carina Augusto / Alamy Stock Photo

Bloomsbury Publishing Plc does not have any control over, or responsibility for, any
third-party websites referred to or in this book. All internet addresses given in this
book were correct at the time of going to press. The author and publisher regret any
inconvenience caused if addresses have changed or sites have ceased to exist,
but can accept no responsibility for any such changes.

Every effort has been made to trace the copyright holders and obtain permission to
reproduce the copyright material. Please do get in touch with any enquiries or
any information relating to such material or the rights holder. We would be pleased to
rectify any omissions in subsequent editions of this publication should they
be drawn to our attention.

A catalogue record for this book is available from the British Library.

A catalog record for this book is available from the Library of Congress.

ISBN: HB: 978-1-3502-8977-2
PB: 978-1-3502-8978-9
ePDF: 978-1-3502-8979-6
eBook: 978-1-3502-8980-2

Typeset by Newgen KnowledgeWorks Pvt. Ltd., Chennai, India

To find out more about our authors and books visit www.bloomsbury.com
and sign up for our newsletters.

CONTENTS

List of Figures	vii
Foreword	viii
Colonial Legacies in Comparative Perspective: A View from Portugal	
Benoît de L'Estoile	
Acknowledgments	xvii

Chapter 1
PORTUGAL'S COLONIAL LEGACIES AND THE (DIS)CONTINUITIES OF
THE COLONIAL PAST IN THE PRESENT   1
    Elsa Peralta and Nuno Domingos

Part I
EMPIRE, NATION, AND MEMORY POLITICS

Chapter 2
MEMORY OF THE EMPIRE AND SPACE OF CELEBRATION: THE CASE
OF THE BELÉM DISTRICT IN LISBON   27
    Elsa Peralta

Chapter 3
NARRATIVES OF TRANSITION AND THE INSTITUTIONALIZATION OF
PORTUGUESE COLONIAL HISTORY: BIOGRAPHY AND
AESTHETIZATION   45
    Nuno Domingos

Chapter 4
LISBON IS BEING REDISCOVERED: THE GOVERNANCE OF CULTURAL
DIVERSITY IN THE POSTCOLONIAL CITY   63
    Nuno Oliveira

Part II
POSTCOLONIAL SPACE, WORK, AND CITIZENSHIP

Chapter 5
GHOSTS OF COLONIALISM IN THE POSTIMPERIAL CITY: A HISTORY
OF INFORMAL SETTLEMENTS IN LISBON, 1970S–2010S   83
    Eduardo Ascensão

Chapter 6
THE USES AND RESISTANCES OF CAPE VERDEAN CREOLE IN THE
MIGRATORY CONTEXT OF THE POSTCOLONIAL CITY　　107
　　Ana Estevens

Chapter 7
DESIGNING SUBORDINATION: A COMPARATIVE SOCIAL HISTORY OF
PAID DOMESTIC WORK IN PORTUGAL　　125
　　Nuno Dias

Chapter 8
BRAZILIAN MIGRATION IN LISBON: PLACE, WORK, AND COLONIAL
REPRESENTATIONS　　143
　　Simone Frangella

Part III
POPULAR CULTURE AND EVERYDAY COLONIAL LEGACIES

Chapter 9
DIASPORA IDENTITIES, COSMOPOLITANISM, AND THE PROMISE
OF CITIZENSHIP: LUSOPHONY THROUGH THE MUSIC OF AFRICAN
DIASPORAS　　163
　　Rui Cidra

Chapter 10
COLONIAL REVIVALISM AND THE BESTSELLING PUBLISHING　　181
　　João Pedro George

Chapter 11
EMBRACING POSTCOLONIAL DIVERSITY? MUSIC SELECTION AND
AFFECTIVE FORMATION IN TAP AIR PORTUGAL'S IN-FLIGHT
ENTERTAINMENT SYSTEM　　199
　　Bart Paul Vanspauwen and Iñigo Sánchez-Fuarros

Chapter 12
NEW LISBON: MUSICAL HYBRIDISMS AND THE REINVENTION OF A
POSTCOLONIAL CITY　　219
　　Marcos Cardão

AFTERWORD: OUTLINE OF A RESEARCH APPROACH TO COLONIAL
　　LEGACIES　　239
　　Nuno Domingos and Elsa Peralta

List of Contributors　　247
Index　　251

FIGURES

5.1	The Quinta da Holandesa settlement near the central area of Areeiro, 1999	84
5.2	Felícia and her daughter by their house, 2008	87
5.3	Residents gather by the collective well, before a makeshift water provision was installed, c. 1990	89
5.4	Forty-four of the fifty most-populated informal settlements in the Lisbon Metropolitan Area, by nationality of the head of the household	93
5.5	The day of an initiative for an electoral information campaign, c. 1991	96
5.6	A policeman looks over a contested demolition and the resulting space, 2008	99
5.7	GIS representation of the PER's population fluxes between informal settlements and housing estates	101
11.1	Album covers of the disks distributed on TAP flights	203
11.2	Video stills from the official music video of "De Braços Abertos"	204
11.3	"Can you hear the fado?"	210
11.4	Video stills from different onboard promotional performances by Lusophone artists	211

FOREWORD

Colonial Legacies in Comparative Perspective: A View from Portugal

Benoît de L'Estoile

After visiting the Monastery of the Jerónimos or the Tower of Belém along the Tagus River in Lisbon—two luxuriant examples of Manueline architecture built in the early sixteenth century in the wake of Portuguese expansion overseas—tourists and locals throng the traditional pastry house Pastéis de Belém to savor its famous custard tarts; on every table, cinnamon is available to pepper the *pastéis*. This gesture commemorates the quest of Portuguese sailors conquering the maritime road to India to bring back to Europe coveted spices such as *Cinnamomum verum*, originally from Sri Lanka. On leaving the pastelaria, visitors may stroll in the nearby Tropical Botanical Garden, formerly Colonial Garden, created in 1906 to host species originating from the Portuguese colonies on various continents. Cinnamon, as well as coffee, chocolate, tea, and sugar, has been so much part of European daily life for centuries that we fail to perceive them as colonial legacies, together with various other materialities—architectural, botanical, and gastronomical.

The present volume offers a welcome critical take on the conspicuous, although sometimes unacknowledged, presence of imperial legacies in various areas of today's Portugal—music, language, work relationships, urban policies, migration, cultural diversity, memory, history and popular culture —, be it in central historical neighborhoods, the shantytowns of Lisbon's periphery, or the airplanes of Portuguese national airlines.

As stated in the introductory chapter to the volume, Elsa Peralta, Nuno Domingos, and other contributors have creatively appropriated a research program on "colonial legacies," which I outlined more than a decade ago. Back then, drawing on Malinowski's insight to study "the past as it lives now," I called for developing an "anthropology of colonial legacies," inviting an exploration of the multiple forms, conscious or not, in which the colonial past is part of our present. I ended my essay expressing the hope that a research program on "colonial legacies" could "open up fruitful avenues for inquiry on 'the past as it lives now,' including ... comparative research on the various ways of dealing with colonial legacies, in former imperial capitals or in former colonial peripheries" (de L'Estoile 2008: 277). This book, of which most chapters focus on Greater Lisbon, offers a substantial contribution to such a research program. It is beyond the scope of a foreword to undertake such an analysis, but I would like to highlight how the Portuguese case offers a privileged instance to study "colonial legacies" in a comparative perspective.

The Past in the Present: Colonial Memories or Legacies?

I am grateful to the editors of this volume for this opportunity to revisit the notion of "colonial legacies." In common parlance, "colonial legacy" is associated primarily with negative traits (such as racist violence, stereotypes, and prejudices) and is used to denounce the persistent remains of colonialism in the present. Thus, Zimmerer (2015) points out "the problem of confronting Germany's colonial legacy" in relation to the issue of recognizing genocide against the Herero and Nama in Namibia. "Colonial legacy" is indeed often used (in the singular form) as a "target notion," that is, as a tool aimed at identifying a pathological or undesirable feature with a view to uprooting it. It is thus often associated with a call to "decolonize" (museums, urbanism, diplomacy, knowledge, street names, etc.). While such use may make sense politically as a tool to denounce unwelcome continuities, it, however, severely restrains the analytical potential of the notion. In the first volume of *History of Sexuality* ([1976] 1979), Michel Foucault, instead of focusing on the repressive (negative) dimension of power, invited us to be on the lookout for its productive effects. Similarly, we need to pay attention not only to colonial violence and processes of appropriation but also to the productive dimension of colonial legacies. Of course, it is not a matter of falling back to the hackneyed issue of the positive or negative effects of colonization in terms of a balance sheet, or of an evaluation from a moral perspective, but rather of developing an analysis of the scope and diversity of what has been "produced" by colonial interactions, both in former colonial territories and in former metropolitan centers.

Many scholars have approached the study of the past in the present under the label of "colonial memories." In a previous book, Elsa Peralta (2017) proposed a fine analysis of "the place of the imperial past" in the city of Lisbon, largely built around the notion of memory. Despite the richness of such works, the semantic field of "legacy" offers a wider heuristic potential than the field of "memory." "Colonial memory" refers to a specific kind of "collective memory," a form of "collective representation" in the Durkheimian sense, associated with a distinctive social grouping (Halbwachs 1992). This notion, however, suffers from limitations. First, it tends to project the characteristics of the individual psyche on to an essentialized "collective mind." "Colonial memory" then typically triggers a number of associated terms belonging to the semantic field of psychology or psychoanalysis, such as forgetting, denegation, amnesia, repression, and so on.[1] While some scholars have seriously tackled the challenges in exploring the interactions between individual and collective memories (for colonial memories in Portugal see Dos Santos 2022), the field of investigation has often been restrained to the sphere of public discourses and representations. Second, this notion, originating in the academic field, has been reappropriated in public discourse, loaded with affective and normative aspects (for instance, when one speaks of a "duty of memory") leading to forms of blurring. For the sake of clarification, I suggest that we refrain from using "memory" as an analytical category, focusing instead on exploring how it is used as a "native" category by various actors in different situations. Finally, as a noun, "memory" focuses more on a (collective) state of mind than on the processes that shape it; part of what is called "memory" could be more fruitfully analyzed as "commemoration" or "remembering practices," thus highlighting issues of process, agency, and visibility.

In my original paper, I insisted on "the indeterminate, open character of the 'legacy.'" Inviting scholars to explore to the full the potential of the metaphor, I stressed the variety of perceptions and emotions it elicited:

> Legacies are not simply "handed down"; they are often claimed and negotiated, but also repudiated, selectively accepted, falsified or challenged. They involve various feelings, nostalgia and jealousy, remembering and forgetting, gratitude or bitterness. They may elicit contestation and negotiation, struggle for recognition and suspicions of illegitimacy. A legacy creates relationships (sometimes quite conflicting) between the various potential heirs: legacy at the same time divides and relates, as suggested by the double meaning of *share*, to divide and to have in common. (de L'Estoile 2008: 270; original emphasis)

After independence, several countries chose new names, often associated with precolonial kingdoms, to mark a break with the colonial past. However, most postindependence nation-states can be described as colonial legacies: of course, not because they would lack precolonial history but because, most of the time, their territorial formation, as well as population, language(s), political and cultural institutions, and so on, has been decisively shaped by colonial experiences and interactions.

The notion of colonial legacies thus opens more perspectives for inquiry than colonial memories. Notably, it suggests including a focus on material culture, on flows of people and goods, and also on so-called immaterial elements such as language, music, food, cultural performances, aesthetics, institutions, legal norms, emotions, and so on. It also involves a reflexive questioning of the very categories with which we try to order and make sense of the world we live in, which often are themselves colonial legacies. Thus, the very notion of "heritage" is often a colonial legacy, which has been reappropriated by postindependence nation-states, with varying degrees of continuity (see, e.g., Roussillon [2010] on Morocco).

Peralta and Domingos stress the historicity of colonial legacies and their transformations across time and space. Indeed, colonial legacies appear more or less salient in different contexts and at different times. Thus, in 2014, German artist Philip Kojo Metz installed in front of the German Historical Museum of Berlin his sculpture "The invisible hero," a vacant pedestal meant to be "a memorial for the Cameroonian soldiers who died in the First World War for the German fatherland." By setting up a conspicuous vacancy, he called attention to an historical episode that had remained completely invisible in the public space and historiography.

Similarly, at the University of Oxford, a statue of the late-nineteenth-century diamond magnate Cecil Rhodes on the street facade of Oriel College, which for decades had been barely noticed by college students, fellows, and visitors, was literally made salient in 2016 by the "Rhodes must fall" movement (Beinart 2019). Conversely, each fall since 2002, in early September in Paris, Saint-Germain-des-Prés becomes a meeting point for an international tribal art fair, called "Parcours des Mondes," attracting galleries and collectors from Europe, the United States, and Australia. While several impressive artifacts are displayed as masterworks, especially the most prestigious ones, they were collected in colonial situations, and the very category of "primitive art" is still used by some galleries. The absence of any explicit reference to colonialism is striking; the occasional mention that an artifact was brought back by an officer, or a colonial administrator, serves but as proof of its "authenticity." In other words, such an event is *not* recognized by its participants as being a colonial legacy. This suggests a research question: which colonial legacies are visible or not and at what time? Among the various colonial legacies, conscious or unconscious, which are the ones that, at a given moment, are recognized as salient or "problematic"? And who are the actors involved in these processes?

In recent years, various individual and collective initiatives endeavored to make colonial legacies more visible in the urban landscape. Thus, a *Historical Guide to an African Lisbon*, highlighting the ancient African presence in Portugal's capital, was recently published in English and Portuguese (Castro Henriques 2021). The Musée pour l'histoire de l'immigration produced a booklet on traces of colonial history in the 12th arrondissement in Paris, where it is located, pointing out street names, architecture, and statues. In Berlin, "decolonial city tours" in German and English are organized in the "African quarter," with the stated aim to "uncover the hidden history of colonialism."[2] A similar "decolonial tour" is also organized in Oxford by students. Such initiatives constitute alternative readings of the public space, modifying the perception of the past in the present by making colonial legacies visible. The colonial past is also made present through images. Thus, Paul Gilroy published *Black Britain: A Photographic History* (2007), a book of photographs explicitly meant to make visible the place of people from African descent in Great Britain, yesterday and today;[3] analogous books have been published in France. Other initiatives such as Facebook pages or websites serve similar purposes.

Colonial legacies (in the plural form) are not univocal, but plural and contradictory, reflecting the complex and contradictory character of the forms of colonial relationship themselves and of the various ways they have been appropriated (or not) subsequently. They are not received passively, but their meaning is actively reinterpreted and renegotiated according to situations. Far from aiming at an inventory of "colonial legacies" in order to eliminate them, the challenge for scholars is to seek to understand the ways in which colonial legacies, both in Europe and in the former colonial dependencies, crucially shape today the modalities of relations and conceptions of self and other, and the ways in which people confront and negotiate them.

Decentering Colonial Legacies: A Peripheral Empire

Near the historical city of Coimbra, a highly popular theme park, called Portugal dos Pequenitos (Portugal of the little ones), offers a miniature summary of Portuguese monuments and original features. Designed by a personal friend of Salazar, the head of the Estado Novo regime, it opened in 1940 as a village of typical regional houses; it was expanded in the 1950s, in conformation with the late colonial affirmation that the "Overseas Provinces" were as much a part of the country as the peninsular ones (Thomaz 2005): thus, along with replicas of the Tower of Belém or the royal castle of Sintra, the Mozambique Pavilion reproduces a Portuguese fortress, the India one a Hindu temple, and the Africa one statues of semi-naked warriors. This form of permanent colonial exhibition was meant to instill in children and their parents the myth that Portugal was in essence an imperial nation, encompassing the peninsular mainland, the islands (such as Madeira and Açores), and "overseas territories." This materialization of empire is still in place, perpetuating among Portuguese people the idea that the "Portuguese world" shares some kind of common destiny. In recent years, museums have become central places where the presence and visibility of colonial legacies have been hotly debated, prompting a wave of critical self-examination. In Lisbon, however, the recently opened Museum of the East (Museu do Oriente) epitomizes a form of nostalgia for Portugal's imperial past, lacking any critical confrontation with it; similarly, the project of a Museum of Discoveries, emerging from the project of a museum on Portuguese as a global language, attracted scholarly critiques for its uncritical ingenuity (Peralta, this volume). Such features suggest that the naturalization of colonial legacies may be stronger in Portugal than in other European countries.

While all of Europe has been involved in colonial relations, the duration of the colonial experience and its impact on national life have been highly differentiated. A specific feature of Portuguese colonial experience is that it lasted longer than in most European countries, from the conquest of Ceuta in Morocco in 1415 to the cession of Macau to China in 1997. This contrasts strongly with Germany, whose direct involvement in colonization was both very late (in the last quarter of the nineteenth century) and terminated early when its possessions were lost during the First World War. To take another case, Sweden's colonial experience was dual: directly over the Sami populations in the North, indirectly through the participation of Swedes in the colonial enterprise of Leopold's Congo Free State, or through missions. These variations account for different modalities of presence of colonial legacies in European countries. Thus, in Germany, for a long time, colonial history occupied a highly marginal place in the national narrative. While for obvious reasons the issue of public memory was saturated with the Nazi past, most Germans were ignoring the fact that their country had been a colonial power. In 2015, the National Museum of German History, in Berlin, explicitly thematized the relationship between the colonial past and the present in its exhibition titled "German Colonialism: Fragments Past and Present," hoping to "lead to the establishment of stable, long-term identities in the sense of contemporary global connections in Germany and in the former colonial territories" (Deutsches Historisches Museum 2015).

Compared with other European countries, Portugal's colonial past is still relatively recent. While Belgian, British, and French colonies in Africa had become formally independent by 1960, the wars of independence started in 1961, and Portuguese migrations to Africa continued well into the 1960s. While many poor Portuguese looked for a better future in the African colonies, where they could exchange subaltern positions at home for comparatively higher ones, others went to Brazil and, from the 1950s on, to Europe. The immigration from former Portuguese colonies in Africa started relatively late in comparison with France, Britain, or Belgium; in the 1970s, the majority of migrants from the colonies were the so-called *retornados* (returnees), who had been living in the African territories, sometimes for various generations, including mestizos and Goanese people. In the 1980s, Portugal, benefiting from its inclusion in the European community, became a labor market for Brazilians; while such a situation may be described as postcolonial, this feature is probably not salient for most Brazilian migrants.

Portugal was the only European empire that had for a time its capital moved to a colony: when Napoleon's armies invaded Portugal in 1807, the king fled to Brazil with his court, government, and national institutions. The singular place of Brazil also surfaces in the peculiar fact that the legitimizing discourse of the late colonial system, *Luso-tropicalism*, had been initially conceived in the 1930s as a national myth for the former colony by a Brazilian thinker, Gilberto Freyre, who became a sort of "organic intellectual" of the Portuguese empire (Thomaz 2002). The claimed exceptional character attributed to the Portuguese, derived from a supposedly more inclusive attitude, both by miscegenation and by incorporation of cultural elements from colonized populations, served to justify the continuation of colonial rule at a time when other European countries had given up most of their former colonial territories. The claim that one's own form of colonial rule is unique (and better than that of the others) is a self-justifying myth common to all colonial powers. Miguel Vale de Almeida (2002) pointed out, while cautioning against slipping into a form of "Portuguese exceptionalism," that it is essential to pay close attention to the specificities of postcolonial Portuguese experience. This dual concern leads to his suggestion regarding the use of the notion of "Grey Atlantic" (*Atlântico Pardo*), at the same time paying tribute to the idea of "Black Atlantic," coined by British cultural studies scholar Paul Gilroy, and explicitly trying to avoid the pitfall of mechanically importing concepts developed in and for the English-speaking world.

Because of academic geopolitics, most analytical frameworks available to think colonial and postcolonial situations are inscribed in specific imperial experiences, such as the US or British ones. As we have seen, while the various European colonial trajectories share generic features, each is also singular. While they provide heuristic questions and hypotheses, they may not be directly adequate to situations rooted in different histories, such as Belgium, France, Spain, or Portugal. A critical comparative perspective is thus an epistemic necessity to make sense of a case.

A crucial challenge is to make an effort to include within this dialogue discussions developed in other places and languages. In other words, the Portuguese case not only provides a "field" to test theories elaborated in English-speaking imperial and postimperial settings but also has the potential to contribute new perspectives to the study of colonial legacies.

While some contributions analyze the experience of migrants from the former empire (Brazil, Lusophone Africa), this volume is centered on Portugal; certainly, the experience of colonial legacies would be different if apprehended from Brazil, Goa, or Guinea-Bissau. Confronting points of view across the Atlantic was precisely the objective of various encounters between Brazilian and Portuguese scholars, interrogating shared legacies, and the content of terms such as "colonial" and "postcolonial" (Bastos, Vale de Almeida, and Feldman-Bianco 2002). They stressed the need to develop concepts and methodologies in dialogue with current international debates on colonialism and postcolonialism, while accounting for the specificities of Portuguese imperial experience. Portugal offers the fascinating paradox of being a peripheral empire: priding itself on being the first modern European empire, it was a poor country at the periphery of Europe, whose elites self-consciously struggled to enhance their status by mobilizing the empire. This is precisely what gives it a powerful potential for decentering more usual perspectives on colonialism and postcolonialism.

The issue of language appears here as a central topic in various chapters. Language is indeed one of the most important colonial legacies, as pointed out by Amílcar Cabral, the independentist leader of Cape Verde: "The Portuguese language is one of the best things that the Portuguese left us, because language is an instrument for people to relate to each other, a means to express the realities of life and the world" (Cabral [1969], quoted by Estevens in this volume). At about the same time, Algerian writer Kateb Yacine famously claimed that "the French language was and still is a war booty." Languages inherited from the colonial past constitute a common medium through which intellectuals, artists, writers, but also migrants, from former colonial peripheries and colonial metropoles, can argue, conflict, and exchange in a space of (partial) shared understandings. "Lusophony" is at the same time a shared medium and the basis for interstate political projects, like the Community of Portuguese Speaking Countries (CPLP), created in 1996, but also for consumption and personal appropriation.

Creole languages are fundamentally colonial legacies. They cannot be "unmade," because they are constitutive of individual and collective ways of being in the world. Such processes of linguistic and cultural appropriation are precisely what French Caribbean intellectuals Edouard Glissant and Patrick Chamoiseau (2009) call "politics of creolization," which consists of saying: "those riches belong to you, all languages belong to you" (2009: 27). A Caribbean perspective suggests that decolonizing cannot aim only at uprooting all "colonial legacies," because they are constitutive of our very being. Estevens's contribution in this chapter shows that the choice by young people of Cape Verdean origin raised in Lisbon to use Creole in their musical works is a performance of a specific identity. Such a case suggests several comparative enquiries: what are the specificities of postcolonial migrations in relation to language? In what ways is the status of Creole among Cape Verdeans in Lisbon's periphery different from the status of Portuguese among Lusitanian immigrants in France? Conversely, how does the fact that some migrants come from former Portuguese colonial territories whose official language is Portuguese affect their relationship with that language?

The various chapters in this volume suggest to what extent daily life is permeated with colonial legacies and how these are deeply ambivalent. As shown by Domingos, the universal celebration of the football player Eusébio (born in Mozambique and becoming in the 1960s a star of the Benfica football club in Lisbon) as a national figure repeats the colonial narrative of assimilation. Similarly, the celebration of Lisbon as a pluricultural and global city, with its vibrant musical scene animated by musicians originating from Africa or from the diaspora, echoes tropes of "Luso-tropicalism." The category of "Lusophone music," played on TAP (Portuguese Air Transportations) airplanes, has however been appropriated by musicians from Brazil and from Portuguese-speaking Africa.

* * *

Recognizing that our contemporary world is largely postcolonial urges upon us the necessity to confront colonial legacies in all their complexity. Focusing on the Portuguese case, the richness and timeliness of this volume invites readers to realize how much colonial legacies are constitutive of today's world, not only among the migrants of former colonized territories but also in urban infrastructures; flows of people, goods, and ideas; our knowledge and perception of the world; and the very tissue of our lives, much beyond what is explicit or conscious. Legacies can be reevaluated, and their meanings change over time, as they are reappropriated by different heirs. Uncertainty regards not only the present and the future but also the past: what was considered certain can become contested or unsettled. The present time is especially interesting in that respect, offering a rich field for future investigations. The peripheral Portuguese empire, challenging us to explore new paths to account for its complexity, has the potential to decenter what has largely become a stereotyped vision of colonialism and offer new insights on colonial legacies.

Notes

1 Thus, Stuart Hall evokes "the amnesia which has overtaken British popular memory of its long imperial past" (2007: 5).
2 https://www.dekolonialestadtfuehrung.de/. Similar bicycle tours are organized in Paris by the association Alter Natives, targeting descendants of migrants from former colonial territories.
3 Stuart Hall writes that "the legacy of that troubled past continues to influence the direction and destiny of the Black British diaspora" (2007: 5).

References

Bastos, C., M. Vale de Almeida, and B. Feldman-Bianco (eds.) (2002). *Trânsitos coloniais: Diálogos Críticos Luso-Brasileiros*. Lisbon: Imprensa de Ciências Sociais.
Beinart, W. (2019). "Rhodes Must Fall: The Uses of Historical Evidence in the Statue Debate in Oxford 2015-6." Paper for "Racialisation and Publicness in Africa and the African Diaspora," African Studies Centre conference, Oxford, June. https://oxfordandcolonialism.web.ox.ac.uk/article/rhodes-must-fall (accessed August 2022).
Castro Henriques, I. (2021). *Historical Guide to an African Lisbon*. Lisbon: Colibri.
de L'Estoile, B. (2008). "The Past As It Lives Now: An Anthropology of Colonial Legacies." *Social Anthropology/Anthropologie sociale*. "Colonial legacies," 16(3): 267-79.
Deutsches Historisches Museum (2015). *German Colonialism: Fragments Past and Present*. Exhibition, Berlin.
Dos Santos, I. (2022). "To Link Life Histories to Historical Narratives: The Place of 'Memory' in Post-1974 Portuguese Society." *Conserveries mémorielles* [Online], no. 25 http://journals.openedition.org/cm/5295.
Foucault, M. (1979 [1976]). *The History of Sexuality Volume 1: An Introduction*. London: Allen Lane.
Gilroy, P. (2007). *Black Britain: A Photographic History*. London: Saqi.
Glissant, É., and P. Chamoiseau (2009). "La créolisation et la persistance de l'esprit colonial." *Cahiers Sens public*, 2(10): 25-33.
Halbwachs, M. (1992). *On Collective Memory*. Chicago: University of Chicago Press.
Hall, S. (2007). Preface to Paul Gilroy, *Black Britain. A photographic history*, SAQI, pp. 5-10.
Peralta, E. (2017). *Lisboa e a Memória do Império: Património, Museus e Espaço Público*. Lisboa: Deriva.
Roussillon, A. (2010). "À propos de quelques paradoxes de l'appropriation identitaire du patrimoine." In R. Cattedra, P. Garret, C. Miller, and M. Volait (eds.), *Patrimoines en situation: Constructions et usages en différents contextes urbains: Exemples marocains, libanais, égyptien et suisse*. Beirut: Presses de l'Ifpo.
Thomaz, O. R. (2002). "Tigres de papel: Gilberto Freyre, Portugal e os países africanos de língua oficial portuguesa." In C. Bastos, M. Vale de Almeida, and B. Feldman-Bianco (eds.), *Transitos coloniais: Diálogos Críticos Luso-Brasileiros*, 45-70. Lisbon: Imprensa de Ciências Sociais.
Thomaz, O. R. (2005). "The Good-Hearted Portuguese People: Anthropology of Nation; Anthropology of Empire." In B. de L'Estoile, F. Neiburg, and L. Sigaud (eds.), *Empires, Nations and Natives: Anthropology and State-Making*, 58-87. Durham, NC: Duke University Press.
Vale de Almeida, M. (2002). "O Atlântico Pardo: Antropologia, Pós-colonialismo e o Caso 'Lusófono.'" In C. Bastos, M. Vale de Almeida, and B. Feldman-Bianco (eds.), *Transitos coloniais: Diálogos Críticos Luso-Brasileiros*, 23-38. Lisbon: Imprensa de Ciências Sociais.
Zimmerer, J. (2015). "The First Genocide of the 20th Century: On the Problems of Confronting Germany's Colonial Legacy." In A. Scriba (ed.) *German Colonialism: Fragments Past and Present*, 138-45. Berlin: Deutsches Historisches Museum.

ACKNOWLEDGMENTS

The editors of this volume acknowledge their appreciation for a number of people and institutions whose contributions have helped to make it happen. First, this book was produced under the project Portuguese Colonial Empire and Urban Popular Culture: Comparing Visions from the Metropolis and the Colonies (PTDC/CPC-CMP/2661/2014), funded by the Portuguese Foundation for Science and Technology (FCT), and was financed by Portuguese national funds through FCT – Foundation for Science and Technology, I.P., under Project UIDB/00509/2020. Our thanks also go to the Institute of Social Sciences and the Center for Comparative Studies of the Faculty of Arts and Humanities, both of the University of Lisbon, for financial and administrative support for the duration of the project and the production of the book.

We are grateful to Ana Estevens, Bart Paul Vanspauwen, Eduardo Ascensão, Iñigo Sánchez-Fuarros, João Pedro George, Marcos Cardão, Nuno Dias, Nuno Oliveira, Rui Cidra, and Simone Frangella for having contributed to this book. Their different disciplinary perspectives, together with their diverse research interests, have greatly contributed to a complexification. This has been a long-term collaboration, with chapters published mostly in Portuguese, which we now intend to make known to an international audience. This is specifically the case of the chapters by Ascensão, Dias, Frangella, Oliveira, and Peralta that were published in Portuguese—although they have been updated and reworked to include more recent dynamics—in *Cidade e Império: Dinâmicas coloniais e reconfigurações pós-coloniais* (edited by N. Domingos and E. Peralta; Lisbon: Edições, 2013).

A word of thanks also goes to Nélia Dias for her insights, inputs, and participation in the colloquium we organized at the Faculty of Arts and Humanities in 2019 on the topic of "colonial legacies." A special thank you also goes to Benoît de L'Estoile for writing the foreword of the book; his work has critically inspired this undertaking. His contribution will allow us to place the Portuguese case within the wider debates and conceptual queries about the range of colonial legacies in postcolonial Europe.

Heartfelt thanks also go to Jean Burrows, who undertook the task of the English-language revision of the book, for her careful and attentive work. Finally, we would like to thank Bloomsbury for the publication of this book, in particular, Rodhri Mogford and Laura Reeves for the way they monitored the whole process, and also the reviewers for their very positive contributions toward improving it.

Chapter 1

PORTUGAL'S COLONIAL LEGACIES AND THE (DIS)CONTINUITIES OF THE COLONIAL PAST IN THE PRESENT

Elsa Peralta and Nuno Domingos

Empire left indelible marks on European material, social, cultural, and symbolic landscapes, not only in those European countries that were former imperial power centers but also in Europe as a whole. Decolonization represented the end of colonial rule but did not efface imperial and colonial categories, mythologies, and embodied experiences and habits. Indeed, empires never entirely die; as structures of power and influence that span vast geographical spaces, empires may formally end, but they remain beyond the end of colonial rule through practices, subjectivities, and discourses. Nevertheless, empires are not pure, universal, abstract, or immutable and do not remain immune to historical and social change, political struggles, and contextual individual and collective strategies. Instead, the legacies of colonialism are drawn in an embattled social field and are mutually constituted by the uneven encounters between disparate social groups.

Placed in the wider scope of European colonial legacies, this book looks at the legacies of the Portuguese empire in today's Portugal, more than four decades after the empire came to an end. The case studies included in this volume look at a wide range of colonial legacies and at how they have been expressed, contested, appropriated, negotiated, and internalized in the social domain. These legacies feed on imperial fantasies and mythologies, persist in old colonial categories and racial classifications, and rearticulate the memories and myths of Portuguese national identity along a line of historical (dis)continuity brought about by the transition from the colonial to the postcolonial.

They are present in the commemorative spaces of the Portuguese capital city where the old imperial myths continue to be reproduced, especially those associated with the first voyages of "discovery" and the "golden age" of Portuguese maritime expansion. In the same vein, the myths of Portuguese colonial exceptionalism, asserted for decades by successive regimes, have been adapted to the globalizing languages and branding operations of Portugueseness, linked to tourism, commerce, and the purposes of the so-called economic diplomacy, thus facilitating the important commercial exchanges between Portugal and its former colonial territories. Colonial legacies are also expressed in postimperial modes of consumption, very much present in popular culture, in a growing publishing market of colonial nostalgia and in the consumption of "Lusophone" music and food, as well as in modes of postcolonial-chic consumption.

Finally, colonial legacies are alive within the citizenship relations with former colonial subjects, whether they are immigrants from former Portuguese colonies, imperial "returnees," or former combatants in Portugal's colonial wars. An analysis of the colonial legacies involves enquiring about the condition of these individuals and groups, who have changed Portugal's demography, the persistence of logics of social categorization and racial segregation inherited from the colonial past and that still operate today, often through categories that euphemize this power and hide situations of labor disqualification, social immobility, and poor housing conditions that affect a large part of the people originating from the former colonies and their descendants living in Portugal today. But this analysis also imposes a consideration of the multifarious ways by which these individuals and groups appropriate colonial categories, imperial representations, and social patterns of relations that are historically shaped, such as hierarchies of race, class, and gender. These patterns also include networks of interpersonal relations that they use to negotiate their own social place within the borders of citizenship and nationness or create with the aim of a better social insertion and for the development of basic livelihoods.

The Afterlife of European Empires

Empires, as well as the relations their existence has established, have affected the colonized as much as they have affected the colonizer. This issue is not new, and many academic studies have underlined the importance of connections across and between empires, the networks established between colonies, and the significance of power centers outside the metropolis.[1] By insisting on the importance of identifying the connections between people from different parts of the world, the power relations that exist between them, and the circuits of production, distribution, and consumption in which they lived, such studies sought to overcome the idealized metropolis/colony pairing by considering both within the same analytical framework (Stoler 1989; Cooper and Stoler 1997). This stimulates a need to bring empire "home." The colonial system was intrinsically related to the emergence of a global economic order based on unequal exchanges and to the role of the modern nation-state in establishing a racialized dual citizenship and shaping the structures of colonial domination on the ground. Indeed, the establishment of an unswerving dichotomy of relations between an exploitative imperial center and an exploited colonial periphery, along with an international division of labor, in which one part of the world supplied raw materials and cheap labor to the other part, was critical for the expansion of capitalist economies that were in need of investment, labor, and material resources for the profitable employment of surplus capital. As such, empire was intrinsic to the construction of European nation-states, imperial projects are part of the history and memory of Europe, and the categories of national and imperial are still deeply entangled (MacKenzie 1999; Thompson 2005; Hall and Rose 2006; Cooper 2014a).

Since empire did have a long-lasting impact on European societies, it is important to keep this connection between the metropolitan and the imperial, but with the aim of interpreting it in the postimperial European landscape. But the afterlife of empire is more than a mere transference of past colonial structures and worldviews to the postcolonial moment. These structures and worldviews went through several reworkings in order to fit the demands of the new world order established after the demise of European colonial empires following the Second World War. Decolonization, as much as colonialism, was a shared European project; ending empire and turning former European imperial powers into postimperial nation-states was as much a part of politics in Western Europe after 1945 as was building the institutional architecture of the European Community. Not only borders but also previous economic relations and citizenship rights had to be redesigned. The disappearance of the colonial empires caused a large movement of people (former colonizers as well as formerly colonized peoples) to head to Europe, while the European integration project encouraged the movement of citizens within the community (Laschi, Deplano, and Pes 2020).

In this changing context, former European imperial centers had to be imagined anew, and the whole of European colonial history had to be renegotiated. Most often, this was done on the basis of a memorial display that still placed empire at the center of national identity definitions (Buettner 2016), which also served as an instrument for the creation of new political constituencies from former imperial governance systems, such as the Commonwealth, Francophonie, and Lusofonia. Here, the negative connotations associated with the exploitative nature of empires are reformulated to appear beneficial to both the colonizers and the colonized and usually structured around ideas of cosmopolitanism, multiculturalism, and intercultural dialogue. In the meantime, global economic exchanges between former colonizers and colonized continue to be extremely unbalanced and exploitative. This construct points to both postcolonial and neocolonial directions. On one hand, it allows former European imperial centers to make the transition to postcolonial nations but without overturning the respective governing myths that stem from imperial history. On the other, it is shaped by rather paternalistic undertones as it discloses the ways in which the colonial expansionist enterprise continues to inform contemporary debates on cultural and social diversity. Such institutional traits deeply influenced the shape of European public spaces and the production of a collective memory of colonialism, something that is most evident in the former colonial metropoles. Their deeply ingrained character, both in policy and commonsense, have become obstacles for the development of a public debate on the legacies of colonialism in the postcolonial period, one that should be backed by systematic research both on the structure of colonial systems and on their manifold afterlives.

In an influential work, Benoît de L'Estoile (2008) conceived the various ways in which the colonial past persists after the demise of European empires as *colonial legacies*, which can be found both in Europe and in formerly colonized countries around the globe. While acknowledging the place of empire in the various

European, national, and shared memory cultures (Rothermund 2015), his concept of colonial legacies purposely goes beyond a mere notion of colonial memory to encompass a wider range of experiences that stem from a complex (and very often contested) set of colonial relations that are still present in the world today. In de L'Estoile's own words, the colonial past is

> embodied in material culture, in monuments, architecture, libraries, archives and museum collections, in alimentary diet, dress and music, but also in continuing flows of commodities, images and people. In perhaps less tangible but no less crucial ways, it shapes politics, economics, artistic and intellectual life, linguistic practices, forms of belonging or international relations. It informs the rhetoric and the categories mobilised when Europeans deal with migrants from other continents, define standards of good governance or conceive development projects, or when people outside Europe deal with European tourists, businessmen, NGO workers or anthropologists. (2008, 267)

The concept of "colonial legacies" thus encompasses a multiplicity of meanings and relationships that were inherited from the relations set under colonialism and have been differently reenacted, appropriated, negotiated, and contested in postcolonial times.

Colonial legacies are present in the public space, materialized in heritage and museums that harbor a representation of national identity very often associated with an imperial past. This is most expressive in former imperial cities whose urban landscapes are saturated with traces of collective memory (Boyer 1996) in their imaginative colonial geographies, in the imprint of exotic architectural styles, and in the monuments built to celebrate imperial triumphs and deeds. But traces of the imperial past can also be found in the social and material arrangements produced by empire, which have affected the industrial, commercial, and urban life as well as the political and social organization of the city space, where civil and political rights are unevenly distributed (King 1990; Jacobs 1996; Varma 2011; Peralta and Domingos 2019).

Colonialism still promotes ethnic, interracial, and class tensions stamped by the concepts of race, ethnicity, and difference inherited from colonial times (Lammert and Sarkowsky 2010), which frame persistent forms of labor exploitation and citizenship disqualification inherited from the colonial experience. These are converted into today's reshaping of the European political field, progressively defined by resurgent protectionism, nationalism, and xenophobia in Europe, which are often accompanied by outbursts of imperial nostalgia associated with the loss of imperial power and with the national decline in the context of wider economic and political arrangements (Lorcin 2013). Moreover, the global demographic change promoted by colonialism was not severed by decolonization. Large flows of people headed for former European metropolises after the collapse of empires, including thousands of repatriates from empire (e.g., Jordi 2003; Peralta 2021) and also numerous immigrants coming from erstwhile colonial domains (Panayi and Virdee 2011). Former colonial knowledge and categorizations are still present in daily interactions, among racialized populations but also among the repatriated colonial settlers whose feelings of resentment have in some cases been exploited by ideological agendas, as in the case of the *Pieds-Noirs* in France and their association with the far right (Eldridge 2010).

The persistence of these colonial relations can also be perceived in more banal ways in the daily life of the former metropolis, culinary practices, music, festivities, and worldviews, which, while often being reproduced within particular domestic spaces or social groups, are also deeply ingrained as part of a supposed national habitus inherited from the imperial past. These practices are increasingly attuned to the market of colonial nostalgia for the lost empire and for bygone colonial lifestyles. This is ever more present in a growing publishing market of colonial nostalgia and in the consumption of *world* music and food, as well as in modes of postcolonial-chic consumption, which reproduce a rather objectified cultural depiction associated with the lost empire.

Colonial legacies have historically taken many configurations. How they were reproduced, negotiated, and contested depended on the geopolitical position of the colonizing nation in the imperial power hierarchies and disputes; the respective model of colonial governance; the empire-specific processes of dominance, appropriation, and exchange operating within colonial societies; the particular way each decolonization process was conducted; and the political, social, and economic processes that defined the postcolonial situation. Only through empirically grounded research is it possible to access the several layers that comprise each specific national configuration and to do so without losing sight of the broader framework of European empires' structures and legacies. The aim of this book is, therefore, to place the Portuguese case in dialogue with other critical cases of European colonial legacies without, nonetheless, disregarding its own specificities. Portugal's relationship with its imperial past, the persistence of this past in the present, and its ensuing consequences for the relationship with postcolonial subjects have attracted growing attention from Portuguese academia.[2] But while this is an increasingly vibrant field of inquiry in Portugal, very much driven by a larger debate on identity politics and by the anti-racism activism that has recently broken out in Portuguese civil society, the Portuguese case is still poorly known outside Portugal and little mentioned in comparative studies on the matter. Through the publication in English of the work we have been developing in this area in close collaboration with several colleagues, we intend to contribute to reversing this situation, while at the same time aiming to establish a research agenda capable of articulating cultural criticism with the analysis of the social structures in which the colonial legacies and their multiple reconfigurations are grounded, reproduced, and contested.[3]

Portuguese Colonial Legacies

Although not widely known, some aspects of the Portuguese case highlight the specificity of its colonial legacies and make it particularly interesting for cross-analysis with other European cases. First, the Portuguese empire was the first and last European empire; it was the most enduring of all, spanning more than five centuries of history from its early stages. Because of Portugal's structural vulnerabilities related to the peripheral role of the country in Europe and its weaker geopolitical position in comparison with other European empires, this *longue-durée* has important implications in terms of the place of empire in the Portuguese national imagination. The relative importance of colonial possessions for Portugal compared with other European imperial centers is an inherent condition for the production of Portuguese nationalism. Empire is thus a key part of the structure of Portuguese nationalism, both past and present (Bethencourt 1999; Matos 2008; Sobral 2014).

Portuguese national imperialism was operated for centuries by intellectual and political elites, having become more apparent since the beginning of the nineteenth century when the liberal monarchy was established in the country. After the independence of Brazil in 1822, in particular, and afterward in the context of the Scramble for Africa by European powers, the perception that Portugal could not exist as an independent nation without its empire became strongly imbedded in Portuguese society (Alexandre 2005–6, 32). The African project took shape with the realization of the Berlin Conference (1884–5), when African territory was divided among the European powers. The idea that colonization would only be justified if it were carried out in such a way as to enhance the development of the colonial territories and if it were based on an effective colonization was gaining more and more weight on the international scene. Portugal, however, lacked the human, financial, and material resources to keep up with the race set in motion by the other European powers and had little political influence in the international context. The old alliance with England,[4] which since the seventeenth century had compensated for Portugal's political vulnerability (at the cost of its economic dependency), was now more uncertain, and a distrust of Portugal's traditional ally gradually grew, cementing Portugal's secondary and peripheral position in an industrialized Europe and the country's condition as a subordinate ally of the British Empire.

At this juncture, there was a growing concern about the future of the Portuguese colonial possessions, and an official discourse was woven around the emphatic reaffirmation of Portugal's "historical right" to possess overseas territories and the Christian design of "civilizing" the populations that lived therein. This claim was justified on the international stage by the fact that Portugal was the pioneer of European maritime explorations, with the first voyages of the Discoveries started in the fifteenth century by Portuguese navigators (Alexandre 2005/2006: 32). Portuguese ambitions were put forward in the famous Pink Map (also known as the Rose-Coloured Map) that Portugal presented at the Berlin Conference. The project consisted in claiming Portuguese sovereignty and effective occupation of all territory between Angola and Mozambique, ensuring land communication between the two colonies and thus facilitating trade and transport of goods. The Portuguese ambitions were, however, thwarted by Great Britain which, in 1890, ordered the Lisbon government to retreat under threat of a break in diplomatic relations and possible military reprisals. Faced with the British Ultimatum, the Lisbon government backed down, and the idea immediately spread that Great Britain had betrayed Portugal by plundering the immense African territory that belonged to it by historical right. This event would trigger a true nationalist and imperial "passion" in the heart of the nation. The legitimacy of the monarchy, considered responsible for the country's decadence, was increasingly questioned by the republicans, whose political ambitions were sustained by the construction of a national-imperialist ideology that would contaminate the collective memory of the nation to this day.

In October 1910, the constitutional monarchy was finally deposed in Lisbon, after years of a republican mobilization in which the imperial question took center stage. During the Republican period (1910–26), a decisive attempt to "nationalize the masses" took place, with the creation of national symbols and their dissemination through school socialization mechanisms, thus spreading through the popular strata and exerting a broader influence on Portuguese formulations of identity. Also, a whole new civil liturgy was created, with a new national flag whose central symbol was an armillary sphere and a new, frankly nationalist and imperial, anthem.

After the fall of the First Republic, the establishment of the military dictatorship in 1926, followed by the institutionalization of *Estado Novo* (New state)[5] in 1933, led to the development of a highly centralized policy based on the uncompromising defense of the Portuguese colonial empire,[6] thus legally enshrined after the promulgation of the Colonial Act (*Acto Colonial*) of 1930.[7] In terms of mass socialization, the Estado Novo created a whole cultural apparatus related to the ideology of imperial nationalism (Domingos 2021), which would result in a true "Imperial Mysticism" (Léonard 1999). Headed by António de Oliveira Salazar, Estado Novo's highly imperialist and nationalist policy resulted in a euphoric exaltation of the nation's imperial quality, one that has remained deeply entrenched in the Portuguese ethos until this day.

While the European democracies that maintained their colonies after the Second World War gradually opened a public space for debate on their colonial past, mostly influenced by the circulation of racialized students and intellectuals[8] (Gopal 2019), Estado Novo's authoritarian policies were crucial for the almost uncontested reproduction of colonial myths in the public sphere until very late. Portugal's "civilizing mission" was the ontological principle always used to affirm the country's "historical right" to own overseas territories—because it was the pioneer of European maritime explorations—and its Christian design to "civilize" the populations within them, supposedly motivated by the "missionary vocation" (Léonard 1999: 13) of the Portuguese people. Adopted by a conservative Catholic regime, the sacralization of the Portuguese civilizing design aimed at creating an image of a "moral" empire for both national and international audiences.

After the Second World War, and in a context of increasing international pressure to decolonize, the Portuguese rhetoric of exceptionality was reworked to meet the demands of the new world order. On the legal plane, this resulted in the obliteration of any mention of the term "colonial" and the redesign of the geopolitical architecture of the nation. In a Constitutional Revision undertaken in 1951, Portuguese colonies were renamed "Overseas Provinces," and Portugal became a multi-continental nation composed of both European Provinces and Overseas Provinces. On the ideological plane, this was accompanied by the redesign of the model of social and racial relations that would characterize the contacts between the Portuguese and the peoples colonized by them. The interracial and intercultural relations developed by the Portuguese overseas had always been guided by ideas of social Darwinism and unambiguous ethnic-racial conceptions (Sobral 2004: 259), ordained during the Estado Novo by the *Indigenato* Statute, which established the legal principle of the inferiority of indigenous peoples.[9] However, support for the idea of a transcontinental nation presumed a rhetoric of racial and cultural equivalence that legitimized the supposed exceptionality of Portuguese colonization and its moral superiority over other European colonialisms.

The new Portuguese overseas (*ultramar*) ideology would find its foundations in the theses defended by Gilberto Freyre (1900–1987), a Brazilian sociologist who had spread his ideas about the particular nature of Portuguese colonialism and the hybrid cultural and racial forms that it favored. Freyre's interpretation was already set out in his book *Casa Grande e Senzala*, published in 1933, and it was reinforced in the 1950s when the sociologist was working closely with the Estado Novo (Freyre 1958). According to him, the Portuguese, unlike other colonizing peoples, have the "capacity to fraternize with Africans, Amerindians and Asians, to love their women, to incorporate their values" (Castelo 2008: 301–2), a predisposition that enhanced the Christian logic of Portuguese expansion and colonization. Freyre's thoughts on the virtues of Portuguese colonialism, a nonracist colonialism that promotes miscegenation, and thus the cultural unity between metropolis and colonies, proved very useful to the ideological legitimation of Portuguese colonial policy in an international context marked by an attitude of growing anti-colonialism (Jerónimo and Monteiro 2013). It is in this particular context that Gilberto Freyre coined the term "Luso-tropicalism" (literally referring to the Portuguese of the tropics), whose foundations—miscegenation, cultural fusion, absence of racist prejudice—would eventually come to form the basis of Portugal's imperial ideology (Castelo 1999; Anderson, Roque, and Santos 2019). The strength of this rhetoric was reinforced by the lack of any public debate, both in the metropolis and in the colonies, that could counter this line of reasoning. The political context of the postwar era had shaped the emergence of political oppositions both in the metropolis and in the colonies. However, whereas in other colonial spaces an African civil society emerged (Cooper 2014b), in the Portuguese context an authoritarian state continued to suffocate African autonomies and did so even more after the colonial wars started in 1961.[10]

After the demise of the Portuguese empire in the aftermath of the April 25, 1974, Revolution that overthrew the dictatorial regime of the Estado Novo, and during the unstable period that followed the revolution, the former empire was a no-name land. Largely motivated by discontent over the situation in the colonies, the downthrow of the Estado Novo inevitably opened the door to decolonizations.

However, the issue of the independence of the overseas territories gathered no consensus, and different interpretations regarding the matter were accompanied by strong political turmoil, both in the metropole and in the colonies. The negotiations between Portugal's representatives and the African national liberation movements paved the way for the independences, which were believed to be peaceful and to allow for a harmonious coexistence among the different colonial populations residing in the newly independent territories. The dreams of a multiracial utopia, for some, or the establishment of a Rhodesian-style white minority government, for others, ended up falling apart for all. During that period, but also before, and most certainly in the period after, the Cold War equilibriums and interferences became major actors in the existence of these territories.

The escalation of violence that erupted in Mozambique after the signing of the Lusaka agreement on September 7, 1974 (due to a military coup attempt led by sections of the Portuguese white minority), and in Angola immediately after the signing of the Alvor Treaty on January 15, 1975 (due to the dispute for power between the three liberation movements[11] with which Portugal had agreed the terms for independence), soon revealed the harsh consequences of colonialism for the colonized peoples but also for the colonizer. More than half a million people who had lived permanently in the colonies returned en masse to the former metropolis, fleeing from the escalating violence that ravaged the newly independent countries. Thousands of soldiers were also demobilized and the nation starts accounting the many dead, wounded, and traumatized in thirteen years of colonial wars in Africa. The ivory tower that had maintained the idea of the exceptionality of Portuguese colonialism was finally torn down. Refugees fleeing the civil wars that ravaged the former Portuguese overseas territories in the postindependence period also started to arrive in Portugal.

Although the Portuguese Nationality Law of 1959[12] unmistakably declared that all those born in Portugal were Portuguese—at a time when the overseas provinces were regarded as an integral part of Portugal—these refugees no longer had access to Portuguese citizenship. As amended by Decree Law no. 308-A/75, which revoked the soil criterion and promoted the blood criterion, Portuguese citizenship was reserved only for individuals who could prove their European ancestry, largely excluding the non-white populations from the former Portuguese colonies and from Portuguese citizenship and sharply revealing the divides hidden in the colonial ideology of lusotropicalism (Kalter 2022).

After the tense political situation that marked the postrevolutionary period, Portugal began to experience a moment of economic growth, which accompanied the country's democratic consolidation. With its accession to the European Economic Community in 1986 and integration into the market economy, there was a tangible improvement in living conditions and a complex process of social change. The urban middle classes grew and schooling rates and the population's general well-being levels increased, despite the structural imbalances of the Portuguese economy, which in the near future proved to be dramatic. The labor market demanded migrant workers, some of whom came from Portuguese-speaking African countries (PALOP) and began arriving in the 1980s. As the country began to take on a multicultural and multiracial face, the former populations of the Portuguese empire were now seen as foreign and immigrant.

In this context, official Portuguese identity policies were being reworked so that they fit into the new political and cultural contexts of liberal democracies. Portuguese nationalism thus went through a deep revision to put the colonial and undemocratic past behind and head out into a new European future (Pinto and Teixeira 2004). Providing a very positive frame to Portugal's colonial experience, the idea of the universalist, humanist, and anti-racist character of the Portuguese empire inherited from the Estado Novo was easily asserted in the postcolonial context to become assumed and reproduced by Portuguese of all social origins and generational strata (Cabecinhas and Cunha 2003).

Key to this operation was the work of the National Commission for the Commemoration of Portuguese Discoveries (CNCDP), created in 1986.[13] Its activities continued until 2002, and these represented a huge state effort to reassert the history of the Portuguese Maritime Expansion as the chief national identity narrative of Portugal. This endeavor culminated in the commemoration of the five hundred years of the "Discoveries" and the staging of the Expo'98 World Exhibition, based on the theme of the "Oceans." Accompanying the activity of the CNCDP, a whole array of spheres of cultural and social reproduction endlessly replicated milder versions of former imperial mythologies. Poetry, literature, politics, cultural production, and the school socialization apparatus all kept enhancing the historical legacy of the Portuguese "Discoveries" as a "gift to modernity," and the former Portuguese empire was conceived as a route to cultural encounters on a world scale and as a metaphor for a modern nation that is multifaceted and tolerant. As a result, the national collective imagination remained largely centered on pride in the history of the "Discoveries," which has remained a touchstone of Portuguese nationalism until this day, with the Portuguese youth perceiving the long imperial history as an adventure and an opportunity for friendship between peoples (Pais 1999).

This reading also proved very accommodating of the neoliberal agendas followed by political representatives to whom it was important that historical inquiries not disturb business practices. Branding operations that conveyed an image of Portugal as an entrepreneurial, modern, and cosmopolitan country, and as an open and tolerant society, are widely exploited by the tourism industry and used to attract foreign investment. Interventions in Portuguese cityscapes together with several actions of public culture have also heavily capitalized on ideas of diversity and interculturality, updating earlier lusotropical myths, which have now been converted into economic and symbolic resources likely to encourage postmodern lifestyles and consumption patterns. In these instances, the destabilizing experiences of race, ethnicity, and class ensuing from previous colonial relations, which are very present in today's Portuguese society, are read in the light of such ideas as multiculturalism or intercultural dialogue. This should be the happy result of a tolerant, nonracist, and hybridizing (imperial) history, perpetuating the myths of exceptionality that have long mediated the Portuguese imperial experience. Converted into a durable form of conceptual violence, the rhetoric of equivalence has thus obscured the legacy of inequality that defined the Portuguese colonial experience (Domingos 2013).

This imperial and postimperial ideology is tightly linked to mechanisms and policies of social regulation and postcolonial governance (Oliveira 2020). The migrant flows from the former colonies to Portugal, and the tensions and ambivalences that characterize the relationship between the white Portuguese populations and the populations formed by people from Portugal's ex-colonies and their descendants, have always been influenced by the legacies of imperial power (Dias 2016; Mapril 2021). Today, the non-European migrant fluxes include not only people from the former colonies—a Lusophone context in which the Brazilians are the largest group—but also people from other regions. Even though the Lusophone migrants are the majority, colonial imaginaries and categories are also applied to people from other migrant nationalities such as Pakistan, Bangladesh, Nepal, and Senegal. In their daily lives, these other migrants also feel the colonial legacies weighing on them. All these migrant populations tend to be perceived from the standpoint of the assimilationist model inherited from the colonial past. This model conveys the idea of a cultural hybridism that characterizes a peaceful coexistence with racial and cultural difference, even if they are usually in stark contrast to the situations of pressing social exclusion often associated with the descendants of migrants from former colonies and the neighborhoods in which they live in the outskirts of Lisbon.

Some influential works on racism in Portugal suggest that the fact that these myths are so deeply internalized by the Portuguese, even if they are not historically accurate, has a benign effect on everyday interracial interactions, helping to prevent more radical and violent forms of racial discrimination (Vala, Lopes, and Lima 2008). But they might as well have worked as a cover-up of these. In fact, following the advance of the far-right in Europe and the world, and also in Portugal, and for the first time since 1974 and the end of the dictatorship, in 2019, a political party with a nationalist and anti-immigration discourse—Chega ("Enough" in English)—had parliamentary representation, being today the third political force in the country. At the same time, situations of police violence against Black people now receive media coverage, and the denunciation of episodes of daily racism have become part of the political agenda, especially since the development of anti-racist and Afro-descendant movements and the election, also in 2019, of three Black women as members of parliament.[14]

In this context, the legacies of Portuguese colonialism and its ideological representations took center stage in the public debate. As before, the management of nationalist representations, which aim to regulate, attenuate, or solve current social, political, and economic problems, and their banal naturalization through popular culture (Cardão 2015) are highly dependent on the cover-up of the actual lived experiences on the ground, in both the colonial and postcolonial contexts. The Portuguese colonial legacies, however, continue to be as deeply dependent on the persistence of the ideological effects of national and imperial propaganda as on the heritage created by its social structures. Such considerations lead us to a second realm of problems and questions involving the Portuguese case.

Portugal was both a European colonial center, and thus belonged to the representational North (Mignolo 2000), and a poor peripheral country, sometimes perceived as belonging to the subaltern South[15] (Santos 2002; Peralta and Jensen 2017) or to the Mediterranean cultural area (Pina-Cabral 1991). As mentioned before, although being an imperial power center, when compared with the other European imperial systems, Portugal has always suffered from a "structural vulnerability" (Alexandre 2005-6: 35). This vulnerability determines the unusual character of Portuguese colonialism—a colonialism dependent on one of the poorest nations in Europe and one produced by a "domestic imperialism" within Europe itself, in which Portugal occupied a dependent position in relation to the British Empire.

In fact, during the period of high imperialism, Portugal had a backward economy based mostly on farming, with poor industrialization, in addition to the fact that it was a small, peripheral country with a population of no more than 5.5 million, many of whom found emigration, especially to Brazil and the United States, the only way to escape the lack of prospects in the country.[16] The dual standing of Portugal as a country of both emigration and immigration testifies to its ambivalent position in the world imperial system and in the world system. Emigration has always been a constant in the country's history, having reached huge proportions between 1850 and 1930, when substantial flows migrated to Brazil, and between 1950 and the fall of the Estado Novo in 1974, when Portuguese emigration reached a peak, heading mostly to Western European countries such as France and Germany that were in need of migrant laborers (Pereira 2014). Also, in this second cycle, thousands migrated to the Portuguese colonies in Africa, mostly to Angola and Mozambique, where they established themselves as settlers (Castelo 2012). The highly uneven distribution of resources in the country, together with the very precarious living conditions of a considerable part of the Portuguese population, was at the origin of these migrations. After the fall of the Estado Novo and in the aftermath of decolonization, more than half a million Portuguese nationals living permanently in the former colonies started returning to Portugal, along with many refugees fleeing the civil wars that plagued the former Portuguese overseas territories in the postindependence period. This colonial transit of settlers, along with the return of the Portuguese military that fought the colonial wars (Antunes 2015), had a great impact in the production of private and public memories on how life was in colonial societies.

From the 1980s on, and especially after Portugal joined the EU in 1986, the economic development of Portugal favored the growth of the labor market and the demand for workers in areas—and regions—not entirely filled by the large Portuguese working classes. This boosted the entry of immigrant workers in the country, most of them from African Portuguese-speaking countries and later coming from Brazil;[17] at the same time, there was a fall in Portuguese labor emigrating abroad. However, when the 2008 economic crisis hit Portugal, thousands of Portuguese started emigrating again; as an "irony of history" (Dos Santos 2017), many of these emigrants headed to Angola, which was going through an economic boom. The consideration of colonial settlers as migrants who moved in parallel with labor and economic migrants in a global economic and social space created by empire, the postcolonial migrant flows heading to Europe from the former colonial world, and, finally, the reverse contemporary emigration of Portuguese people to former colonies are all phenomena that strike imperial imaginaries and reverse North/South power relations (Slater 2004).

Very easily, however, Portugal's structural condition, defined by its economic and political vulnerability, could lead to the reinforcement of the nationalist mythology of cultural exceptionalism. To avoid such claims, it is fundamental, first, to stress that Portuguese colonialism was not gentler or more lenient. As some authors argue, such fragility, which predominantly meant the lack of capital to support the Portuguese colonial enterprise, was the main factor responsible for the use of methods of extreme violence and exploitation (Isaacman 1996; Pélissier 2004). Until the end of the African Empire, coercion was a main element of Portuguese rule (Penvenne 1995; Keese 2015; Curto, Cruz, and Furtado 2016; Cruz 2020), and systemic racial discrimination was far from being eliminated, despite the political and legal changes from the late 1950s on. Moreover, the persistence of forced labor in the Portuguese colonies until well after the Second World War was probably the best example showing how Portuguese exceptionalism was not benign (Allina 2012; Jerónimo 2015; Monteiro 2018). Second, in postcolonial Portugal, economic deprivation, poor housing, and imperfect access to social care and civic and political participation are more relevant to interpreting the life of migrants and racialized populations than the culturalist discourse so present in diverse public and private institutions, which invokes history and ontological national qualities to create a representation of social harmony and exchange. Despite the vital changes brought about by the constitutional legal framework that emerged from the April 25 Revolution and the development of a weak but inclusionary welfare state, in Portugal, as in other European countries that were formerly imperial power centers, we find the ongoing material structures of inequality and embattled immigrant suburbs are today significantly questioning the governing myths of the nation, as shown by groundbreaking work on these topics (e.g., Malheiros and Vala 2004; Ascensão 2015a; Cardão 2015; Carmo and Estevens 2017; Cachado and Frangella 2019; Cidra 2021).

Despite the relevance of this research and the work of social and political movements, there is still a lack of grounded research on racialized populations, whose lives and patterns of insertion in Portuguese society continue to be poorly known. If the study of Portuguese colonial legacies must inevitably be placed within a broader enquiry into the legacies of European colonialism, this placing should not be reduced to the mere adoption of international theories and frames of analysis. New research would certainly be helpful for a better understanding of these legacies, their place in Portuguese postcolonial lives and subjectivities, and therefore the struggles implicated in overcoming centuries-old inequalities and discriminations.

Grounding Our Subject

This book is divided into three parts, each focusing on an area of Portuguese national life where colonial legacies are expressed, performed, and internalized, although many crossovers can be made between the chapters arranged in each of these parts. In several of these chapters, Lisbon takes center stage. As the political and symbolic center of the Portuguese empire, Portugal's capital was heavily discursively invested, and to that extent, the concentration of colonial legacies in the city space is incomparably bigger than in other Portuguese cities. In addition, Lisbon was the main Portuguese receiving point, first during decolonization, and then from the mid-1980s on, of people coming from the former Portuguese colonies, a presence that has no parallel in other Portuguese cities, either from the point of view of social relations therein established or from the point of view of the occupation and use of the city space. Finally, while other Portuguese cities were reimagined in postimperial times on the basis of other histories and cultural referents, Lisbon continued to be strongly invested with an imperial symbolism, this being a strong mark of the strategic image that was intentionally imprinted in the city. Whereas other Portuguese cities might have lacked the financial and institutional resources to invest in a differentiated image capitalizable in an international market of capital cities, Lisbon sought to position itself as a marketable destination for international tourism, and to that extent it has depended heavily on inherited colonial legacies. More than any other Portuguese city, Lisbon shows the confluence between imperial imaginaries, governance of intercultural and racial relations, and capitalist trends of urban economic restructuring, highlighting the complexities inherent to processes of rehabilitation of colonial legacies in the present time. On the other hand, despite the centrality of Lisbon, the several case studies in the book deal mainly with the relationship between the national, the imperial, and the global and therefore often go beyond any specific location in terms of the analytical breadth of the study of colonial legacies. In general, therefore, contemporary Portuguese spaces, as well as former colonial territories, are empirical sites for the investigation of imperial legacies, since they were the target of the political agendas of public and private institutions that worked to disseminate representations and shape practices. The most important of these were probably those that emerged from modern mass society, from the universal school system to modern mass media.

In the first part of the book, entitled "Empire, Nation, and Memory Politics," we reflect on how various official institutions and policies reproduce Portuguese colonial legacies in the public sphere. This reproduction is present in the official politics of memory, in the discourses about urban space and city buildings, in the materiality of things, in museums and monuments. They are also part of the language of various institutionalized fields, such as those which, through specific narratives about heritage, architecture, or sports, reproduce the foundations of lusotropicalism and subtly maintain a discourse of colonial supremacy. Finally, we also examine how colonial legacies are reproduced through the imaging of cities such as Lisbon, which are today interlinked with ideas of multiculturalism and intercultural dialogue that are capitalized by processes of gentrification, property speculation, and tourism promotion. Indeed, despite assigning to the state a key role in managing postcolonial representations of empire, this section emphasizes the convergence between official policies and the interests of private actors guided by market dynamics.

Elsa Peralta's chapter opens this section by looking at how the area of Belém, in Lisbon, became a "memorial landscape" in which, explicitly and implicitly, an official memory of Portuguese colonialism was put in place. Through her ethnographic journey in the area, she explores the creation of public memories as an ongoing process of re-narrativization of the historical past, in which the central state, the city council, and civil society constantly build-up, contest, and debate its content and meaning.

Next, Nuno Domingos's chapter explores how two "narratives of transition"— the biographical construction of Eusébio da Silva Ferreira, the famous Mozambican football player, and the current narratives on the history of Portuguese modern colonial architecture—embedded in institutional practices and discourse, naturalize an exceptional version of Portuguese colonialism. More subtly than the official mnemonic repertoires transmitted by official state institutions, these vehicles of historical narration sanction a return to the past that is less intrusive and conflictual.

Concluding this first part, Nuno Oliveira examines how, in Lisbon, cultural diversity has become a vehicle of urban governance. He argues that the nationalistic construction of the idea of a singular Portuguese culture, which is supposedly multicultural and multiracial, as a legacy of lusotropicalism is today a driving force in processes of touristification and gentrification, leading to logics of urban restructuring resulting from the capitalist dynamics of globalization.

The postcolonial experience is also expressed in the lives of those who moved from the former colonies to the metropolis, whether returned settlers or African immigrants and their descendants. In Part II of the book, focused on "Postcolonial Space, Work, and Citizenship," the integration of these individuals in contemporary Portugal is questioned and the continuities and discontinuities of well-established historical experiences examined. The ongoing rationale of labor and educational disqualification, reinforced by forms of racism, puts many of these people in a position of social subordination that has historically characterized colonial relations, despite the postcolonial changes brought about by democracy. The occupation of these individuals in menial forms of labor and the ambiguous and often disruptive and violent relation with state institutions are clear markers of these continuities.

Eduardo Ascensão opens this second part of the book. Focusing on the outskirts of Lisbon, he introduces us to the lives of immigrant communities from the former Portuguese colonies in Africa. His aim is to understand how institutional policies, the labor and housing markets, and a set of everyday practices reproduce forms of social and racial discrimination, suggesting the existence of continuities with the colonial power structure. Still, Ascensão reveals how, in this framework of state governmentality, immigrants and other inhabitants find forms of class solidarity through vindicatory actions or forms of sabotaging the power of the state.

Next, Ana Estevens explores the creative uses of colonial legacies by the postcolonial population. In particular, she addresses the current uses of the Cape Verdean Creole language in Portugal. Cape Verde migrants and their descendants (most of whom live in the outskirts of Lisbon in dire housing conditions), use Creole in family, work, and daily leisure interactions as a means of building community relations. Marginalized within the Portuguese linguistic field, Creole has also become a cultural vehicle for youngsters to communicate their urban experiences of exclusion, as demonstrated by the growth of digital communities developed around local rap music inspired by imaginaries of resistance and artistic creation imported from American popular culture.

Nuno Dias's chapter follows, proposing a history of the political construction of domestic work in Portugal. The situation of domestic workers in Portugal also reveals how, despite important differences in the democratic period, certain forms of labor exploitation still persist. The author suggests there is a class homology in the structural position of domestic work in three different urban contexts, namely the largest cities of Portuguese imperial Africa, the metropolitan Portuguese cities involving internal migrations from the countryside, and currently these same cities but now involving economic migrants who came from the former Portuguese colonies. In an intersectional approach, Dias crosses the progressive feminization of domestic work with its prevalent ethnicization. Performed today mostly by immigrant women, their class position is furthermore derived from the classification of domestic work as "unskilled labor," configuring a space where gender is consigned to domesticity, informality, and isolation, limiting the horizons of collective action.

In the final chapter in this section, Simone Frangella presents evidence to show how colonial legacies have several dimensions and involve different populations, many of whom establish relationships with local people, often on the basis of previously negotiated colonial assumptions. Her chapter examines how the Brazilian migrant populations living in the Lisbon neighborhood of Arroios have transformed this central urban area. According to Frangella, the stereotypical representations that the Portuguese had of Brazilians, which invoke old colonial images and categorizations, were critical to the urban and labor integration of these migrants, revealing the many ambivalences that accompany the processes of updating and manipulating national identity images in transnational migration.

Part III of the book, entitled "Popular Culture and Everyday Colonial Legacies," looks at Portuguese colonial legacies in popular commercial culture. Uncritical cosmopolitan and multicultural perspectives are today commercial vehicles of current colonial rhetoric. Works of this kind have a conspicuous consumer in the repatriated settler population from Africa, but they are also consumed by much larger groups and appeal to Portuguese society as a whole. This is because it has been brought up on the myths of empire through school socialization and several mediums of state propaganda, both past and present. However, these legacies do not circulate uncritically since they are subject to innumerable appropriations, negotiations, contestations, and subversions. Based on a series of interviews conducted with African musicians, the chapter by Rui Cidra explores how the concept of Lusophony is currently appropriated and used. He argues that whereas the postcolonial creation of a Lusophone community—which consists of the Portuguese-speaking countries—was an attempt by Portugal to recover some of its imperial greatness and boost business networks, the specific appropriations of the concept show a more complex situation. In their professional lives, musicians from former Portuguese colonies have reinterpreted the notion of Lusophony to suit their particular interests and strategies, giving evidence to the polysemic nature of the meanings attached to it.

The current Portuguese literary production on colonial themes is the subject of João Pedro George's chapter. He analyzes how the historical genres that defined the development of popular literature throughout the world are being used by a number of Portuguese authors to revisit the colonial past. Most of these books—which are very popular—recreate a representation of Africa as an exotic and savage place where white settlers have various experiences and adventures; others revisit the return of the Portuguese settler from Africa in the wake of decolonizations, appealing to an emotional response from interested audiences by exploring the dramatic nature of the events. Even when these narratives introduce a critique of the colonial situation, these books have usually marginalized the African characters, thus highlighting how the publishing market frames the experiences of class and race and the historical experience of Portuguese colonialism through the same explanatory tropes and cultural imaginaries inherited from the colonial period, perpetuating them in society at large.

In their chapter, Bart Vanspauwen and Iñigo Sánchez-Fuarros analyze the role that TAP—*Transportes Aéreos Portugueses*, the Portuguese flag carrier airline company—had in the production of an imperial representation of Portugal. While investing in travel routes that reproduce the old imperial map, TAP reinforces the idea of a Lusophone community defined by notions of *mestizaje* and hybridity and mutually enriching cultural practices. Given the hymn "With Arms Wide Open" in 2011—in which Portuguese *fado* singer Mariza, the Angolan *semba* musician Paulo Flores, and Brazilian singer Roberta Sá sing in one voice—the authors investigate some strategies by which TAP creates postcolonial connections between Portugal and the Portuguese-speaking world on board, thus showing how diversity management today is a space of convergence between old imperial myths and a current neoliberal framework.

Closing Part III of the book, Marcos Cardão's chapter demonstrates how the redefinition of Lisbon's identity is not limited to official strategies of institutional governance that use urban branding to promote cultural diversity. The presence in Lisbon of several entrepreneurs of "dance music," in close dialogue with different genres of what is generally termed "African music" (such as Afro House, *zouk*, *kuduru*, *funaná*, *batuque*, *tarraxo*, and *kizomba*), has contributed to the redefinition of Lisbon's soundscape. Cardão describes this process, relating the uses of alternative music to the reinvention of Lisbon as a cosmopolitan and postcolonial city. His main purpose is to highlight the role that the music department of a multinational company, the Red Bull Academy, had in the production of Lisbon's new identity.

The analysis of the legacies of Portuguese colonialism in the postcolonial period is not exhausted in this book and the chapters included in it. However, we wanted to focus on the ways in which state agencies, both local and central, converge with the interests of large economic corporations, the strategic and creative use of colonial categories in the processes of negotiating symbolic spaces, and the importance of citizenship and labor relations as central for the analysis of how the structures and ideological frameworks of the colonial past continue to live on today.

Notes

1 Especially relevant to this are, among others, the contributions of Eric Wolf (1982) and Sidney Mintz (1985).
2 Among the authors who developed relevant research on the subject are Almeida (2002), Ribeiro (2004), Oliveira and Castelo (2006), Sanches (2006), and Domingos and Peralta (2013).
3 Large or small parts of the chapters in this book have been published elsewhere, mostly in Portuguese. Substantial parts of the texts by Ascensão, Dias, Frangella, Oliveira, and Peralta have already been published in Portuguese, although they have been updated and reworked to include more recent dynamics (see Domingos and Peralta 2013). Domingos's chapter is a substantially modified version of Domingos (2016). Parts of earlier versions of Ascensão's chapter have also been published in Ascensão (2015b).
4 The Anglo-Portuguese Alliance (or Luso-British Alliance) between the Kingdom of England (succeeded by the United Kingdom) and the Kingdom of Portugal. It is the oldest diplomatic alliance in the world still in force. It was sealed in 1386 by the Treaty of Windsor.
5 The Estado Novo was an authoritarian, Catholic, colonialist political regime which ruled Portugal from 1933 until April 25, 1974. It succeeded the military dictatorship established with the coup of May 28, 1926, which overthrew the First Republic (1910–26). Estado Novo was the most enduring of the European dictatorships born in the 1920s.
6 At this time, the Portuguese empire comprised the following territories: Azores, Madeira, São Tomé and Príncipe, Cape Verde, Guinea-Bissau, Angola, Mozambique, Goa, Damão and Diu, East Timor, and Macau.
7 Decree no. 18570, *Diário do Governo*, July 8, 1930. The "Colonial Act" would later be incorporated into the Constitution with the revision of 1933, thus being installed as one of the cornerstones of the national law.
8 The case of Casa dos Estudantes do Império, a housing facility built in Lisbon to receive colonial overseas students, was a minor but important laboratory of study to demonstrate the influence of this human and cultural flux for the political and intellectual debate in the Portuguese context during Estado Novo (Castelo and Jerónimo 2017).
9 During the Estado Novo, the rights and, above all, duties of the indigenous peoples of the Portuguese colonies were established by the *Estatuto do Indigenato*, which classified three population groups—the white, the assimilated, and the indigenous peoples.

10 In 1961, an anti-colonial movement was born in Angola, marking the beginning of what became known as the Portuguese Colonial War. The war of independence in Guinea began on January 23, 1963, on the initiative of PAIGC (African Party for the Independence of Guinea and Cape Verde), a party founded in 1956 by Amílcar Cabral. In Mozambique, guerrilla operations began in 1964.
11 The People's Movement for the Liberation of Angola (MPLA), the National Liberation Front of Angola (FNLA), and National Union for the Total Independence of Angola (UNITA).
12 *Lei da Nacionalidade Portuguesa* no. 2098, 1959. DG no 172/1959, I Série, July 29.
13 For details of the activities of the Commission, see Oliveira (2003) and Curto (2015).
14 Romualda Fernandes (Partido Socialista [Socialist Party]), Beatriz Gomes Dias (Bloco de Esquerda [Left Bloc]), and Joacine Katar Moreira (Livre [Free]).
15 An illustrative example of this happened in the context of the global financial crisis. In the financial market media and in the national media of the more affluent parts of Europe, the derogatory acronym PIGS (Portugal, Italy, Greece, and Spain) came to symbolize an attitude that, although an immediate product of the current crisis, was also a case of the resurfacing of a much deep-rooted representational history—a re-materialization of domestic European orientalism that entails a subalternization of the southern part of the continent.
16 Between 1890 and 1930, one million Portuguese emigrated to these destinations (Pinto 2000: 5).
17 In 1960, the percentage of Africans in Portugal in the total number of foreigners was only 1.5 percent, but in 1981, that figure stood at 44 percent (Pires 1999: 199).

References

Alexandre, V. (2005–6). "Traumas do Império: História, Memória e Identidade Nacional." *Cadernos de Estudos Africanos: Memórias Coloniais*, 9/10: 23–41.
Allina, E. (2012). *Slavery by Any Other Name: African Life under Company Rule in Colonial Mozambique*. Charlottesville: University of Virginia Press.
Almeida, M. V. de (2002). "Longing for Oneself: Hybridism and Miscegenation in Colonial and Postcolonial Portugal." *Etnográfica*, 6(1): 81–200.
Anderson, W., R. Roque, and R. V. Santos (2019). *Luso-tropicalism and Its Discontents: The Making and Unmaking of Racial Exceptionalism*. Oxford: Berghann.
Antunes, M. J. L. (2015). *Regressos Quase Perfeitos: Memórias da Guerra em Angola*. Lisbon: Tinta da China.
Ascensão, E. (2015a). "Slum Gentrification in Lisbon, Portugal: Displacement and the Imagined Futures of an Informal Settlement." In L. Lees, H. B. Shin, and E. López-Morales (eds.), *Global Gentrifications: Uneven Development and Displacement*, 37–58. Bristol: Polity.
Ascensão, E. (2015b). "The Slum Multiple: A Cyborg Micro-History of an Informal Settlement in Lisbon." *International Journal of Urban and Regional Research*, 39(5): 948–64.
Bethencourt, F. (1999). "A Memória da Expansão." In F. Bethencourt and K. Chaudhuri (eds.), *História da Expansão Portuguesa*, vol. 5, 442–80. Lisbon: Círculo de Leitores.
Boyer, M. C. (1996). *The City of Collective Memory: Its Historical Imagery and Architectural Entertainment*. Cambridge, MA: MIT Press.

Buettner, E. (2016). *Europe after Empire: Decolonization, Society, and Culture.* Cambridge: Cambridge University Press.
Cabecinhas, R., and L. Cunha (2003). "Colonialismo, Identidade Nacional e Representações do 'Negro.'" *Estudos do Século, XX*(3): 157–84.
Cachado, R., and S. Frangella (2019). "House and Mobility: Portuguese Hindus and Brazilians in Lisbon in Face of Housing Constraints." *Archivio antropologico mediterraneo,* Anno XXII, n. 21(2).
Cardão, M. (2015). *Fado Tropical: Luso-tropicalismo e cultura de massas.* Lisbon: Unipop.
Carmo, A., and A. Estevens (2017). "Urban Citizenship(s) in Lisbon: Examining the Case of Mouraria." *Citizenship Studies,* 21(4): 409–24.
Castelo, C. (1999). *"O Modo Português de Estar no Mundo": O Luso-tropicalismo e a Ideologia Colonial Portuguesa 1933–1961.* Porto: Afrontamento.
Castelo, C. (2008). "O Outro no Labirinto Imperial: Orientalismo e Luso-Tropicalismo." In R. M. do Carmo and R. L. Blanes, *A Globalização no Divã,* 295–315. Lisbon: Tinta da China.
Castelo, C. (2012). "Colonial Migration to Angola and Mozambique: Constraints and Illusions." In E. Morier-Genoud and M. Cahen, *Imperial Migrations: Colonial Communities and Diasporas in the Portuguese World,* 137–56. Basingstoke: Palgrave Macmillan.
Castelo, C., and M. B. Jerónimo (eds.) (2017). *Casa dos Estudantes do Império: Dinâmicas Coloniais, Conexões Transnacionais.* Lisbon: Edições 70.
Cidra, R. (2021). *Funaná, Raça e Masculinidade. Um trajetória colonial e pós-colonial.* Lisbon: Outro Modo.
Cooper, F. (2014a). *Africa in the World: Capitalism, Empire, Nation-State.* Cambridge, MA: Harvard University Press.
Cooper, F. (2014b). *Citizenship between Empire and Nation: Remaking France and French Africa, 1945–1960.* Princeton, NJ: Princeton University Press.
Cooper, F., and A. L. Stoler (1997). *Tensions of Empire: Colonial Cultures in a Bourgeois World.* Berkeley: University of California Press.
Cruz, B. P. (2020). *(Des)controlo em Luanda: Urbanismo, Polícia e Lazer nos Musseques do Império.* Lisbon: Outro Modo.
Curto, D. R. (2015). "A Memória dos Descobrimentos, da expansão e do império colonial." In J. B. Monteiro and N. Domingos (eds.), *Este País não Existe,* 95–107. Porto: Deriva.
Curto, D. R., B. P. da Cruz, and T. Furtado (2016). *Políticas Coloniais em Tempo de Revoltas—Angola circa 1961.* Porto: Afrontamento.
De L'Estoile, B. (2008). "The Past As It Lives Now: An Anthropology of Colonial Legacies." *Social Anthropology,* 16(3): 267–79.
Dias, N. (2016). *Remigração e Etnicidade. Trânsito colonial entre a África de Leste e a Europa.* Lisbon: Mundos Sociais.
Domingos, N. (2013). "A desigualdade como legado da cidade colonial: racismo e reprodução de mão de obra em Lourenço Marques." In N. Domingos and E. Peralta (eds.), *Cidade e Império: Dinâmicas Coloniais e Reconfigurações Pós-coloniais,* 59–112. Lisbon: Edições 70.
Domingos, N. (2016). "Les reconfigurations de la mémoire du colonialisme portugais: récit et esthétisation de l'histoire." *Histoire@Polotique,* 2(9): 41–59.
Domingos, N. (ed.) (2021). *Cultura Popular e Império: as lutas pela conquista do consumo cultural em Portugal e nas suas colónias.* Lisbon: Imprensa de Ciências Sociais.
Domingos, N., and E. Peralta (eds.) (2013). *Cidade e Império: Dinâmicas Coloniais e Reconfigurações Pós-coloniais.* Lisbon: Edições 70.

Dos Santos, I. (2017). "Migrer du Portugal en Angola: Perception de la Migration et Rapport au Passé Colonial. Quelques Pistes de Réflexion." *Cahiers de l'Urmis*, 7: 1–16.
Eldridge, C. (2010). "Blurring the Boundaries between Perpetrators and Victims: Pied-Noir Memories and the Harki Community." *Memory Studies*, 3(2): 123–36.
Freyre, G. (1933). *Casa Grande e Senzala. Formação da Família Brasileira sob o Regime da Economia Patriarcal*. Rio de Janeiro: Record.
Freyre, G. (1958). *Integração Portuguesa nos Trópicos*. Lisbon: Junta de Investigações do Ultramar.
Gopal, P. (2019). *Insurgent Empire: Anticolonial Resistance and British Dissent*. New York: Verso.
Hall, C., and S. Rose (2006). *At Home with Empire: Metropolitan Culture and the Imperial World*. Cambridge: Cambridge University Press.
Isaacman, A. (1996). *Cotton Is the Mother of Poverty—Peasants, Work, and Rural Struggle in Colonial Mozambique, 1938–1961*. Portsmouth, NH: Heinemann.
Jacobs, J. M. (1996). *Edge of Empire: Postcolonialism and the City*. London: Routledge.
Jerónimo, M. B. (2015). *The "Civilising Mission" of Portuguese Colonialism, 1870–1930*. Basingstoke: Palgrave Macmillan.
Jerónimo, M. B., and J. P. Monteiro. (2013). "Internationalism and the Labours of the Portuguese Colonial Empire (1945–1974)." *Portuguese Studies*, 29(2): 142–63.
Jordi, J.-J. (2003). "The Creation of the Pieds-Noirs: Arrival and Settlement in Marseilles, 1962." In A. L. Smith (ed.), *Europe's Invisible Migrants*, 61–74. Amsterdam: Amsterdam University Press.
Lammert, C., and K. Sarkowsky (eds.) (2010). *Travelling Concepts: Negotiating Diversity in Canada and Europe*. Wiesbaden: Springer VS.
Laschi, G., V. Deplano, and A. Pes (eds.) (2020). *Europe between Migrations, Decolonization and Integration (1945–1992)*. London: Routledge.
Léonard, Y. (1999). "O Império Colonial Salazarista." In F. Bethencourt and K. Chaudhuri (eds.), *História da Expansão Portuguesa*, vol. II, 2–30. Lisbon: Círculo de Leitores.
Lorcin, P. M. (2013). "Imperial Nostalgia; Colonial Nostalgia: Differences of Theory, Similarities of Practice?" *Historical Reflections*, 39(3): 97–111.
Kalter, C. (2022). *Postcolonial People: The Return from Africa and the Remaking of Portugal*. Cambridge: Cambridge University Press.
Keese, A. (2015). "Developmentalist Attitudes and Old Habits: Portuguese Labour Policies, South African Rivalry, and Flight in, 1945–1974." *Journal of Southern African Studies*, 41(2): 237–53.
King, A. (1990). *Global Cities: Post-imperialism and the Internationalization of London*. New York: Routledge.
MacKenzie, J. M. (1999). "Empire and Metropolitan Cultures." In A. Porter (ed.), *The Oxford History of the British Empire*, 5 vols., vol. III: *The Nineteenth Century*, 270–93. Oxford: Oxford University Press.
Malheiros, J. M., and F. Vala (2004). "Immigration and City Change: The Lisbon Metropolis at the Turn of the Twentieth Century." *Journal of Ethnic and Migration Studies*, 30(6): 1065–86.
Mapril, J. (2021). "Placing the Future: Onward Migration, Education and Citizenship among Portuguese-Bangladeshi in London." *International Migration*, 59(6): 109–27.
Matos, S. C. de (2008). *Consciência Histórica e Nacionalismo—Portugal, séculos XIX e XX*. Lisbon: Livros Horizonte.
Mignolo, W. D. (2000). *Local Knowledges/Global Designs: Coloniality, Subaltern Knowledges and Border Thinking*. Princeton, NJ: Princeton University Press.

Mintz, S. (1985). *Sweetness and Power: The Place of Sugar in Modern History*. New York: Viking.
Monteiro, J. P. (2018). *Portugal e a Questão do Trabalho Forçado. Um Império sob Escrutínio (1944-1962)*. Lisboa: Edições 70.
Oliveira, A. de (2003). "The Activities of the CNCDP: A Preliminary Assessment." *e-JPH*, 1(1): 1-12.
Oliveira, N. (2020). *Diversidade(s): paradigmas, modelos e governança*. Lisbon: Tempos Sociais.
Oliveira, P. A., and C. Castelo (2006). "Memórias Coloniais." Special Issue of *Caderno de Estudos Africanos*, 9/10.
Pais, J. M. (1999). *Consciência Histórica e Identidade: os Jovens Portugueses num Contexto Europeu*. Oeiras: Celta.
Panayi, P., and P. Virdee (eds.) (2011). *Refugees and the End of Empire: Imperial Collapse and Forced Migration in the Twentieth Century*. New York: Palgrave Macmillan.
Pélissier, R. (2004). *Les Campagnes Coloniales du Portugal 1844-1941*. Paris: Pygmalion.
Penvenne, J. M. (1995). *African Workers and Colonial Racism: Mozambican Strategies and Struggles in Lourenço Marques, 1877-1962*. London: James Currey.
Peralta, E. (ed.) (2021). *The Retornados from Portuguese Colonies in Africa: Narrative, Memory, and History*. London: Routledge.
Peralta, E., and N. Domingos (2019). "Lisbon: Reading the (Post-)Colonial City from the Nineteenth to the Twenty-First Century." *Urban History*, 46(2): 246-65.
Peralta, E., and L. Jensen (2017). "From Austerity to Postcolonial Nostalgia: Crisis and National Identity in Portugal and Denmark." In S. Jonsson and J. Willén (eds.), *Austere Histories in European Societies: Social Exclusion and the Contest of Colonial Memories*, 74-91. Abingdon: Routledge.
Pereira, V. (2014). *A ditadura de Salazar e a emigração. O Estado português e os seus migrantes (1957-1974)*. Lisbon: Temas & Debates.
Pina-Cabral, J. de. (1991). *Os Contextos da Antropologia*. Lisbon: Difel.
Pinto, A. C. (2000). "Portugal Contemporâneo: Uma Introdução." In A. C. Pinto (ed.), *Portugal Contemporâneo*, 1-38. Madrid: Ediciones Sequitur.
Pinto, A. C., and N. S. Teixeira (2004). "From Atlantic Past to European Destiny: Portugal." In W. Kaiser and J. Elvert (eds.), *European Union Enlargement: A Comparative History*, 112-30. London: Routledge.
Pires, R. P. (1999). "O Regresso das Colónias." In F. Bethencourt and K. Chaudhuri (eds.), *História da Expansão Portuguesa*, 5 vols., vol. V, 182-96. Lisbon: Círculo de Leitores.
Ribeiro, M. C. (2004). *Uma História de Regressos: Império, Guerra Colonial e Pós-Colonialismo*. Porto: Edições Afrontamento.
Rothermund, D. (ed.) (2015). *Memories of Post-imperial Nations: The Aftermath of Decolonization, 1945-2013*. Cambridge: Cambridge University Press.
Sanches, M. R. (2006). *Portugal não é um país pequeno Contar o "Império" na Pós-colonialidade*. Lisbon: Livros Cotovia.
Santos, B. S. (2002). "Entre Próspero e Caliban: Colonialismo, Pós-Colonialismo e Inter-Identidade." *Luso-Brazilian Review*, 39(2): 9-43.
Slater, D. (2004). *Geopolitics and the Post-colonial: Rethinking North-South Relations*. Oxford: Blackwell.
Sobral, J. M. (2004). "O Norte, o Sul, a Raça, a Nação—Representações da Identidade Nacional Portuguesa (Séculos XIX-XX)." *Análise Social*, XXXIX(171): 255-84.
Sobral, J. M. (2014). *Portugal, Portugueses: uma identidade nacional*. Lisbon: FFMS.

Stoler, A. L. (1989). "Rethinking Colonial Categories: European Communities and the Boundaries of Rule." *Comparative Studies in Society and History*, 31(1): 134–61.

Thompson, A. (2005). *The Empire Strikes Back? The Impact of Imperialism on Britain from the Mid-nineteenth Century*. Harlow: Pearson.

Vala, J., G. Lopes, and M. Lima (2008). "Black Immigrants in Portugal: Luso Tropicalism and Prejudice." *Journal of Social Issues*, 64: 287–302.

Varma, R. (2011). *The Postcolonial City and Its Subjects: London, Nairobi, Bombay*. London: Routledge.

Wolf, E. (1982). *Europe and the People without History*. Berkeley: University of California Press.

Part I

EMPIRE, NATION, AND MEMORY POLITICS

Chapter 2

MEMORY OF THE EMPIRE AND SPACE OF CELEBRATION: THE CASE OF THE BELÉM DISTRICT IN LISBON

Elsa Peralta

Over several decades and under successive regimes, cities and towns in Portugal were subject to a continuous inscription of a memory alluding to the empire in the public space. Museums, monuments, commemorative events, statuary, and toponyms were created all over Portugal with the aim of reproducing the imagined realities of the empire in the metropolis, perpetuating them to the present day. But although this memorial action was replicated a little all over the country, it was in Lisbon, the former capital of the empire, that it was most expressive. In Lisbon, it is the geographical area that corresponds to the parish of Belém, in the western part of Lisbon, that is the most paradigmatic case of inscription and condensation in the national public space of a memory alluding to the Portuguese colonial empire. Functioning as a symbolic synthesis of national identity, this area houses a "memory complex" associated with the Portuguese imperial experience and offers a privileged observatory for questioning the complexities inherent to the composition and dissemination of public memories.

This chapter explores the process of composing a public memory in Belém from the nineteenth century to the present day. First, it focuses on the antecedents of this process, underlining the role played by both monumental heritage and museums in the symbolic thematizations of national identity. It then discusses the lasting impact that the 1940 Portuguese World Exhibition left on the configuration of Belém as a space of mythification of Portuguese identity. It ends with a discussion of the ongoing postcolonial re-narrations about the empire in the Belém space. The importance of tourism and the commodification of the national past are emphasized, which, although leading to its progressive depoliticization, still contains the possibility of contestation and articulation of counter-memories.

The Belém Memory Complex

Concentrating the most representative examples of the monumental architecture associated with the period that state propaganda named "Portuguese Discoveries,"[1] the Belém District is the part of Lisbon and Portugal where a public memory associated with the Portuguese empire is most expressive. The most emblematic components of this cluster are the examples of Manueline art located there—Jerónimos Monastery and Tower of Belém—two distinctive symbols of the master national narrative associated with the history of the Portuguese maritime expansion, both classified as world heritage by UNESCO in 1983. Around these two icons are large gardens—Belém Tower Garden, Vasco da Gama Garden, and Afonso de Albuquerque Garden—used for recreational purposes either by the many tourists visiting the area or as part of the leisure habits of the inhabitants of Lisbon. Both groups enjoy it as a naturalized, everyday space in which the "Discoveries," the navigators, the monuments, the museums are part of a "habitual" memory of living the city.

On the left of the Jerónimos Monastery, facing west, there is the Belém Cultural Center, a building of minimalist architecture showcasing works of modern and contemporary art for the consumption of an urban and cosmopolitan audience. On the same side is the Gulbenkian Planetarium, owned by the Navy Museum, which is housed in a wing of the Jerónimos Monastery. In another area adjacent to the Jerónimos Monastery we find the National Archaeological Museum. The monastery stands on one side of a huge square, the Praça do Império (Empire Square). On the right of the monastery is a row of old residential buildings that survived the successive spatial reorganizations to which the area was subjected. These survivors now accommodate several restaurants, very popular with tourists. This row of restaurants is on the street adjacent to the Vasco da Gama Garden, which houses a monument in honor of Vasco da Gama,[2] a playground, and a wooden structure with exotic oriental ornamentation, called the Thai Pavilion. This was a gift from Thailand to Portugal in the context of the celebrations of five hundred years of Luso-Thai relations. It was inaugurated in February 2012 in a ceremony that celebrated the uninterrupted good relations between the two countries since the age of the maritime expansion.

Across the street, in Belém's central block, is a pastry shop selling Belém's famous *pásteis de Belém* (custard tarts), where local residents, visitors, and tourists line up. Behind are the Tropical Gardens, with fewer visitors, where one can find several native species brought from the Portuguese colonial domains. Continuing east, there is the Belém Palace, the official residence of the president of the Portuguese Republic, and to its left is the new Museu Nacional dos Coches, a museum that houses a collection of royal carriages and cars. It has been there since 2015, in another building of modern architectural design. To the north, outside the monumental cluster, lies the residential area of the parish, a substantial part of which is occupied by the Bairro do Restelo, an urban development dating from the 1940s. Single-family dwellings predominate, many of them converted into the headquarters of diplomatic representations of various countries. This area is also home to the National Museum of Ethnology, a museum created by decree in 1965 as the Overseas Ethnology Museum. As in the monumental area, the streets there are often named after navigators, historical figures, or places alluding to the "Discoveries," such as Dom Vasco da Gama Avenue, the Squares of Diu, Goa, and Malaca, or Bartolomeu Perestrelo and Damião de Góis Streets, among many others.

Separated from this cluster by the railway and Marginal Avenue, with access through an underground passage, the monumental ensemble extends toward the river Tagus where the Belém Tower and its gardens are located. The area is popular with tourists, hence the many souvenir stalls set up there, and also with children on school visits. At weekends, it also serves as a leisure area for Lisboners. To the west of this ensemble is the Monument to Overseas Combatants, erected in honor of the Portuguese soldiers who fell in the colonial wars (1961–75). This space is not much used, except on commemorative days. To the east, in an area marked by port activity, restaurants, bars, and nightclubs, there is the Museum of the Orient, a museum owned by the Orient Foundation, set up in 1988 by the Portuguese administration of Macau in exchange for the exclusive right to operate the gambling business in the colony, with the purpose of developing and continuing "the historical and cultural ties linking Portugal and the Orient, specifically China."[3] Accordingly, the Museum of the Orient opened its premises in 2008, with an artful collection testifying to the relations between the Portuguese and East Asian peoples since the sixteenth century. The museum is not widely visited and attracts a mostly specialized audience interested in the topics covered by the conferences, workshops, or shows held inside.

Near the river is also the Museum of Popular Art. It is a modernist-style building whose facades display panels depicting scenes of rural life and work. It was built for the Portuguese World Exhibition that took place in Belém in 1940. Next to it is a pavement with a rose compass (*Rosa dos Ventos*), which encircles the Monument to the Discoveries, a caravel-shaped monument, with the bow facing the river. It displays a number of historical figures associated with the maritime "Discoveries," headed by Prince Henry, The Navigator (1394–1460), considered the great promoter of the Portuguese maritime enterprise. And, finally, there is the Tagus river, which provides the scenic backdrop to the multiple layers of time that make up the Belém memory complex.

The Composition of a Memory Complex

The National and the Imperial

This exhaustive set of memorial references produces a space of national glorification whose composition has been operating over time and is the result of unraveling memorialization actions that have given the space the configuration it has today. The area of Belém has long had a significant symbolic power related to the "Discoveries" in the collective imagination, as it was from there that Vasco da Gama's armada left on July 7, 1497, to try and find a sea route to India. But the parish only developed from nineteenth century on as a number of industrial units were established there, near the monuments and occupying the areas adjacent to them. The railway was also built by then, and this brought a physical barrier into the landscape, which has separated the monumental zone from the river since then (Elias 2004: 55).

It was during this period—which coincides internationally with the intensification of disputes for domination of the African continent in the context of the Berlim Conference (1884–5), and domestically with the growing challenge to the monarchy by the increasingly influential Republican Party—that the first monumentalization actions of the Belém space took place, with the establishment there of museums and the adoption of conservation measures to refurbish the monuments. In the nineteenth century, the Jerónimos Monastery was in a state of partial ruin. Its restoration as a magnificent representative of the "golden age" of the "Discoveries" came after the establishment of liberalism in Portugal, especially from the moment when a foreigner, Francisco Adolfo Varnhagen, used the designation "Manueline style" in 1842. He used it to define a decorative, sculptural, and mobile art style developed during the reign of King Manuel I (1495–1521), whose role in the expansion of the Portuguese empire was crucial. Since then, the Manueline style has been considered the unique expression of the "national style" (Bethencourt 1999: 444) and Jerónimos Monastery its masterpiece. It was then necessary to refurbish it. Restoration and remodeling work started in 1860 and lasted until the beginning of the following century. Much of the body of the previous building was modified by neo-Manueline revivalist interventions that introduced maritime-themed decorative elements, sublimating the memorial effect of the monument.

The symbolic rehabilitation of the monastery goes hand in hand with the mythification of Luiz Vaz de Camões (c. 1524/1525–June 10, 1580), author of the sixteenth-century epic *Os Lusíadas*, the magnum opus of the "Portuguese people" and its maritime saga. The commemorations of the Camões Tercentenary were held on June 10, 1880, an initiative largely resulting from the action of the Republicans, which thus highlighted the contrast between the glories of the past symbolized by Camões and the decay of the present symbolized by the monarchy. As part of the celebrations, the bones of the poet and those of the navigator Vasco da Gama were transferred to the Jerónimos Monastery. At a time when Portugal was seeing its African possessions threatened by European powers—which would culminate in the British Ultimatum of 1890, when the British government urged Portugal to withdraw the claim to imperial sovereignty over the territories between Angola and Mozambique—a commemorative cycle dedicated to the glorification of the national epic was inaugurated.[4] The objective was to strategically remind its international competitors of the historical rights of the Portuguese in the partition of Africa and, at the same time, to foster national enthusiasm for the imperial cause (Alexandre 1999: 177). This set of memorial actions would culminate in 1910—the same year of the implantation of the Republic in Portugal—in the classification by decree of the Jerónimos Monastery as national heritage, thus turning it into a major symbol of Portuguese national-imperialist ideology. Belém was then also definitively established as a center of political power, when the former Royal Palace of Belém was designated in 1912 as the official residence of the president of the Portuguese Republic.

The memory of the expansion and the imaginary geographies of the empire were then also perennially inscribed in the symbolic landscape of the area of Belém in a very expressive way through the toponymy and, to a lesser extent, through the statuary. In 1880, the year of the commemoration of the Camões Tercentenary, Dom Vasco da Gama Square appeared in the area, and in 1901, Afonso de Albuquerque Square was built, with a statue of this viceroy and governor of India placed in its center. Shortly afterward, in 1930, a statue to Afonso de Albuquerque was also erected in the city of Porto, joining it to the statue of Prince Henry, which had also been erected in this city in 1894. This period was also marked by the creation, all over Portugal, of new toponyms associated with the maritime expansion and the empire. In Belém, the Bartolomeu Dias Street was established in 1911, in honor of the fifteenth-century navigator.

Along with the monumentalization of Belém's urban space, the first intentions were expressed to set up museums on the site. Once the historical value of the Jerónimos Monastery was enshrined, the question soon arose of installing a museum in the unoccupied spaces adjacent to it. The writer, politician, and geographer Luciano Cordeiro (1844–1900)[5] proposed installing the Torre do Tombo (National Archive) on one side of the body of the monument to function as a "rich and genuine repository of the life of the nation in all its elements and in all its evolutions." This space would also be the "depository of the remains of the Portuguese Discoverers and Navigators" (Cordeiro 1895. 19, 27). For the writer Ramalho Ortigão (1836–1915),[6] the monastery, "in its high expression of faith, adventure and glory" (Ortigão 1897: 8–9), was the ideal place to establish a naval museum.

In any case, the museum intended to be set up in the Jerónimos Monastery would be national in character and house a comprehensive representation of Portugal and the Portuguese people (Branco 1995). The different forms that this representation was taking, in both the discourses and debates on the subject, and in the concrete actions that were developed, would depend strongly on the particular readings of Portuguese culture and identity held by specific agents—individual or institutional—involved in the process.

Navy, archeology, ethnology, and the colonial stand out as the main thematic areas and competing disciplinary domains in the ongoing identity definitions and in the appropriation of the building attached to the Jerónimos Monastery. The Navy Museum was started in 1863 when it was decreed that a collection should be constituted, related to Portuguese maritime activity, to "collect, enjoy and properly classify the glorious monuments of our maritime history" (José Silvestre Ribeiro, cited in Gouveia 1997: 62), and it was thus an obvious candidate to occupy the space. However, difficulties in its institutionalization as a national museum delayed this solution for several decades.

This period also saw a project begin to take shape to create a colonial museum, reflecting the growing importance of this theme in Portuguese life. The Colonial

Museum, containing collections of "colonial products" gathered on "scientific explorations" organized by the Overseas Directorate-General, even had its regulations approved in 1871,[7] but the collections thus constituted were eventually transferred to the Lisbon Geography Society. Founded in 1875, and explicitly dealing with what was termed the "African problem" (Sociedade de Geografia de Lisboa 1950: 40), from the outset, the promoters of the Geography Society declared their intention to set up a museum with ethnographic objects collected from the African colonies. This museum began to take shape in 1884, and because its orientation approached that of the state-created Colonial Museum in 1871, it was decided that the collections gathered in the meantime by state explorations would be transferred there. The Colonial and Ethnographic Museum has been operating in the premises of the Society of Geography at Portas de Santo Antão Street, in Lisbon, since 1892, displaying a collection of products and objects related to the history of the expansion in and exploration of the African continent, with the natural riches and ethnographic traditions of the peoples of the colonies and the metropolis (João 1999: 391).

The progressive affirmation and disciplinary autonomy of archeology and ethnology in this period make these two disciplinary areas also stand out as important candidates for the thematic occupation of the museum space that was intended to be created in the Jerónimos Monastery. The Portuguese Ethnological Museum had been created in 1893 on the proposal of the Portuguese archeologist and ethnographer José Leite de Vasconcelos, from ethnographic and archeological items that he and his colleagues had collected. This museum was temporarily housed in the building of the Lisbon Academy of Sciences, but because of difficulties of space the collection was eventually transferred to the Jerónimos Monastery in 1903. The existence of a collection of ethnographic and archeological objects already constituted by Leite de Vasconcelos thus ended up determining which thematic area would occupy the vacant space in the Monastery. In 1906, the museum was opened to the public, legitimizing that space as a museum dedicated to the origins of the Portuguese people, where archeological materials complemented by ethnographic objects predominate.

However, this symbolization of national identity around the Portuguese people and their remote origins would soon be under discussion. The retirement of Leite de Vasconcelos in 1929 and his replacement by Manuel Heleno as director of the museum prompted a review both of the museum's disciplinary vocation and of the version of the national identity contained therein. In particular, this discussion involved the disciplinary affirmation of ethnography, sidelined in the museum by the predominance of archeology and also the claim for a broader representation of Portuguese national identity that included the reality of the situation overseas (Gouveia 1997: 153). The imperial is then claimed as inseparable from the national, which would be expressed by the museum, including a section of indigenous ethnography in the predominantly archeological collection on the national roots of the Portuguese people. This aspiration reflected the claim for the creation of a colonial museum run directly by the state—considering that the existing one had been assigned to the Geography Society—which was justified on the basis of the long imperial history of Portugal. However, the creation of such a museum was delayed for many decades, as we will see later.

In this period, the colonial theme was also beginning to enter the city space through broader and less explicit forms. One example was the planting of many exotic species from Brazil, Africa, and Asia in the city, constituting a very visible yet indiscernible memory of the Portuguese expansion in the city space, which thus acquired a complexion of colonial city. This purpose was also achieved by the creation of botanical gardens. In Belém, the Colonial Garden was created in 1912 and the Colonial Agricultural Museum was inaugurated in 1929. Finding no expression in the national museums, the colonial theme was thus referred to the question of the exploration and development of the colonial economy.

Lisbon, the Imperial City

With the establishment of the military dictatorship in 1926, followed by the institutionalization of the Estado Novo (New state) regime in 1933, a true monumental glorification of the empire was undertaken throughout the country, particularly in Lisbon, which reconfigured itself in this period as an imperial city. In this glorification, the Jerónimos Monastery and the Belém area became the key parts in the dramatization of the regime's "Imperial Mysticism" (Léonard 1999). One of the most definitive examples of this glorification was the Portuguese World Exhibition, held in Belém in 1940 (from June 23 to December 2). It received more than three million visitors, mostly Portuguese, at a time when Europe was being plagued by the Second World War (Corkill and Almeida 2009). Designed to mark the double commemoration of the founding of the nation in 1143 and the restoration of independence from Spain in 1640, the exhibition, considered the largest propaganda event of the Estado Novo, was a very important vehicle for the diffusion and validation of the nationalist-imperialist ideology of Salazar's regime (Almeida 2005).

Having taken two years to build, the exhibition entailed a profound rearrangement in the monumental space of Belém, leaving long-lasting marks on the urban landscape of Lisbon. The Jerónimos Monastery was the central element around which the exhibition space was conceived and a large square was created— the Praça do Império (Empire Square)—which was the focal point of the exhibition. The modernist design of the space was brought by the architect Cottinelli Telmo (1897–1948), who was responsible for several major works under the Estado Novo. The entire public and political space of Belém was then organized from this ornamental cluster. On the one hand, by highlighting the monumental features of this part of the city, symbolically allusive to the theme of the "Discoveries" and the "golden age" of Portuguese history; on the other, the historic city was at the same time affirmed as a political center, both national and imperial (França 1980: 39). In concrete terms, the intervention there resulted in the demolition of the whole urban fabric that was inappropriate to the monumental glorification that was taking place. Part of the historical housing core of the Belém area disappeared, to open up an area of 560,000 square meters intended to provide sites for participants in the exhibition. Furthermore, the groups of houses that interrupted the continuous view of the body of the monastery when viewed from the riverside were also demolished. The "real" city was destroyed and in its place the "symbolic city of Portuguese history" built, as defined by the Commissioner-General of the Exhibition Augusto de Castro (cited in Corkill and Almeida 2009: 393). It was in this space, which extends to the river by crossing the railway via a footbridge decorated with crusaders, that the exhibition project was established, comprising a set of pavilions that showcased the history, culture, and economic activities of the regions and colonies of Portugal. In its design, the exhibition conceived the empire as an impregnable part of the nation and presented it in its "sanitized version" (397), with a view to extolling the civilizing qualities of Portuguese colonialism.

Without the filter of historiographical rigor, the result was a kind of historicist museum-park that included a colonial section installed in the Colonial Garden. This section included various pavilions featuring the overseas provinces, with maps, photographs of indigenous life, showcases of local products, replicas of "typical" streets (such as streets in India and Macao), with its most important monuments (such as the Church of St. Francis Xavier of Goa and a Chinese temple of Macao). There were also reconstructions of the villages and dwellings of the indigenous peoples of the colonies, which even included "human samples" of different African peoples. A mythical and abstract representation of the national identity linked with the Portuguese maritime expansion, and exalted through the figures of the solitary heroes who made the collective epic, was combined with another one that was more anchored in an idea of the popular, both rural and colonial. Both modes, the monumental and the ethnographic, often acquired a modernist tonality, brought about by the architectural design of the space.

History blended with ethnography, both with very selective elements of the modern (Corkill and Almeida 2009: 395), resulting in a true bric-a-brac of memorial objects belonging to different temporal and geographical scales, but which came together to make up a memory complex designed as representing the "Portuguese world." As in Boyer's reading, the *city of collective memory* was thus built with the same fictional devices that serve to build a museum, based on the selection of fragments of historical information to construct a representational totality. Without its curator's "fabulations," this totality "simply crumbles into a random show" (Boyer 1996: 132).

In the case of the Portuguese World Exhibition, its functional disintegration was precipitated by the theatrical and ephemeral character of the buildings. The time available for the construction of the exhibition project determined that practically all the built structures were temporary. The closing of the exhibition made it clear that the project was provisional, a situation that was aggravated by many structures being damaged by a heavy storm that occurred shortly after it closed. The space was then entrusted to a commission (*Comissão Administrativa do Plano de Obras da Praça do Império*—CAOPI), which was responsible, in collaboration with the Lisbon City Council, for planning the redevelopment of Praça do Império and the rest of the exhibition space (Elias 2004: 105). Some pavilions were demolished while others were kept with the prospect that they might become permanent. The cultural and tourist use of the space was also foreseen, and lease contracts were signed with the purpose of giving the vacant spaces a use. However, most of these contracts were not renewed, which worsened the abandonment of part of the former exhibition park. In 1945, CAOPI was eventually wound up before the spaces had been fully redeveloped.

Several projects later emerged to consolidate the Belém area as a space of national glorification. The Portuguese World Exhibition had already placed the emphasis on the imperial theme, which in turn reopened the debate about the profile of the museums to be installed in the area. The creation or installation of a museum related to the theme of maritime "Discoveries" in the still vacant parts of the Jerónimos Monastery was again called for. Duarte Pacheco (1900–1943), minister of public works and mayor of Lisbon, then proposed that two museums should be installed in the vacant side sections of the Monastery—an Ultramarine Museum and the Navy Museum—keeping the already existing Portuguese Ethnological Museum in the center. However, the only museum that was eventually established in Belém was the Museum of Popular Art, a folk art/ethnographic museum which was installed in one of the vacant pavilions of the Exhibition in 1948. Without their own representational space, the maritime and colonial themes then became fixed largely through the monumental heritage—Jerónimos Monastery and Belém Tower—and toponyms. In other words, it was the materiality of the built landscape that cemented them, not an explicit narrative interpretation such as that made in a museological context.

Indeed, it was in toponymy that the regime's action was most vigorous in spatially inscribing a comprehensive memory of the empire. With even greater emphasis than in the previous period, during the Estado Novo the marks of the empire were extensively incorporated into the city's "imaginative geographies" in an enduring celebration of the imperial feats of national history. The practice of inscription of geographical names of the empire began in 1933, when the names of parts of the empire were assigned to streets in the district known as Colónias, then recently built in Lisbon city center, with the Streets of Angola, Cabo Verde, Ílha de Sao Tome e Príncipe, Macao, Mozambique, Timor, or Zaire.[8] This action in the toponymy would also serve as a symbolic response of the regime to international pressure on Portuguese colonial domains. For instance, following the independence of India in 1947 and in response to the demand for the integration of Portuguese India into the Indian Union, in 1948, the government created the Damão, Diu, and Goa Squares in Belém, as well as several other toponyms all linked to the Portuguese expansion to India, such as India Avenue, Dom Vasco da Gama Avenue, São Francisco Xavier Street, Fernão Mendes Pinto Street, Damião de Góis Street, Dom Manuel I Square, among others.[9]

In the postwar aftermath, and in an international environment marked by increasing independence pressures on Portuguese possessions in Africa, the colonial theme was once again the subject of various symbolic investments by the Estado Novo. In 1951, a plan was devised to convert Belém into a space of overseas (*ultramar*) representation, in accordance with the requirements of Portuguese foreign policy (Ferreira 1987). This plan would center on the construction of an overseas palace and would include a complex of buildings under the Ministry of Overseas Territories: Overseas Museum, Higher Institute of Overseas Studies, and Institute of Tropical Medicine. The plan, as conceived by architect Luís Cristino da Silva (1896–1976), never came to fruition, but a conception of Lisbon metropolis, replacing Lisbon capital of the empire, did increasingly take shape in the Belém area and its neighboring spaces. In particular, the construction of three buildings achieved this, characterized by an institutional architecture intended to accommodate functions and services related to the overseas administration: the Overseas Ministry, designed in 1960 and located in Restelo (today the Ministry of Defense); the Institute of Hygiene and Tropical Medicine (completed in 1958); and the Overseas Hospital, designed in 1967 (today Egas Moniz Hospital). The last two are on Junqueira Street in Belém. Also on this street, in the Burnay Palace, the Higher Institute of Social Sciences and Overseas Politics (ISCSPU), formerly the Colonial School, opened its premises in 1962. A functional feature was thus added to a more commemorative one in the layout of the space of Belém, contributing to its symbolic effectiveness as a center of imperial power.

However, the issue of rehabilitation of the spaces abandoned by the Portuguese World Exhibition still had to be dealt with, along with the indecisions and postponements regarding the creation of the Overseas Museum. In order to resolve this impasse, in 1956, the government decided to assign to the Navy Museum facilities in the Jerónimos Monastery, which would then accommodate two tenants: the Portuguese Ethnological Museum (rebaptized as the National Museum of Archaeology and Ethnology in 1965), and the Navy Museum, which opened to the public in 1962, with a plan enshrining an interpretation of the national identity associated with Portugal's maritime vocation through its naval history.

In 1958, a new urbanization plan was drawn up, again by Cristino da Silva, although all that remains of the implementation of this plan was the construction in 1960 of a monument in honor of Prince Henry to mark the fifth centenary of his death: the Monument to the Discoveries. Originally, the monument was a temporary structure exhibited at the Portuguese World Exhibition of 1940, the work of architect Cottinelli Telmo (1897–1948) and sculptor Leopoldo de Almeida (1898–1975). It was eventually destroyed in 1943, before being turned into a definitive structure in concrete and stonework. The monument is a representation of a stylized caravel bow, facing the river Tagus, with sculptures of thirty-two illustrious characters, including kings, navigators, missionaries, intellectuals, and conquerors, topped by the mythical figure of Prince Henry, who symbolically holds a caravel in his hands. Other symbols adorn the monument, such as the huge sword cross that stands the full height of the building or the drawing of a large rose compass, with a world map in the center, depicted on the floor. At the same time, Praça do Império was also restored, with the inclusion of flower beds that represent the coats of arms of the capitals of the provinces of metropolitan Portugal and of the empire, in alphabetical order, from the coats of arms of the Province of Angola to the coats of arms of the city of Viseu.

The Colonial Museum, renamed Overseas Museum, never actually settled in the nation's reverential space of Belém. Its approximate achievement came years later, as a result of the work of the anthropologist Jorge Dias (1907–1973) and the group assigned to the Center for Studies in Ethnology. The important collections acquired in Mozambique, which made it possible to compile an exhibition about the Maconde people, justified the creation of a museum specializing exclusively in the field of ethnology. In 1965, the Overseas Ethnology Museum was created by decree, but ironically, it was only in 1974—the year when the regime was overthrown and the way for decolonization opened—that the construction of a building located in Restelo, outside the monumental area of Belém, was completed. The museum opened its doors to the public in 1976, by then in the democratic period, and it was renamed National Museum of Ethnology in 1990, in keeping with its topical name. The word "colonial" was thus permanently removed from national semantics.

Cosmopolitanism and National Branding

After the end of the Estado Novo, the space of Belém went through another recomposition. This again began with the Jerónimos Monastery as well as with a classification act: in 1983, the monastery, together with the Belém Tower, were inscribed on the UNESCO World Heritage List. Regarding the monastery, UNESCO justifies this classification by the fact that these monuments are "directly associated with the Golden Age of the Discovery and the pioneer role the Portuguese had in the 15th and 16th centuries in creating contacts, dialogue and interchange among different cultures."[10] Since UNESCO is an institution that represents a culture of peace, democracy, and cooperation, its classification was a permanent act of praise and prestige, legitimizing the space of Belém as one of commemoration of the nation, neutral to the political configurations that modeled it (Harrison and Hitchcock 2005).

Since then, two perspectives have been decisive in the composition of Belém's space and in the configuration of the discourses on the memory of Portugal's imperial past in the national public space. First, there is a pedagogical perspective on the history of the nation, conveyed by the most diverse sectors of Portuguese society, interested in pointing out the full democratic inclusion of the country in the European context. Second, there is a perspective of commodification, in which the past gains an exchange value in the cultural and tourist consumption market. As hallowed spaces in the national mythical landscape, the Jerónimos Monastery and Belém Tower were used to hold the most significant events in matters of foreign relations and cultural policy developed by the Portuguese state after the end of the Estado Novo. On June 12, 1985, the Treaty of Accession of Portugal to the European Economic Community (EEC) was signed at the monastery.[11] On June 10, 1987, the president of the republic honored the "Portuguese Discoverers" at a ceremony held in the Belém Tower Gardens to mark the official opening of the National Commemorations of the Portuguese Discoveries, entrusted to a specially created Commission, which was active until 2002.

The cultural and the historical were again appropriated by politics, with various cultural institutions under the seal of state power together with its economic partners acting as agents in constructing narratives about the national imagined community. Jerónimos Monastery, Belém Tower, and the Monument to the Discoveries are, as they were before, the major agents of this representation. It is, therefore, in the *artifact* of the monument itself that in large part lies the interpretation of the Portuguese imperial past in the symbolic space of Belém. This results in an inert and repetitive memory, which gives "to the fiction of the past," as Marc Guillaume argues, "the guarantee of its visibility and materiality" (2003: 143). This fictional effect is further facilitated by the shortage of informative texts or other interpretative materials within the monuments themselves that would foster a deeper understanding of Portuguese maritime—and imperial—history.

To these protagonists another was added, materializing the re-narrativizations under way in the democratic period in matters of national identity. The construction of the Belém Cultural Center (CCB) in 1988 would fulfill a significant symbolic function, as it would allow the arrangement of Belém's urban space to be resumed, with a definitive intervention in the empty spaces left by the Portuguese World Exhibition of 1940. But it would also allow the materialization of a very modern and cosmopolitan version of the Portuguese national identity. Built in 1992 to host the Portuguese Presidency of the European Community and later to develop cultural activity, the CCB once again represented an affirmation of Belém as a center of political power, not only in relation to the national whole but also in relation to the European context, where Portugal was then seeking a new political and symbolic standing. A foundation was created to manage the CCB, and it was named the Discoveries Foundation. Once again, the national history and the glorious past of the nation were used to bless and legitimize cultural policies.

Establishing itself as a frame of reference in terms of cultural offerings of an erudite character, but aimed at the general public, the CCB stated its political objectives of spreading access to cultural goods and consolidating a market of cultural consumption in the Portuguese capital. This is what M. Christine Boyer has termed "contemporary arts of city-building": the art of building stylized landscapes and standardized environments as "vital instruments enhancing the prestige and desirability of place" (Boyer 1996: 4–5). This is achieved by investing in the construction of new public spaces, capable of helping to define a cosmopolitan and differentiating image of the city—and of the country—in order to make it competitive in a postindustrial context characterized by a consumer global culture. Here, cultural objects and heritage are defined according to the rules of the leisure, entertainment, and tourism markets (Balibrea 2003: 33).

A privileged context for observing this increasing tendency to commodify the national past, at the expense of the deflation of its ideological context, are the different proposals for creating a museum alluding to the theme of the "Discoveries" and the Portuguese maritime expansion in the Belém area. The proposal to create a museum of this nature was first promoted in 2006 by Isabel Pires de Lima, minister of culture in the seventeenth constitutional government led by the Socialist Party, when she launched the project for the creation of the museum Mar da Língua Portuguesa (Sea of Portuguese Language)— Interpretative Centre of the Discoveries. The aim of this new museum was to highlight the fact that Portuguese is the fifth most spoken language in the world, with about two hundred million speakers, the "most visible permanent result" of the Portuguese expansion in the fifteenth and sixteenth centuries, while, at the same time, turning it into "one of the most visited" museums in Lisbon.[12] Focusing on the issue of the diffusion of the Portuguese language, the museum, which would be interactive in nature, would also be a "museum of the sea," a terminology that proves a new reconfiguration of the semantic meanings attributed to the period of the "Discoveries." Thus, the proposal can be read as an attempt to finally create a museum to represent this historical period, albeit in a poetic guise that allows the removal of the political, social, and economic processes involved. This is the same mechanism identified by Nélia Dias when analyzing the knowledge technologies used in the Quai Branly Museum, which allow the colonial past to be transposed through aesthetic mechanisms that eliminate its political dimension (Dias 2008: 305). The project also proposed the installation of this new museum in the premises of the Museum of Popular Art, a survivor of the Portuguese World Exhibition of 1940, which was effectively abandoned. Notwithstanding, this proposal was received with huge criticism. A civic movement was created in defense of the Museum of Popular Art, and in June 2009, a colloquium was held to discuss its existence (Leal 2009). The project to create the Museum Mar da Língua Portuguesa was eventually shelved.

However, the idea of creating a museum of this kind was revived later. In April 2010, another minister of culture, Gabriela Canavilhas, of the eighteenth constitutional government led by the Socialist Party announced that a new Museum of the Discoveries would occupy the space previously used by the National Museum of Archaeology (the former Portuguese Ethnological Museum created by Leite de Vasconcelos), which would be transferred to Cordoaria Nacional, an exhibition space outside Belém's central monumental nucleus. According to the minister, the new museum aimed to tell "our epic of the Discoveries made by the sea and travels"[13] and would be a project shared between the Ministry of Culture and the Navy. In fact, the project presupposed the expansion of the Navy Museum into the Archaeology Museum space and also assumed the Navy Museum would be reorganized to highpoint a component relating to the "Discoveries" and the Portuguese expansion.[14] Once again, an intense controversy was triggered around the expulsion of the Archaeology Museum from the Jerónimos Monastery. The Archeologists' Society worked to prevent the museum from leaving its historical premises and launched a public petition to prevent this outcome.[15] However, the scenario of profound budgetary restraint that was sparked in the meantime delayed the implementation of several projects. The transfer of the National Archaeological Museum to Cordoaria Nacional was postponed and the intense controversy surrounding the displacement of the Archaeological Museum from the nation's symbolizing center immediately ceased. The idea of creating a Museum of the Discoveries was, however, revived at the end of 2011, when members of the nineteenth constitutional government led by the Social Democratic Party (PSD) decided to ponder another use for the building that was then being built to house the Museu dos Coches (Coach Museum). This other use would be that of a travel and language museum, similar to the previously advanced proposals, extolling the Portuguese civilizing legacy in the world through the diffusion of language and other cultural forms.[16] This intention was never realized, and in 2015, the Museu dos Coches was inaugurated in the building designed for it.

The intention to create a museum on the theme of the "Discoveries" was to be realized not in Lisbon but in Porto. Furthermore, instead of a public investment, it was a venture undertaken by Mystic Invest, a private Portuguese financial company operating in the travel and tourism sector. The result is the interactive museum World of Discoveries, a theme park based on the history of the "Portuguese Discoveries" that opened in Miragaia, Porto, in 2014. Recreating life-size characters and scenarios in a very childish way, including a part of the visit made in a small boat that sails through the continents explored by the Portuguese, this museum can be understood as an extreme version of the tendency to commodify the Portuguese imperial past in the service of the tourism industry.

But Lisbon would not set aside its intention of having a museum dedicated to the "Portuguese Discoveries" under the municipality's seal. In 2017, a new proposal for the creation of a Museum of the Discoveries was made, this time by the hand of the mayor of Lisbon, Fernando Medina (from the Socialist Party). The proposal had been included in his electoral program for the City Council and advocated, still in very general terms, the creation of a "poly-nucleated structure in the city that includes some existing spaces/museums and some others to create anew that promote a reflection on that historical period [that of Portuguese maritime expansion] in its multiple approaches, be it economic, scientific, or cultural, in its most and least positive aspects, including a core dedicated to the theme of slavery."[17] According to the proposal, this structure would be named Museum of the Discoveries. A heated reaction to this proposed name broke out immediately. More than one hundred academics, historians, and social scientists from national and foreign institutions signed and published an open letter in the *Expresso* newspaper entitled "Why a museum dedicated to Portuguese 'Expansion' and the processes it has unleashed cannot and should not be called 'Discoveries Museum.'" According to the signatories of the letter, the name "Discoveries" "crystallizes a historical inaccuracy," since the word "discovery" . . . "only refers to the perception of reality from the point of view of the European peoples," whereas "for the non-Europeans, the idea that they were 'discovered' is problematic." In conclusion, it is also considered that "at a time when debates on Portuguese colonial history intensify, . . . it is important that a new museum would also be a reflection of this problematizing richness."[18]

Indeed, while the previous proposals have been criticized on the basis of disciplinary arguments and in view of defending the ownership of established knowledge areas such as archeology and ethnography over the representation of national identity, now, for the first time, the arguments put forward were ideological, calling for a less fictional and more problematizing representation of

Portuguese imperial history. In the aftermath of the financial crisis that Portugal lived through, and in an international scenario of growing ideological polarization around identity politics, Portugal also finally opened up the field for a debate on the legacies of Portuguese colonialism.

Concluding Remarks: Persistence and Contestation

Although there is an increasing tendency to commodify the national past, which contributes to deflate its ideological content, there is also, especially in recent years, the emergence of areas of contestation and articulation of counter-memories. Voices claiming for the recognition of the facets of Portuguese colonialism that contradict the dominant representation around its supposed kindness in comparison with other European colonialisms have become increasingly eloquent. Slavery, forced labor, but also the colonial wars and the return of settlers from Africa are suggesting new ways of remembering the colonial past and have increasingly focused attention on the "wounds" of Portuguese colonialism. In Belém, the exhibition "Return: Traces of Memory" was held in 2015, proposing to reflect on decolonization and the return of nationals from former Portuguese colonies, which occurred in 1975.[19] In 2017, the National Museum of Archaeology was part of the cycle "Testimonials of Slavery: African Memory" held in the context of the Lisbon 2017 Ibero-American Capital of Culture event, organizing and displaying an exhibition on the subject.[20] The Exhibition "Racism and Citizenship"[21] was organized under the same event and held in the Monument to the Discoveries. At the same time, several associations of Afro-descendants active in the field of memory were created, such as the Djass Association, which in 2017 submitted an application to the Participatory Budget of the Lisbon City Council, with the proposal to create a Memorial to Enslaved People in Lisbon.[22]

All these initiatives were unprecedented in calling for a more problematizing and critical memory of the long Portuguese imperial history that does not refer solely to the "golden age" of the "Discoveries." Furthermore, they took place in consecrated spaces of the Portuguese official memory, with the support of the political and media spheres. However, even if a postcolonial critique has inevitably permeated the symbolic space of the city of Lisbon, the Portuguese imperial past rests a memorial reference for national identity, remaining very resistant to different interpretations. This is made evident by the heated debates that rage daily around the legacies of the Portuguese colonial empire, with one faction brandishing the uncompromising defense of Portugal's sacred imperial heritage and the other clamoring for the decolonization of practices, representations, and knowledges. Even if this debate is most often centered in the city of Lisbon, with the rest of the country remaining largely absent from it, it has not failed to irreversibly assert a space for the representation of memories and experiences of the Portuguese colonial past, other than the sacralizing readings that have made up the discourse of Portuguese national-imperialism for several decades.

Notes

1. Period corresponding to the intensive maritime exploration undertaken by the Portuguese during the fifteenth and sixteenth centuries.
2. Vasco da Gama (c. 1460s–1524) was a Portuguese navigator and the first European to reach India by sea.
3. https://www.foriente.pt/files/acto_instituicao.pdf (accessed October 30, 2021).
4. In addition to the commemorations of 1880, this cycle includes Portugal's participation in the Colombian centenary (1892), the fourth centenary of the birth of Prince Henry (1894), the discovery of the maritime route to India (1898), the "discovery" of Brazil (1900), the conquest of Ceuta and the anniversaries of Afonso de Albuquerque (1915), Fernão de Magalhães (1921), Camões (1924), and Vasco da Gama (1925).
5. Founder of the Lisbon Geographical Society and noted for his fierce defense of Portugal's interests in Africa.
6. One of the main figures of the so-called seventies generation (*Geração de 70*), a nineteenth-century academic movement that revolutionized various dimensions of Portuguese culture, from politics to literature.
7. Decree-law, January 26, 1871.
8. With April 25, 1974, and the consequent Portuguese decolonization, the "neighborhood" was renamed the District of the New Nations, although colloquially it was always referred to as Bairro das Colónias. Later on, in another political context, in the 1960s and 1970s, cities and towns in Mozambique, Angola, Guinea, and Cape Verde were used for naming the streets of another Lisbon district, the Bairro dos Olivais.
9. Being very expressive in Lisbon, the creation of toponyms allusive to the empire or to the maritime "Discoveries" was neither exclusive to the capital of the country nor restricted to the dictatorial period, having continued during the democratic age. In fact, a study done for the *Observador* newspaper shows that there are 343 toponyms named after Vasco da Gama and 246 after Prince Henry and that the "Discoveries" theme is one of the most used in Portuguese toponymy, especially in Lisbon and the Algarve. See Rocha (2018).
10. https://whc.unesco.org/en/list/263 (accessed December 4, 2021).
11. The Jerónimos Monastery was also the venue for the signing of the Treaty of Lisbon on December 13, 2007.
12. "Mar da Língua nasce no Museu de Arte Popular," Diário de Notícias, October 31, 2006, https://www.dn.pt/arquivo/2006/mar-da-lingua-nasce-no-museu-de-arte-popular-648128.html (accessed December 6, 2021).
13. *Público*, April 14, 2010.
14. *Público*, April 14, 2010.
15. The news of the transfer of the Archaeological Museum was received with indignation by various sectors of society and a movement of Friends of the Archaeological Museum was set up to support keeping the Museum in the Jerónimos Monastery. See http://gamna.blogspot.pt/2010_07_01_archive.html (accessed March 20, 2013). An online petition was posted requiring that the Archaeological Museum remain at Jerónimos. See http://www.peticao.com.pt/museu-national-of-archeology (accessed March 20, 2013). A similar petition was also posted online against transferring the Navy Museum's estate to a new museum. See http://www.peticaopublica.com/Peticao Ver.aspx?pi=P2010N2153 (accessed March 20, 2013).

16 *Público*, September 29, 2011.
17 http://www.cm-lisboa.pt/fileadmin/DOCS/Publicacoes/publicacoes-digitais/Presidencia/Programa_Governo_Lisboa_2017-2021.pdf (accessed October 30, 2019).
18 *Expresso*, April 12, 2018.
19 http://www.cm-lisboa.pt/noticias/detalhe/article/retornar-tracos-de-memoria-em-exposicao (accessed November 30, 2015).
20 Um Museu, tantas coleções! Testemunhos da Escravatura. Memória Africana (museunacionalarqueologia.gov.pt) (accessed August 1, 2017).
21 http://www.padraodosdescobrimentos.pt/pt/evento/racismo-e-cidadania/ (accessed August 1, 2017).
22 https://www.facebook.com/associacao.djass/posts/1759579381004239 (accessed December 1, 2017).

References

Alexandre, V. (1999). "Nação e Império." In F. Bethencourt and K. Chaudhuri (eds.), *História da Expansão Portuguesa*, vol. 4, 90–142. Lisbon: Círculo de Leitores.
Almeida, J. C. (2005). *Celebrar Portugal: A Nação, as Comemoração Públicas e as Políticas de Identidade*. Lisbon: Instituto Piaget.
Balibrea, M. P. (2003). "Memória e espaço público na Barcelona pós-industrial." *Revista Crítica de Ciências Sociais*, 67: 31–54.
Bethencourt, F. (1999). "A memória da Expansão." In F. Bethencourt and K. Chaudhuri (eds.), *História da Expansão Portuguesa*, vol. 4, 442–80. Lisbon: Círculo de Leitores.
Boyer, M. C. (1996). *The City of Collective Memory: Its Historical Imagery and Architectural Entertainments*. Cambridge, MA: MIT Press.
Branco, J. F. (1995). "Lugares para o povo: uma periodização da cultura popular em Portugal." *Revista Lusitana* (Nova Série), 13–14: 145–77.
Cordeiro, L. (1895). *As Obras dos Jerónimos: Parecer Apresentado à Comissão dos Monumentos Nacionais*. Lisbon: n/e.
Corkill, D., and J. C. P. Almeida (2009). "Commemoration and Propaganda in Salazar's Portugal: The *Mundo Português* Exposition of 1940." *Journal of Contemporary History*, 44(3): 381–99.
Dias, N. (2008). "Double Erasures: Rewriting the Past at the Musée du Quai Branly." *Social Anthropology*, 16(3): 300–11.
Elias, H. (2004). "A Emergência de um Espaço de Representação: Arte Pública e Transformações Urbanas na Zona Ribeirinha de Belém." *On the w@terfront*, 6. http://www.raco.cat/index.php/Waterfront/ article/viewFile/216971/289615 (accessed July 30, 2010).
Ferreira, V. M. (1987). *A Cidade de Lisboa: de Capital do Império a Centro da Metrópole*. Lisbon: Publicações Dom Quixote.
França, J. A. (1980). "1940: Exposição do Mundo Português." *Colóquio Artes*, 2.ª série, 45: 34–47.
Gouveia, H. C. (1997). "Museologia e Etnologia em Portugal: Instituições e Personalidades." PhD thesis, FCSH, Universidade Nova de Lisboa, Lisbon.
Guillaume, M. (2003). *A Política do Património*. Lisbon: Campo de Letras.
Harrison, D., and M. Hitchcock (eds.) (2005). *The Politics of World Heritage: Negotiating Tourism and Conservation*. Wiltshire: Cromwell.

João, M. I. (1999). "Organização da memória." In F. Bethencourt and K. Chaudhuri (eds.), *História da Expansão Portuguesa*, vol. 4, 376–402. Lisbon: Círculo de Leitores.

Leal, J. (2009). "Da arte popular às culturas populares híbridas." *Etnográfica*, 13(2): 67– 80.

Léonard, Y. (1999). "O Império Colonial Salazarista." In F. Bethencourt and K. Chaudhuri (eds.), *História da Expansão Portuguesa*, vol. 2, 2–30. Lisbon: Círculo de Leitores.

Ortigão, R. (1897). *A Conclusão do Edifício dos Jeronymos: Parecer da Commissão Approvada em Sessão de 23 de Junho de 1897*. Lisbon: Comissão Nacional dos Monumentos, Imprensa Nacional.

Rocha, R. P. (2018). "De Cunhal a Salazar: Há ideologia nos nomes das ruas de Portugal (e muito mais)." *Observador*. https://observador.pt/especiais/de-cunhal-a-salazar-ha-ideologia-nos-nomes-das-ruas-de-portugal-e-muito-mais/ (accessed December 21, 2021).

Sociedade de Geografia de Lisboa (1950). *75 Anos de Actividades ao Serviço da Ciência e da Nação: 1875–1950*. Lisbon: Sociedade de Geografia de Lisboa.

Chapter 3

NARRATIVES OF TRANSITION AND THE INSTITUTIONALIZATION OF PORTUGUESE COLONIAL HISTORY: BIOGRAPHY AND AESTHETIZATION

Nuno Domingos

Imperial history has been essential for the production of a Portuguese national memory. After April 25, 1974, when a military coup overturned the Estado Novo regime (1933–74) and paved the way for the end of the colonial wars and the independence of the former colonies, imperial celebration instantly collapsed. Gradually, however, new allusions to the colonial past have begun to emerge during the Portuguese democratic period. The ongoing reintroduction of colonial memory as a fundamental dimension of the Portuguese national history recycles the images and rhetoric put forward by the ideology of Portuguese colonial exceptionalism, advocated since the 1950s by the Estado Novo regime. These lusotropicalist tropes reclaim the universal character of Portugal and emphasize how the country was a leader of a multicultural globalization and how it was able to create a specific experience in the colonized territories, usually defined as a cultural exchange. This general representation allows for the long imperial era within the national chronology to be retained, creating a linear Lusophone time.

Entrenched as an unchallenged account taken as given, this master narrative is renarrated today through diverse institutional arenas. Dependent on a larger field of national power, but using specific idioms, categories, and chronologies, some of these institutional mediums have a unique capacity to naturalize national ideology.[1] More specifically, they become very effective in establishing a bond between the colonial and postcolonial periods. Therefore, their internal historical accounts work as successful "narratives of transition." Based on two case studies, this chapter stresses how the mechanisms and dynamics of particular institutional spheres, permeated by the state ideology but not part of its typical ideological apparatus, are very effective devices in the mediation and reproduction of an official imperial account. The biography of a famous Mozambican football player and the formal and aesthetic interpretations of the modernist architectural works the Portuguese left in their former African colonies are the examples chosen in this chapter to illustrate how the inner logics of institutional mediations manufacture "imperial narratives of transition."

My first case study is the official biographical construction of Eusébio da Silva Ferreira, the Mozambican football player who rose to prominence in the 1960s, both as part of his club, Sport Lisboa e Benfica, and as part of the Portuguese national team. After his death in 2014, Eusébio was officially recognized as a national hero, and his remains were relocated to the National Pantheon in Lisbon. Celebrities from popular culture, such as football players, were typically absent from the traditional gallery of national heroes, which was filled with statesmen, military officers, explorers, intellectuals, and scientists whose biographies became efficient means to celebrate the past and, more specifically, the imperial past. However, Eusébio's case demonstrates how popular culture can lend the nation's official memory a narrative texture that is flexible enough to produce a virtuous imperial narrative of transition. His biographical account is rooted in the celebration of football talent and embedded in the communitarian bonds and affections produced by football-enhanced identities and by the power popular culture has in the banalization of collective norms and values (Löfgren 1989; Billig 1995; Edensor 2002).

The second case examined here is the role heritage studies has in the making of imperial narratives of transition. During the Estado Novo, the evocation of heritage, used as a touristic asset, was primarily a matter of political propaganda. Nowadays, even if the study of national heritage is not directly propagandist, it nonetheless constitutes one of the principal mediations highlighting the empire's material legacy. In the democratic period, this "heritage machine" (Gonzalez 2019) continued to produce historical representations and shape the strategies of several institutions. Following this lead, I will focus on the particular example of the current academic account of the legacies of modern Portuguese architecture and urban planning in the former imperial territories. In the case of this imperial narrative of transition, the promotion of Portuguese colonial exceptionalism is shaped by technical and aesthetic descriptions of the material legacy left by the Portuguese throughout their overseas territories. Grounded in the interpretation and celebration of the formal and aesthetic achievements of scientists, artists, and architectural schools, current scholarly analysis of Portuguese architectural heritage ends up reifying the national framework that gives value and distinction to that heritage, inevitably translated in the laudatory history of Portuguese authors, styles, and schools. Among the colonial themes most commonly studied by Portuguese scholars, national heritage has always been one of the dominant means of representing the imperial imagination.[2]

While reproducing a mediated historical representation of nation and empire, the narratives of transition analyzed here become powerful means of conceptual violence; they produce reality through the naturalization of an official national account and turn all the dimensions of the Portuguese colonial experience that cannot be celebrated invisible, namely the radical inequities that defined colonial societies and constitute, by and large, the most profound Portuguese imperial legacy.

Empire and Nation

The interpretation of the empire's role in the development of national bonds is an extension of the wider debate on the origins and dynamics of the formation of a Portuguese identity.[3] Within the political field, celebratory imperial representations, aiming to strengthen internal cohesion, were a means to communicate with the Portuguese population. These efforts became more active from the 1820s onward, when territorial and ethnic nationalism arose (Matos 2008a), and peaked in the context of the English Ultimatum of 1890, when the British government objected to Portugal's desire to reclaim imperial sovereignty over the territories between Angola and Mozambique. The strong entanglement between national and imperial pride persisted during the rise of the Republican Movement, which led to the fall of the Portuguese monarchy in 1910, throughout the first Republic (1910–26), and during the Estado Novo dictatorship (1933–74). While criticizing the contour of colonial policies, political oppositions to the Estado Novo recognized Portuguese sovereignty over its imperial possessions until well after the end of the Second World War (Neves 2008). The extensive identification that Portuguese political actors had with the imperial worldview did not depend only on the profound convictions of leaders educated in the nationalistic atmosphere, not even on their declared and undeclared interests: the empire was a political capital and a vehicle to transmit ideas and values to the national population, and, therefore, its existence was non-negotiable. Moreover, the Portuguese political context under the Estado Novo dictatorship, unlike what happened in other colonial metropoles (Gopal 2019), blocked the access of anti-colonial narratives in the public sphere.

In one of the first works on the Portuguese colonial system published after the 1974 Carnation Revolution, the historian Valentim Alexandre (1979) highlighted how most of the studies on colonialism carried out during the Estado Novo regime put forward a whole range of nationalist myths. Among these myths was the theory that the Portuguese were the first to abolish the slave trade. Another myth, based on the official appropriation of Gilberto Freyre's (1951, 1958, 1961) lusotropicalist theory in the 1950s, was the alleged cultural tendency of the Portuguese to create multiracial societies.[4] In the same period, the idea of adaptability and plasticity of the Portuguese people was present in essays on national identity, such as, for example, in the work of the anthropologist Jorge Dias (1955).[5] Few researchers had denounced the contradictions between the official discourse promoted by the state since the 1950s and the reality on the African colonial terrain.[6]

Imperial nationalism was more vigorously challenged when the colonial wars (1961–74) broke out, inciting divisions within the Portuguese ruling classes and a more diverse and openly internal anti-colonialist opposition (Cardina 2011). The consensus concerning the empire's place in the construction of national grandeur was interrupted following the events of April 25, 1974. During the revolutionary period, the political forces defending a swift decolonization had achieved hegemony within the state apparatus and in the political and cultural fields (Pinto 2001: 80). Nonetheless, such ideas were met with resistance. Right-wing political organizations and some of the settlers who left the colonies in 1974 and 1975 called for maintaining ties between Portugal and its former colonies, demanding a different type of decolonization, one that would prolong Portuguese tutelage (83). Although the mainstream right-wing parties co-opted the majority of the voters who had lost something with the decolonization process, they did not demand any kind of sovereignty over the former imperial space. Plans to recover a Portuguese imperial authority thus had no political representation, except for small far-right groups (Marchi 2015). Several polls conducted since the April 25 political transition suggested that most Portuguese considered the actual process of decolonization fair, even if they did not agree with it.[7]

After 1974, other national imaginaries proposed from within the political field replaced the representations of Portuguese imperial grandeur. Projects that envisioned a socialist and revolutionary Portugal, on the one hand, and a European Portugal stabilized in the framework of a liberal democracy (as happened from 1976 onward), on the other, put aside such imperial imagination (Pinto 2003). On African ground, new local actors quickly marginalized the former colonial ruler, as the Cold War became more relevant to explaining the origins of the civil wars that devastated Angola and Mozambique after decolonization.

If Portugal was no longer a relevant regional actor, imperial memory was not something that could instantly vanish from nationalist representations. Little by little, economic and institutional relations with the former colonies were reestablished, old networks resurged, and with them new economic opportunities grew. National diplomacy, reinforced by Portugal's entry into the European Economic Community in 1986, provided the Portuguese state with an intermediary role between Europe and countries in Africa, Latin America, and Asia. In 1996, the creation of the Comunidade de Países de Língua Portuguesa (CPLP; Community of Portuguese Language Countries), justified by a narrative of historical proximity and cultural exchange, proposed a Lusophone imaginary (Margarido 2000). As a strategy for negotiating imperial memory, Lusophony offered a particular perspective on the relations between Portuguese-speaking spaces and encouraged the historical and political recognition of what was positive and acceptable in the past, so that it was possible to create a favorable institutional relationship for diplomacy and business. Through different means and using distinct rhetoric, a hegemonic colonial memory reinforced the idealized past disseminated by the ideology of exceptionalism.

Colonial imaginaries were crucial dimensions of the splendor and historicity of diverse institutional arenas in Portugal, including the military, the Catholic Church, and scientific and cultural organizations, all intrinsically linked with colonial enterprise and imperial and national identity.[8] Several Portuguese spheres of activity whose history is shaped by the imperial experience are still struggling to open a more in-depth discussion about the legacy that colonialism left in their current practices and worldviews.[9]

The politically elected democratic institutions were unable to challenge an established historical account that seems to be shared by a significant portion of the Portuguese population.[10] The end of Portuguese colonial power in Africa did not mean the end of the place of the imperial narrative in the nationalist construction. However, so that a certain representation of the past—a pastoral one (Williams 1973)—still remained, the Estado Novo's imperial rhetoric style had to be abandoned. Today, the propagation of a heroic account of Portugal's history that survived the end of the dictatorship and the end of the African empire relies on narratives that can successfully form a bridge between the colonial and the postcolonial time.

Eusébio: Popular Culture's Hero

Eusébio da Silva Ferreira, a Mozambican-born football player and one of the greatest heroes of Portuguese popular culture, died in January 2014. The relocation of the player's body to the National Pantheon, a monument where some of the most illustrious representatives of the Portuguese nation rest, was the last act in a process that officialized the player's biography (Domingos 2019).[11] The unprecedented institutional celebration of a football player was justified by his extraordinary sporting talent, used at the service of the national football team at a rather special time. Eusébio was initially recognized as a national hero in the 1960s, when the authoritarian Estado Novo regime was struggling to maintain the empire in Angola (1961), Guinea-Bissau (1963), and Mozambique (1964), and at a time when almost all former African colonies were achieving their independence. Champion of S. L. Benfica and the Portuguese national team in the 1960s, Eusébio was not the most obvious choice to join the family of national and imperial heroes. He was only a remarkable football player.

Eusébio does not owe his career to extraordinary talent alone. Born in the Mafalala slum, in the poor and racially segregated suburbs of Lourenço Marques, the capital of Mozambique (today's Maputo), Eusébio soon fell in love with the game, practiced since the beginning of the twentieth century in the outskirts of this city (Domingos 2017). In these suburbs, a group of clubs gathered in 1924 and founded the Associação de Futebol Africana (AFA; African Football Association). Inspired by South African sports associations and competitions, the AFA brought together Black and mestizo players from the periphery, who were not allowed to play in the league organized by the Lourenço Marques Football Association, created in 1923 by a group of settlers' clubs. The two associations operated in Lourenço Marques till 1959, when the Portuguese administration shut down the AFA, considered then an inconvenient vestige of official racialism. This happened one year before Eusébio went to Lisbon to play for Benfica.

Unlike other players who have never been able to reveal their talent outside Lourenço Marques's urban periphery, Eusébio benefited from the relative political opening of the late colonial period and progressed from suburban games to the city center championship. At the time, football was experiencing a process of professionalization, and the search for good athletes partially transcended racial obstacles (Domingos 2017). Transferred to the metropolitan league, some African players rapidly became celebrities. Successful examples, such as Matateu and Mário Coluna, stimulated the development of an imperial football market

(Cleveland 2017). Eusébio only won Benfica's second European Cup in 1962, but his performances were so impressive that he was soon considered one of the best football players in the world (Armstrong 2004).

Eusébio's international status was confirmed when the Portuguese national team won the third place in the 1966 World Cup in England and he was crowned the top scorer. His remarkable performances have made Portugal's name ring around the world. In Lisbon, the unprecedented glorification of a Black African has granted popular culture an emerging role in the construction of modern nationalism.[12] The Estado Novo soon tried to use these triumphs to its advantage. A rarity among European national teams, Portugal's multiracial one could effectively represent the image of an exceptional colonialism (Coelho 2001; Cardão 2015), an imperial imagined community brought to the multitude of football fans. Exploited by the mass media as a means to obtain more audiences and profits, football's imaginary became a subtle and effective ideological tool and Eusébio the greatest protagonist of this particular representation of Portugueseness on the field.

The Institutionalization of a Biographical Account

The quintessential place of the national hero, the empire experienced a renaissance before the end of the nineteenth century. That was the time of the "centenarians": the third centenary of the death of Luís de Camões (1524–1580), the national poet who narrated the greatness of Portugal in *Os Lusíadas*, in 1880; and the fourth centenary of the arrival of Vasco da Gama in India in 1898 (Sobral 2014). At that time, travelers who first explored the African hinterland were also widely celebrated—Serpa Pinto (1846–1900), Hermenegildo Capelo (1841–1917), and Roberto Ivens (1850–1898)—as were the contemporary leaders of the African military campaigns who paved the way to twentieth-century colonialism, such as Mouzinho de Albuquerque (1855–1902) and António Enes (1848–1901). Built on these exemplar biographies, imperial subjectivities were instilled by state institutions, by a canonical written culture, gradually accompanied by iconography—essential in a country where the majority of the population was illiterate—, by the public inscription of a celebratory past, by official ceremonies, by an array of scientific and cultural productions, and also by the commercial circulation of colonial products (Curto 1993; João 2002; Bethencourt 1999; Trindade 2008; Matos 2014). Brought about by the political appropriation of the work of Gilberto Freyre, the lusotropical representations of the Portuguese world spread through the cultural and sports industries in the 1950s and 1960s (Cardão 2015).

Although a football game could be compared to a battlefield, Eusébio did not belong to the genealogy of imperial heroes publicized by the school system and the propaganda apparatus, all white men, overseas explorers, military leaders, missionaries, and colonial administrators (Paulo 2000; Araújo and Maeso 2010). He was also not the classic protagonist of a popular nationalist historiography, which relied heavily on the use of the biographical genre, whose dramatic potential and linear structure made the national narrative more attractive (Matos 2008a).[13]

Yet, his enormous popularity and international projection were not insignificant. For the Estado Novo, he was no longer just an essential name in the history of football but an important protagonist and a product of the circumstances of the national time.

His official promotion to the rank of national hero required, however, an appropriate biography that could describe his sporting achievements, already widely known, while also capable of shaping him as a man. This civilian facade was decisive in building a more reasonable narration of national and imperial history. This proper biographical account was initially written a few years after Eusébio's arrival in Lisbon in late 1961, when he came from his hometown, Lourenço Marques. In 1966, the publication of his autobiography, ghostwritten by Fernando Garcia, a journalist at the Emissora Nacional (the national radio broadcaster), laid the main elements that would produce a certified chronology of Eusébio's life story that, to a great extent, endured until his death (Ferreira 1966).

According to this description, Eusébio was a young man who grew up in the poor but picturesque suburban neighborhoods of Lourenço Marques, which are depicted in the book using a series of exotic elements: the colorful markets, the local traditions, and the traditional clothes worn by women (Ferreira 1966: 6). His devoted mother, Elisa Anissabeni—who, like her son, had the *indígena* status, given by the Portuguese colonial state to the "non-civilized" population—was responsible for his education. His father, a mestizo railroad worker from Angola, died when Eusébio was only eight years old. As the book tells us, Eusébio was a devout Catholic and a dedicated student who revealed his talent during the games played in his district of Mafalala. Before he joined Sporting of Lourenço Marques, he knew little about Lourenço Marques's city center, because, according to his autobiography, he was very attached to his neighborhood (7). At seventeen, he was already a local idol. He made the leap to Lisbon with a controversial transfer to Benfica. Beyond his great sporting prowess, other factors helped propel his public persona, including his enlistment in the Portuguese army in 1963 and his virtuous marriage with Flora Bruheim who had also come from Mozambique. Extensively covered by the press, his marriage was described as the romantic culmination of a great love, with Eusébio portrayed as a typical head of the family in the Estado Novo's patriarchal society.

There was a central moral to this autobiographical depiction: Eusébio's success did not affect his simplicity and humility. More than his qualities as a football player, simplicity and humility were what best defined the kind-hearted national hero who had come from the lower rungs of society and achieved a public status through popular culture. These features, however, also defined the idealized behavior of the assimilated African in the Portuguese empire. More generally, one could say that these qualities met the behavior that was expected of the respectable working classes; they were the sort of features that must persist in order for the processes of social mobility not to disturb the status quo.

Staged in an idealized social and historical context, Eusébio's life history become a medium through which history is built and naturalized, basically in accordance with the common lusotropicalist ideals.[14] Conversely, so that this pastoral is effective, all the biographical aspects that disclose meaningful counter-pastorals must be purged.

According to his sanctioned biographical account, Eusébio did not grow up in the segregated neighborhoods of Lourenço Marques, where malnutrition and deadly diseases were common and the mortality rate seven times higher than that of the "cement city" (the city center) (Rita-Ferreira 1967–8). Eusébio was not part of a community of people who were victims of continuous violence, forcibly removed from the city center, controlled and monitored, exploited as cheap labor, forced to emigrate to the South African gold and diamond mines to survive. According to this exemplary biography, he did not grow up in a city where the local African population did not have the same civil, legal, and political rights as the white settlers, where they could not use the same leisure spaces, the same schools, the same hospitals, and the same transports as the Europeans.

While this imperial representation, trivialized by the life of a football player, was built at a time when the Estado Novo's censorship was very vigorous, this archetypal tale has survived the empire's fall. After 1974, Eusébio remained very popular, becoming an official symbol of the national team and of Benfica; he was also Benfica's assistant coach for a long period. He occasionally supported political parties and candidates, almost always center-right, but his value as an electoral asset was not significant. On many occasions, he said his "politics was football" (Armstrong 2004: 263). Such disinterest in politics strengthened the consensus around his person, reinforced after his death.

His death produced a phenomenon of national commotion and popular participation, particularly manifest during his epic funeral. The spontaneous fervor that characterized popular reactions to Eusébio's death was gradually systematized by the mediatized speeches of the professionals of representation (Bourdieu 1987: 14). The voices of politicians, media commentators, notable figures from different spheres of Portuguese society, and representatives of official Portuguese football bodies spoke in unison, reinforcing the representation of the great athlete and the simple and humble man. Some of these figures immediately argued for the need to officialize a national emotion around Eusébio.

Through a unanimous decision, the Portuguese parliament decided that Eusébio's body would be transferred to the National Pantheon, home to several national heroes. The words that justified his presence in the Pantheon immortalized a biography that became an homage to Portuguese history, as the Mozambican player was considered

> a milestone in the diffusion and globalization of the image and the importance of Portugal in the world . . . [He was] immediately recognized all over the world, attached to the image of Portugal thanks to his personality, his affability and his humility . . . Sporting successes, however, do not impress more than his human side: glory never rose to his head and all who knew him admired his simplicity, his humility and his sense of solidarity. Let us not forget the human qualities that have made him a reference in sharing and helping others . . . [He gave] his face and his image to various campaigns of solidarity, expression of his authentic

and natural affability and enthusiasm. (Assembleia da República Portuguesa Resolution, No. 1232/XII, 24/2/2015)

Eusébio's rise to the rank of national hero depended on talent but also on qualities that must be interpreted within the history of Portuguese colonialism. The exhibition organized by the Parliament in 2015 in his honor evoked, through the display of diverse memorabilia, all the known stages of his exemplary biography. More than forty years later, the biographical accounts of Eusébio, endorsed by the state and widely disseminated by the media, reproduced the narrative account established in the 1960s, when Portugal was ruled by a dictatorship that was fighting for the remains of its African empire. Keeping colonial history intact was an indispensable element in the construction of the popular culture national hero. In 2015, Portugal lacked consensual heroes. In a context of serious economic and financial crisis, the eulogy of Eusébio could bind the feeling of national unity. Official speeches at the ceremony staged at the National Pantheon emphasized Eusébio's universality and his human example, which went beyond any political and ideological divide.[15]

The institutionalization and objectification of Eusébio's biographical account, while recognizing his mastery in an activity cherished by a large portion of the Portuguese population and not only among closed-off elites, has become an efficient channel to reproduce, through the creation of specific representations of the colonial past, an imperial narrative of transition. If official biographies of national heroes are illusive by definition, in the Portuguese democratic period Eusébio's biographical account became far more operative in reproducing colonial memory through wide social networks than the extensively celebrated lives of statesmen and military leaders during the Estado Novo, most of whom are today known only as names on street plaques.

The Empire's Aesthetization

As in the case of Eusébio, the production of exemplary biographies is also a key feature of the second imperial narrative of transition analyzed here. Where in Eusébio's case the chronological thread follows the history of football and sporting conquest, now the heroes are the modern architects and urbanists and their "schools" who left a significant patrimonial heritage in the Portuguese colonial territory in Africa. The histories of these men seem to be long forgotten, but recent academic research has brought their brilliant lives and work back into the chronology of their specific fields of activity. Along with the invocation of their lives and work, however, came a narrative on the Portuguese colonial empire.

During the late colonial period, a group of Portuguese modernist architects and urban planners left a significant mark on the colonial territories, most notably in Angola and Mozambique. Despite José Manuel Fernandes's (2002) pioneering research, which tried to highlight the professional and artistic worth of these men, their work in Africa has remained largely unknown. The members of this "African generation," as Fernandes called them, included modernist authors such as Francisco Castro Rodrigues, Vasco Vieira da Costa, Fernão Simões de Carvalho, and João Garizo do Carmo. Narrated by academic scholars, this generation's heroic collective history became what Bourdieu (1985) branded a "sociodicy," a social odyssey that reinforced and distinguished the subjects of interests of a particular field of activity and their processes of institutionalization.

If the history of Portuguese architecture had marginalized these authors, then the disclosure of their African itineraries has made it necessary to rethink the very history of the discipline in the country.[16] For academic specialists, the exposure of individual and collective trajectories and the emphasis on the articulation of their works with international trends rapidly became a major research goal.[17] Thus, these heroic African journeys ought to be acknowledged and included within the chronological and symbolic limits of the modernist movement, where they rightly belong. Accordingly, the detailed formal and aesthetic description of their major works in Angola, Mozambique, and Guinea-Bissau reveal how fair this late acknowledgment was.

Research on modernist construction in Africa has enshrined the category of "tropical architecture" (Frey and Drew 1956) in which the work of the Portuguese "African generation" could be inserted. Justified by the need that architects had to adapt their works to the tropical climate, which suggested a new variant of modernism, the word "tropical" worked as a historical euphemism—a technical expression that allowed scholars to avoid the more contentious "colonial." Nonetheless, this acquaintance with the international avant-garde was not enough to emphasize the singularities of these Portuguese African experiences. In the end, it was the national flavor of this tropical variety of modernism that allowed these professionals the opportunity to carve out a place for themselves.

Thus, these modernist works that went tropical were ultimately defined by their original Portuguese matrix, acknowledged by current scholars as a Luso-African architecture molded by the cultural contexts of tropical Portugueseness (Fernandes 2011; Magalhães and Gonçalves 2009; Milheiro 2012).

Hence, a vague idea of Portuguese culture justified the existence of a new variety of modernism born in the colonial spaces ruled by the Portuguese. A mark of distinction for the work of architects and urban planners, but also for their current interpreters, national culture was essential to interpret the itinerary of the "African generation," an asset that should be preserved from any kind of political contamination. Still, at a certain point, these current academic accounts had to give some explanation on how the history of Portuguese modernist architects and urban planners in Africa connected with the political context of the Estado Novo dictatorship and its exploitative, racist, and violent imperial rule.

Some analysis claimed that these professionals achieved an aesthetic and political autonomy during the Estado Novo, in the metropolis as through the empire (Fernandes 2002; Milheiro 2012). In connection with this thesis, it was suggested that this autonomy had been conquered as part of a political resistance, as some of the most relevant architects belonged to the political opposition (Fernandes 2002). Finally, other analysis argued that the regime was under a process of change, becoming less repressive and open to new ideas. This was noticeable on the colonial ground when the state launched several infrastructure projects and hired modernist architects to design them (Milheiro 2012).

Woven through descriptions of professional biographies of architects and urban planners and their more significant works, such explanations tried to insulate aesthetic and formal chronologies from other historical contextualization. For the colonial state and private investors, however, buildings and urban plans had their proper functions and uses: they were not art pieces, chosen for their stylistic excellence, but critical elements of political and economic projects.[18] The aesthetic and formal chronology proposed by the internal history of specific fields do not run in parallel with the political and economic chronology of colonialism. On the contrary, they were deeply interlinked. The assessment of these bonds calls for research on the social and historical life of this colonial heritage, something that, in the Portuguese context, is far from achieved.

The Colonial Life of Cities and Buildings

Beyond the formal discourse, imperial buildings and structures tell other stories, which were passed over in silence. The most striking are those that give an account of a colonial urban history based on the production of plans that, until very late, were based on segregationist models. In this regard, the trajectory of the architect João Aguiar, who was responsible for the Colonial Urbanization Office (1944–51, which became, from 1951, the Overseas Urbanization Office) is emblematic. He was one of the main theoreticians of Portuguese urban planning and the author of many urbanization plans of Portuguese African cities until the late colonial period. His ideas reveal that the stylistic and technical options of urban planners and architects supported specific political objectives (Aguiar 1952). They aimed to create modern and functional urban centers where housing plans were supposed to reproduce social, professional, and racial hierarchies. Within these urban plans, African populations were displaced and relocated so that economic and labor needs as well as a more effective social control could be achieved (Aguiar 1952). The modernization policies followed by the colonial state from the late 1950s onward, stimulated by economic development plans and increased private investment, demanded infrastructures for which the contribution of architects and planners was paramount (Pereira 2012; Cruz 2020). Despite the personal political stances of some of the modernist architects and urban planners in opposition to the dictatorship, this was the colonial ground in which they worked (Domingos 2013). Hence, the increasing demand for experts in urban interventions was inevitably related to political and economic colonial programs (Ferreira 2006).

In the absence of a historical contextualization that sets the terms under which Portuguese modern heritage was erected, the reader of research works on the history of the trajectory of architects and urban planners in Africa is left predominantly with formal descriptions of well-organized and constructed modern colonial cities—such as Luanda, Lobito, Bissau, Lourenço Marques, and Beira—where even today one can find the traces of modern Portuguese architecture and urban planning. The visions of modern and cosmopolitan colonial cities proposed by these architectural geographies are almost indistinguishable from the current public discourse of members of the settler populations in those same urban areas.

What is left out of the image, similarly to what happened in the case of the biographical account of the football idol Eusébio, is the actual life that defined segregated urban environments, generally divided between a white center where the settlers lived and had the opportunity to access all kinds of infrastructures and a Black suburb that soon became a slum.[19] The process of heritagization of these colonial cities produces an urban representation that excludes the peripheral areas; the "informality" and "spontaneity" of the suburban constructions, supposedly neither planned nor organized, is, for several experts, stylistically irrelevant. Thus, the emphasis on the aesthetic brilliance engenders a representational colonization of African cities well after the end of colonialism.

In these aesthetic chronologies, the urban colonial contexts become devoid of sociability, of power relations, and even of some of their basic spatial components. Consequently, modern urban descriptions that celebrate the end of formal historicism—to use a term invoked in specialized research to criticize the propagandistic nature of Estado Novo architecture—end up reproducing the historical pastoral created by the dictatorship. Even if such works praise the universal logic of international architectural styles, they come to subordinate the history of these styles to the master narrative of national history, and, therefore, they continuously naturalize and objectify a representation of Portuguese exceptionalism through the conceptual and thematic perspectives dominant in a specific field of research. Filtered by a formal idiom, analysis of material heritage tends to uncritically reify the chronology, themes, and problems of national history.

Conclusion

The mythical biographical construction of a talented football player and the aesthetic representation of the colonial terrain through the language of national heritage illustrate how the ideology of Portuguese colonial exceptionalism is reproduced through the mediations defined by the idioms, chronologies, categories, and systems of classification dominant in specific social and institutional worlds.

Football's popularity became a powerful resource for national representation and mass communication. The vehicle of an imperial historical narrative, the victorious trajectory of Mozambican player Eusébio da Silva Ferreira became a way of ordering the colonial past and made this narrative extensively present in a broader public sphere. Appropriated by an official national account, football's history became a certified producer of national history. A similarly linear historical reasoning emerges from the research programs of specialized academic fields on Portuguese imperial heritage. Usually circulating among a confined readership, these accounts, despite being primarily concerned with formal and aesthetic analysis, end up ratifying a nationalistic historical representation already shared by the majority of the Portuguese population. Moreover, some of these scholarly works support entertainment media narratives and touristic commercial agendas based on laudatory interpretations of the imperial Portuguese heritage.[20]

Craftier than the official and traditional mnemonic repertoires channeled by official state institutions, these mediations consent to the manufacture of a new postcolonial imperial exaltation, one that would be subtler, less assertive, and conflicted. Absent from these pleasant perspectives of imperial rule is the basic structure of colonial power relations, mostly based on violence, economic extraction, and racist domination. In this context, inequality was the basic Portuguese colonial legacy. As the empire became an uncritical category of knowledge and interpretation, this legacy became imperceptible.

Notes

1 The following sentence by Pierre Bourdieu could be applied to these examples:

> What is at stake here is the power of imposing a vision of the social world through principles of division which, when they are imposed on a whole group, establish meaning and a consensus about meaning, and in particular about the identity and unity of the group, which creates the reality of the unity and the identity of the group. (1991: 221)

2 Major research on the subject still preserves a patrimonial perspective of the colonial past, such as the publication of the series of books *Património de Origem Portuguesa no Mundo*, coordinated by the historian José Mattoso, an important inventory of the buildings left in the ancient possessions of the empire, which, despite its concern in setting a historical context, follows this pattern (Mattoso 2012).
3 Among the works that have discussed this issue since 1974 are Albuquerque (1974), Mattoso (1985), Bethencourt and Curto (1991), Leal (2000), Godinho (2004), Matos (2006, 2008b), Neves (2008), Trindade (2008), Sobral (2014), Sobral and Vala (2010).
4 On the reception of Freyre's work in Portugal, see Castelo (2001) and Castelo and Cardão (2015).
5 On Dias, see West (2005).
6 The anthropologist Marvin Harris (1958) was probably the first.
7 According to the study of Mário Bacalhau, cited by António Costa Pinto, in 1978, 70 percent of the Portuguese considered that independence should be given to the colonies, while safeguarding the rights of the Portuguese settled there. Only 2.2 percent believed that the war should have continued (Pinto 2001). Francisco Bethencourt quotes a survey published in the newspaper *O Jornal* (April 19, 1984), in which 69 percent of Portuguese agreed with decolonization and 22 percent were opposed to it. However, more than 73 percent disagreed on how the decolonization was done (Bethencourt 1999: 480). More recently, a survey on the fortieth anniversary of April 25 seemed to confirm these figures: 68 percent considered that decolonization was a totally or fairly resolved subject (Lobo 2014: 19).
8 The strength of the logic of symbolic consecration within the military institution implied, for example, that soldiers who were against the colonial war and colonialism

still recognize the values, duties, and hierarchies typical of the military institution. This means that colonial lands continue to be represented as places of military heroism, camaraderie, and esprit de corps. The frequent gatherings of former soldiers build, singularly, this imperial representation as a moment of institutional consecration, based on strong emotional bonds (Peralta 2014). For the Catholic Church, the religious conversion of African populations, effective in innumerable parts of the empire, is still a reason for celebration, regardless of the discussion that one could have on the role the church played in the colonial system (Jerónimo 2012). Similarly, the history of Portuguese science is intrinsically linked with the imperial conquest. On the case of Portuguese social sciences, see West (2005), Pereira (2005), and Ágoas (2012: 338–9).

9 The thin lines that separate academic work, scientific dissemination, and official historical accounts are particularly evident when one refers to national history. The agenda of the National Commission for the Commemoration of Portuguese Discoveries (1986–2002) renewed, at the highest level, the interest in maritime "discoveries." The activity of this commission is a source of discussion and controversy up to this day (Curto 2014: 95).

10 The available data on the formation of national pride in various European countries revealed that Portuguese self-importance comes principally from the country's history (91.9 percent of responses) (Sobral 2010: 98). Other parameters, which typically characterize civic patriotism, had less impressive results: only 18.9 percent were proud of the social security system and 38.7 percent of their democracy (Leal 2010: 76).

11 Reopened in 1965 by the Estado Novo, the National Pantheon received in 1966 the bodies of Almeida Garrett, Guerra Junqueiro, João de Deus, Manuel de Arriaga, Óscar Carmona, Sidónio Pais, and Teófilo Braga. After April 25, the bodies of Humberto Delgado, Aquilino Ribeiro, Amália Rodrigues, and Sophia de Mello Breyner Andresen were placed there. The body of Eusébio saw its burial in the Pantheon confirmed by the draft resolution no. 1232/XII.

12 On the history of Black populations in Portugal, see Tinhorão (1988) and Henriques (2009).

13 Matos (1998) describes the genres that typically made up this historiography: general histories of Portugal, historical narratives related to certain past episodes (not to be confused with historical novels), biographies, schoolbooks, small commemorative texts in newspapers and almanacs, and pamphlets where the historical argument prevails.

14 For a historical deconstruction of this perspective, see Penvenne (1995) and Zamparoni (1998).

15 At the ceremony, the Portuguese president, Aníbal Cavaco Silva celebrated Eusébio's modesty using words very similar to the ones in the official decree that justified the player's burial in the Pantheon.

16 Under the "architecture" entry in the dictionary of the history of Portugal, there is no reference to the colonial spaces. See Portas (1999: 118–26).

17 As in Fernandes (2002) and Milheiro (2012).

18 Moreover, they disregard the dependency these professionals had on political demands to develop their careers.

19 In 1963, Lourenço Marques's architect, Pancho Guedes, denounced the plight of the "reed city" in a newspaper article entitled "The sick city," describing the severe conditions in which the poor and servants where living: the suburban populations survived "without sewers, water or electricity, among ponds and piles of rubbish.

Their houses are precarious shacks made of old zinc, tins, boxes and reed. These shacks are infested with mice and rats, cockroaches, fleas, and bedbugs" (1963: 6–7).

20 A primetime television program asked viewers to vote for the best "wonders" that the Portuguese have left around the world, marvels chosen by a group of professors and researchers and directed by the historian Pedro Dias. Other academics protested this selection, which gave pride of place to military buildings and churches, and which freed itself from the historical contextualization necessary for the viewer to better understand the functions and uses of these spaces within the framework of the Portuguese colonial project. Using a similar model, a previous television show had proposed a vote on the most important Portuguese in history ("the great Portuguese"). Among the list of names from which one was supposed to vote were a considerable number of historical characters related to the imperial saga.

References

Ágoas, F. (2012). "Estado, Universidade e ciências sociais: um programa de pesquisa." In M. B. Jerónimo (ed.), *O Império Colonial em Questão*, 338–9. Lisbon: Ediçoes 70.

Aguiar, J. A. de (1952). *L'Habitation dan les pays tropicaux/Housing in Tropical Countries*. Lisbon: Federation Internationale de L'Habitation et de l'Urbanisme.

Albuquerque, M. de (1974). *A Consciência Nacional Portuguesa*. Lisbon: Author's Edition.

Alexandre, V. (1979). *Origens do Colonialismo Português Moderno*. Lisbon: Sá da Costa.

Araújo, M., and S. R. Maeso (2010). "Explorando o Eurocentrismo nos manuais portugueses de História." *Estudos de Sociologia*, 15(28): 239–70.

Armstrong, G. (2004). "The Migration of the Black Panther: An Interview with Eusébio of Mozambique and Portugal." In G. Armstrong and R. Giulianotti (eds.), *Football in Africa, Conflict, Conciliation and Community*, 247–68. Hampshire: Palgrave.

Assembleia da República Portuguesa (2015). Resolution no. 1232/XII, February 24.

Bethencourt, F. (1999). "A Memória da Expansão." In F. Bethencourt and K. Chaudhuri (eds.), *História da Expansão Portuguesa*, vol. 5, 442–80. Lisbon: Círculo de Leitores.

Bethencourt, F., and D. R. Curto (eds.) (1991). *A Memória da Nação*. Lisbon: Livraria Sá da Costa.

Billig, M. (1995). *Banal Nationalism*. London: Sage.

Bourdieu, P. (1985). "The Genesis of the Concepts of Habitus and Field." *Sociocriticism, Theories and Perspectives*, II(2), December: 11–24.

Bourdieu, P. (1987). "What Makes a Social Class? On The Theoretical and Practical Existence of Groups." *Berkeley Journal of Sociology*, 32: 1–17.

Bourdieu, P. (1991). "Representation: Elements for a Critical Reflection on the Idea of Region." In *Language and Symbolic Power*, 221–8. Cambridge, MA: Harvard University Press.

Cardão, M. (2015). *Fado Tropical: O Luso-tropicalismo na Cultura de Massas*. Lisbon: Edições Unipop.

Cardina, M. (2011). *Margem de Certa Maneira: O Maoísmo em Portugal 1964–1974*. Lisbon: Tinta da China.

Castelo, C. (2001). *O Modo Português de Estar no Mundo: O Luso-tropicalismo e a Ideologia Colonial Portuguesa (1933–1961)*. Porto: Afrontamento.

Castelo, C., and M. Cardão (eds.) (2015). *Gilberto Freyre: Novas leituras do outro lado do Atlântico*. São Paulo: Edusp.

Cleveland, T. (2017). *Following the Ball: The Migration of African Football Players across the Portuguese Colonial Empire, 1949–1975*. Athens: Ohio University Press.

Coelho, J. N. (2001). *Portugal: A Equipa de todos nós. Nacionalismo, futebol e media*. Porto: Afrontamento.

Cruz, B. P. da (2020). *Des(control em Luanda): Urbanismo, Polícia e Lazer nos Musseques do Império*. Lisbon: Outro Modo.

Curto, D. R. (1993). "Língua e memória." In *Historia de Portugal*, vol. 3: *No alvorecer da modernidade, 1480–1620*, 357–73. Lisbon: Circulo de Leitores.

Curto, D. R. (2014). "A memória dos descobrimentos, da expansão e do império colonial." In B. Monteiro and N. Domingos (eds.), *Este País não Existe*, 97–109. Porto: Deriva.

Dias, J. (1955). *Elementos Fundamentais da Cultura Portuguesa*. Coimbra: Tipografia Atlântica.

Domingos, N. (2013). "A desigualdade como legado da cidade colonial: racismo e reprodução de mão de obra em Lourenço Marques." In N. Domingos and E. Peralta (eds.), *Cidade e império: dinâmicas coloniais e reconfigurações pós-coloniais*, 59–112. Lisbon: Edições 70.

Domingos, N. (2017). *Football and Colonialism: Body and Popular Culture in Urban Mozambique*. Athens: Ohio University Press.

Domingos, N. (2019). "The Death of a Football Player: Eusébio and the Struggle for Portuguese History." *Práticas da História: Journal on Theory, Historiography and Uses of the Past*, 8: 163–97.

Edensor, T. (2002). *National Identity, Popular Culture and Everyday Life*. Oxford: Berg.

Fernandes, J. M. (2002). *Geração Africana: Arquitectura e Cidades em Angola e Moçambique, 1925–1975*. Lisbon: Livros Horizonte.

Fernandes, J. M. (2011). *Arquitectura e Urbanismo de Matriz Portuguesa*. Lisbon: Caleidoscópio/Universidade Autónoma.

Ferreira, A. R. F. (2006). "Obras públicas em Moçambique: Inventário da produção arquitectónica executada entre 1933 e 1961." [Public works in Mozambique: Inventory of architectural work carried out between 1933 and 1961.] Master's dissertatiory, Departamento de Arquiteclura, Faculdade de Ciências e Tecnologias, Universidade de Coimbra.

Ferreira, E. da S. (1966). *O Meu nome é Eusébio*. Mem Martins: Europa-América.

Frey, M., and J. Drew (1956). *Tropical Architecture in the Humid Zone*. New York: Reinhold.

Freyre, G. (1951). *O Mundo que o Português Criou*. Lisbon: Livros do Brasil.

Freyre, G. (1958). *Integração Portuguesa nos Trópicos*. Lisbon: Junta de Investigações do Ultramar.

Freyre, G. (1961). *O Luso e o Trópico*. Lisbon: Comissão Executiva das Comemorações do Quinto Centenário do Infante D. Henrique.

Godinho, V. M. (2004). *Portugal: a Emergência de uma Nação*. Lisbon: Colibri.

Gonzalez, P. A. (2019). *The Heritage Machine: Fetishism and Domination in Maragateria, Spain*. London: Pluto.

Gopal, P. (2019). *Insurgent Empire: Anticolonial Resistance and British Dissent*. London: Verso.

Guedes, P. (1963). "A Cidade Doente." *A Tribuna* (9/6/63): 6–7.

Harris, M. (1958). *Portugal's African "Wards": A First-hand Report on labor and Education in Moçambique*. New York: American Committee on Africa.

Henriques, I. C. (2009). *A Herança Africana em Portugal*. Lisbon: CTT.

Jerónimo, M. B. (2012). *A Diplomacia do Império: Política e Religião na Partilha de África (1820–1890)*. Lisbon: Edições 70.
João, M. I. (2002). *Memória e Império: Comemorações em Portugal (1880–1960)*. Lisbon: Fundação Gulbenkian.
Leal, J. (2000). *Etnografias Portuguesas (1870–1970): Cultura Popular e Identidade Nacional*. Lisbon: Publicações Dom Quixote.
Leal, J. (2010). "Ser português: um orgulho relativo." In J. M. Sobral and J. Vala (eds.), *Identidade Nacional, inclusão e exclusão social*, 67–80. Lisbon: Imprensa de Ciências Sociais.
Lobo, M. C. (2014). *As atitudes dos portugueses em relação aos 40 anos do 25 de Abril*. Lisbon: Fundação Calouste Gulbenkian.
Löfgren, O. (1989). "The Nationalization of Culture." *Ethnologia Europaea*, XlX: 5–23.
Magalhães, A., and I. Gonçalves (2009). *Moderno Tropical: Arquitectura em Angola e Moçambique*. Lisbon: Tinta da China.
Marchi, R. (2015). "A identidade de Portugal no discurso da direita radical: do multirracialismo ao etnonacionalismo." *Estudos Ibero-Americanos*, 41(2): 422–42.
Margarido, A. (2000). *A Lusofonia e os Lusófonos: Novos Mitos Portugueses*. Lisbon: Edições Universitárias Lusófonas.
Matos, P. F. de (2006). *As Cores do Império: Representações Raciais no Império Colonial Português*. Lisbon: Imprensa de Ciências Sociais.
Matos, P. F de (2014). "Power and Identity: The Exhibition of Human Beings in the Portuguese Great Exhibitions." *Identities: Global Studies in Culture and Power*, 21(2): 202–18.
Matos, S. C. de (1998). *Historiografia e memória nacional, 1846–1898*. Lisbon: Colibri.
Matos, S. C. de (2008a). *Consciência Histórica e Nacionalismo—Portugal, séculos XIX e XX*. Lisbon: Livros Horizonte.
Matos, S. C. de (2008b). "Naçao." *Ler História*, no. 55: 11–124.
Mattoso, J. (1985). *Identificação de um País: Ensaio sobre as Origens de Portugal*, 2 vols. Lisbon: Editorial Estampa.
Mattoso, J. (ed.) (2012). *Património de Origem Portuguesa no Mundo*. Lisbon: Fundação Gulbenkian.
Milheiro, A. V. (2012). *Nos Trópicos sem Le Corbusier, Arquitectura Luso-africana no Estado Novo*. Lisbon: Relógio D'Água.
Neves, J. (2008). *Comunismo e Nacionalismo em Portugal—Política, Cultura e História no Século XX*. Lisbon: Tinta da China.
Paulo, J. C. (2000). "Da 'educação colonial portuguesa' ao ensino no Ultramar." In F. Bethencourt and K. Chaudhuri (eds.), *História da expansão portuguesa*, vol. 5, 304–33. Lisbon: Temas e Debates.
Penvenne, J. M. (1995). *African Workers and Colonial Racism: Mozambican Strategies and Struggles in Lourenço Marques, 1877–1962*. London: James Currey.
Peralta, E. (2014). "O Monumento aos Combatentes: A performance do fim do Império no espaço sagrado da nação." In P. Godinho (ed.), *Antropologia e Performance*, 213–36. Castro Verde: 100 Luz.
Pereira, R. M. (2005). "Conhecer para Dominar, O desenvolvimento do Conhecimento Antropológico na Política Colonial Portuguesa em Moçambique." PhD thesis, FCSH-UNL, Lisbon.
Pereira, V. (2012). "A economia do império e os planos de fomento." In M. B. Jerónimo (ed.), *O império colonial em questão (secs XIX-XX): Poderes, saberes e instituições*, 261–95. Portugal: Edições 70.

Pinto, A. C. (2001). *O Fim do Império Português*. Lisbon: Livros Horizonte.
Pinto, A. C. (2003). "The Transition to Democracy and Portugal's Decolonization." In S. Lloyd-Jones and A. C. Pinto (eds.), *The Last Empire: Thirty Years of Portuguese Decolonization*, 1–17. Bristol: Intellect.
Portas, N. (1999). "Arquitectura." In A. Barreto and M. F. Mónica (eds.), *Dicionário de História de Portugal*, vol. X, 118–26. Porto: Figueirinhas.
Rita-Ferreira, A. (1967–8). *Os Africanos de Lourenço Marques*. Lourenço Marques: Separata das Memórias do Instituto de Investigação Científica de Moçambique.
Sobral, J. M. (2010). "Dimensões étnicas e cívicas e glorificação do passado em representações da identidade nacional portuguesa numa perspectiva comparada." In J. M. Sobral and J. Vala (eds.), *Identidade Nacional, inclusão e exclusão social*. Lisbon: Imprensa de Ciências Sociais.
Sobral, J. M. (2014). *Portugal, Portugueses: uma identidade nacional*. Lisbon: FFMS.
Sobral, J. M., and J. Vala (eds.) (2010). *Identidade Nacional, inclusão e exclusão social*. Lisbon: Imprensa de Ciências Sociais.
Tinhorão, J. R. (1988). *Os Negros em Portugal: Uma presença silenciosa*. Lisbon: Caminho.
Trindade, L. (2008). *O Estranho Caso do Nacionalismo Português*. Lisbon: Imprensa de Ciências Sociais.
West, H. G. (2005). "Invertendo a Bossa do Camelo: Jorge Dias, a sua Mulher, o seu Intérprete e eu." In M. R. Sanches (ed.), *Portugal não é um País Pequeno*, 141–90. Lisbon: Cotovia.
Williams, R. (1973). *The Country and the City*. New York: Oxford University Press.
Zamparoni, V. (1998). "Entre Narros e Mulungos: colonialismo e paisagem social em Lourenço Marques, c.1890–c.1940." PhD thesis, Universidade de São Paulo.

Chapter 4

LISBON IS BEING REDISCOVERED: THE GOVERNANCE OF CULTURAL DIVERSITY IN THE POSTCOLONIAL CITY

Nuno Oliveira

This chapter examines the processes involved in incorporating cultural diversity in the local space through governance mechanisms specific to the entrepreneurial city in a postcolonial context. I have made use of the territory of Mouraria—a neighborhood at the historical center of Lisbon—and the local authority's intervention there to identify the construction of an "urban scene" with its symbolic material role in the urban development of the city. This in turn has its own specificity, with images and postcolonial social realities being adjusted to strategies of capitalist exploitation of territories and the consequent commodification of ethnic identities. In the construction of a Lisbon brand, the definition of its image comes across as immersed in a rhetoric of Portuguese intercultural continuity based, in part, on a generic lusotropicalism, which, according to Almeida (2000: 182), condenses an ancestral cultural matrix into new cultural forms and objects. In this respect, two overlapping domains will be underlined.

First is the domain between the postcoloniality of cities and their cosmopolitanism. Paraphrasing Keith (2005), the postcolonial reality both embodies the imperial legacy and expresses the spatial and temporal interpretations inherent to the multiple aspects of globalization. Thus, the relationship between the postcolonial and the cosmopolitanism of today's cities would be more than tangential, produced by temporal sequence; rather, it is a profound overlap between juxtaposed temporalities. The cosmopolitanism of today harks back to the empire of yesteryear, and this would be revived in its representations and languages, now tamed by aesthetics, in the new urbanism of the postcolonial city.

Second, the ways in which immigrants collaborate in making the places where they live have been highlighted in the literature (Glick Schiller 2018; Radice 2009; Schuch and Wang 2015). This must be coordinated with another finding that shows how cities and governance strategies have highlighted the diversity that these same immigrants embody. This encounter produces space, and in it is rooted a significant part of the urban planning logic of the inner city.

The first and second sections of this chapter offer a theoretical review of some contributions to the understanding of the role of culture and its autonomization in cities' governance. They emphasize that the cultural diversity brought by immigrant collectives and the expression they assume in the public space must be considered against the backdrop of governance processes at the local level. In this respect, they discuss the notion of governance of diversity as policy and practice of the local as opposed to a norm-based approach. In the third section, I present the case of Mouraria as paradigmatic of these trends; namely, regarding the return to the center and its symbolic meaning. In the fourth and fifth sections, I examine in more detail some of the most emblematic cultural practices that were carried out in that area with the intention of "showcasing" the cultural diversity of the city center. Finally, I discuss how these manifestations can be read as intercultural props that buttress cultural policies. While this is not a new insight, I argue that in the case of Lisbon such policies and initiatives are informed by a particular narrative.

Local Aspects of the Governance of Cultural Diversity

What we mean by diversity governance should be explained in two stages. First is a matter of scale. Under globalization conditions, cities occupy the positions of the main nodes in the systems of cultural and capital flows, thus replacing modern nation-states. Sassen (1991) has highlighted urban space as a concentration of social difference, insofar as both the hegemonic economic culture and the multiplicity of cultures and identities are inscribed in it. In this context, urban society has become the most significant integration social context in view of the need for new forms of regulation and governance posed by globalization processes.

Second, at the institutional level, the local space is a focus for the concentration of state power (Magnusson 1985; Keil 2003). This approach has given the municipality new regulatory power, a power that is not sovereignty like that of the nation-state but one of accommodation between the privatizing entrepreneurship of the post-Fordist urban model and the construction of consensus and promotion of cooperation and solidarity between the various social, economic, and political actors present in the urban space.

By this, I mean that the governance of diversity must be viewed from the local level and as the result of complex processes involving a multiplicity of actors. These actors are involved in different interpenetrating spheres of action, and therefore they do not exist as exclusive domains that are analyzed as merely economic, or cultural, or social dynamics. The sense that cultural diversity is something that needs to be managed has gained the status of a harmonized institutional culture (Wood and Landry 2008), offering very similar organizational applications and visibility strategies in international urban centers (Oliveira 2020).[1]

Cultural diversity governance has generally been associated with the ability of procedures and institutions to respond to the demands for cultural recognition of ethnic minorities and migrants (Koenig and de Guchteneire 2007). The underlying premise of this perspective is an expansion of the rights of these groups, envisaged alongside the harmonized application of human rights in contemporary liberal democracies. The governance of cultural diversity is thus regarded as an adjustment between an expansionist legal standard and the cultural needs of minority ethnic groups in the context of the nation-state. However, this perspective obliterates the link between the processes of development and growth of cities and the expression of cultural diversity, the role of the latter in the diffusion of an image of the city, and the way in which this diversity is managed in the appropriation and dispossession of public space. In fact, by focusing on a perspective of expanding the rights of minorities and immigrants, its analysis fails to integrate the strategies characteristic of the governance of the entrepreneurial city, as shown by Harvey (1989).

On the other hand, because the processes identified here are inscribed in the life and spatial distribution of the city, planning emerges as the instrumental form of governance of diversity in urban space. Indeed, the postcolonial city is a planned and governed city; it is not only the meeting point for more-or-less interdependent differences, whose actors negotiate spatialities deliberately and spontaneously within their ecology. It is planned because it links a metropolitan rationality with the practices of its technicians, which gives it an overall vision; and governed because despite the situated multiplicity (Amin 2008) that constitutes it, it is a complex of authority structures coordinated in permanent balances of power.

This is why city planning encounters diversity through the problematization grid that produces visibility or invisibility for immigrant populations in the urban public space. It is therefore directly concerned, in its formulation of urban policies, with defining, separating, and adjusting what belongs to the public space and what is confined to the private. And so the question that urban planning has tried to answer is how to make the multicultural city compatible with the marketized, gentrified, and regenerated city within the parameters of the symbolic economy.

Finally, the autonomization of culture as a functionality of planning is a recent process that can be located in the progressive expansion of the aestheticization of some spaces articulated with capitalist investment. In urban terms, this process was associated with the "commodification of cities," a process that is underpinned by global competition, urban regeneration, and the interaction between public policies and private markets (Hannigan 1998; Logan and Molotoch 1987). Urban regeneration has largely concentrated on the recovery of the inner city accompanied by urban gentrification movements, with the occupation of these spaces by a middle and upper middle class. Although the details differ, this general pattern seems to be replicated in major European and North American cities. This "return to the center" engaged in by the "gentrifiers" is accompanied by an international revaluation of the city centers, taking into account the attraction that they can exert on a tourist contingent resulting from commodification strategies of the city and its investment dynamics. Taking advantage of cultural diversity based on its aesthetizing aspects, that is to say, those facets that can be integrated in the rationale of culturalization of the urban intervention or regeneration, is a strategy that has been spreading (Oliveira 2020; Raco and Taşan-Kok 2020; Raco 2018). The visibility of this diversity, taken as an outcome of an emerging multiculturalism, by no means happens independently of the discursive and material investments that try to appropriate it for an image of the urban, ideologized, because it often conceals asymmetrical relations and is a bearer of a rhetoric of the legitimation of these same relationships. This is what we will now try to show, putting forward some elements illustrating not only its presence but also its functionality and using the recent interventions in Mouraria to identify a process guided by certain parameters that seem to sustain widespread models of "governance of cultural diversity." In the following, we will give some contextual data of the space on which our analysis falls, paying particular attention to the composition of the foreign population and diversification trends of that same territory.

Lisbon Is Being Rediscovered: Mouraria in the Symbolic Return to the Center

Lisbon is the main focus of attraction for immigrants in Portugal, with more than half of the total migratory influx making it their destination. But it is also a city in rapid decline and suffering demographic aging, with negative growth balances in almost all parishes (only four showed positive changes in the resident population). In this context, the immigrant population has contributed to the population balance in Lisbon, moving its concentration, especially since 2000, from the outskirts to the inner city (Rodrigues 2010: 154).

Considering the population trend according to nationalities, the contribution of foreigners to the demographic "recovery" of the area considered here is quite clear, if we look at the period between 1981 and 2011, the year of the last census at the time of writing. In fact, while the Portuguese segment of the population is still on an overall downward trend (−16 percent and −11 percent in Mouraria and Eixo Almirante Reis,[2] respectively), the foreign population is growing significantly in both, with increases of around 247 percent and 124 percent, respectively.

Moreover, according to data from INE—Statistics Portugal, the foreign population accounted for about a quarter of the residents in Mouraria (24.3 percent). These figures are much more significant than those recorded for Lisbon as a whole (where foreign residents amount to less than 6 percent of the population). This confirms that we are looking at an area with a strong concentration of immigrants, both in the Eixo Almirante Reis (which corresponds to 2.1 percent of the municipal area, accommodating 5.9 percent of the city's resident population and 13.5 percent of foreign residents) and in Mouraria (which occupies only 0.2 percent of the municipal area, hosting 0.8 percent of the residents and 3.4 percent of foreign residents).

A neighborhood with a peculiar tradition within the city of Lisbon, linked to the birth of fado—Lisbon's music style—and to the symbolic aura of the Christian reconquest and the Moorish presence within its walls, since the 1970s, it has been favored by immigrants, both for settling as residents and for setting up businesses. Migratory waves have followed one after the other, diversifying the local population ethnically and culturally. The inflow of international migrants began with people from the Indian subcontinent to whom the Almirante Reis-Martim Moniz neighborhood was ineradicably linked, mainly through commercial activities, as shown in the early works of Malheiros (1996). They were followed by Africans and more recently by Chinese, Slavs, Brazilians, Bangladeshis, and Nepalese. Growing ethnicization has become part not only of its social composition but also of the perceptions of it by the citizens of Lisbon and its visitors.

While Mouraria is traditionally recognized as a neighborhood (*bairro*), this recognition has no counterpart in any administrative area. In fact, it is the historical result of the combination of memories, stories, and fluid identifications that prevailed in the popular imagination and became an identifiable spatial and cultural entity. Mouraria owes its name to the period of Christian reconquest when the Moors were driven out from Lisbon. The remaining Arab population was confined to an area of the medieval city called Mouraria in 1147. Therefore, to use an analogy with a contemporary term with some freedom, Mouraria began as a ghetto, despite there being thriving economic activity between Christians and Muslims (Menezes 2005).

At the same time, it was also a region of migrations. Mouraria received several migratory waves from the countryside, particularly poor farmworkers in search of social mobility. The demographic changes that occurred from the nineteenth century and extended into the twentieth helped to increase the concentration of population in the old quarters of the city, where several pockets of poverty developed.

According to the 2011 census, based on the population of the three main parishes that compose the social territory traditionally designated as the Mouraria neighborhood (Socorro, São Cristóvão, and São Gonçalo), the nationalities that are residing there have changed significantly over recent decades. In 2001, the census data recorded an important presence of African and Asian immigrants, reaching 31 percent and 36 percent of the resident foreign population, respectively, and only 10 percent of immigrants from America. In comparison, in 2011, the most significant nationalities were Asian (62 percent of resident foreigners), with India and China standing out. Immigrants from these countries represent 13.4 percent and 13.1 percent, respectively, of the foreigners. Meanwhile, "other countries" from Asia, not specified in the available data and where they are included, namely, Bangladesh and Nepal, which started to show a great relevance in the city. Immigrants from mainland Europe represent 14.6 percent of the foreigners living in Mouraria, anticipating a growing phenomenon of transnational gentrification. African immigrants, meanwhile, decreased to 14.2 percent of the resident population of Mouraria, and 9.4 percent of the foreigners came from America (8.7 percent if we consider Brazil alone).[3] Despite these changes in the demography of migrations in this territory, the most represented populations in Mouraria are still immigrants from the Asian continent, with 62 percent, followed by Europeans. Immigrants in this territory are over-represented in the retail trade, although it is questionable whether we can speak of this space of social and economic relations as an ethnic enclave, because of its remarkable rotation of nationalities and geographical origins.

Mouraria is also a territory of disparities, differences that are reinforced when comparing national citizens and immigrants.[4] The aging population includes 53 percent of the national residents aged over sixty-five years, which contrasts with 8 percent of immigrants in the same age cohort. In effect, it is verified that in average terms this territory is more aged than the city, with the aging index[5] in Lisbon being 186 compared with 227 in Mouraria.[6] Thus, the aging index for foreigners is only 21 in Mouraria, quite significantly different from the values for the total resident population. To a certain extent, this accompanies the tendency of the city, where foreign residents have an aging index of only 46. The exception to this pattern is found in European citizens with aging indices that are close to 100, that is, where the number of old people almost equals that of young people. The aging population is therefore counterbalanced by the rejuvenation brought by immigrants.

But simultaneously, and without making any distinction of national origins, 58 percent of the classic family dwellings in the parish of Socorro (the heart of Mouraria) are overcrowded. In 2009, 7 percent of the population of Mouraria benefited from the Social Integration Income and more than 3 percent from the Solidarity Supplement for the Elderly. If we add to this 7 percent of the population covered by unemployment benefit, we have a total of 17 percent of the population benefiting from some type of social benefit or the other. The retail trade in the area, however, has experienced a strong development due to the action of the immigration networks. Bastos, in 2004, had inventoried two hundred shopkeepers of ethnic origin for the Martim Moniz area alone (cited in Mendes 2012). According to evidence collected during the fieldwork,[7] shopkeepers maintain the image of trade in ethnicized products enjoying increasing demand, such as jewelry from India, cuisine from Southeast Asia, and Brazilian, African, Arab, Indian, and Chinese food products, which represent the variety of the local population.

This coexistence of different "mourarias" means that the imaginaries that construct and reconstruct it in the perception of residents and outsiders are diverse and historically produced. In this process of making it visible, the municipality has insisted that the history of the traditional Mouraria is a good symbolic receptacle for the more recent Mouraria of interculturalism and the melting pot.

Despite previous attempts to rehabilitate the area, the spaces and social practices associated with it converged to social settings of exclusion, bringing together marginality, illicit acts, homelessness, prostitution, and drug trafficking. In this context, rehabilitating that territory would have to obey a criterion of wholesomeness, that is to say, a revalidation of the social forms found there, redefined and now based on an identity that would positively differentiate the neighborhood. It is in this sense that factors such as centrality, diversity, patrimonialization, and aestheticization competed to redefine Mouraria's image and were key to the urban intervention process. As a historic quarter, Mouraria has been the target of a regeneration program instigated by the Lisbon City Council (CML), which was called Programa de Acão Mouraria (Mouraria Action Program) and financed through QREN (National Strategic Reference Framework [NSRF]) funds. The excerpt that follows, taken from the strategic vision for the city of Lisbon as it was outlined in an official document, refers to the main strands of intervention:[8]

> The ongoing regeneration . . . is very important as the driving force of the regeneration dynamics of this strand . . . for establishing new commercial activities, especially those of a multicultural and ethnic nature, in close collaboration with the immigrant communities present (Slavic, Guinean, Hindu, São Tomense and Cape Verdean . . . On the other hand, it is necessary to rebalance this . . . attracting population and activities, and keeping urban planning in line with the tertiarization and installing productive activities in technology–based sectors and the knowledge economy.

Associated with this aspiration, the program funded by the NSRF included the regeneration of the public space, the rehabilitation of various buildings, and a program of social enrichment of the residents, which was called the Programa de Desenvolvimento Comunitário da Mouraria (Mouraria Community Development Program). The program was proposed in 2010 so that the positive impacts of urban intervention could influence the people and communities living in Mouraria, with a view to alleviating the "conditions of exclusion and poverty and promoting greater openness to the city."[9] The two programs, one with greater material scope, the other mainly concerned with social intervention, ran in parallel. But the intervention in the memory and social representations associated with the neighborhood, whether of endogenous or exogenous origin, will also be an "object of rehabilitation," the result of an ongoing symbolic production that has served as the basis for a Lisbon branding whose leitmotif is the diversity of this territory.

(Inter)cultural Activities as Public Space Occupation

Of the initiatives aimed at an explicit convening of cultural diversity in the public space of this area of Lisbon, the Todos Festival and the Fusion Market are particularly noteworthy. The Todos Festival epitomizes this logic. The Festival Todos—Caminhada de Culturas and other initiatives of the same nature are imbued with emblematic potential by being associated with a CML office whose designation presages this aspiration: Lisboa, encruzilhada de Mundos (Lisbon, crossroads of worlds). The aim of the festival is to create synergies, approximations, and recognitions through performance art and the occupation of public space (Estevens 2017). In this context, the collaboration of the inhabitants themselves is sought and the cultural and human resources already in that territory (artists, bands, musicians) are combined with cultural equipment and artists from outside the neighborhood. This festival celebrates "the multiculturalism of the city and the intercultural dialogue between its people," thereby helping to "raise the level of self-esteem of the foreign communities living in Lisbon" (Gabinete Lisboa Encruzilhada de Mundos, director in CML, 2016). In the words of the mayor of Lisbon, it is a "relevant cultural manifestation open to the artists and creators from the city, with the political importance of affirming Lisbon as an open, tolerant and multicultural city that is its identity mark."[10] As one of the cultural entrepreneurs involved in the organization underlines, the festival emerged in a context of urgency to create in the city an event where interculturality was present and to show that Lisbon could be claimed as a city interested in interculturality (Oliveira and Padilla 2017: 7).

The first three years of the festival took place in Mouraria, Martim Moniz, and Intendente, which became the favored area for pursuing that strategy[11] as it was held in conjunction with GABIP Mouraria (Intervention support office) and the Associação Renovar a Mouraria (local residents' association). It subsequently diversified its location, following a pattern that corresponds to areas undergoing gentrification (such as São Bento, Poço dos Negros, Santa Catarina, and, more recently, Colina de Santana).

This event has had a very significant projection and participation, being central to asserting "Lisbon as a city committed to the dialogue between cultures, between religions and between people of different origins and generations."[12] In the words of its leaders, the festival "has contributed to the destruction of territorial ghettos linked with immigration, opening the entire city to everyone interested in living and working there."[13] In fact, what was already evident in the first few editions of the festival is still valid today; Todos is fully integrated in the touristic and cultural agenda of the city.

At the 2014 edition of the Mouraria and Intendente Festival, one of the most popular artistic displays was the collection of photographs representing people from the neighborhood (native people) with immigrants, as family portraits. The collection was displayed in visible places such as window balustrades, doors and outside walls, and advertising billboards. Such an exhibition sought to base the necessary construction of a community cultural context on an aesthetic sense, where interactions of mutual recognition strengthen social and neighborly ties. In one of the news items of the presentation, "everyone . . . [was invited] to visit, meet and interact with the inhabitants of this area of the city," with the purpose of fighting the fear of what we do not know, "getting to know one another."

> This dimension of the experiential, of the construction of empathy, is quite clear in the statements of a municipal official according to whom . . . local conditions for interculturality to work are beginning to be created . . . I don't know how many people who live in Lisbon—starting with me—have ever been into that area, why? It's the strange, it's the other, it's the fear; let's give it a go. (Interview with CML official, February 2011)

Todos thus emerged as the collateral for a practical recognition of the interculturality of the city of Lisbon. In the words of Robert Palmer, the director of culture and cultural and natural heritage of the Council of Europe, on the occasion of the celebration of Lisbon's joining the network of intercultural cities of the Council of Europe, the city would have "an exemplary character in intercultural relationship and dialogue" and the expression of that would be, precisely, the Todos

Festival (Câmara Municipal de Lisboa 2011). In fact, under the suggestive name of "Intercultural Corridor," one of the actions of this program aims at the "crosscutting enhancement of interculturality" through initiatives such as Há Mundos na Mouraria (There are worlds in Mouraria) linked with the Festival Todos (All festival), whose objective was to spread awareness of the "historical and cultural worlds of Mouraria and intends to disseminate the various cultural manifestations of the peoples of the world, both through the exhibition of the various artistic, cultural and gastronomic areas, and through the committed participation of the community in drawing up the program and in the functioning of the festival."[14] In this regard, the interculturality promoted by Todos is not a body that is foreign to the city's imaginary; rather, it is constructed as an integral part of that same imaginary. And it is with this objective in mind that the various actors involved work to reformulate the image of Mouraria as a stigmatized space, in an attempt to make it appealing not only for tourism but also for gentrifiers, while ensuring the cohesion of the social fabric within the neighborhood itself.

In this context, the urban regeneration was undertaken in order to turn the "stigmatized" Mouraria—of illicit trades and marginality of the people—into an appealing place for visitors, integrating it into tourist routes by offering a "cultural tourist route."[15] It combines ethnic diversity with the tradition of the social vernacular associated with fado and the picturesque quality of its geography and architecture, such as that symbolized by cultural facilities such as Casa da Severa, in tribute to the origins of fado in Mouraria, or initiatives like the Fado Competition promoted by the Associação Renovar a Mouraria. The focus on traditional, popular, and vernacular aspects is accompanied by the modernizing intervention resulting from the installation of university residences or creative hubs such as the Mouraria Innovation Centre (CIM), aimed at accommodating creative industries.[16] Similarly, the implementation of the so-called Fusion Market, established in Martim Moniz, a large square opening onto the territory of Mouraria and Almirante Reis, merges the two dimensions of the vernacular and the modern. As a project implemented by a cultural entertainment company, it is described in tourist guides as being "in the most multicultural square in Lisbon, Martim Moniz, [where] one can travel the world without leaving the center of Lisbon. In one of the areas of Lisbon with the most foreign communities, the *Mercado de Fusão* [Fusion Market] brings the planet closer together."[17] Even at the time of its presentation, it was stated that it intended to offer "activities dominated by the idea of multiculturalism," deepening a "recent vocation [of Mouraria] as a place for the meeting of peoples and cultures."[18]

Attempts at cultural theming had already been part of previous attempts to rehabilitate the area. During the mandate of João Soares (mayor of Lisbon between 1995 and 2002), a Chinatown was planned for the Mouraria area, taking advantage of the synergies between an immigrant Chinese population that was settling there and the traditional commercial potential of Martim Moniz and adjacent areas. However, this idea was eventually abandoned. In fact, in contrast to the experiences associated with "ethnic districts," the neighborhood is not linked to any particular community, as would be the case of a Chinatown. Efforts of this kind have always been systematically frustrated, as they contradicted the directives of the public authorities. In 2007, when this possibility was raised by a Chinese business association (Menezes 2009) and by some influential politicians, it was not only rejected by the Lisbon City Hall authorities but also faced resistance from Portugal's largest anti-racist association (SOS Racismo), with the allegation that it was an attempt to create a "ghetto." Thus, ethnic definitions of the place are supposedly inhibited in favor of an image of pure diversity, where places and foreigners intersect in interrelationships that are not limited to exclusive ethnic belonging.

But while this intention was abandoned, in part because the Chinese population itself would disperse and new immigrant populations from Southeast Asia would settle there, the theming was continued, extended now to demonstrating interculturality through the social and demographic recomposition of the neighborhood. While the global strategy is assumed to be fundamentally homologous between geographically and historically differentiated urban territories, as we can see from other experiences in globalized cities, in this case it is rooted in a symbolic, imagetic, and social specificity that should be highlighted.

Interculturality and Historical Authenticity—Postcolonial Imaginaries

If diversity is a prop that is increasingly used in the cultural policies of cities, in Lisbon it is expressed through a particular narrative. This matrix is organized around the celebration of an assumed historical ballast that finds its roots in a postcolonial lusotropicalism (the theme of the "crossroads of worlds").

Much of this narrative is crossed by recovering the tropes of multiracialism, as exemplified in statements such as "Martim Moniz, place of 'mixture' par excellence" or the slogan of the Todos festival itself: "Viajar pelo mundo sem sair de Lisboa" (Traveling the world without leaving Lisbon). In its original formulation and denoting the postcolonial burden surrounding the initiative, it read, "Traveling the world *again* without leaving Lisbon." Because this burden, we speculate, is perceived by the actors involved in its creation, the "again," with its all-too-clear imperial associations, was removed while maintaining the semantics of travel, of displacement, dear to the images of transculturation and contact with the other (Pratt 1992).

If, on the one hand, the recovery of the neighborhood largely involves its redefinition—albeit without any memorial ballast—as an intrinsically intercultural space—"Martim Moniz, a place of 'mixture' par excellence"—on the other hand, the construction of such a narrative, and suffering from an excess of presentness, is functional in the construction of a more comprehensive narrative, symbolized in the trope of "Lisbon the crossroads of Worlds," which is invested with all the melancholy in the sense that Gilroy (2004) gives it, of the lost imperial greatness. In effect, "Lisbon the crossroads of worlds" raises a whole set of memories forged in the imperial imaginary of yesteryear—imaginary that is always refractory to the violence of the colonial relationship established between colonizer and colonized, and always reconfigured as a direct result of a lusotropical nature, in which Portugal would be, by ancestral and mythical definitions, the "true" melting pot of cultures.

Its particular inscription can be seen in the literary collaboration of the Angolan writer José Eduardo Agualusa with the Lisbon City Hall. It is in the literary itinerary of Lisbon, entitled *Lisboa, cidade de Exílios: o mundo em Lisboa* (Lisbon city of exiles: The world in Lisbon), written on the occasion of the Oceans Festival in 1999, that the theme of the endogenous diversity of Mouraria is first mentioned. We can read there that Mouraria was the place chosen by D. Afonso Henriques[19] "to settle the free Moors." In a chapter entitled "Lisboa de todas as cores—United Colors of Lisbon," the writer drafts an identity for Mouraria, and consequently for the rest of Lisbon, which is affirmed as culturally and ethnically hybrid from its very beginnings. And to leave no doubt as to its hybrid nature, the description of its shopping mall appears as a metaphor for lost imperial grandeur. The Mouraria shopping center is reputed to be a place of travel through the old territories of the Portuguese empire:

> Inside, in a single afternoon, you can visit almost the entire former Portuguese Empire. The strong fragrance of spices drives the air crazy. The great adventure of the Portuguese Discoveries inevitably comes to mind; it was to renew the tired taste of European cuisine that Vasco da Gama set sail for India, inaugurating a new trade route and changing the world's destiny.[20]

Further on, "Africa appears near the heart of Lisbon," maintaining its physical and bodily proximity from the first slaves to the present day—the percentage of Africans, the author points out, has remained at roughly 13 percent since the slave trade began. Therefore, a miscegenation vocation that dilutes the Arabs in the national body followed by the Africans, diluted despite their Black presence in the heart of the city. Agualusa's Mouraria in 1999 did not yet denounce a gradual replacement of migrant populations, so neither the Brazilian presence nor that of Southeast Asians is noted. But the way these small stories rewrite the big story can be heard by comparing it with another Lisbon itinerary, from the middle of the past century, with a special Romanesque twist. In Book III of the 1940 *Peregrinações em Lisboa* (Pilgrimages in Lisbon), one of the contributions to note among Olisiponian studies, the purposeful way in which this Lusotropical discourse is used is not yet present.[21]

The Lisbon of the mixture is only in class terms, that is, an urban geography that mixes ordinary people's and aristocratic origins. Mouraria also emerges as a place of contradictions, not between tradition and modernity but between aristocratic and popular Lisbon instead. In this relationship, the "impurities" in the history of Lisbon, and particularly of Mouraria, are maintained; and as such the Lisbon of the succession of peoples and tendencies is reported in a much rawer (and realistic) way and resistant to lusotropicalist sanitization. It describes how the Arabs were separated from the rest of the population for reasons of racial purity—relations considered impure with the Saracens were forbidden. The Moorish houses, in fact, scattered throughout the main towns of the Tagus valley, were places of "ghettoization" of the Moors, expelled from the old citadels after the reconquest where they remained as slaves and later as *forros* (freemen) but, as Mattoso says (1993: 354), "all politically and socially diminished," despite being considered "naturals of the kingdom." The fact is that not only were they separated, but later on, when the Jews were expelled in the fifteenth century, their cemetery was devastated after D. Manuel I[22] (the Fortunate) took over Mouraria and expropriated the *almocávar* (the name for Lisbon's Arab cemetery), whose slabs were later used to build the Todos os Santos Hospital that was handed over to the Companhia de Jesus (the Jesuits). The same happened with the old mosque that D. Manuel turned into a building for the Dominican nuns in 1539. Still under the sign of impurities, we can mention that Severa was not only a prostitute but also of gypsy origin, and the illicit and troubled love affairs between this woman of the people and members of the Portuguese aristocracy. The aristocratic Mouraria is contrasted with the Mouraria of the scoundrels, prostitutes, hustlers, vagrants, and fado singers, and it is added that neither of the two exists except in the imagination of the people of Lisbon. The interest of this story lies in the fact that it is a narrative that is not submerged in the tropes of lusotropicalism—neither the narrative of genetic continuity, as defined by the Brazilian sociologist Gilberto Freyre at about the same time,[23] nor the colonial imagination of imperial panoptics through which, like exhibitions, travel routes, and aesthetic representations, the "imperial gaze" perceived the world, just as today's tourist routes promise us a view of the empire in a day.

In this way, the instant memory of an intercultural neighborhood is extremely operative in the recovery of a well-defined imaginary. In this regard, this particular discursive formation, which includes not only the discourses of writers and advertisers but also the shows, the performances, and the various modes of occupation of the public space through cultural initiatives, emerges as a concrete manifestation of "generic Lusotropicalism" (Almeida 2000: 182), that is, the reappropriation of lusotropical tropes in a postcolonial matrix.

This matrix is present in several formulations that make up the image of Lisbon conveyed by tourism marketing. From the brand image of the "value strategy" presented for 2010 by the Lisbon Tourism Association, where the idea is reproduced that the Portuguese capital "started globalization by connecting Europe to the World," to the systematic invocations of multicultural capital that integrate the various tourism campaigns or regional development strategies, fixing itself in the iconic phrase of the ATL Strategic Plan 2011-14, "Lisbon, a cosmopolitan and tolerant capital marked by the discovery of new worlds and original for its hospitality and multiculturalism."[24] In the opening note to this plan, the then mayor underlines the "mixture" that characterizes the city "of past and future, of celebration and nostalgia, of roots and travel, of modernity and memory, of character and cosmopolitanism, and of unity and diversity that makes it unique" (Almeida 2000: 3).

We can even extend the analogy. It is in this way that Mouraria is included in this imagetic production as a mark of interculturality, a configuration that becomes autonomous from the social and daily life of the local Mouraria to gain a space apart in the tourist imagination. If the exotic of the empire was found in its sui generis modeling of a pacified space of encounter between peoples and races, in the oscillation between the strangeness of the distant and the proximity of the familiar, in which the Other objectified by the imperial gaze is therefore kept at a safe distance, the exotic Lisbon rediscovers itself in the same way in the presence of the strangely distant and familiar. In the space of the encounter of national tradition, urban historical heritage, and vernacular cultural expressions, with the images of cultural diversity, ethnicized by virtue of this encounter. Motifs like the walks through the streets of Mouraria offered to tourists, giving them the opportunity to see an entire world concentrated in the alleyways of a single neighborhood, invoke the imperial passion for itineraries and grand exhibitions that placed before the ethnocentrically surprised gaze of the visitor the world as it could be encompassed by the imperial panoptic vision (or fantasy of that vision).

Urban tourism seeks the exotic, and the exotic displays its characteristics all the more as its form is displaced from the context of its expression. A typical Bangladeshi food store in an alley in a neighborhood that still retains traces of Moorish architecture is the unusual combination offered to tourists. Today's Mouraria offers this hybrid, and for this reason it now features on the desirable routes of international tourism. The postcolonial city thus reconfigures itself as a meeting place between the trends of urban economic restructuring resulting from the capitalist dynamics of globalization and the folding of the empire upon itself. In other words, the mapping capacity that empires exercised outside the metropolis in order to better dominate their territories is now turning to spaces inside the metropolis and replicating this social and ethnicized mapping of yesteryear. It is not a question of replicating imperial modes of domination and subjugation in the postcolonial and postimperialist city; rather, it is a question of reorganizing difference from spaces that in the past took their time to be known, mapped, and controlled, applying new principles of mapping, knowledge, and control to this displaced difference.

We thus encounter the use of culture for urban marketing and image-making purposes combined with the celebratory discourse of interculturality in local cultural policies. In turn, a recommended reconfiguration of identities, both of the spaces and the groups that inhabit them, leads to a combination of the commodification of ethnic identities and their strategic use to improve social cohesion in specific territories, with reflections on the public symbolization of ethnicized populations as they are integrated into the imagetic and commercial circuits of the city. The strategies for mobilizing cultural diversity, with their attempt to generate a unique and competitive offer in the international tourism market, end up producing, paradoxically, the same harmonized and replicated result in different urban contexts.

Immigrant populations have officially figured in this economic scenario of value generation, largely in terms of festivalization (as in the Notting Hill Carnival or Berlin's Karneval der Kulturen and other events, among which we would include the Todos—Caminhada de Culturas [All—cultures walk]). As a result, the production of cultural policies that were intended to celebrate and protect ethno-cultural diversity through the administrative grid of granting and expanding rights (including cultural ones, as a new modality in the palette of citizenship rights) is now, broadly speaking, more geared toward emphasizing their economic potential. Thus, the governance of cultural diversity in the urban space implies a necessary concession to the ability to generate value and the suitability of these activities to an urban development model that largely involves turning the local state into a facilitator of the symbolic economy and of the globalized culture of consumption arising from the increase in tourist flows, thus replacing its traditional role as a service provider.

The formula in fact comes close enough to the search for an urban scene that recreates the spirit of the city. The reconstruction of traditional spaces of sociality as the mark of a neighborhood authenticity, the simulation of a particular universal as a generic representation of a specific urban space, and the role of performative activities to give a sense of a participation that is as shared as it is generic—is that not what we find being built in Mouraria? Thus, from a marginalized neighborhood, where the imposition of order hardly got results, to an exotic object that returns the "true essence" of Lisbon—the mixture, the hybrid, the endless journey of the exploits of the old Portuguese—the production and planning of this territory seems to fulfill the same function.

Conclusion

The urban governance of cultural diversity poses, from the outset, a problem of visibility, that is to say, invoking Scott (1998), a problem of legibility by the state. Visibility, in this context, means which symbols gather consensus as legitimated in the public space and which ones are in dispute. Because the various cultures that the city is home to tend to be subsumed into a comprehensive practical version of an urban model that stems from the logics of the symbolic economy, it is the cultural expressions that are most suited to it that are offered the greatest visibility. The cultural events around cultural diversity sponsored by local authorities are an illustration of this. Their dissemination is all the more effective and the investment in the production of a set of "interculturalized" images is all the greater regarding the intention to define urban politics within the molds of the symbolic economy and its spatialization (Oliveira and Padilla 2012).

Postcolonial identities are nuanced by postimperial narratives; not least because the postcolonial city is usually a postimperial city. We can even think that the cultural politics of place and identities are imbued with the legacy of imperialist ideologies and practices, as Jacobs (1994: 4) intends. Local space is a privileged place for the mobilization of these identity configurations; it is there that their investments become visible and liable to be interpreted by the actors involved. It is important to keep in mind, however, that contrary to what a certain benign interculturalism would have us believe, this field of interpretations is not politically innocent. And in this respect, some interpretations have greater legitimacy than others, to the extent that they are confined by certain configurations of power.

The diverse city, with its cosmopolitan narrative, the praise of the hybrid, is nevertheless still linked to differential arrangements for creating visibility of what that same diversity should be. The aestheticization of diversity, implicit in the technology of urban planning, corresponds to the most immediate and effective way of commodifying it for specific segments of urban tourism or for the creation of exotic places suited to the search of the new postindustrial middle classes for authenticity and difference.

Notes

1. This trend is confirmed by the program to harmonize the urban guidelines of European cities known as 'intercultural cities."
2. A long avenue that links downtown Lisbon to northern neighborhoods.
3. *Source*: Serviço de Estrangeiros e Fronteiras (SEF), 2017 (https://sefstat.sef.pt/Docs/Rifa2016.pdf).
4. Presentation of the Plano de Desenvolvimento Comunitário da Mouraria (Mouraria Community Development Plan), CML, taken from http://www.aimouraria.cm-lisboa.pt/pdcm.html (accessed July 21, 2012).
5. Aging index = (Older population/young population) x 100, where the population aged sixty-five and over is considered old and the population under fifteen is considered young.
6. Data from the 2011 General Population and Housing Census.
7. *Diversidades, espaços e migrações* (Diversities), FAMI project in collaboration with CIES from ISCTE-IUL, CIUAD from the Faculty of Architecture, and CRIA, Center for Research in Anthropology.
8. Visão Estratégica, Lisboa 2002–12. Eixos de desenvolvimento urbano, Lisbon: CML, 2007, p. 75, http://ulisses.cm-lisboa.pt/ data/002/009.
9. Program presentation, CML website: http://www.aimouraria. cm-lisboa.pt/pdcm.html (accessed July 21, 2018).
10. Mayor of Lisbon at the opening of the 2017 edition of the Festival: http://www.cm-lisboa.pt/noticias/detalhe/article/festival-todos-na-colina-de-santana.
11. The temporary installation of the mayor's office in this area should be highlighted as a clear sign of political commitment to the new symbolic importance of this "return to the center."
12. http://www.festivaltodos.com/intro/home.
13. http://www.festivaltodos.com/intro/home.
14. Lisbon Municipality site presenting Há Mundos na Mouraria, http://www.aimouraria.cm-lisboa.pt/valorizacao-socio-cultural-e-turistica/festi-val.html (accessed January 2016).
15. On the CML website, the page about the QREN Action Program (NSFR), Mouraria, says that "the appreciation of the historical and architectural heritage of the buildings and public spaces of the neighborhood of Mouraria . . . as well as the intercultural characteristics of the lower part of Mouraria, will allow Mouraria to be included in the city's tourist routes."
16. The introductory note on the Lisbon City Council website (http://www.cm-lisboa.pt/centro-de-inovacao-da-mouraria-mouraria-creative-hub [accessed August 18, 2019]) has the following:

> The Mouraria Innovation Center / Mouraria Creative Hub is Lisbon's first incubator to support business projects and ideas from the creative industries ... We provide fully equipped workstations, a wide network of mentors, tailored training and consultancy, access to financing solutions and support for the commercialization of products and services. All this just a 5-minute walk from Martim Moniz.

17 Taken from the Turismo de Lisboa/Lisbon Tourism website https://www.visitlisboa.com/en/places/fusion-market-mercado-de-fusao (accessed September 22, 2019).
18 "Martim Moniz is to have restaurants and an intercultural market" (*Público*, May 10, 2012).
19 The first Portuguese king (?–1185) who founded Portugal in 1143.
20 Agualusa (1999).
21 See *Peregrinações em Lisboa/Descritas por Norberto de Araújo; acompanhadas por Martins Barata* (Lisbon: Partnership A. M. Pereira, 1938-9), Livro III.
22 The Portuguese King (1469–1521) who impersonates the golden period of Portugal's overseas expansion.
23 *Casa-Grande & Senzala de Freyre* was published in Brazil in 1933. Freyre wanted to tell a sui generis story of the encounter between the West and the Tropics through his notion of lusotropicality. See, inter alia, Araújo (1994).
Plano Estratégico 2011–2014 da ATL, 2010, Deloitte Consultores, p. 326.
24 *Plano Estratégico 2011–2014 da ATL*, 2010, Deloitte Consultores, p. 326.

References

Agualusa, J. E. (1999). *Lisboa: cidade de exílios: O mundo em Lisboa*. Lisbon: CML, Festival dos Oceanos.
Almeida, M. V. (2000). *Um Mar da Cor da Terra*. Celta: Oeiras.
Amin, A. (2008). "Collective Culture and Urban Public Space." *City: Analysis of Urban Trends, Culture, Theory, Policy, Action*, 12(1): 5–24.
Araújo, R. B. de (1994). Guerra e Paz. *Casa-Grande & Senzala e a obra de Gilberto Freyre nos anos 30*. Rio de Janeiro: Editora 34.
Estevens, A. (2017). *A Cidade Neoliberal: Conflito e arte em Lisboa e em Barcelona*. Lisbon: Le Monde Diplomatique e Deriva editores.
Gabinete Lisboa Encruzilhada de Mundos. (2016). *CML, Revista Lisboa*, no. 18: 21.
Gilroy, P. (2004). *After Empire: Melancholia or Convivial Culture?* London: Routledge.
Glick Schiller, N. (2018). "Introduction. Multiscalar City-Making and Emplacement: Processes, Concepts, and Methods." In A. Çağlar and N. Glick Schiller (eds.), *Migrants and City-Making: Multiscalar Perspectives on Dispossession*, 1–32. Durham, NC: Duke University Press.
Hannigan, J. (1998). *Fantasy City: Pleasure and Profit in the Postmodern Metropolis*. London: Routledge.
Harvey, D. (1989). "From Managerialism to Entrepreneurialism: The Transformation in Urban Governance in Late Capitalism." *Geografiska Annaler* B, 71: 3–17.
Jacobs, J. M. (1994). *Edge of Empire: Postcolonialism and the City*. London: Routledge.
Keil, R. (2003). "Globalization Makes States: Perspectives on Local Governance in the Age of the World City." In N. Brenner, B. Jessop, M. Jones, and G. MacLeod (eds.), *State/Space: A Reader*, 278–95. Malden, MA: Blackwell.

Keith, M. (2005). *After the Cosmopolitan*. Abingdon: Routledge.
Koenig, M., and P. de Guchteneire (eds.) (2007). *Political Governance of Cultural Diversity: Democracy and Human Rights in Multicultural Societies*, 3–17. London: Ashgate.
Logan, J. R., and H. L. Molotoch (1987). *Urban Fortunes: The Political Economy of Place*. Berkeley: University of California Press.
Magnusson, W. (1985). "Urban Politics and the Local State." *Studies in Political Economy*, 16: 111–42.
Malheiros, J. M. (1996). *Imigrantes na Região de Lisboa: Os Anos da Mudança*. Lisbon: Edições Colibri.
Mattoso, J. (1993). "História de Portugal: A Monarquia Feudal." In J. Mattoso (ed.), *História de Portugal*. 169–97. Lisbon: Editorial Estampa.
Mendes, M. M. (2012). "Bairro da Mouraria, território de diversidade: entre a tradição e o cosmopolitismo." *Sociologia, Revista da Faculdade de Letras da Universidade do Porto*, thematic number: 15–41.
Menezes, M. (2005). "Património urbano: por onde passa a sua salvaguarda e reabilitação?" *Uma breve visita à Mouraria, Comunidades e Territórios*, 11: 65–82.
Menezes, M. (2009). "A Praça do Martim Moniz: Etnografando lógicas socioculturais de inscrição da praça no mapa social de Lisboa." *Horizontes Antropológicos*, 15(32): 301–28.
Oliveira, N. (2020). *Diversidade(s): Paradigmas, modelos e governança*. Lisbon: Mundos Sociais.
Oliveira, N., and B. Padilla (2012). "A diversidade como elemento de desenvolvimento/atração nas políticas locais urbanas: contrastes e semelhanças nos eventos de celebração intercultural." *Sociologia, Revista da Faculdade de Letras da Universidade do Porto*, thematic number: Immigration, diversity and cultural conviviality: 129–62.
Oliveira, N., and B. Padilla (2017). "Integrating Superdiversity in Local Governance: The Case of Lisbon's Inner-City." *Policy and Politics*, 45(4): 605–22.
Pratt, M. L. (1992). *Imperial Eyes: Travel, Writing and Transculturation*. London: Routledge.
Raco, M. (2018). "Critical Urban Cosmopolitanism and the Governance of Urban Diversity in European Cities." *European Urban and Regional Studies*, 25(1): 8–23.
Raco, M., and T. Taşan-Kok (2020). "A Tale of Two Cities: Framing Urban Diversity as Content Curation in London and Toronto." *Cosmopolitan Civil Societies: an Interdisciplinary Journal*, 12(1): 43–66.
Radice, M. (2009). "Street-Level Cosmopolitanism: Neighbourhood Shopping Streets in Multi-ethnic Montréal." In S. Velayutham and A. Wise (eds.), *Everyday Multiculturalism*, 140–59. Basingstock: Palgrave Macmillan.
Rodrigues, W. (2010). *Cidade em Transição: nobilitação urbana, estilos de vida e reurbanização em Lisboa*. Celta: Oeiras.
Sassen, S. (1991). *The Global City*. Princeton, NJ: Princeton University Press.
Schuch, J., and Q. Wang (2015). "Immigrant Businesses, Place-Making, and Community Development: A Case from an Emerging Immigrant Gateway." *Journal of Cultural Geography*, 32: 214–41.
Scott, J. C. (1998). *Seeing Like a State: How Certain Schemes to Improve the Human Condition Have Failed*. New Haven, CT: Yale University Press.
Wood, P., and C. Landry (2008). *The Intercultural City: Planning for Diversity Advantage*. London: Earthscan.

Part II

POSTCOLONIAL SPACE, WORK, AND CITIZENSHIP

Chapter 5

GHOSTS OF COLONIALISM IN THE POSTIMPERIAL
CITY: A HISTORY OF INFORMAL SETTLEMENTS IN
LISBON, 1970S–2010S

Eduardo Ascensão

In the late 1980s, fifteen years after the Portuguese democratic revolution, it was estimated that around 200,000 people lived in informal settlements in the country (AML 1997; Númena 2003: 143; Ascensão 2015a: 52). This was the peak of a long process of internal migration to the Porto and Lisbon metropolitan areas since the 1960s and immigration to Lisbon since the mid-1970s from the newly independent Portuguese-speaking African countries Cape Verde, Guinea-Bissau, Angola, Mozambique, and São Tomé and Príncipe. The most vulnerable of these populations had been priced out of the housing market and immigrants were left out of the eligible pool for the diminutive public housing system; in effect, they had been "led" to the interstices of the urban fabric to look for or build the accommodation they could not find or afford in the regular city. Informal settlements were then tacitly accepted by the state because of its inability to provide housing for everyone. The state turned a blind eye while the white Portuguese internal migrants and the Black African postcolonial immigrants who constituted the urban poor settled in shanties or similar structures in areas that had become unprofitable for agriculture but were not yet subject to the instruments of urban planning such as surveying or zoning (Salgueiro 1977; Rodrigues 1989; Nunes and Serra 2004; Pinto 2015).

Up to this point, the immigrant populations that had settled in the preexisting settlements had been invisible to the state, in the sense that they were not accurately recorded in the census or other statistics, nor did municipal authority workers such as town surveyors have a precise idea of how many illegal dwellings, or illegal citizens, existed de facto outside of the state's sight. But for those fifteen years, in close contact with the white Portuguese populations who had initially set up the settlements, immigrants from former colonies had moved in, built, and upgraded their dwellings. Choosing the location was an individual event, in the sense that they were often "personally directed" by a Portuguese colleague at the workplace who told them where they could build a shack in which to live without risking its demolishment by the authorities, an event repeated many times over. This made it a "structural event," in the sense that these immigrants—at first mostly men without their families, who worked in construction and helped build most of the infrastructure of democratic Portugal—settled in whatever available urban space there was, provided it was close enough to jobs. Then, continuing over the years to invest income to upgrade their shanty houses and "bring over" the rest of the family, they set in motion a process that increasingly tied them to the space they had settled in. The largest shantytowns became micro-neighborhoods of their own. As time elapsed, the slum or ghetto stigma was associated with these areas more and more, and a second-class citizen status emerged, one that was especially acute for those who were Black (Fikes 2009), but which extended itself to other ethnic groups, such as the Hindu populations of the Quinta da Holandesa (Figure 5.1) and Quinta da Vitória settlements, which had originated from Goan migration first to Mozambique and then to Lisbon (Trovão 1991; Cachado 2013).

Seen broadly, such urban conditions reproduced the social organization of colonial cities such as Luanda, Lourenço Marques, or Bissau, where, for much of the twentieth century, the large Black majority lived outside the planned city center in areas without municipal infrastructure known as *musseques* in Luanda, the *caniço* in Lourenço Marques, or *bairros indígenas* in Bissau (Silveira 1989; Domingos 2013; Silva 2015). The ghost of urban colonialism—segregation and the lack of infrastructure for populations that were essentially regarded as labor for the

Figure 5.1 The Quinta da Holandesa settlement near the central area of Areeiro, 1999. Photograph by Pedro Letria.

colonial regime—was present in the way Lisbon's peripheries were interspersed with shantytowns after 1974. This is not a specificity exclusive to Portugal's postimperial history. In fact, this type of urban segregation, arising as a reflex of previous colonial structures of domination extending to the housing context of postcolonial migrants immediately after decolonization and becoming integral to the urban growth of a postimperial city, can be compared to Algerian or other Maghreb immigrants settling in the *bidonvilles* of Paris in the 1960s (Cohen 2011). An important difference, however, was that here postcolonial migrants shared their urban condition with the poor white Portuguese populations with whom they lived. The element of class thus needs to be understood—along with race, or better, the migration of poor Black people from a former colonial territory—as forming a dual layer of factors behind the growth of urban informality in Lisbon during the period.

In any case, the way the colonial element was present in the urbanization process of Lisbon's shantytowns is not restricted to a broad reading of their emergence; rather, it took more defined and concrete forms. Some of the people living in these shantytowns had traveled and worked across the colonial landscape or been conscripted to the Portuguese army to fight against the liberation armies before coming to Lisbon. Their condition as subalterns of the Portuguese empire was clearly, if differently, replicated in the postimperial city. Their offspring would then endure a long period of infra-citizenship—born in Portugal, they were not entitled to full citizenship as the *jus sanguis* nationality laws made them foreigners, even if they had never visited their "home country." For many years, they carried blue ID cards instead of the regular yellow ones. Physical and social separation went hand in hand with a process of "othering" of Black people, especially those who "lived in the slums" (*os que vivem nas barracas*). Finally, housing inequalities persisted even as Lisbon started to come to terms with its postcolonial status and, from the mid-1990s onward, moved toward an acceptance and celebration of its multicultural nature. The rehousing of slum dwellers was a protracted process in many settlements, in some cases spanning more than twenty years, one that often involved displacement to public housing estates located in more peripheral areas—once again there are parallels between this last element and the location of postcolonial migrants in the *banlieues* of former imperial centers such as Paris or Brussels and, though differing slightly, in suburban London.

Tracing Colonial Associations in the Postimperial City

This chapter illustrates some of the associations and postcolonial memories King refers to as "affecting the use of space in the postcolonial city" (2009: 326), shown from the viewpoint of the people who were the historical agents in this urbanization process: the residents of these settlements. It proposes that there was a colonial ghost in the process, something that is clear in general terms—the urban poor from former colonies constituted one of the biggest contingencies in these shantytowns[1]—but which deserves to be detailed, as it takes multifaceted forms and leads to different interrogations. However, unlike authors who approach the historical continuities and discontinuities of the postcolonial and postimperial city from the viewpoint of architectural knowledge or the translation of urban planning techniques and paradigms from colonial to postcolonial contexts (e.g., King 2009; Kusno 2010), I reflect on the colonial nature of the relationship between the residents of informal settlements, so often invisible historiographically, and the rest of the city. I will do so through what I refer to as micro-biographies on migration, work, and the everyday life of residents from one informal settlement in particular, the Quinta da Serra neighborhood in the Loures municipality, in the outskirts of Lisbon, which nevertheless illustrate aspects that occurred in other places within the constellation of informal settlements that existed in the city for three decades.[2]

Internal Migration and Informal Urbanism

The first inhabitants of Lisbon's informal settlements were rural white Portuguese migrants who came to Lisbon in the 1960s and early 1970s. Most informal settlements in the city began either with the illegal use of legally owned agricultural land for housing or with illegal squatting on private or public land—both serving the same purpose, with the latter setting up a twofold illegal status in settlement (Beja-Horta 2006). Many such settlements were located along the different sections of an old military road, by then disused (Gaspar 1989: 91). Historically, the road had encircled the city slightly outside the municipal boundaries, thus providing a set of conditions for settling, namely, a high degree of invisibility from state authorities while in sufficient proximity to jobs (Salgueiro 1977).

Felícia was one of these first inhabitants. Born in 1958 in the north of mainland Portugal, in the Trás-os-Montes region, the eldest of four siblings, she started working from an early age as a cleaner and domestic worker, having not completed formal education beyond the fourth grade. When she was eighteen years old, she married an iron welder, and they moved into a shack built on top of his parents' house, in what was only a provisional solution. One year later, they moved next door to the wooden shack that belonged to his godmother, which they decided to tear down shortly afterward in order to build a brick house on the plot. This was the same house that Felícia was living in in 2008 with two of her four children, after having divorced her husband (interview, 2008; Figure 5.2).

Felícia shared this type of trajectory with many young women from the countryside who were domestic workers in the homes of bourgeois families during the dictatorship (Brasão 2012). They would often live with their employers, sleeping in dedicated inner rooms; emancipation from such arrangements would most of the time mean moving to a rented room or, when that was economically unviable, into shantytowns. Felícia's arrival in Quinta da Serra is an illustration of the housing alternatives for the white Portuguese underclass during the Estado Novo, a condition that extended into the first decade of democracy. Her move also coincided with the first official documents that mention poor housing conditions

Figure 5.2 Felícia and her daughter by their house, 2008. Photograph by the author.

in the area (Sacavém Parish Council 1977), drawing attention to "hundreds of people living in shacks without the hygiene standards to which they are entitled [under article 65 of the Constitution]." Interestingly, her daughter's skin color, the result of an interracial relationship she had after her divorce, illustrates the multicultural life that existed in many informal settlements at the time, when such mixed couples were almost nonexistent in the wider society.

That said, the temptation to see such interracial relationships as evidence of a color-blind Portuguese exceptionalism along lusotropicalist lines should be avoided. Conversely, these relationships, no matter how few they were, should not be dismissed. What was happening was an encounter based on class more than on any other element. Later developments in the public housing estates that these Black and white populations were rehoused in—and where younger generations have greatly overcome race distinctions—suggest precisely that: race divides are trumped by a shared "underclass" identity.

Through the Colonial Landscape to Lisbon: Migration and Networks of Arrival

The next group of settlers in Quinta da Serra and other settlements included immigrants who, before 1975, had had a career working across the colonial landscape, including as "indentured laborers" in São Tomé and Príncipe's cocoa and coffee plantations—part of a flow of labor and "a forced migration movement by which Cape Verdeans could choose between death due to malnutrition in Cape Verde or death due to exhaustion in the plantations" (Batalha 2004: 132)—or working for colonial police forces (see Ascensão 2013, 2015b). The majority arrived between 1978/79 and 1985, directly from Cape Verde, Guinea-Bissau, or São Tomé. They came to Lisbon, at first using "boss's containers" for accommodation before moving to a shantytown. The move to a shantytown was not disassociated from the broader social structures of both the country of arrival—such as racist practices in rental accommodation—or the country of origin—for instance, Cape Verdean class and ethnic divisions. Batalha (2004) distinguishes between a first generation of Cape Verdean migrants to Lisbon in the 1960s—a better-educated and middle-class population, who in urban terms settled in a more dispersed way, in regular housing stock and would typically be employed in jobs either in public services or in municipal companies—and a second, shantytown-settling, working-class population, usually employed in construction (men) and fish peddling or domestic cleaning (women) (see also Fikes 2009).

The latter population was the one that contributed to the settlement's growth. Starting with arranging a place to build a shack in the middle of agricultural allotments, over the next decade they oversaw the densification of the settlements to the point where every plot or subplot was being used for a shack or a house. Most of the informal technologies (such as electricity tapping or water wells; see Figure 5.3) were first put in place by them. For many years, too, they taught new residents how to build their shacks, in communal occasions that followed the Cape Verdean tradition of *djunta mon* (joining hands) (see also Weeks 2012).

Cape Verdeans replicated in Lisbon the form of urban settling that poor populations had experienced in their country of origin—which, it must be noted, involved great architectural ingenuity and building ability. Francisco was part of this early cohort, and his personal migratory trajectory was closely tied to Portuguese late colonialism. He was born in the city of Praia, on the island

Figure 5.3 Residents gather by the collective well, before a makeshift water provision was installed, c. 1990. Photograph by Father Valentim Gonçalves.

of Santiago, Cape Verde, in 1929. After working in agriculture, he moved to construction, working first as a bricklayer in 1960 and then as a foreman from 1963 onward. Between 1965 and 1969, he worked in East Timor, building housing estates for the colonial administration. In Dili, he worked first on a residential complex for civil servants, "then, when we were done, they sent us to another side, Suai, to build houses for the chiefs of the outpost" (interview, 2008). He and his coworkers were relocated by military personnel, which shows the strength of being assigned and displaced to different places of work according to colonial needs. Francisco spent the next five years in Angola, still working in construction, but this time having been joined by his wife and children. Following Angolan independence in 1975, and with the political situation tense for Cape Verdeans (who were the target of animosity as they had historically been employed in the lower rungs of the colonial administration), he consequently moved back to Cape Verde:

> We couldn't take it anymore. I sent the wife and children to Cape Verde. I stayed ... Then, on the eve of Cape Verde's independence, I thought about going back too ... you couldn't send money, everything was blocked ... I managed to get a ticket for the boat with a friend, and I went. I took thirty *contos* [thirty thousand escudos] in the coat lining! You couldn't transfer money, nothing. And if I took the money in my pocket, they would keep it. I took it in dollars ... I arrived with thirty thousand escudos, of small diamonds that I had sold. (Interview, 2008)

He returned to Cape Verde and used the money to buy a plot of land where he could build a house, pay family debts, and start a business with a friend. They made iron beds and washbasins. From 1975 to 1978, the business flourished before going into rapid decline. In 1983, Francisco moved to Lisbon where he stayed with his eldest son in a cheap apartment in Almada at first, before moving to Quinta da Serra in 1985 as they were unable to pay the rent of the apartment.

In Francisco's case, we see how low-skilled work in civil construction during the colonial period was followed by a move to Lisbon as an escape from the recurrently difficult economic situation in Cape Verde, followed by taking up residence in an informal settlement immediately or sometime after arrival. Together with other older residents of Quinta da Serra mentioned earlier, Francisco's journey through the colonial landscape and move to Portugal to work in civil construction perfectly illustrate the few options for work available to a poor Cape Verdean in the forty years following 1950. At different times in his life, Francisco simply worked on what was available to a *badiu* from Santiago without formal education, work "designed" to a greater or lesser degree by the colonial system. And because the Portuguese empire survived longer than those of the other European colonial powers, one could encounter people who had lived through it in the postimperial city as late as 2008.

Disappointment upon Arrival and Parallels between Former Life in the Colonies and in Lisbon

The possibility of being able to build a shack as one wanted and among fellow countrymen was often nullified by the realization that life in Lisbon had turned out to be far harder than they had envisaged:

> We came to build a better life but, for the majority of us, had we known we would have stayed put instead. But by then we had no way of getting back to our homeland. By then, I didn't have the money for the flight back ... If I told what I went through during the first years to people back home they would get scared (laughter). And when we go back we don't let them know what we've been through here ... There was work back then, that was easy, but we had no place to live ... I went through a lot to have this little shack, which is not much but has provided shelter. It helped raise my children. (Interview, 2008)

Dóia, the woman who expressed these feelings, had at first lived with the father of her four children in a wooden shack, but "he drank and got himself into too much trouble" and so she decided to leave. The house she lived in until 2010 was for the most part built with the help of her mother as well as other residents who helped lay the foundations, erect the walls, and place the roof. Dóia undertook the remaining tasks herself, "after work, every day, slowly, sometimes until three in the morning" (interview, 2008).

The parallels between life in the peripheries of colonial cities and their new settings in Lisbon did not go unnoticed. Another female resident of Quinta da Serra, Utelinda, who was born in Guinea-Bissau, recalled her mother's work washing and ironing clothes for "Portuguese ladies" in Bissau during the colonial war, and described life during her teenage years:

> We didn't have electricity ... Bissau proper had electricity, where the Portuguese lived ... All we had were oil lamps ... so at night we'd listen to stories told by the elders. (Interview, 2009)

This brief excerpt tells us of the social geography of Bissau during the late colonial period. During that period, urban plans were an integral part of a highly segregated society, instituting a complete spatial separation between the white colonialist city center and the suburban ring (Silveira 1989; Silva 2015). There was no infrastructure in Bissau's urban periphery, with the exception of two neighborhoods (Santa Luzia and Bairro da Ajuda) built by the colonial administration for a minority among the urban poor. Such projects were part of the late colonial development plans (*Planos de Fomento*) devised, first, to stabilize the workforce needed for the developing colonial economy and, later, to appease populations as the wars of liberation went on in the rural areas. And yet, while the two neighborhoods amounted to a few hundred dwellings, the whole of Bissau's periphery was estimated to have over thirty thousand inhabitants at the time (Acioly 1992: 16).[3] Housing provision in the "European quarters" was not extended to the rest of the city: the colonial administration regulated housing for natives exclusively through legislation that enforced distances and hygienic principles or that let traditional African typologies be used. Utelinda regarded the lack of infrastructure in Quinta da Serra as a mirror to her early life in Bissau.

Encountering the Structural Forces of Regularization: The Divergent Urban Trajectories of Clandestinos *and* Barracas

Coming back to Lisbon, an explanatory detour is needed to understand why some informal settlements in Lisbon became increasingly dense and dilapidated, in other words "slums," while others were subject to infrastructure upgrade and regularization, eventually becoming acceptable residential environments. Throughout the 1960s and 1970s, Lisbon's outskirts were marked by another illegal but tacitly accepted type of housing, the *clandestino*, usually a one-family house erected without planning permission on legally owned lots or on subplots divided by illegal developers and sold to the residents (Salgueiro 1977; Guerra and Matias 1989).[4] Casal de Cambra in the Sintra municipality or Quinta do Conde in Sesimbra are two examples (on the former, see Castela 2011). Crucially, many of those buying or selling plots constituted a significant portion of the local politicians' electorate.

Clandestinos overlapped for many years with informal settlements of shack dwellings (*barracas*), and public policies did not distinguish between the two until 1993, with the Special Rehousing Program (Plano Especial de Realojamento; hereafter referred to by its abbreviation, PER), and 1995, with dedicated legislation for the land regularization of these areas, from then on referred to by the acronym *AUGI—Áreas Urbanas de Génese Ilegal* (urban areas of illegal genesis) (Raposo and Valente 2010). But even before that, they were already experiencing diverging trajectories. In fact, and to oversimplify, many shantytowns started out as clandestinos; they simply worsened over time while the others gradually improved. The original builders of both types of settlements lacked resources. Yet, whereas some were subsequently legalized and developed infrastructure and municipal services such as rubbish removal (often through political trade-offs with local authorities), others began to deteriorate.

Land tenure was one of the key factors in this division between improving and deteriorating neighborhoods. Where land was owned by its inhabitants and illegally built upon, processes of political trade-offs between local authorities and populations with a view to legalization could occur. Where land was owned neither by inhabitants nor by public bodies, it was subject to urban economics, in the sense of a push for clearance, rehousing of populations to more peripheral sites, and residential development for better-off populations. Quinta da Serra is an example of the latter. The land was initially owned by different individuals until it was bought by a public-listed construction company interested in developing and profiting from it. Tenure insecurity was always a factor in the neighborhood. A second key factor was the working and migration trajectory of populations, or their class position. The less educated and lower class the populations were, the less able they were to engage with political parties or administrations on an equal footing, and the less likely they were to realize all the legal implications of squatting—or they did realize but had no other choice.

Overall, the overwhelming majority of the population of clandestinos was white Portuguese, and those postcolonial Black immigrants who had not settled in regular housing stock had in large part squatted in areas of private property—together with their low-income Portuguese counterparts, as mentioned earlier. This resulted in a separation of the two illegal typologies along racial lines—one typology with access to the instruments for improvement, overwhelmingly inhabited by white people, while the other had very few conditions for improvement or upgrade, in reality threatened by demolition and displacement, inhabited by Black, white, and Roma populations.

A similar trend arises even when clandestinos are taken out of the equation and the focus is exclusively on *bairros de barracas*. Whereas some of the early shantytowns "discovered" after the revolution were either improved by the program SAAL (Ascensão 2016), with residents' participation, or rehoused through other schemes of the then housing institute FFH—Fundo de Fomento à Habitação (Bandeirinha et al. 2018), the remaining ones faced a context of diminishing expenditure on public housing over the next decade and were left to their own devices, growing throughout the early 1980s with new Black postcolonial residents

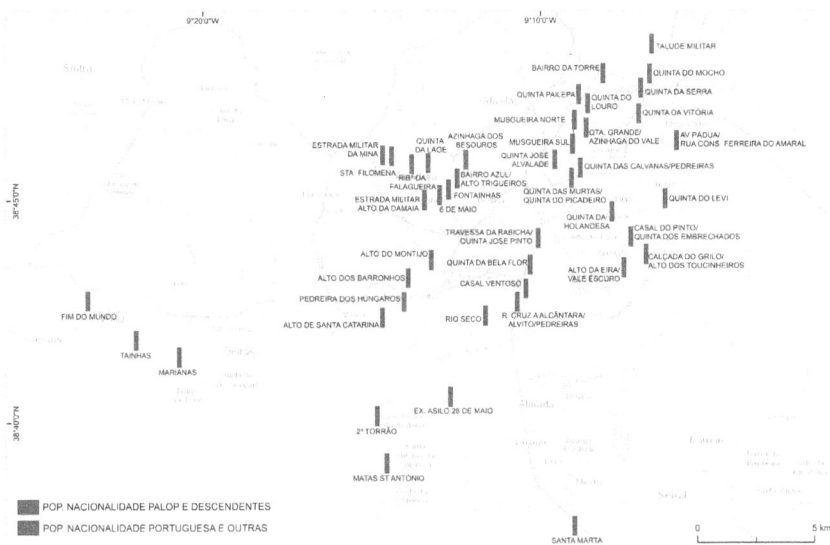

Figure 5.4 Forty-four of the fifty most-populated informal settlements in the Lisbon Metropolitan Area (comprising 58 percent of the total population), by nationality of the head of the household. *Source*: Instituto da Habitação e da Reabilitação Urbana (IHRU). Map by Miguel Leal.

moving in. Then, in the late 1980s, the Lisbon City Council became the first in the metropolitan area to reinitiate rehousing—and shantytowns in the municipality were in the majority inhabited by white Portuguese people. The settlements located in municipalities further away were the ones with larger percentages of Black populations (Figure 5.4).

Those with secure tenure and politically savvy community leaders and those located in municipalities that had land available for development saw swift rehousing by the PER; the others saw protracted processes of clearance and rehousing. The latter were settlements with very high percentages of Black populations.[5] In other words, the whiter and more politicized populations saw their housing problem addressed earlier than the populations who were blacker and less engaged with local party politics. It was as if the settlements with Black populations were left until last. This has not been sufficiently studied in part because census methodologies do not allow for ethno-racial data gathering, but it is a key research gap that deserves investigation.

Racialized Outcomes from "Non-racist" Practices

As life went on, shack dwellers experienced recurrent instances of racism in everyday life. Perpetrated by Portuguese society at large, they were more deeply felt when they resulted from the decisions and procedures of official institutions, which seemed to be continually detrimental to slum dwellers, in particular Black residents, despite official claims to the contrary.

Take the following two examples. In 1993, the first collective relocations in Quinta da Serra were carried out. As the highway's toll booths had to be relocated further north, the Portuguese Roma population who lived alongside it had to move. The relocation was carried out by JAE—Junta Autónoma das Estradas, the government's roads department. Rehousing, land clearance, and ad hoc compensations were carried out swiftly by the construction company involved in the works—sometimes this was just an envelope with cash to convince a reluctant family to move out. Two years later, in 1995, a larger relocation scheme was put in place to allow for the highway connection to the new bridge and the new ring road (the CRIL), both due to be ready by 1998, the year of the Lisbon World Exposition, Expo '98. This time, the remaining Roma and a large number of white Portuguese as well as Cape Verdeans were relocated to the large housing estate of Quinta da Fonte (also known as Apelação). Following these relocations, the remaining population of Quinta da Serra was overwhelmingly Black. Over the years, this would foster a recurring question among residents:

> Down here there used to be a lot of whites. The whites all got their house, we [got] nothing. Everyone went away, only the black man stayed. It's always like that ... I sometimes wonder if they think we are stupid. (Interview, 2007)

Although the population who was rehoused had approximately equal numbers of Portuguese Roma, white Portuguese, and Cape Verdeans, the area necessary for the CRIL access way was where the majority of individuals belonging to the first two groups resided, resulting in Black Cape Verdean and Bissau-Guineans forming the overwhelming majority of those who remained. Over the next fifteen years, nothing was done in terms of resettlement for the latter two groups, leading many to refer to this period as introducing a kind of "de facto racism" in the relocation process (see, in detail, Ascensão 2015a).[6] Their perception is that this was just one of several "racialized-results-not-caused-by-racist-practices" that they would suffer during the rehousing process. To an extent, the complaint concerns structural forms of racism, albeit exemplified by focalized (but repeated) racialized results.

The second example is also of an individualized nature, though repeated many times over, and it involves difficulties in accessing public services and navigating state bureaucracies. Seen from the eyes of an NGO worker who often accompanied teenagers when they needed official certificates:

> I've witnessed, yes, I've witnessed acts of non-acceptance [or *não-aceitação*]. I can't say it's racism because racism is not a very concrete thing and I don't have facts to say that. Yet common procedures that are easy to do for a Portuguese person become impressive[ly hard] for the population. For example to have the *cartão de utente* [national health card] or to ask for a simple residence certificate ... Suspicion, too many obstacles, obstacles that are difficult to overcome. That I saw, yes. (Interview, 2008)

Living in an informal settlement and being Black became a mark people bore in social interactions. It was as if the racist ghost of colonialism came back as a shadow that fell on social interactions and which framed almost everything. Surraia, one of the first people in Quinta da Serra to enter higher education, recalls how during her time at university she was never very willing to reveal exactly where she lived to her colleagues:

> I remained in . . . It's not shame . . . Well, perhaps it's shame, yes. You get afraid people will look down on you, "Oh, she lives in . . .," or that a strange situation happens where something is stolen and you are the first one accused. (Interview, 2008)

The feeling of shame described stems from the social image of informal settlements, which arose from years or decades of negative portrayal in media and policy, often deliberate. For instance, Crozat (2003) analyzed the case of the Pedreira dos Húngaros neighborhood and revealed how these representations "performed" to make policy decisions regarding clearance easier, in a multistaged and complex sequence of events that he summarized into the different steps of "indifference," "compassion," the "dangerous" theme, and "indifference" again. This social image was then internalized by residents, in the form of shame such as Surraia's. This element took on intense relevance when people engaged with the rest of the city, for instance, in the assumption that for a job application "it's just better not to put your address and instead put a friend's" (field notes, 2008), or in the use of the parish council designations that corresponded to your slum "pocket"—Prior Velho for Quinta da Serra, Buraca for Cova da Moura, Miraflores for Pedreira do Húngaros, and so on.[7]

Collectively, the urban existence of these populations in postimperial Lisbon was still not postcolonialized; and the link between racism, periphery, and social stigma was eventually extended beyond the informal settlement and into the public housing estate where these populations were rehoused (Alves 2016; Raposo et al. 2019). This tells us that the long shadow cast by colonialism has not yet dissipated.

Communal Organization and the Intermittent Nature of Associational Life

In the face of such stigma, collective organization was key to fight for improvements in the settlements. In Quinta da Serra, the Residents' Association was at the center of activities that sought to improve life for the population. Electoral information campaigns (Figure 5.5), assemblies to discuss issues related to rehousing or citizenship status and illegal immigrants' rights, and, at a later stage, a tentative childcare center that was abandoned and eventually resumed, as well as parties or cultural events, were organized in cooperation with different organizations, from the local parish to immigrants' associations.

The Residents' Association in particular went through different periods of intense activity followed by passivity and decline, becoming more

Figure 5.5 The day of an initiative for an electoral information campaign, c. 1991. Photograph by Father Valentim Gonçalves.

formalized in its later years as an intermediary with the High Commission for Immigration for youth activities through the Escolhas project to be funded in the neighborhood.[8]

> I was one of the founders of the association. We started it in order to have someone to represent us. The need for that kept appearing so that's how the association started. Then it fell, then it rose again, then it fell once again. It used to be stronger, have more life. Nowadays I am not so up to date. I've retired myself from it. But the teaching support they have now is a great step. But soon enough, those disgraceful people couldn't leave it alone, they took the computers, they took everything [refers to the burglary and the theft of computers by a youth gang from the neighborhood]. And now the activity is in danger. (Interview, 2008)

The first part of this citation portrays a stop-go struggle for insurgent citizenship (Holston 2009) and typifies what Bachmann (2005: 43) calls the episodic and discontinued nature of social organizations in developing urban metropolises; these tend to be centered around specific goals (such as infrastructure improvements or funds for education projects), but once these are achieved, they recede. Central governments often grant specific concessions in order to appease pressures for structural overall demands such as securing land tenure, or in this case solutions for swift in situ rehousing. The second part points to episodes of sabotage from some inhabitants, who might not have an interest in areas becoming open to the rest of the city because such openness could jeopardize the drug dealing they are involved in in these areas.

Governmentality Descends on the Settlements

Finally, when the PER was introduced, a new element started to emerge in the relationship between the state and informal settlers, that of the instruments and mechanisms of governmentality, surveillance, and social control instituted in the settlements.

Previously, the process of settlement itself had shifted between the "invisibility" that enabled people to build their shacks hidden from authorities—sometimes over a short period of time such as a weekend, erecting a precarious dwelling they would then upgrade from the inside over a longer period of time, what I refer to as "indoor bricklaying" (Ascensão 2015b: 958)—and a "minimum possible visibility" that permitted access, in stages and over time, to different levels of citizenship. Inhabitants had to develop some sort of legal relationship with those authorities in order to get documentation to work, get children into school, or access health services. This relationship was fraught with uncertainties, leading residents to delay visits to health centers for fear of being repatriated.[9]

It was as if the previous politics of invisibility necessary for the urban poor in colonial cities to deal with authorities had been transported to postimperial Lisbon. Colonial authorities continually counted native populations according to needs related to instituting "spaces of calculation" for the economy or the urban area (Rabinow 1989; Mitchell 2002) but left many uncounted if that would entail providing health, infrastructure, or better housing; and native populations had to navigate such shifting realities.

The PER too, enacted to eradicate slum dwellings, had first to count them. Technologies of control were increasingly applied to the areas, first with simple counting and census-like registration (which were a prerequisite for councils to enter the program and in some cases were outsourced to university research centers, e.g., CET 1992); then with corrections and updates to such quantification; and finally with the development of social surveys (e.g., CML 2005) as a way to manage the populations. All these instruments of measurement applied to the neighborhoods were an important part of the process of a population being rendered increasingly visible to the state. What we saw from pre-1993 to the 2000s was the transformation of poor urban populations from unknown, unmonitored quantities into subjects of a modern state.

However, not all were properly counted. Despite a methodology that sought to minimize data variation, the combination of how it was put into practice, scarce human resources, and context left the surveys prone to error:

> The original PER survey was done with a margin of error, so to speak. If we think of this "floating population" that circulated to where construction work existed, in the Algarve, Porto . . . They eventually settled here, but when the survey

was carried out they were either working away, or spending time back home . . . Sometimes they are easy cases to establish [that they resided in Quinta da Serra in 1993] . . . The survey was done in the best possible way, but there were thousands and thousands of shanties, 5,000 in Loures alone. (Interview, 2007)

One of the most important problems concerned the individuals who had arrived after 1993 and were thus not eligible for the PER. This was because the program had instituted a fixed matrix regarding the number of "households-by-municipality," with reference to the date of the original survey, so as to prevent the indefinite building of shacks by poor people with a view to rehousing. As an example, this meant that the 4,298 households surveyed in 1993 in the municipality of Loures were a "locked" figure—and changes (called "extensions" [*desdobramentos*]) were seldom allowed.

This led to cases such as Armindo's. Part of the neighborhood's early cohort—he was one of those who had worked in São Tomé's plantations in the 1960s and had been a policeman in Angola in the early 1970s—he had settled in Quinta da Serra in 1977. His wife and eldest son had joined him in the 1980s, though his two youngest sons only came in 1994. As they grew and became independent, each child built a separate area around their father's house, as if a separate home for their nuclear family, each one accessed from a kind of inner courtyard. Eleven people were living in Armindo's extended family house in 2008. The household corresponding to this house had been surveyed in 1993, but only Armindo, his wife, his eldest son, and his nuclear family were eligible for rehousing. Armindo's two others sons, their wives, and their children were considered "non-PER." Besides the atomization of households of extended families, the numerical atomization of the PER survey delineated residents' rehousing possibilities. This led to his refusal to comply with the rehousing options he been offered:

> I will only move out once my two sons' situation is resolved. What do they think? I would sign [the compensation agreement] on a Tuesday, on Wednesday they would say "the money is in your account," by Thursday or Friday the shacks would go down. That I don't want . . . I will go back home, but only after their situation is secured. [My sons] are not going from here to another piece of rubbish. (Field notes, 2008)

In the penultimate sentence, he is referring to an option some municipal schemes had of straight compensation for the shack and relocation to the country of origin. Armindo preferred this option as, his working career over, he thought that rehousing in Apelação would be a nightmare and a move under the PER-Famílias scheme (a subsidy for home-ownership instead of council housing tenancy) did not suit his wishes. The overall reasoning concerning his sons' predicament, however, applies to all three options. Whatever he did would have an immediate impact on them, who would then be left without a home. In addition, Armindo mentioned the implicit value in the choice of compensation over the other options: this way he would "cost less" to the state—15 percent of the average price of a new dwelling, or indeed nothing given it was to be funded by the land owner (who was working with the city council to facilitate clearance)—so he would have liked that goodwill to be, in principle if not in exact value, to go to his sons. He knew the logic behind this argument was too individualized to be taken on board by the authorities, yet he used it nonetheless. It was a "family logic": he was willing to move back to Cape Verde if that meant his sons could "collect" some of his housing entitlement. Armindo's refusal to leave is a personalized illustration of what Scott (1990) terms as the silent resistance to numerical forms of governmentality, using the only power he had left—to not go away.

Such forms of resistance took on different shapes (see other "hidden transcripts" in Cachado 2013), but by way of the different "counting methodologies" and their various ways of trying to deal with fluidity, on the one hand, and the PER's fixed matrix of cases, on the other, parts of the population disappeared in "official" terms. They remained non-PER despite living in the settlements for years—indeed, many of them would move from one settlement to another as they were cleared. It also led to cases where people "sold" their shack to others with the implicit promise that they too would be rehoused. When that proved not to be true, evictions ensued that could have simply followed the correct administrative procedures but instead were violent life events for those whose only shelter were the demolished shacks, leaving them with nowhere to go. These demolitions occurred individually (Figure 5.6) or collectively (Pozzi 2017).

Zooming out, the way rational and numerical governmentality was applied to the settlements had a considerable element of what Foucault (2003, or 1977; see also Graham 2012) termed the boomerang effect, that is, the way colonial techniques of control related to military strategy and, crucially, urban planning, were imported to the imperial space, in a process resembling internal colonialism:

> New ideas for *controlling troublesome neighborhoods or classes*; of monitoring, disciplining, or imprisoning subjects; of dealing with disease, hygiene and education; and for *governing, counting and registering populations* were all shaped heavily by imported colonial experience. (Graham 2012: 38; emphasis added)

Figures 5.6 A policeman looks over a contested demolition and the resulting space, 2008. Photographs by the author.

In the Portuguese colonial landscape, military techniques of control had included the clearance and realignment of native villages (Henriques and Vieira 2013; Curto et al. 2016), while urban planning ones had included the masterplans that established a clear intra-urban segregation between Africans and Europeans (Domingos 2013; Silva 2015). Yet here segregation, clearance, and absence of formal housing alternatives were part of a context that was no longer a colonial one. "Lisbon 1975-to-2010" was a postimperial context, but at least as regards these urban poor populations it was not a "postcolonialized" or "decolonized" one, in the sense that long-standing structures of oppression had not been sufficiently dismantled. They subsisted in small but, due to their cumulative nature, forceful ways. When seen as part of *longue durée* historical processes, that previous colonial subjects were still treated as such in the postimperial city is not surprising—it can be attributed to the tail end of colonialism, if you will. But seen from the life trajectory of these people, the injustices were clear: some of them had experienced the forces of colonialism firsthand, but even after migrating to the postimperial city their place in society and their subjectivity were still traceable back to the colonial past.

Conclusion

In this chapter, I have attempted to show some of the different associations between colonial and postcolonial histories and the emergence of informal settlements in Lisbon, a process that in part carried traces of urban colonialism. This was particularly clear in the period from 1975 to the enactment of the PER in 1993, with invisibility and an unequal relationship with the state shaping a subjectivity closer to that of the colonial subject than of the postcolonial citizen. But even after that date, and despite the considerable public expenditure to address the housing predicament of these populations, the PER (as an indirect means of the Portuguese state) instituted a top-down relationship with slum dwellers resulting in incredibly complex patterns of displacement to public housing estates located in more peripheral areas. It involved the break-up of established communities and their splitting into different locations, a movement of dispersal that came after counting and numbering. Such an analysis is beyond the scope of this chapter, but research based on official data recently made available provides clear evidence of a phenomenon of splintered displacement (Ascensão et al. forthcoming; see Figure 5.7).[10]

In the face of such a complex social process of migration, informal urbanism, and the construction of a modern democratic society, my final words are to celebrate the people who helped build contemporary Portugal under conditions of great economic and housing hardship discussed in this chapter. They deserve recognition for their initiative, architectural ingenuity, collective resistance in the face of unequal relationships with the state, and for their part in building a multicultural Portuguese society.

Figure 5.7 GIS representation of the PER's population fluxes (green lines) between informal settlements (red dots) and housing estates (blue dots). *Source*: IHRU. Digital atlas by "exPERts" research project.

Notes

1 When the state enacted the Special Rehousing Program (Plano Especial de Realojamento, hereafter referred to by its abbreviation, PER) in 1993, there were 984 informal settlements in the Lisbon Metropolitan Area, comprising 32,333 households. Of these, those with a head-of-household with nationality from one of the five PALOPs (Portuguese-speaking African countries) constituted 34 percent of all households. Compared with the percentage of immigrants relative to the overall population which ranged from 3 to 9 percent (depending on the different municipalities), this meant that postcolonial migrants were significantly overrepresented among the residents of informal settlements. The same overrepresentation persisted in 2001 (Malheiros and Vala 2004: 1084).
2 This chapter is based on ethnographic research conducted in Quinta da Serra between late 2006 and 2008, with follow-up visits until 2012. It draws on fifteen in-depth interviews with informal settlers and twenty-seven with institutional actors. Writing was financed by Portuguese national funds through FCT—Foundation for Science and Technology (DL57/CT/11960/2018).
3 See more: https://www.technoscienceslumintervention.org/bissau (last accessed August 18, 2021).
4 In the Mediterranean basin, *clandestino*s share many features with *viviendas marginales* in Spain, *borghetti* in Italy, or *afthereta* in Greece.
5 There are too many examples to list. Some large settlements with protracted and/or unjust processes were Quinta da Vitória (Cachado 2013), Quinta da Serra (Ascensão 2015a), Santa Filomena (Pozzi 2017), Bairro 6 de Maio (Sampaio 2018),

among others. Indeed, as late as 2020, settlements such as Jamaika or Santa Marta de Corroios in Seixal, 2º Torrão in Almada, Barruncho in Odivelas, Bairro da Torre in Loures or Quinta da Lage in Amadora had not yet seen their rehousing scheme fully implemented.

6 A process mired in gross neglect from the upper hierarchy of the Loures City Council. This neglect existed alongside the honest efforts of workers from different departments in the city council, who faced the daily implementation of rehousing without having real solutions to the situation. Both the recommendations of the municipal master plan prepared by the Department of Planning and Urbanism and work at the local level were rendered useless by a lack of decisions from the municipal executive—the key one being the lack of acquisition or expropriation of land to rehouse the population. See CML (1994) and CML/DPU (1997).

7 This sophisticated use of language was common in many settlements. For instance, the rap collective TWA—Third World Answer, originally from Pedreira dos Húngaros, chose to title their debut album using the Cape Verdean Creole word for Miraflores, Miraflôr. For them, it was something more than merely trying to escape the slum stigma: through their conscious decision to use Creole while not circumscribing it to "Pedreira," they avoided ethnicization of the "slum" part; asserted that Miraflores was by then more than the white middle-class residential part; and underlined that they were a part of it.

8 The Escolhas (Choices) program was initiated after a media-induced moral panic about "dangerous neighborhoods" took off in the aftermath of the car-jacking of a famous actress by a gang from a housing estate in Setúbal. The dangerous label then became associated to other housing estates and informal settlements. The silver lining was that the program turned out to be an important instrument for youth in these areas to have small community centers that provided different training and artistic education modules, such as studios for young musicians.

9 Bentes et al. (2004) and Gonçalves et al. (2003) revealed the use of hospitals or local health units by African communities in general was strongly dependent on their visa/residence status.

10 Based on data from the Instituto da Habitação e da Reabilitação Urbana (IHRU), the website PER Atlas maps the entirety of the fluxes from informal settlement to public housing estate and provides evidence in support of this statement. See http://expertsproject.ics.ulisboa.pt/ and http://expertsproject.ics.ulisboa.pt/analise.html (last accessed August 18, 2021).

References

Acioly, C. (1992). *Settlement Planning and Assisted Self-Help Housing: An Approach to Neighbourhood Upgrading in a Sub-Saharan African City.* Delft: Technische Universiteit Delft.

Alves, A. R. (2016). "(Pré)Textos e Contextos: Media, Periferia e Racialização." *Política & Trabalho*, 44: 91–107.

AML—Área Metropolitana de Lisboa (1997). *Caracterização do Programa Especial de Realojamento na Área Metropolitana de Lisboa*. Lisboa: AML.

Ascensão, E. (2013). "A Barraca Pós-colonial: Materialidade, memória e afeto na arquitectura informal." In N. Domingos and E. Peralta (eds.), *Cidade e Império: Dinâmicas coloniais e reconfigurações pós-coloniais*, 415–62. Lisboa: Edições 70.

Ascensão, E. (2015a). "Slum Gentrification in Lisbon, Portugal: Displacement and the Imagined Futures of an Informal Settlement." In L. Lees L, H. B. Shin, and E. López-Morales (eds.), *Global Gentrifications: Uneven Development and Displacement*, 37–58. Bristol: Policy.

Ascensão, E. (2015b). "The Slum Multiple: A Cyborg Micro-history of an Informal Settlement in Lisbon." *International Journal of Urban and Regional Research*, 39(5): 948–64.

Ascensão, E. (2016). "Interfaces of Informality: When Experts Meet Informal Settlers." *City*, 20(4): 563–80.

Ascensão, E., M. Leal, C. Sofia, and A. Estevens (forthcoming). "Splintered Displacement: The Urban Dispossession Effects of a Rehousing Program." Environment and Planning A: Economy and Space.

Bachmann, B. (2005). "Les enfants de la même agonie." In M. Davis (ed.), *Planète Bidonvilles*, 51–114. Paris: Ab Irato.

Bandeirinha, J. A., T. Castela, R. Aristides, and J. G. Alves (2018). "O Fundo de Fomento da Habitação de 1969 a 1982: ordenamento, alternativas e mercado." In R. Agarez (ed.), *Habitação: cem anos de políticas públicas em Portugal, 1918-2018*, 235–80. Lisboa: IHRU.

Batalha, L. (2004). *The Cape Verdean Diaspora in Portugal: Colonial Subjects in a Postcolonial World*. Lanham, MD: Lexington.

Beja-Horta, A. P. (2006). "Places of Resistance: Power, Spatial Discourses and Migrant Grassroots Organizing in the Periphery of Lisbon." *City*, 10(3): 269–85.

Bentes, M., C. Dias, C. Sakellarides, and V. Bankauskaite (2004). *Health Care Systems in Transition—Portugal*. European Observatory on Health Systems and Policies.

Brasão, I. (2012). *O Tempo das Criadas: A condiçao servil em Portugal (1940-1970)*. Lisboa: Tinta da China.

Cachado R. (2013). "O registo escondido num bairro em processo de realojamento: o caso dos hindus da Quinta da Vitória." *Etnográfica*, 17(3): 477–99.

Castela, T. (2011). "A Liberal Space: A History of the Illegalized Working-Class Extensions of Lisbon." Doctoral dissertation, UC Berkeley.

CET (1992). *Levantamento e Caracterização Urbanística dos Bairros de Barracas do Concelho de Loures (CET Report n. 12)*. Lisboa: CET.

CML (1994). *Plano Director Municipal de Loures: Projecto de Plano, Habitação e Emprego*, vol. 2, tome 8. Loures: CML (Masterplan).

CML (2005). *Estudo Sociológico da população Residente nos Núcleos PER—Quinta da Serra, Quinta das Mós e Talude Militar*. Loures: CML/DMH/Grupo de Estudos Sociais.

CML/DPU (1997). *Revisão do Plano de Urbanização do Prior Velho/Sacavém, Cadastro de Propriedade*. File DPU/7242 (detailed plan).

Cohen, M. (2011). "Les bidonvilles de Nanterre: Entre 'trop plein' de mémoire et silences?" *Diasporas*, 17: 1–22.

Crozat, D. (2003). "Enjeux de la manipulation de l'image d'un bidonville (Pedreira dos Hungaros a Lisbonne)." *Travaux de l'Institut de Geographie de Reims*, 115: 163–82.

Curto, D. R., T. Furtado, and B. P. Cruz (2016). *Políticas Coloniais em Tempo de Revoltas: Angola circa 1961*. Porto: Afrontamento.

Domingos, N. (2013). "A desigualdade como legado da cidade colonial: racismo e reprodução de mão-de-obra em Lourenço Marques." In N. Domingos and Peralta (eds.), *Cidade e império: dinâmicas coloniais e reconfigurações pós-coloniais*, 59–112. Lisboa: Edições 70.

Fikes, K. (2009). *Managing African Portugal: The Citizen-Migrant Distinction*. Durham, NC: Duke University Press.

Foucault, M. (2003, or 1997). *Society Must Be Defended: Lectures at the Collège de France (1975–1976)*. London: Allen Lane.

Gaspar, J. (1989). "Aspectos da urbanização ilegal nos países mediterrâneos da OCDE." In C. M. Rodrigues (ed.), *Clandestinos em Portugal—Leituras*, 82–91. Lisboa: Livros Horizonte.

Gonçalves, A., S. Dias, M. Lunck, J. Fernandes, and J. Cabral (2003). "Acesso aos cuidados de saúde de comunidades migrantes." *Revista Portuguesa de Saúde Pública*, 21(1): 55–64.

Graham, S. (2012). "Foucault's Boomerang: The New Military Urbanism." *Development Dialogue*, 58: 37–48.

Guerra, I., and N. Matias (1989). "Elementos para uma análise sociológica do movimento clandestino." In C. M. Rodrigues (ed.), *Clandestinos em Portugal: Leituras*, 92–123. Lisboa: Livros Horizonte.

Henriques, I. C., and M. P. Vieira (2013). "Cidades em Angola: construções coloniais e reinvenções africanas." In N. Domingos and E. Peralta (eds.), *Cidade e império: dinâmicas coloniais e reconfigurações pós-coloniais*, 7–58. Lisboa: Edições 70.

Holston, J. (2009). *Insurgent Citizenship: Disjunctions of Democracy and Modernity in Brazil*. Princeton, NJ: Princeton University Press.

King, A. D. (2009). "Postcolonial Cities." In R. Kitchin and N. Thrift (eds.), *International Encyclopedia of Human Geography*, 321–6. Oxford: Elsevier.

Kusno, A. (2010). *The Appearances of Memory: Mnemonic Practices of Architecture and Urban Form in Indonesia*. Durham, NC: Duke University Press.

Malheiros, J. M., and F. Vala (2004). "Immigration and City Change: The Region of Lisbon in the Turn of the 20th Century." *Journal of Ethnic and Migration Studies*, 30(6): 1065–86.

Mitchell, T. (2002). *Rule of Experts: Egypt, Techno-politics, Modernity*. Berkeley: University of California Press.

NUMENA (2003). *National Analytical Study on Housing: RAXEN Focal Point for Portugal*. Lisboa: Númena.

Nunes, J. A., and N. Serra (2004). "Decent Housing for the People: Urban Movements and Emancipation in Portugal." *South European Society & Politics*, 9(2): 46–76.

Pinto, P. R. (2015). *Lisbon Rising: Urban Social Movements in the Portuguese Revolution, 1974–75*. Manchester: Manchester University Press.

Pozzi, G. (2017). "Cronache dell'abitare. Pratiche di costruzione informale e rialloggiamento forzato nel quartiere Santa Filomena (Lisbona)." *Antropologia*, 4(1): 49–69.

Rabinow, P. (1989). *French Modern: Norms and Forms of the Social Environment*. Cambridge: MIT Press.

Raposo, I., and A. Valente (2010). "Diálogo social ou dever de reconversão? As áreas urbanas de génese ilegal (AUGI) na Área Metropolitana de Lisboa." *Revista Crítica de Ciências Sociais*, 91: 221–35.

Raposo, O., A. R. Alves, P. Varela, and C. Roldão (2019). "Negro drama: Racismo, segregação e violência policial nas periferias de Lisboa." *Revista Crítica de Ciências Sociais*, 119: 5–28.

Rodrigues, C. M. (1989). "Eficiência e equidade na produção de espaço clandestino." In C. M. Rodrigues (ed.), *Clandestinos em Portugal: Leituras*, 69–81. Lisboa: Livros Horizonte.

Sacavém Parish Council (1977). *Document to Loures City Council, no subject*, dated April 1.

Salgueiro, T. B. (1977). "Bairros clandestinos na periferia de Lisboa." *Finisterra—Revista Portuguesa de Geografia*, 12(23): 28–55.

Sampaio, C. (2018). "Ficar sem tecto: as demolições no Bairro 6 de Maio." In A. Carmo, A. Estevens, and E. Ascensão (eds.), *A cidade em reconstrução: Leituras críticas, 2008-2018*, 109–19. Lisboa: Outro Modo.

Scott, J. C. (1990). *Domination and the Arts of Resistance: Hidden Transcripts*. New Haven, CT: Yale University Press.

Silva, C. N. (2015). "Colonial Urban Planning in Lusophone African Countries." In C. N. Silva (ed.), *Urban Planning in Lusophone African Countries*, 7–28. Farnham: Ashgate.

Silveira, J. (1989). "La spatialisation d'un rapport colonial: Bissau, 1900–1960." In M. Cahen (ed.), *Bourgs et villes en Afrique Lusophone*, 74–97. Paris: L'Harmattan.

Trovão, S. (1991). *A comunidade hindu da Quinta da Holandesa: um estudo antropológico sobre a organização sócio-espacial da casa*. Lisboa: LNEC (Laboratório Nacional de Engenharia Civil).

Weeks, S. (2012). "'As You Receive with One Hand, So Should You Give with the Other': The Mutual-Help Practices of Cape Verdeans on the Lisbon Periphery." MSc dissertation, Instituto de Ciências Sociais, University of Lisbon.

Chapter 6

THE USES AND RESISTANCES OF CAPE VERDEAN CREOLE IN THE MIGRATORY CONTEXT OF THE POSTCOLONIAL CITY

Ana Estevens

The immigrant community from Cape Verde is the oldest to reside in Portugal. Cape Verdean immigration began at the end of the 1960s and is essentially labor based. It derives from the historical, political, and economic ties that were established in colonial times and the supposed proximity of the Portuguese language. At this time, Cape Verdean citizens moved to mainland Portugal from overseas to work in civil construction and public works. This made up for the shortage of labor (Pereira 2010) caused by Portuguese emigration[1] and the colonial wars (1961–74), which led to the departure of a large part of the country's young male population. From 1975 onward, the decolonization processes intensified the migratory flows from the former colonies, also including Angola, Guinea-Bissau, and São Tomé and Príncipe.

The migratory context of the Cape Verdean citizens determined their socio-occupational positions and their places of residence. The largest immigrant community with origins in the former Portuguese empire—employed predominantly in low-skilled jobs, particularly domestic services and construction—is concentrated in the outskirts of Lisbon. Many live in neighborhoods with poor housing conditions, which have remained unchanged over the years. As Sónia Pereira has noted, the low-skilled positions that Cape Verdean immigrants have come to occupy have influenced "the formation of their collective and individual identities in the national context" (2010: 103), with consequences for their social integration and the segregation they suffer. Although Portugal is well ranked in the Migrant Integration Policy Index (MIPEX) 2020 for the way in which its policies ensure equal opportunities and rights for all citizens, complaints of discriminatory situations continue to this day.

Placed in this migratory context, which is linked to Portugal's colonial history, this chapter examines the social uses of Cape Verdean Creole. This is the language spoken by a large majority of Cape Verdean immigrants and their descendants in their close relationships, at home and at work, in contemporary Portuguese society. It is important to note that although Portuguese is the official language of

Cape Verde, Creole is the most widely spoken language. In Cape Verde, however, this prominence is marginalized because Portuguese came to be the language of power and social mobility, used by state institutions and predominant in the school system. Creole is thus assigned the role of subaltern language. Both in Cape Verde and in the diasporic context, Creole is linked to class belonging, used in family contexts, leisure sociabilities, and in working environments where Cape Verdeans prevail. In Portugal, it also became a vehicle for recounting the urban daily life and experiences of social and racial exclusion as it applies to marginal territories that are considered excluded (Malheiros 2000).

In this chapter, I will focus specifically on the current uses of Cape Verdean Creole, considering music, particularly rap, and its use in the daily lives of its speakers.[2] The relationship of Cape Verdean immigrants with music has been the subject of several studies (Contador 2001; Cidra 2008, 2021; Monteiro 2011). This chapter aims to contribute to this discussion by interpreting the main tensions arising in the use of Creole in the Lisbon Metropolitan Area (LMA). It is assumed that Creole is used in certain contexts as a political instrument and practice, particularly in the framework of popular culture and in the context of the production of rap sung in Creole. Rap, a musical style created in the 1970s in New York, emerged in Portugal in the 1990s and was quickly adapted to the reality of Portuguese urban fringes; in those circumstances, it was used to denounce social and ethnic discrimination, violence, inequality, and poverty. Within the Cape Verdean community, Creole became a language of the local rap and a significant medium of resistance.

Considering that music is an important vehicle of social integration and transformation, and that it can trigger critical questioning and change in social and power relations (Marcuse 2007), particularly in relation to mobility options or exclusion and inclusion processes of immigrants (Turino 1993), I wish to examine the following questions in this chapter:

1. What is the practical and symbolic condition of Creole in contemporary Portuguese society?
2. In this context, to what extent is speaking Creole an act of resistance and political positioning?
3. For what purposes is Creole used in rap music?

Data used in this analysis essentially include semi-structured interviews conducted with three interlocutors at different times, the interlocutors being a sociolinguist and Creole teacher, an associative leader of the main Cape Verdean associations in Portugal, and a rap musician. It was complemented with ethnographic fieldwork and archival research collected between 2014 and 2019.

The Cape Verdean Creole

Cape Verdean governments have been promoting the country's closer relationship with the European Union since the 1990s, with Portugal being an important link in this process. Since 2007, the archipelago has had a special partnership with Brussels.[3] This desire for close ties is not new and has been materialized in different ways. Cardina and Rodrigues (2021) describe how Cape Verdean memoryscape has been developing an anti-anticolonial memory, which emerges as an alternative to the memory that prized the struggle against Portuguese colonialism. This is a further step in the political and cultural approach to Portugal and Europe. The authors identify this change from the 1990s,[4] with the policies developed by the Movement for Democracy (MpD). After having risen to power and dethroned the historical African Party for the Independence of Cape Verde (PAICV)—the party that waged the colonial struggle, then under the acronym PAIGC (African Party for the Independence of Guinea and Cape Verde[5])—the MpD sought to "establish new national narratives, new national heroes and new State symbols" (5). Among these, Cardina and Rodrigues highlight the changes in the country's flag (the colors ceased to be those associated with Pan-Africanism [yellow, green, and red] and became closer to the colors and design of the flag of the European Union), in the anthem (all references to the liberation struggle disappeared), in the currency notes and coins (the figure of Amílcar Cabral and other African revolutionaries disappeared), and in the statues and busts (figures from colonial times were restored); even the names of the streets that referred to the liberation struggle were replaced. The authors consider that "at the same time, there was a public backlash against the PAIGC and those combatants that had occupied important political positions during the single-party regime" (5). The changes made by the MpD after coming to power in 1991 were thus depoliticizing and emptying out the colonial context. The devaluation of Creole and its teaching-learning programs played a relevant role in this process of depoliticization.

During the liberation struggle, Amílcar Cabral, the historical leader of Cape Verde, valued the use of the local Creole. However, he also recognized that it was important for Cape Verdeans to study Portuguese in order to be empowered. In due course, when conditions would allow it, Creole would be taught and learnt. In one of his speeches, in 1969, Cabral referred to the use of local languages in Cape Verde and Guinea:

> We combat all opportunism, even in culture. For example, there are comrades who think that it is better to teach in *fula*, in *mandinga* or in *balanta*. That's very nice to hear, but it's not possible yet. How are we going to write in these languages now? Who knows their phonetics? We don't know yet, so we have to study them first, even Creole. To teach in a written language you need to have a correct way of writing it, for everyone to write it in the same way. But many comrades, with opportunistic sense, want to go ahead with Creole. We are going to do that, but after we have studied Creole well. Now, our written language is the Portuguese language. Therefore, it is worth speaking both Portuguese and Creole. We are not more sons of our land because we speak Creole . . . Let us have a real sense of our culture. The Portuguese language is one of the best things that the Portuguese left us, because language is an instrument for people to relate to each other, a means to express the realities of life and the world. (Cabral [1969] 2020: 82–3)

The awareness of the importance of education and the mastery of the Portuguese language was very present in the vision of the PAIGC. Cabral considered that Creole had not evolved as much as Portuguese. He focused on the fight against illiteracy, aware of the power of knowledge and the gap, in terms of development, between his country and the metropolis.

According to data from the National Institute of Statistics of Cape Verde[6] in 1970, the literacy rate[7] was 39 percent (53 percent for men and 15 percent for women), while in 2017 this figure had increased substantially to 89 percent. Amílcar Cabral was murdered in 1973 and did not have the chance to follow this evolution or attempt to formalize a Creole that could be spoken and written by all. In 1998, the MpD government approved a decree-law[8] that stated that Creole is the national language and mother tongue of Cape Verde, reserved for informal communications, mainly in the area of speech. Taking it as a "daily language," the government believed that it should be standardized and applied, on an experimental basis, through the Unified Alphabet for the Writing of the Cape Verdean Language (ALUPEC), where its bases are drawn from.[9] In 2005, the PAICV government approved a resolution[10] that conditions should be created for the officialization of Creole, in a strategy to enhance the Cape Verdean language and the progressive construction of a real bilingualism.

Portuguese has been the official language of Cape Verde since independence. It is taught in schools and used for official documents, by the press and for most printed objects. With its different variations, Creole is only considered a "mother tongue," although it is widely used not only in the daily life of the archipelago's inhabitants but also to a large extent in the diaspora. The distinction between official language and mother tongue has raised many questions in Cape Verde. Over the years, the teaching-learning policy of Creole and its "regulation" has varied according to who is at the head of the government. Considering the difficulties of teaching-learning Portuguese, the PAICV usually tries to implement measures that reinforce bilingual teaching. However, when the MpD governs, the Portuguese language is once again favored and is taught to children as early as possible.[11]

The teaching-learning process of Portuguese in Cape Verdean schools raises considerable challenges. On the one hand, these are related to the need for a better use of Portuguese, and on the other hand, they concern a certain degradation of Creole. According to the sociolinguist and Creole teacher Hans-Peter (Lonha) Heilmair, "The Cape Verdean government insists that Portuguese will be spoken, because Portuguese is very important, but it does not undertake measures to ensure an acceptable quality of Portuguese. When they write in Portuguese, [the Cape Verdeans] do not have a good command over the complexity of sentences" (interview with Hans-Peter "Lonha" Heilmar, 2019). Similarly, Ondina Ferreira, a Cape Verdean writer who has been arguing that the Portuguese in Cape Verde should be taught from childhood, warned about the "little ease with which the educated Cape Verdean speaker expresses himself in Portuguese."[12] The writer considered that Portuguese is "the language of union that allows us to communicate with the CPLP countries"; she also enhanced the interest of several countries

(China, India, and Japan) for Portuguese as a "business language," predicting "a bright future, of full globalization and worldization" for this language.

In December 2016, the Cape Verdean minister of education, Maritza Rosabal Peña, of the MpD, announced a reinforcement of the teaching of Portuguese, a language that would now be taught as a second language with the aim of strengthening its expansion in the country. This announcement was controversial and forced the government to issue a statement on the matter, explaining that, as the speakers do not master "the Portuguese language with the same competence and fluency with which they master the Creole language," it was necessary to adopt a methodology that assumed Portuguese was a second language, and that "scientific treatment should be given to the linguistic interferences and to the error, through the adequate and opportune use of the Mother Tongue," which was already foreseen in an ordinance of 1993.[13] The need for such policies shows that although Portuguese is the official language of Cape Verde, its spoken fluency is not comparable with Creole. That is why the government considers that Portuguese should be introduced as early as possible.

Despite being the language spoken in Cape Verdean daily life, Creole is also starting to move away from its more or less formal basis; is being progressively decreolized and its lexical structures, syntax, and morphology are influenced by Portuguese, which brings consequences for both languages. As stated by the linguist Lonha Heilmair:

> 98% of people speak Creole in their daily lives. The language of the people is effectively Creole and they speak Portuguese in some situations. For example, in the court, at school, in solemn moments they have Portuguese. Otherwise it is Creole, but the quality of the Creole is suffering a lot. When they go to a more formal Creole, a formality that has been forging itself, there is always the idea of being as close as possible to Portuguese. And this ends up destroying the very structure of Creole. It gets to the point where people are no longer able to speak and to free themselves from this weight. Even if they want to, they can't. This is serious and shows that either something is done at the level of education/training, introducing some elements where Creole can become Creole again, or else Creole will be lost. (Interview with Hans-Peter "Lonha" Heilmar. March, 2019)[14]

This dynamic of valorization and devaluation of Creole reveals its marginal and subaltern position. Speaking Portuguese fluently and correctly is an instrument of power to which only the upper middle classes have access, enabling their children to receive an education abroad.[15] The social distance is intensified when the use of a language is forced. In this case, it is not only a question of not being able to speak a language but also of creating a gap with another culture, that of the desired Europe. In Portugal, among the immigrants but also among their children already born in the former metropole, Creole is also a subaltern language reproduced within communitarian interactions but generally ignored by public policies and institutions. For some youngsters, however, it became a public instrument of resistance.

The City and Their Immigrants: What Context Are We Talking About?

In 2018, Cape Verdeans represented 7.2 percent of the foreign resident population in Portugal, only surpassed by Brazilians (21.9 percent) (Observatório das Migrações, 2019). Lisbon and Setúbal[16] concentrate the highest number of resident immigrants in Portugal. In 2019, data from the Foreigners and Borders Service (SEF) revealed that in these districts resided, with some kind of legal status (and excluding those who acquired Portuguese nationality), about 53 percent of the documented foreign population in the country. The majority of immigrants living in these regions come from Brazil, Cape Verde, Angola, China, and Guinea-Bissau. Romania, Ukraine, India, and São Tomé and Príncipe are other origins with relevant statistical significance. This mosaic reflects the history of immigration to Portugal. Based on colonial networks established previously, this migratory process was characterized, in a first phase, by a "traditional" migration, mainly coming from Cape Verde still in the colonial period, and in the postindependence period from other Portuguese-speaking African countries (Angola, Guinea Bissau, and São Tomé and Príncipe); in a second phase, beginning in the 2000s, there was new flow, originating from Brazil and Eastern European countries; and finally, more recently, new fluxes, composed of migrants coming from Asian countries, notably India, China, Pakistan, Bangladesh, and Nepal, which have become very significant (although this flow already existed, it gained greater expression in the past decade).

According to the 2011 census, the municipalities in the LMA with the highest number of immigrants are Lisbon (30 percent), Sintra (18 percent), Cascais (12 percent), Amadora (10 percent), and Loures (9 percent). The housing distribution of African citizens is defined by the predominance of public social housing and also pockets of the so-called nonclassic housing, that is, self-construction, in peripheral urban areas. In addition, these residents occupied certain labor niches (construction, domestic service, cleaning services, restaurants, and hotels) and generally had lower incomes (Malheiros and Mendes 2007; Pereira 2010; Malheiros and Fonseca 2011), which consequently pushed them to more marginal territories of the LMA. In a study by DEPIAP—CEPAC (Departamento de Estudos e Documentação sobre Imigração Africana em Portugal—Centro Padre Alves Correia 1995) referred by Pereira (2010: 109–10), Cape Verdean immigrants were most concentrated in the municipalities of Amadora and Oeiras, both located in the greater Lisbon. Oeiras, in the Alto de Santa Catarina neighborhood, had approximately 2,520 Cape Verde citizens living there. In Amadora, the Azinhaga dos Besouros (2,429), Alto da Cova da Moura (2,340), and Estrada Militar do Alto da Damaia (2,126) neighborhoods had the largest number of Cape Verdean citizens. With the exception of Cova da Moura, all these neighborhoods were demolished and their inhabitants relocated in social housing quarters.

In this peripheral housing environment, Creole is the most spoken language in the daily lives of thousands of people. In a questionnaire applied to 537 foreign citizens residing in LMA conducted in 2015,[17] about 12.10 percent reported having Cape Verdean Creole as their mother tongue. However, it is essential to insist that not only immigrants but also their descendants, now Portuguese citizens, speak this language in various contexts of proximity (at home and at work). Despite the relevance of this language, the bilingual teaching-learning Portuguese-Crioulo is generally nonexistent in the school system in Portugal. Even though there have been projects such as the Escola Multilingue (multilingual school)[18] (implemented in two primary schools in Vale da Amoreira, Moita, between 2008 and 2013), these experiments, despite their good results, are exceptional. The implications of this situation can be seen in the social mobility of students coming from these social and cultural contexts and in the perpetuation of social and territorial marginalities, which are manifest in the migratory belts of the LMA.

An image of criminality, insecurity, and strong stigmatization was built around the self-build neighborhoods, which did not disappear with the demolitions and the rehousing of their residents in the 2000s. Places like the Pedreira dos Húngaros, Arrentela, or Cova da Moura have a negative symbolic territorial connotation that is immediately linked to their residents. These neighborhoods are also associated with violent situations, including police violence. However, when one examines the figures released by the Direção-Geral da Política de Justiça (Directorate-General for Justice Policy), of the Ministry of Justice, which the Portuguese Observatory of Migrations (2019) publishes in its annual statistical report, it is noticeable that in 2018 the foreigners' crime conviction rate is very similar to that of the Portuguese population. For example, for the crime of theft/violence, the conviction rate is 69 percent for Portuguese citizens and 70 percent for foreign citizens. When the crime is simple or qualified, the values are, respectively, 49 percent and 60 percent for Portuguese citizens and 52 percent, in both cases, for foreigners. Regarding domestic violence, the conviction rate is 54 percent for Portuguese citizens and 48 percent for foreigners. These numbers contrast with collective perceptions spread by the tabloid media. Discrimination associated with skin color is still very marked in Portugal. According to the European Social Survey, for the cumulative total of responses between 2004 and 2016, about 16 percent of foreign citizens surveyed in Portugal consider that they belong to a group discriminated against on the basis of color or race, nationality or ethnic group, a figure that is higher than the 11 percent estimated for the EU22 average.[19]

It was in this scenario of discrimination and social, racial, and residential segregation that a set of artistic manifestations emerged from the outskirts of Lisbon. One of the most significant of these manifestations materialized in the production of rap music in the 1990s. Back then, the first rap groups were formed, in a juvenile environment, "a bit all over the AML, mainly in neighborhoods on the outskirts of the city" (Cidra 2010: 619); for those youngsters, rap became "a central element of their sociabilities" (619). In 1994, the publication of the album *República*[20]—a compilation of various artists and groups—was a critical event for the popularization of the genre. In this period, as Cidra states, "rap groups gained prominence as participants in events related to urban marginality and gang life, or as voices of resistance against a government that paid little attention to the problems of racism and social exclusion" (619). Their music and lyrics depicted dense historical backgrounds and collective memories, such as the time of the

Colonial War and decolonization, and "events or occurrences coming from life in the neighborhood or, even in the city, in the most vulnerable fringes" (Simões 2019: 28).

Popular Culture in a Migratory Context: Rap in Creole

For Martiniello and Lafleur (2008), in the context of immigration, music-making and listening is used to recreate the culture of the motherland, to remind the migrant of the place where they came from, and to affirm their ethnic identity in societies where they are, or feel, marginalized. Furthermore, this process can, and often does, include the creation of new musical forms as a reaction to the new place of settlement, and as a recreation of identities or views about the daily life (Turino 1993; Baily and Collier 2006). This is especially evident in the second or third generations. However, for Martiniello and Lafleur (2008), music is not only "culture" and/or art but also used as a means of political expression, and in the context of immigration this becomes more evident. Actually, music can also be looked at from a point of view that considers its political significance as an expression of cultural activism, contestation, and resistance, and as a form of political expression that reflects power relations and creates spaces for political claims, resistance, and alternative ideologies, thereby giving visibility to issues pertaining to immigrants and their descendants.

In contemporary cities, the arts and culture have played a key role in deepening processes of social cohesion and integration. More specifically, they were especially relevant for promoting individual and collective self-esteem, the (re)construction of local and social identities, and strengthening the sense of belonging (Miles 1997). For some authors they also enhance and allow the search for a future outside more traditional routes, resonant movements that bring to light mechanisms that are otherwise relegated to invisibility within processes of urban development (Ruby 2002; Panelli 2004; Smiers 2005; Stepanik 2019). Therefore, artistic creation can be one way of finding new answers and highlighting essential elements for better urban development. Moreover, they become the means to counter or reverse the reproduction of inequality and disadvantage by constituting a stimulus to increasing personal and collective confidence, collective learning, and critical thinking, thus contributing to the erasure of the negative connotations associated with certain communities and places (Contador 1999; Fradique 2003; André and Abreu 2006, 2009; Barbosa 2011). Some processes of the institutionalization of artistic and cultural practices, however, also demonstrate how governments and different businesses interests benefit from culture's symbolic power to develop their agendas. Today we are witnessing an appropriation of a symbolic and multicultural narrative, but one that is empty of content. Thus, for instance, the cultural realm was a fundamental element in diverse processes of urban transformation, resulting in severe gentrification in some neighborhoods (Estevens [2017] and Oliveira in this volume). As Cidra and Cardão explain elsewhere in this volume, the development in Portugal of musical practices played by African artists coming from the former empire and their descendants is deeply embedded in processes of appropriation, co-option, and negotiation. Within this artistic context, old colonial representations and renewed Lusophone images are manipulated to conquer audiences and new urban dwellers alike (Mata 2006). For many artists in this field the use of the Portuguese language is an important asset. The use of other languages, particularly Creole, is less visible; when played to Portuguese audiences, music in Creole gains an inevitable flavor of exoticism. Nothing similar happens with the use of Creole in rap music.

The use of the Creole language in musical production within Lisbon suburban neighborhoods is a vibrant expression of protest that also gives insights for a policy of social and urban equality. Thus, the musical use of Creole highlights the socioeconomic condition of these citizens, expressed through their mother tongue; these Creole lyrics created narratives that allowed a better understanding of the social, cultural, and power relations that were being constructed in the territory, in this case in the neighborhoods on the outskirts of LMA. Music in Creole, as a meeting medium of these dynamic relations, is a straightforward answer to stigmatization and discrimination, or a warning call to remind us that the same language was used by Cape-Verdeans in the past to give an account of colonial exploitation and slavery practices and to symbolically confront the colonial regime.

But in what ways, in the tensional/conflictual context of postcolonial Lisbon, can one consider that speaking, singing, and writing in Creole is a form of resistance?

All the work developed by numerous rappers from the fringes of LMA highlights the centrality of resistance as a creative device; and this begins with denunciation. The geography of rap in Creole has been spreading across the most peripheral territories of the LMA since the late 1990s. For LBC Soldjah, a rapper from Cova da Moura [Amadora's neighborhood], rap sung in Cape Verdean Creole is fundamental because

> doing hip-hop in Creole is a way of resisting assimilationist policies . . . the depersonalization of the individual, not only immigrants, but personally, when the individual is black or gypsy . . . we sing in Creole because a language has the weight of an entire civilization . . . For us, to sing in Creole is fundamental, it's very important. Why were the slaves forbidden to speak the language? Other African languages were also forbidden. Or the Romani of the gypsies. Why are there no gypsies speaking their language in Portugal? Because it is a historical process of persecution. This is cultural segregation. These are domination processes, there is always an imposition . . . Colonialism also has values and has a culture; it tries to homogenize everything. (Interview with LBC Soldjah, January 2014)

In his lyrics, in Creole, this idea becomes unmistakable. In the song "Tudu pobri é um soldjah,"[21] (All the poor are soldiers), he talks about the poverty situation of many citizens and how only with knowledge and discipline can one move forward. In the song "Guetto Aljazeera,"[22] he denounces the daily criminalization in the media of the inhabitants of the Cova da Moura neighborhood, subjected to frequent situations of racism. In "Amílcar Cabral,"[23] a song sung along with rappers Kaya and Chullage, he denounces situations of discrimination regarding the immigration of Cape Verdeans to Europe, social injustice, and xenophobia. Chullage is one of the rappers from Arrentela (Seixal) that uses Creole. More recently, on his latest album of 2019, the song "Fidju Maria"[24] pays homage to Black women and their working condition in Lisbon; he specifically focuses on all the workers who take care of other women's children so that they can be emancipated, highlighting the need for class consciousness as a political tool.

The geography of this resistance is being drawn in the voices of rappers from the peripheral municipalities of LMA. From Arrentela (Seixal) to Cova da Moura (Amadora), passing through Mira-Sintra (Sintra) or Vale da Amoreira (Moita), many have played an important role in the production and dissemination of music in recent years. For all of them, digital media have been paramount in this process of dissemination. Through the digital channels, where the number of views of their clips and audio songs is high on the various platforms, they can communicate with foreign audiences and even with international media.[25] Take the case of Loreta, a rapper from Mira Sintra (Sintra), who has thousands of views on YouTube. His song "Bu atitudi muda" (Change attitude), where he expresses the idea of having a life path that is consolidated over the years, has had 1,120,239 views. As Pardue (2012) argues, rap has left the neighborhood(s) and is listened to by thousands of people all over the world, establishing a relationship between the local and the global and a circulation through the main media.

In the context of the production of rap music on the outskirts of Lisbon, and namely in neighborhoods with a migratory origin, a group of artists who use Creole as a means of expression emerged. On the other hand, Cape Verde's musical field, with its different genres, is mainly composed of musicians who sing in Creole.[26] But in both places, there is a discourse of resistance that is carried out through music and in which the use of language is a distinctive element.

Mário de Carvalho, an associative leader of one of the main Cape Verdean associations in Portugal, emphasized in an interview (2015) that Creole is always present when Cape Verdeans are chatting together:

> There is always this preservation of the Creole language . . . But look, this has a lot to do with the message that we pass on. We transmit that Creole is your language and should not influence your capacity of integration or evolution in terms of getting something here in Portugal, in terms of employment, and we have to value the language in this sense. I think it has to be an asset! (Interview with Mário de Carvalho, April 2015)

Despite this idea of preservation of Creole, there is a very present tension in the daily lives of many Cape Verdean immigrants and their descendants. If, on the one hand, they continue to speak Creole in their daily lives, there is also a stigma in relation to their origin, their skin color, or their place of residence that leads them to distance themselves from their mother tongue, even if unconsciously. Thus, speaking Portuguese or another European language is a very relevant instrument of social mobility and citizenship, a linguistic capital (Bourdieu 1991) that cannot be equaled by Creole, a disqualified language in the Portuguese linguistic market.

Nha Dalina, a 61-year-old Cape Verdean citizen who has been living in Portugal for thirty-four years, had only had contact with the written Portuguese language through the literacy classes that she attended in the neighborhood, because in her family only the boys, the *fidjus matxus*,[27] had the opportunity to go to school (Matias 2016: 170). For her, the valorization of the "learning and acquisition of multilingual skills in Portuguese, and especially in European languages," and the need for the estrangement of her children from their mother tongue, despite the fact that she is a speaker of Creole, is evident. It was in Creole that she stated:

> They [their children] did not learn Creole. Thank God! . . . They don't dare to speak Creole . . . With me they only speak in Portuguese . . . because we live in the land of the Portuguese, don't we? . . . What I asked the Lord, do you see? . . . a daughter speaks English, speaks French. One speaks . . . The other also speak French, speak English. She took an English course and always speaks in English. (Matias 2016: 170)

Creole as Form of Resistance

In contrast to Portuguese, Creole is considered, in many contexts, a worthless language. Those who emigrate want to move away from it to give their descendants a better future, considering the teaching-learning of Portuguese and other European languages a clear advantage over Creole. In fact, this evidence enforces the idea historically constructed by Portuguese imperial nationalism and Cape Verdean nationalism for those who emigrate, that Cape Verde is closer to Europe than to their fellow African countries. If there is a heritage that is stigmatized at our destination and also in the country of origin, why should we consider it and not abandon it? If this heritage reminds us of a past of misery, which now further affirms its basis of colonial or postcolonial segregation in the migratory territory of destination, why continue to use this language? As an element of power, the linguistic capital offered by mastering the official language of the country of origin, the same as in the country of destination, is advantageous. Because of imperial power relations and colonial oppression, Portuguese was a means of power and social mobility both for Cape Verdeans in Cape Verde and for immigrants and their descendants in Lisbon.

Soraia Simões, in her book *RAPublicar: A Micro-history That Made History in a Postponed Lisbon: 1986–1996*, says that there is an expression of belonging, identity and territoriality that accompanies and "crosses the experiences of its protagonists and those of their families or cultural heritages in the constant processes of reterritorialization imposed by their diasporas since always, even from the linguistic point of view" (2017: 27). This author sees Cape Verdean Creole as one of the elements that express belonging and heighten the creations "on the daily life circumstances of their artistic-cultural community in the local and global context." If Creole is the language of everyday life in Cape Verde, in Portugal it is also the everyday language of many immigrants, as noted by Mário de Carvalho (2015): "If we are with Portuguese people we will all speak Portuguese but if we meet a Cape Verdean on the street we automatically speak Creole!" (interview with Mário de Carvalho, April 2015).

But as Machado, Matias, and Leal point out, the current use of Creole is an element of cultural disadvantage, especially in the school context:[28]

> Indicators concerning the social class of the students' families and the schooling of their fathers and mothers, privileged indicators of social origin, show the sense of the correlations classically found by the sociology of education at an international level in the 1960s and 1970s by researchers such as Bourdieu and others and later replicated in Portugal . . . Levels of education and failure rates both change in an impressively regular way according to these indicators, improving when there is more economic, professional and educational capital in the families and worsening when there is less of it. (2005: 704)

Comparing the school results of Portuguese children and children of Cape Verdean origin, they concluded "that the effect of class condition overlapped the effect of ethnic belonging" (704). That is why, as "Lonha" Heilmar noted,

> the parents' desire is in the sense that their sons learn the language of the host country. The first generation spoke Creole and the parents spoke Creole at home. The mother tongue of the sons was still Creole. From the second to the third generation, this is only partly maintained. It is also maintained by relationships; they receive people from Cape Verde who speak Creole, there is Creole again. (Interview with Hans-Peter "Lonha" Heilmar, March 2019)

Despite this evidence, Matias identifies an "absence of policies for the language appropriate to the sociolinguistic context of schools" (2017: s/p). She also mentions, in another research work, that "few have been the linguistic and sociolinguistic concerns that migration phenomena raise—even if these have been extensively identified by a vast number of specialized works" (2017). However, this was once a reality in schools where the number of Cape Verdean students or Cape Verdean descendants was high, as "Lhona" Heimar in an interview exemplifies with his own experience:

> When I taught the teachers from a school in Damaia [municipality of Amadora] they had 5000 students, more than 4000 were Cape Verdean. There the situation was the inverse. The Portuguese and Angolans had to learn Creole, otherwise they didn't understand. Everyone spoke Creole. The teachers also wanted to learn to speak Creole and to understand the mechanisms of Creole interference in the Portuguese spoken and written by the students in the class. That is how my classes started in that school. There was a strong desire to learn. There were

as many as 20, 25 teachers in the classes, and this went on for years. The lingua franca of the school was Creole. Today that is no longer the case. (Interview with Hans-Peter "Lonha" Heilmar, March 2019)

This is because there is a general understanding in Portuguese.

With a few exceptions, Cape Verdean literature has been written in Portuguese. In music the situation is the opposite, and Creole is predominant. For Alberto Carvalho (quoted in Fortes 2014),[29] a professor who specializes in Cape Verdean literature, the Cape Verdean writers, "wherever they live, incorporate in their writing not only the Cape Verdean contents but also expressions and Creole language in order to create an effect of popular authentication, rooting, colloquiality, spontaneity, familiarity. It is a kind of seal that is periodically glued" (Fortes 2014). However, he draws attention to the fact that although Creole is

> a language fully mature from the historical, philological, grammatical, lexical point of view, it has a very determined range of intervention, rooted in the islands and, of course, in the many places of emigration, sometimes with an impressive number of speakers. But this empirical reality of mainly popular scope, does not translate into an equivalent socio-political and cultural weight . . . In places of emigration, the working people lack time, motivation and activist training to spread the Creole language, except, of course, in music and the remarkable fact of its consideration as a minority language.

When confronted with the question "is using Creole a form of resistance?" "Lonha" Heilmar replied in an interview,

> I think so. When you don't do that in everyday life it's because there are so many situations where it's convenient to speak Portuguese, when you go into artistic creation, song, literature, etc., then yes, you insist on the root and you continue to create in Creole. While we still know it, this happens and then there is a will to relearn Creole. It is a way of manifesting cultural resistance. (Interview with Hans-Peter "Lonha" Heilmar, March 2019)

For the rapper LBC Soldjah (interviewed in 2014), it is a sharp form of resistance, because politics "talk a lot about integration or tolerance but they don't give a shit. Integration for integration's sake . . . integration, I am wrong with my culture, I need to civilize myself, another culture . . . the way they play with semantics is very good, like games with words but in practice."

Concluding Remarks

Contrary to the widely held belief that the use of Creole is a retreat to Black ancestry, to the roots, there seem to be obvious continuities in the use of this language in daily life both in Cape Verde and in the diaspora. Overall, this highlights certain patterns of disqualification, whether social or territorial. The romanticization of the language of origin, so often reinforced by the Portuguese-speaking elite, forgets that this root reminds ordinary people about the economic, social, or political difficulties (such as hunger, drought, lack of work, inequality, or poverty) that led many Cape Verdeans to emigrate, to wish for a better life for their children, and to distance themselves from their origins. This romanticization can be taken to the limit when the valorization of a certain music sung in Creole, such as the *mornas*, a Cape Verdean musical genre, considered by UNESCO as Intangible Cultural Heritage of Humanity in 2019, happens simultaneously with the devaluation and spurning of the social uses of this language that is the mother tongue of thousands of people.

In Cape Verde, there is a clear difficulty in articulating the mother tongue spoken by all, albeit with variations between islands, and the learning-teaching of Portuguese, the official language. This process has led to various disturbances at the teaching level, which affected professional progression and social mobility. Furthermore, the status of the Creole language in Portugal is not clear. Although it is known that Creole is one of the most widely spoken languages in the LMA, this fact is not completely accepted as a basic condition for bilingual teaching in schools in urban zones where Creole is dominant; such misrecognition ends up encouraging and replicating situations of socioeconomic and territorial marginality.

Despite the tensions that have defined the uses of Creole, most Cape Verdean music, both in the archipelago and in the diaspora, continues to be produced in Creole. The inclusion of African musical traditions sung in Creole inside the world music circuits and their cosmopolitan audiences coexists with their uses as narratives of denunciation that focus attention on the social, economic, and political contexts of their interpreters and local communities. In Lisbon, music in Creole, rap in particular, is an act of resistance that politically narrates and gives visibility to the socioeconomic and spatial segregation that still persists in many territories of the postcolonial city. In the many suburban neighborhoods, music in Creole is a tool for the reinforcement of local sociability and identities that, within those confined urban spaces, become an important mechanism of belonging.

Notes

1 Emigration intensified in Portugal from the 1960s onward. There are several reasons for this, including poverty, lack of employment, especially in rural areas, and the dictatorial regime that was established in the country. See, for example, Pereira (2014).
2 This chapter arises from exploratory research work that is part of the project Sharing Space—Research on Intercultural Cities and Collective Space, FP7 Research Framework PEOPLE Marie Curie-2012-IRSE. The following works resulted from this project: Gavazzo et al. (2016) and Estevens et al. (2017).
3 The main axes of this partnership are political cooperation and the areas of security, regional integration, the knowledge society, and the fight against poverty. The current Cape Verde prime minister, Ulisses Correia e Silva, elected by the Movement for

Democracy in 2016, wants to strengthen this partnership in the fields of economy, trade, investment, and security relations, changing the special partnership to a strategic partnership regime. See https://eur-lex.europa.eu/legalcontent/PT/TXT/HTML/?uri=LEGISSUM:r13018 (accessed June 23, 2021).
4. On January 13, 1991, the MpD won the legislative elections, and in 1992, it began to change the national symbols.
5. During the colonial period, the PAIGC, founded in 1956, fought for the liberation of Guinea-Bissau and Cape Verde. After the independence of these territories, a coup d'état in Guinea, led by Nino Vieira in 1980, led to the end of the PAIGC, and the PAICV was formed in Cape Verde.
6. http://ine.cv/wp-content/uploads/2018/07/independencia_cv-1.pdf.
7. Considering the population aged fifteen years or more.
8. DL 67/98 of December 31.
9. The discussion about ALUPEC is long, and in the present context, this text does not intend to develop it.
10. Resolution n.º 48/2005 14/11/205.
11. Despite this partisan dynamic, there are exceptions even within governments that highlight the country's mother tongue. In an interview with *Diário de Notícias*, Abraão Vicente, the current minister of culture and creative industries of Cape Verde (2016–), in 2017, regarding the VII Meeting of Portuguese Language Writers, said: "Creole is the greatest heritage built by Cape Verdeans . . . Creole should have the dignity of being the official language of Cape Verde and the first step will be its symbolic officialization. The Constitution itself says so in article nine. http://web.archive.org/web/20200302021526if_/https://www.dn.pt/artes/abraao-vicente-o-crioulo-deve-ter-a-dignidade-de-ser-a-lingua-oficial-de-cabo-verde-8881572.html (accessed June 23, 2021).
12. https://www.publico.pt/2014/07/27/culturaipsilon/opiniao/entre-o-crioulo-e-o-portugues-1664265 (accessed June 23, 2021).
13. Edict n.º 53/93, 6/9/1993. This decree-law follows the Law of the Education System in 1990, which defined the objective of "promoting the adequate use of the Portuguese language, as an instrument of communication and study" (Law no. 103/III/90 29/12/90; in 1990, the party in government was the MpD). This law was already amended in 2018, with the purpose of providing "pre-school education [from four years old] with curricular content and teaching materials that allow familiarization with the Portuguese language and preparation for entry into the 1st year of basic education" (Boletim Oficial da República de Cabo Verde de 7 de Dezembro de 2018, p. 1934).
14. Seeking to address some of the problems that arose in the 2013/2014 school year, the government elected by the PAICV decided to implement a bilingual education project. Initially, this project began in two primary schools on the island of Santiago (Ponta D'Água, in the city of Praia, and Flamengos, in Calheta) with two classes, extending to two more classes in Tarrafal in the following school year, as explained by Lonha Heilmair:

> Everyone speaks Creole but those who had a bilingual education were taught in Creole and Portuguese. They learned to write, the alphabet, the spelling rules and it was a success. But at the moment the project is in its fifth year. It may be possible to do the 6th year but there is a tremendous lack of funds and it will only be in two or three classes out of the seven that existed. Even so it is very little . . .

but there has never been formally the regular teaching of Creole in Cape Verde. There were many things that were wanted to be done [after independence]. It may have happened at some point in the literacy campaigns that Creole was used. That was at the height of the struggle and the implementation of Independence, in the early years but there are no systematic records. Then it never entered the school curricula. (Lonha Heilmair, interviewed in 2019)

15 This is a discussion found in other postcolonial contexts, where the language of the former colonizer acquires a prominent role. An example of this process, in another territorial context, is the case of Bolivian immigrants, speakers of Quechua or Yamara, in Argentina (Estevens et al. 2017).
16 The Lisbon Metropolitan Area extends across the districts of Lisbon and Setubal. However, the Foreigners and Borders Service (SEF) only provides disaggregated data at the district level, making it impossible to collect this information in greater detail and at a county scale.
17 This questionnaire was applied within the framework of the project CRISIMI—O Impacto da Crise Económica sobre as Condições de Vida e Dinâmicas de Inserção Laboral dos Imigrantes em Portugal, financiado pelo Alto Comissariado para as Migrações. For more information, see https://www.om.acm.gov.pt/documents/58428/177157/Estudo_OM+60.pdf/f06d4a45-02b7-408b-a8b8-e273ff41cf6e (accessed June 23, 2021).
18 http://www.iltec.pt/pdf/wpapers/EM_projeto.pdf (accessed June 23, 2021).
19 This average value is for the twenty-two countries of the European Union that provided answers to this questionnaire with a sample over 150.
20 "The phenomenon of popularity of one of the songs presented in the phonogram, Nadar, by the group Black Company, gave a sudden visibility to rap, which until then had been commented on by the media for reasons unrelated to the musical production" (Cidra 2010: 619).
21 https://www.youtube.com/watch?v=ucTlA4XhNA0 (accessed June 23, 2021).
22 https://www.youtube.com/watch?v=1MLVViwN_K8 (accessed June 23, 2021).
23 https://www.youtube.com/watch?v=Vb_OqtmVcH4 (accessed June 23, 2021).
24 https://www.youtube.com/watch?v=9Y-Yzrlv1LI (accessed June 23, 2021).
25 https://www.youtube.com/watch?v=oFn7oJz__z8 (accessed June 23, 2021).
26 The lyrics of the *mornas* of Eugénio Tavares are considered the first written records of Creole.
27 Translate *fidjus matxus* as male sons.
28 The authors are referring to Seabra (1994).
29 https://www.publico.pt/2014/07/27/culturaipsilon/noticia/o-portugues-e-para-o-caboverdiano-um-guardachuva-excelente-1664304 (accessed June 23, 2021).

References

André, I., and A. Abreu (2006). "Dimensões e Espaços da Inovação Social." *Finisterra*, XLI(81): 121–41.

André, I., and A. Abreu (2009). "Social Creativity and Post-Rural Places: The Case of Montemor-o-Novo, Portugal." *Canadian Journal of Regional Science/Revue canadienne des sciences régionales*, 32(1): 101–14.

Baily, J., and M. Collier (2006). "Introduction: Music and Migration." *Journal of Ethnic and Migration Studies*, 32(2): 167–82.

Barbosa, C. (2011). "A música rap e espaços de representação juvenil negra em Portugal." *O Cabo dos Trabalhos: Revista Electrónica dos Programas de Doutoramento do CES/ FEUC/ FLUC/ III*, Coimbra no. 5: 1–20.

Bourdieu, P. (1991). *Language and Symbolic Power*. Cambridge: Polity.

Cabral, A. ([1969] 2020). "Análise de alguns tipos de resistência." In I. Galvão, J. Neves, and R. Lopes (eds.), *Análise de alguns tipos de resistência/Amílcar Cabral—Ed. revista e comentada*. Lisbon: Outro Modo Cooperativa Cultural.

Cardina, M., and I. N. Rodrigues (2021). "The Mnemonic Transition: The Rise of an Anti-anticolonial Memoryscape in Cape Verde." *Memory Studies*, 14(2): 380–94.

Cidra, R. (2008). "Produzindo a música de Cabo Verde na diáspora: redes transnacionais, world música e múltiplas formações crioulas." In P. Góis (ed.), *Comunidade(s) Cabo-verdiana(s): as Múltiplas Faces da Imigração Cabo-verdiana, colecção Comunidades*, 105–26. Lisbon: Alto Comissariado para a Imigração e Diálogo Intercultural.

Cidra, R. (2010). "Hip-Hop." In S. Castelo-Branco (ed.), *Enciclopédia da música em Portugal no século XX*, 618–23. Lisbon: Círculo de Leitores/Temas e Debates.

Cidra, R. (2021). *Funaná, raça e masculinidade: Uma trajetória colonial e pós-colonial*. Lisbon: Outro Modo Cooperativa Cultural.

Contador, A. (1999). *Cultura Juvenil Negra em Portugal*. Oeiras: Celta.

Contador, A. (2001). "Music and the Identification Process among Young Black Portuguese." *Sociologia* (36): s/p.

Estevens, A., N. Gavazzo, and S. Pereira (2017). "Música en las ciudades interculturales: Estrategias de visibilidad de los jóvenes migrantes en Lisboa y Buenos Aires." *SSIIM Paper Series*, vol. 17, December, UNESCO Chair on Social and Spatial Inclusion of International Migrants—Urban Policies and Practice, Università Iuav di Venezia.

Fradique, T. (2003). *Fixar o movimento: representações da música rap em Portugal*. Lisbon: Publicações Dom Quixote.

Fortes, T. S. (2014). "Português é para o cabo-verdiano um guarda-chuva excelente." *Público*, July 27. https://www.publico.pt/2014/07/27/culturaipsilon/noticia/o-portugues-e-para-o-caboverdiano-um-guardachuva-excelente-1664304 (accessed June 23, 2021).

Gavazzo, N., A. Estevens, and S. Pereira (2016). "Music: A Tool for Socio-political Participation among Descendants of Bolivian Immigrants in Bilbao, Spain and Buenos Aires, Argentina." In J. Sardinha and R. Campos (eds.), *Transglobal Sounds: Music, Identity and Migrant Descendants*,133–54. New York: Bloomsbury Academic.

Machado, F. L., A. R. Matias, and S. Leal (2005). "Desigualdades sociais e diferenças culturais: os resultados escolares dos filhos de imigrantes africanos." *Análise Social* (176): 695–714.

Malheiros, J. M. (2000). "Urban Restructuring, Immigration and the Generation of Marginalized Spaces in the Lisbon Region." In R. King, G. Lazaridis, and C. Tsardanidis (eds.), *Eldorado or Fortress? Migration in Southern Europe*, 207–32. London: Palgrave Macmillan.

Malheiros, J. M., and M. L. Fonseca (2011). *Acesso à habitação e problemas residenciais dos imigrantes em Portugal* (vol. 48). Lisbon: Observatório da Imigração, ACIDI, IP.

Malheiros, J. M., and M. Mendes (eds.) (2007), *Espaços e Expressões de Conflito e Tensão entre Autóctones, Minorias Migrantes e Não Migrantes na Área Metropolitana de Lisboa*. Lisbon: ACIDI, Colecção Estudos n. 22.

Marcuse, H. (2007). *A dimensão estética*. Lisbon: Edições 70.
Martiniello, M., and J.-M. Lafleur (2008). "Ethnic Minorities' Cultural Practices as Forms of Political Expression." *Journal of Ethnic and Migration Studies*, 34(8): 1191–335.
Mata, I. (2006). "A crítica literária africana e a teoria pós-colonial: um modismo ou uma exigência." *Ipotesi*, Juiz de Fora, 10(2): 33–44.
Matias, A. R. (2016). "Nha Dalina: Nha konta stória di–Nha." In S. L. Amândi, P. Abrantes, and J. T. Lopes, *A Vida entre nós: Sociologia em Carne Viva*, 166–75. Porto: Deriva Editores.
Matias, A. R. (2017). "Diversidade linguística em Portugal e a (in)visibilidade das línguas silenciadas—o caso da língua caboverdeana nas escolas portuguesas." Comunicication in *II Colóquio Internacional Raça, Identidade, Mundialização: Desmentidos coloniais, dominações e transformações. Um diálogo entre a psicanálise e as ciências sociais*. Lisbon: ISPA.
Miles, M. (1997). *Arts, Space and the City: Public Art and Urban Futures*. London: Routledge.
Monteiro, C. A. (2011). *Música Migrante em Lisboa: Trajectos e práticas de músicos caboverdianos*. Lisbon: Mundos Sociais.
Oliveira, C. R., and N. Gomes (coord.) (2019). *Imigração em números. Indicadores de integração de Imigrantes. Relatório Estatístico Anual*. Lisbon: Observatório das Migrações.
Panelli, R. (2004). *Social Geographies*. London: Sage.
Pardue, D. (2012). "Cape Verdean Creole and the Politics of Scene-Making in Lisbon, Portugal." *Journal of Linguistic Anthropology*, 22(2): E42–E60.
Pereira, S. (2010). *Trabalhadores de origem africana em Portugal: Impacto das novas vagas de imigração*. Lisbon: Edições Colibri.
Pereira, V. (2014). *A Ditadura de Salazar e a Emigração: O Estado Português e os Seus Emigrantes em França (1957–1974)*. Lisbon: Círculo de Leitores/Temas e Debates.
Ruby, C. (2002). "L'art public dans la ville." http://www.espacestemps.net/document282.html (last accessed March 20, 2014).
Seabra, T. (1994). "Estratégias Familiares de Socialização das Crianças. Etnicidade e Classes Sociais." MA dissertation, ISCTE, Lisbon.
Simões, S. (2017). *RAPublicar: A micro-história que fez história numa Lisboa adiada 1986–1996*. Lisbon: Editora Caleidoscópio.
Simões, S. (2019). *Fixar o (in) visível: os primeiros passos do RAP em Portugal (1986–1998)*. Lisbon: Editora Caleidoscópio.
Smiers, J. (2005). *Arts under Pressure, Promoting Cultural Diversity in the Age of Globalization*. London: Zed.
Stepanik, H. (2019). "On Notions of (In)Visibility and Diaspora Space: The Case of Batuku as a Popular Practice in Lisbon." *Vienna Journal of African Studies*, 36(19): 75–100.
Turino, T. (1993), *Moving Away from Silence: Music of the Peruvian Altiplano and the Experience of Urban Migration*. Chicago: University of Chicago Press Books.

Chapter 7

DESIGNING SUBORDINATION: A COMPARATIVE SOCIAL HISTORY OF PAID DOMESTIC WORK IN PORTUGAL

Nuno Dias

Body, Class, and Labor

At the beginning of the twentieth century, William Du Bois introduced the "color line" concept in his book *The Souls of Black Folk*, an expression that left its indelible mark on the race relations debate in the United States. According to Du Bois, the new century would be defined by the dividing line of skin color. In retrospect, more than one hundred years after his observations, it is undeniable that his prediction has materialized, even if only in part. From the colonial regimes and the systems of racial difference and hierarchy built within them, through Western narratives of ethnogenesis and civilizational exceptionalisms, to the rigidity of racial segregation that still defines the borders of the US society, and the social conflicts in northern economies due to postwar and postcolonial economic migration, few concepts proved to be as analytically useful as the "racialization" one.[1]

Modernity—more precisely industrialization, urbanization, and the bureaucratic development of the colonial enterprise—resulted in complex practices and processes of organization and design through the classification of territories and populations, globally developing production along the axis of racial differentiation and/or class. Such categorization reified and crystallized identity affiliation, vertically fleshing out a hierarchy of social privilege legitimated by skin color or other vulgar features (be it the racial primitivism of the colonial subject or the uncivilized nature of the metropolitan working classes). This seems to corroborate Du Bois's assertion that the relationship between the idea of blackness and US identity would determine the overall evolution of US society.

Despite the differences in the Marxian and Weberian proposals of class analysis, they share an important common ground: class is a consequence of economic activity and plays a central role in constituting and organizing capitalist societies (Dworkin 2007: 15). It is this primordial dovetailing that transforms the concept of class into an important instrument for deconstructing discursive processes regarding what societies "objectively" are and what type of social formations "objectively" explain the way in which they are organized—in other words, what type of relations between individuals and groups of individuals are indispensable to society.

The concept of class (and the Hegelian root explicit in the Marxist interpretation) suggests a mindset of conflict, apparently incompatible with the idea of compromise and stability inherent to the socio-democratic model. This could go some way to explaining the intermittency in academic relevance of Marxist theory in curricula or, at least, the decline in its use. It is equally true that throughout the second half of the twentieth century a series of more or less empirical authors and proposals have challenged the criticism, omissions, and shortcomings that have been attributed to Marxist theory, in particular the concept of class, as a preferred framework within which to analyze inequality.[2] Simultaneously, the analytical space in which attempts are made to harmonize these theoretical frameworks is a result of the dynamics that have emerged from a postwar imperial decline and the crumbling of the inclusivity fantasies nurtured by the vast bureaucratic and rhetorical machines of Western empires.

According to Oliver Cox (1948), modern racial structures are a consequence of capitalism. Furthermore, capitalism does not exist without merchandise and the intensity of its development increases proportionally to the commercialization of its fundamental fuel: labor. This requirement is fully achieved in and from Africa, where physical dissimilarities served the formation of a moral economy that sustained the post-slavery labor regimes. This exploitation of the racialized subject under colonial capitalism is also what makes Cox's theory relevant in postcolonial migrations. The relationship between capital and labor forged in colonized territories migrates with the subaltern to the former metropolises. African and Asian immigration to Europe challenged the idealized international solidarity of the working class. Populist politics organized around exclusivist narratives of national identity and against the perils of ethnic differentiation and social fracture.[3] In this context, class as a preponderant criterion of social organization and mobilization was disputed by media and political usage of "alternative" criteria (such as race, ethnicity, gender, generation, etc.). If one considers ethnicity and race to be possible modalities of social relations, among others, such as nationalism or tribalism, based on the perception of a shared ancestralism, it is not difficult to accept that these divisions can be shaped by other modalities of affiliation and group identification, namely, economic or political.

Therefore, in the sense that some authors assumed that class affiliation would prevail over nationalism, others have, reactively, defined ethnicity as a "primordial" social connection (Geertz 1963). Edna Bonacich, one of the authors who has worked extensively on and developed the areas where these two dimensions of analysis—race/ethnicity and class—intersect, created a conceptual framework to deal with the apparent contradictions and complexity of group formation processes, on the basis of diverse observations. She has also focused on relations within and between groups in capitalist societies where ethnic and/or racial categories are constitutive of social reality (1999: 166–94). In an academic context where class and ethnicity are recurrently discussed according to the types of solidarity that are more spontaneously "mobilized," and hence authentic, Bonacich downplayed the discussion regarding the role that workers of the dominant group played in labor conflicts and the demotion of migrant workers from the political struggle (187–8). For Bonacich, the idea of a segmented labor market[4] relates to global capitalist processes and the structural imbalances between nations, largely depending on structures of colonial (under)development and the incapacity of these workers to resist exploitative processes. The availability of these workers and their readiness to cross national borders engender competition reactions that change the morphology of the labor market. Bonacich suggests approaching all class relations generated within imperial complexes as a system. In this sense, as capitalism develops, the price of labor tends to increase, which, consequently, causes capital to seek cheaper labor to maximize profits. Theoretically, it is thus important to resist more exclusivist notions of class, reformulating the idea of class struggle so that, analytically, the racial/ethnic complex is perceived as part of this conflict.[5] It is therefore essential for this analysis to understand to what extent the formation and replication of a racial/ethnic order have been historically and continuously decisive for the accumulation of capital.

In Portugal, both in the colonies as well as in the mainland, the process of transitioning from an agrarian-based economy to an industrialized and salaried one, in which new protagonists are "pushed" toward urban areas, is evident in the disorganized and insalubrious growth of cities and their capacity to attract rural populations from the interior. Thus, industry's labor demand and, more importantly, control over this workforce are also accomplished through the conversion of women and young men into low-cost labor—simultaneously complexifying the system of exchanges to which reproductive functions are subjected. Placed in the sphere of reproductive tasks, traditionally understood to be extrinsic to production, even when paid, this study will examine the debate around the questions of ethnicity and class and their importance as instruments for analyzing social structures and, within these structures, the political formation of social groups. Domestic work and its particular sociohistorical configuration make it possible to illustrate, in the Portuguese case, the way in which political dynamics of identity, class, ethnic/racial, and professional production intersect and are perpetuated in different geographical and temporal contexts. This chapter discusses paid domestic work in three sociohistorical contexts: Portuguese colonial territories during the twentieth century until decolonization in 1975; Portugal metropole urban settings during the same period; and postcolonial Portugal. Setting out from the figure of domestic employees, it will examine the mechanisms producing structural subordination—based on an ethnic reference or a class reference or both—in capitalist societies.

Urban Colonialism: Gender, Masculinity, and Servants

Reproductive tasks being carried out by individuals outside the family is a common feature throughout time and space, usually derivative of rigid social stratification schemes. Historically, this service was also provided by slaves and under other forms of enforced labor. Over time, the vast and variable list of social categories involved in reproductive tasks and servitude, as well as access to them as a commodity, was consolidated in perceived notions of social status and prestige (Veblen 1899). While it is true that the relationship between servitude and slavery is probably mutually constitutive, it is also true that, after slavery was formally abolished, with modernity came significant changes. To grasp this process, we analyze racial and gender categories during colonialism and the way it interconnects with labor organization in colonial territories—and how, in domestic service, these categories were reinforced by capitalist logics that required the formation of labor reserves accessible to colonial settlement, mainly in urban environments.

The colonial enterprise, after the Berlin Conference, resulted in the rapid growth of urban centers that served as entrepôts, connecting the colonies with the homeland and the rest of the world. This required the construction of infrastructure, streamlined transport to take people from one place to another, and a territorial organization that accentuated distances between residences and work. In Portuguese colonial history, the fin de siècle marked a turning point in labor relations. Jeanne Penvenne (1995), in her discussion on the case of Lourenço Marques, the capital city of colonial Mozambique, demonstrates the existence of a triangle linking urban development, work, and discipline (physical, moral, and political). This triangle molded the relationship between colonists and the Black communities, unfolding in the early twentieth century and defined over the course of the following decades. Analyzing domestic servitude in the context of the Portuguese empire and East Africa also entails reconstituting an important part of the history of colonial cities and how notions of masculinity and race developed during the twentieth century. In 1904, one in six urban jobs consisted of domestic service, and by 1933, domestic servants represented one-third of the city's voluntary workforce (55). During the first half of the twentieth century the same system was found in most African territories colonized by Europeans. A gender pattern accompanied the increasing number of African domestic servants in white settlers' households in the early 1900s. In Mozambique, as in the rest of East Africa, young men were assigned mostly tasks performed inside and around the house (Pariser 2015). The racial demarcation of the colonial occupational structure was noticeable in the 1928 census in which "95% of the entire salaried work force engaged in domestic tasks consisted of African men and women, clearly indicating the subordinate nature attributed to this kind of work in the minds of employers" (Zamparoni 1999: 151).

There was a close relationship between race and the possible standard of comfort. Domestic work represented the dubious nature of the proximity with white colonists: on the one hand, it provided access to a racially circumscribed and privileged space as well as the codes needed to be able to navigate those settings; on the other, it meant being cheek by jowl with their employers' capricious authority (Zamparoni 1999: 54). Historians describe the genesis and evolution of a system of labor relations that depended on compulsory mechanisms of production, control, and discipline of rural populations, for whom urban work (inside homes, in ports, or in construction) was imposed with colonial inevitability (Domingos and Peralta 2013). The coercive schemes designed to incorporate autochthones populations into the monetary economy[6] reflected the arbitrary and violent nature of colonial authority. These schemes were one of the main instruments supporting the development of capitalist ventures under the flag of colonial development. Although Penvenne refrains from explaining this transition as a disaffection of means of production, especially since some of these "migrant" workers retained access to land and some livestock (1995: 6), this is precisely the image that comes to mind: the growing and progressive transfer of rural labor to urban contexts due to a forced introduction into the salaried economy.[7] This was a forced entry that appeared to racially determine the different stages of the productive process and, naturally, the consequent underlying reproductive tasks. With the racial proximity in cities, segmenting political mechanisms emerged, bringing order to the colonial city and to the distribution of the symbolic resources that define the ways of participating in it. The stratified categories became increasingly more complex over the course of the twentieth century, reflecting the growing need for a compliant and mobile labor force. The resistance of the indigenous population to integration into a post-slavery salaried system, and an apparent repeated and generalized disregard by these populations for the commitments and schedules that salaried work entailed, provoked indignation and complaints by employers to the official authorities. These complaints impacted formal policies. It was necessary to civilize by means of discipline through and for work.[8]

One of the characteristics of the productive process in capitalist economies, and the organization of work it entails, is the disciplining of the labor force. In colonial contexts, this was associated with organizing violent methodologies to anchor the indigenous populations in modern spaces. This was met with resistance, from the workers, reluctant to be part of a workforce, which had to comply with arduous labor on large plantations, as well as from the Black elite, who questioned and opposed the demands of white traders and farmers supported by legislation based on racial criteria (Freudenthal 2001: 448). The labor relations evoked by apparently conflicting descriptions—at times highlighting the docile and passive nature of Blacks who had been absorbed into violent work routines while at others describing their savage nature and propensity toward laziness and vices (Macedo 2012: 304–9)—proved a mainstay of the social and political construction of the "native" figure, which continues to extend well beyond the end of the colonial regime, despite all its incongruence and tensions. Notwithstanding the distinct symbolic nature of the subordinated categories observed in colonies and metropoles, the practical vocation of the work systems that were established and regulated produced somewhat similar regimes, as can be illustrated by domestic service. As Marta Macedo has stated, the deadly illnesses present in the plantations of São Tomé and Príncipe, apart from sleeping sickness, are the ones that affect workers from European factories (304–9). This was due to workers being subjected to overwork, insalubrious conditions, and malnutrition. These conditions gave rise to discourse and practices related to hygiene, both in the colonies and in the metropole, which sought to mitigate the impact of working conditions on the physical availability of labor.

It is interesting to note that the importance of educating the indigenous population to carry out tasks subordinately, discreetly and invisibly, particularly domestic tasks, and the clash between this intention and the difficulty of ensuring discipline influenced the dominant moral framework applied to female domestic workers in the metropole. In the colonies, from 1899 onward, work was legally cited as a "moral obligation" of all men and women between fourteen and sixty years of age (Newitt 1997: 341)—a situation linked to the need for state intervention to implement the theoretical assumptions of liberalism by decree.[9] However, even though there was a high demand for domestic workers, the average remuneration of these occupations remained at the bottom of the pyramid and the workers continued to be vulnerable to the whims of employers, although some variables could change according to the region. Probably due to this—in some cases a domestic worker could receive less for his or her work than a laborer recruited under coercive schemes—the majority of domestic servants were young boys who used domestic work as a means to enter the urban labor market, viewing it as training for better paid professions in the urban economy (Zamparoni 1999: 60). The prevalence of males in domestic work also partially reflects the delicate area and danger that physical proximity with colonists represented, from the point of view of managing personal identity. Zamparoni disputes the proposed justification for the marginal number of Black women in domestic work in the colonies, attributing it exclusively to a perceived lack of sexual inhibitions on behalf of white women and the danger that Black women would therefore represent cohabiting with their husbands. This stands in contrast to the European context, where the accentuation of the sexual division of labor occurred simultaneously with the processes of honing the bourgeois model of sociability, which naturally reconciled femininity and domestic activities. According to Zamparoni, this was also true for the arguments that this type of work could have been rejected by African women due to the exceptionally active control of those who carried out domestic tasks or alternatively because of a moral disdain associated with domestic tasks (166).

In Zamparoni's view, this gender imbalance was more a dynamic of resistance, a result of the defense mechanisms of local populations regarding the social role of women in indigenous societies, as they were responsible for reproduction and raising children as well as domestic chores. Only older women would seek out domestic work, usually as washerwomen or nannies. This although, especially after the 1940s, the Estado Novo (1933–74) implemented active policies to attract more women to domestic work, with a view to solving the problem of indiscipline among young male servants (Zamparoni 1999: 148). However, despite the administration's efforts, the number of women in domestic service was never enough to transform the paradigm of domestic workers. This was due, first, to Black women not viewing domestic work as simply a steppingstone to access a better paid profession; in professional terms, it would always be the end in and of itself. Second, female domestic workers—washerwomen and nannies—were not only the worst paid but were also the ones who saw their salaries reduce over time, leading them to opt for factory work in cashew processing units (which was equally poorly paid), if they were allowed to do so (151).

Nevertheless, other studies show that, for the first half of the twentieth century, domestic service was not socially disdained and was associated with a certain prestige (Eastman 1994)—a reality that changed after the war with transformations in the overall nature of domestic service and the way people managed home budgets, resulting in less differentiation between tasks and lower remunerations—a shift that, in Dar es Salaam, led to domestic workers unionizing (Pariser 2015).

The development of the colonial economies took place within imperial systems, where colonies and the metropole interacted, albeit sometimes in an environment fraught with political tension, within an identical, parallel capitalist logic, in which processes of subordinate social group formation are noticeably similar. This means that more than distinct conceptual and operational realities, race and class combined to produce analytically comparable logics of dependence and social obedience. On the one hand, the conventional dynamics of a conflict, which pitted opposing class interests against each other, were evident in the tensions that arose between labor and capital, both in the colony—with Black workers facing white employers—and in the homeland, where the white working class was pitted against white employers. On the other hand, the rhetoric that sustained the repressive mechanism mobilized to contain the organization of Black workers was different from the rhetorical and material tools used to respond to the demands of white workers (Penvenne 1995: 82). Paraphrasing Zamparoni (1999: 168), what could be a better arena to hone the frontiers of racial and class boundaries between colonial subjects, settlers, and colonizers than the insular world of domesticity?

Serving in the Metropole

The aim of comparing historically overlapping social realities is based on the idea of a simultaneous process of easier access to domestic service in two specific political settings: the colony and the metropole. Subsequently, we examine the legacy and continuities of both these environments in the contemporary postcolonial intertwining of domestic service and migration. To this end, it is important to identify the conditions in which domestic work became part of the habitus of bourgeois society and a bourgeois aspiration in the metropole, and to try to capture the impact of this transformation on the political design of the domestic worker. The processes of social reproduction based on the class logic personified by the female domestic workers migrating from rural areas to the main cities, particularly Lisbon and Porto, share some features with those that saw young Black Mozambican boys "serve" and form a significant part of the colonial "racial projects" (Leal 2006: 63–79). The similarities lie particularly in the narratives, discourses, and concerns of employers.

While commenting on popular culture as a primary topic of Portuguese anthropological research during the nineteenth century, deeply committed to the issue of a national identity, João Leal highlighted the deprecating nature of descriptions reserved for peasants and their habits, attire, and other everyday practices—"stupid," "crude," "rustic," "indigent," "bums," and so on. While this disdainful portrayal of peasants and their rural milieu, of their "primitive pottery," reflects a turn-of-the-century obsession with national decadence, it also points to some idealized notions of certain elites regarding lower social classes and their place in the balance of virtues and defects of the national identity (Leal 2006: 65–70). This image of rusticity mirrors reservations regarding the aptitudes and ethics of metropolitan female domestic workers.

The stereotypical female domestic worker during the period of the Estado Novo was a girl from a poor rural family, who was often illiterate (Meersschaert 1986: 633–42). Consistent elements of the trajectories of the servile workforce in both contexts include: their expectations of the urban world and the personal and family shock engendered by the transition; the absence of alternatives and the inevitability of a servile condition; learning behavioral codes; work schedules; required responsibilities; and discipline. In a process comparable to the social and political construction of the Black population as the "stereotype" of contaminated alterity, female servants were socially represented in the metropole as a seed of social disruption (Brasão 2010: 81–110). The "question of the maids" and the moral panic regarding the harmful influence these women had in a pristine bourgeois house—documented by Inês Brasão in her meticulous research on servile conditions during the Estado Novo—were the result of the creation of a "class viewed as typically being disobedient, lacking in moral and physical hygiene, with pretensions of imitating the class they serve (at least in appearance), unable to mind their tongues, physically frail, with low productivity, incapable of looking after others and not very 'Catholic' habits" (2016: 12).

The abundance of deprecating impressions attributed to a specific group, which was thus homogenized, and their amplification were undoubtedly linked to the group's growth in the labor class[10] and the consequent perceived threat due to differences (in this case differences in social status and not skin color) between the ones who serve and the ones being served. Just like in the colonies, the recognition of disparities between the privileges attributed to different social groups and the belief that authority and discipline worked to deter the latent possibility of a reversal in social roles resulted in even more intense characterizations of the subordinated groups as not being worthy candidates for social mobility. The importance of docility and servitude training for female servants also entailed the mobilization of the bureaucratic apparatus. Even though the idea (which persisted during the 1950s and 1960s) of registering domestic maids seems not to have been widespread in practice, its objective was to conform the rebellious "class" to the principles of the National Labor Code. In 1958, Adelaide de Carvalho (1958) spoke in the name of employers and published a piece dedicated to the "problem of maids" in which she lamented the "loss of the rights of employers, victims of abuse and calamities," perturbed by what she felt was a "conflict between nannies and maids." Apart from the strength dedicated to formulating a proposal to create professional identity cards and a registry for maids, this booklet identifies the conflict underway as a class conflict. For the author, "servants" now behaved like a group lacking the spirit of subjection of the "maids of yesteryears." They were like a "revolutionary sect" that did not respect the codes of obedience and deference due to employers (11, 33) and whose lax morality and demands seem more serious in cities where their insolence is evident in class associations, even demanding that their professional category be renamed, promoting the term "employees" over "maids."

The salient difference in the trajectories of both classes seems to be based on their repertoire of demands, varying between the metropole and the colonies. The temporary way Black domestic workers in Mozambique viewed their activities would have made it hard for them to mobilize on the basis of an awareness of professional class. It is precisely this volatility that hinders the formation of a "class for itself." In the case of maids in the metropole, this mobilization became more expressive in 1921, during a period of sectorial and general strikes as a reaction to the persistent formal marginality to which they were subjected. This was the context in which new initiatives to form associations emerged, with the general objective of expanding efforts to defend the interests of servants. This also encompassed maids in private houses and resisted the project to regulate servile activities as well as the creation of a professional booklet paid for by the maids themselves.[11] On August 17, 1921, a massive meeting of the class associations representing hotel and restaurant staff, culinary professionals, and waiters and housekeeping staff at hotels and private houses marked the start of a strike against the "booklet regulation," which resulted in the arrests of members of the Maids Association and clashes between them and the police.[12]

The female domestic workers' struggle continued throughout the dictatorship—mainly concentrated in protests for the recognition of their professional status according to the labor code—and continued after the fall of dictatorship. The entire process of trying to constitute an associative space to organize female domestic workers in the form of a union, as well as the underlying struggles, particularly those that reflected the profound tensions revealed after the Carnation Revolution, had yet to be achieved. Historically, these rural migrants, handed over by their families sometimes at a tender age and on relatively vague terms, who embodied the image of maids in the past century and their representation as simple women in terms of attire and intelligence—undeniably different from their urban and/or sophisticated employers—were the precursors of the Other embodied in foreign domestic workers. The traditional lack of prestige and value associated with the servile condition and domestic work, along with means of reflecting the difference forged during the colonial period, will enable a better understanding of the evolution of the link between domestic service and immigration in a postcolonial context.

Servitude and Migration in the Postcolonial Nation

Several collective efforts have been made to structure concepts in order to interpret and analyze the social transformations that took place in Portuguese society after the Carnation Revolution.[13] Although the immediate aftermath of the revolution ushered in a period of great social political polarization and instability reflected in the tension between labor and capital in contemporary Portuguese history, the main trends that have molded Portuguese society in the past four decades have mostly been analyzed by social scientists at the level of a positivist obsession with the creation of a methodological-conceptual framework cataloguing social dynamics of Portuguese society rather than a critical theoretical-interpretative commitment capable of analyzing models of social organization and predominant production relations as results of a conflict between concrete political agents and ideas. Concepts such as that of an unfinished (Machado and da Costa 1998) or peripheral (Santos 1985) modernity—including studies on the growth of middle classes, the tertiarization of the economy, the expansion of the welfare state, new values and lifestyles that coexist with patterns of reduced social mobility and persistent social inequalities—which indicate a possible restoration of the class structure in Portuguese society, appear, in this sense, excessively tangled in the functionalist analyses of social systems, thus ignoring the possibilities of interpreting the structural transformations that took place in society at the time. Similarly, questions such as the phenotype segmentation of the labor market and the "opportunities structures" have not been sufficiently examined.

As an integral and necessary part of this process, the economic migration that took place in the postcolonial period formed the core of a new public Western construction of "racialized" alterity. This is an encounter without the filtered mediation of a colonial label, which represented a stabilizing hierarchy for collective concerns, albeit with a catchy heading that causes moral panic foretelling social conflict (Guibentif 1991: 63–74).

At the beginning of the industrial period, (new) bourgeois models of managing domestic space emerged and expanded in cities, where the social division of servile work was reconfigured beyond the servile paradigms defined within the aristocracy. In a somewhat similar manner, the economic, social, and political transformations associated with globalization and the postcolonial context once again took domestic work outside the arena of material privileges exclusive to more affluent social groups. The recruitment of female domestic workers, a process that in Portugal benefited primarily from the expectations of upward social mobility, which rural families nurtured with regard to the urban monetary economy, became international and began to be reoriented from the 1980s onward toward the growing female immigrant population. The significant increase in recent decades of the number of families hiring female domestic workers took place in the wake of a varied set of social changes: female emancipation and access to education; growing female employment; the tertiarization of the economy; the demographic evolution in Western nations; and, naturally, the existence of available labor in global circuits (Anderson 2007: 250).

The "mechanization of the domestic unit" and the "commodification of reproductive labor" (Catarino and Oso 2000) have created a gateway for the socially unprotected contingent of labor migrants coming from outside the Schengen area.[14]

Moreover, in a context of an accentuated demographic aging and the dismantling of the social services of the welfare state, it is this labor that is sought after to fulfill the need to accompany the elderly population, thus diversifying and sophisticating the type of services expected from this class.[15] Despite the differences observed in the models of labor relations, for example, in forms of contracts, between those doing cleaning and those who prepare meals and—especially—caregivers (who have the greatest probability of having more stable contracts),[16] phenotype factors, nationality, and legal status continue to be decisive in determining the social position of immigrants in highly ethnic labor markets—the domestic work sector is no exception, quite to the contrary. In a sector that continues to be represented as exceptional, considering an alleged closer interpersonal intimacy between employees and employers, the scope of arbitrariness and the predominance of informal arrangements only seem to confirm the precarious nature of workers and their secondary role in negotiating the work relationship. The widespread perception that domestic work is marked by informal arrangements with negative consequences for those working in this area has in fact contributed toward a global mobilization in the sense of promulgating legislative initiatives that dignify the conditions in which domestic work takes place and is politically perceived.[17] On the other hand, what appears to be a colonial legacy regarding the perception of the white majority concerning certain social groups in terms of neatness, cleanliness, and civility seems to continue to condition the choice of employees and/or the type of tasks assigned to them, reinforcing the differentiated value attributed to different social groups. This depreciative game maintains the intersection between logics of class and "racialization" in the labor market. In Portugal, an exploratory survey of corporate supply in the domestic services and care sectors revealed that some companies justify different prices on the basis of the assumed better quality of the work of Portuguese domestic workers.[18] Another report mapping human transits in Portugal indicates discrimination based on ethnicity to be one of the main problems affecting domestic workers, since "families tend to prefer domestic workers from Eastern Europe or Brazil to the detriment of Africans" (Pereira and Vasconcelos 2007: 41), insinuating that, more than cultural differences, phenotype seems to influence possible sociability in this segment of the labor market. Moreover, it corroborates the theory that skin color continues to be a key marker in terms of access to opportunities in the labor market, formal and informal.

In the case of the domestic services sector, the paternalist provision framing the work done in the private realm still seems to hinder regulation. In this sense, the domestic space continues to be an exception, consecrated judicially by means of a public bourgeoisie perception of the material implications implicit in a relationship between employers and female domestic workers.[19] There seems to be an almost universal tendency to perceive employer/employee relations in the sphere of domestic service outside the generic framework of labor law. Paid domestic service is commonly referred to as echoing family affection based on such notions as duty, gratitude, altruism, and responsibility, there being a dominant tendency on the part of employers to transform the labor relationship into a moral contract where the economic benefit is a privilege (Nare 2011).

In Portugal, the sectorial distribution of immigrant labor reflects global trends and is concentrated above all in the construction, domestic work, and retail commerce sectors and other types of activities, particularly in the less qualified segments of the labor market, representing between 6 percent and 7 percent of labor in the country (Peixoto 2008). From the 1990s onward, less qualified professional groups have significantly outnumbered other professional groups (Baganha, Ferrão, and Malheiros. 2002: 109). From a regional and local point of view, the levels of ethnicization in labor markets are also different. While the Lisbon Metropolitan Area and the Algarve concentrate the bulk of foreign workers, it is also true that in recent years there has been a tendency toward a greater geographical dispersal of immigrant populations. Official data shows that immigrants from Portuguese-Speaking African Countries (PSAC) and Eastern Europe work mainly in the construction sector (14.8 percent), hotels and restaurants (11.7 percent), and services (9.6 percent). We should emphasize that the latter have a strong presence in the agriculture, forestry, hunting, and fishing sectors and extraction and processing industries (Carneiro 2006). Both for women from PSAC and for immigrants from Eastern Europe, the main professional activity is that of "unqualified workers in the service and commerce sectors," which includes domestic services for private individuals and company cleaning services.[20]

The overrepresentation of domestic work on the list of professional activities by immigrant women has been mentioned by most of the authors studying postcolonial migrations in Portugal. However, this unanimity is not a consequence of an in-depth analysis of the apparent self-explanatory correlation. The existence of an initial survey regarding the supply of immigrant domestic work in Portugal (Guibentif 2011) enabled the preparation of a preliminary table characterizing this universe and, most importantly, a comparison of this supply with the indigenous scenario, without purporting to be representative. Domestic work is recognized as a sector marked by informality—both at the level of labor relations and regarding the relationship between workers and the state. This factor, namely informality, often limits a worker's choice to make social security contributions or not. The low salaries and the precariousness of labor relations; the nonpayment of salaries and the difficulty in claiming payments, associated with obstacles raised with regard to proof of a labor relationship in the absence of a work contract and with payments made in cash; and situations in which domestic workers only realize later that the contracts they signed stipulate a salary lower than that which was agreed upon verbally are all common occurrences among immigrant domestic workers, which the results of the survey also indicate.

Similarly to the situation of young male domestic workers in Mozambique, the characteristics that make the domestic sector unattractive as a long-term occupational project are the same as those that seem to consolidate the sector as a privileged area for recruiting female immigrant workers, who are not highly regarded and have recently entered the host society's labor market. Whether they stay in domestic service in the long term depends on a combination of variables (age, plans to return to the home country, family, qualifications, etc.). The prevailing informality and the isolation inherent to developing a significant part of this activity inside private homes can likewise justify the residual mobilization of immigrant female domestic workers converted into initiatives of an associative nature,[21] undermining the potential of female domestic workers to criticize the structural conditions in which labor relations are negotiated and in which the work is carried out.

Concluding Remarks

The Great Recession and Covid-19 recession are auspicious to the recovery of conceptual tools and academic traditions that critically reflect on established modes of social organization and that are politically involved with the transformation of social reality. This chapter aims to contribute toward this trend by highlighting three specific and interconnected historical contexts to analyze the equivalence of political processes of exclusion and disqualification, based on race, gender, and class, in the production of the paid domestic worker. Contemplating the intersection between ethnicity/race and class based on the professional structure in three different contexts merits a more in-depth analysis of the dynamics underway and, above all, the political relationship of forces responsible for the prevalent configuration of these dynamics. Modern industrial cities are hubs that attract populations from peripheral areas—colonial, metropolitan, or global—with fewer material resources, later incorporated into the circuits of capitalist economies by means of largely coercive measures. The participation of these individuals as salaried workers in a central economy is measured by new categorical horizons, frontiers of interaction, those that are a "product of a juridical act of delimitation, and which produce a cultural difference in the same way that they are the product of this" (Bourdieu 1994: 115). In this sense, ethnicity/race and class are political categories, and it is necessary to keep in mind that as tools that order and classify, these categories are invariably subordinate to "practical functions" and are oriented toward producing social effects (115). In other words, they are part of the political struggles that validate everyday orientations and meanings and, more importantly, their producers.

The triptych presented here suggests continuity between contexts, evident, for example, in a paternalism shared by maids in the metropolis and servants in the colonies. This dovetails with the experience of postcolonial immigrants—whether mediated by ethnicity or an imagined ideal of class. Recognizing and interpreting this structural homology results in a critical reflection on the constitution, nowadays, of professional identities and the relevance of political processes of production, segmentation, and the social hierarchy of these identities. The present context of intense social conflict at least paves the way to clarify positions regarding the exceptional structural circumstance of domestic workers within the legal framework of labor relations. This could result in the intensification of concerted initiatives by such workers to put pressure on key public and private institutions in these processes.

Notes

1. The concept of "racialization" describes the process by which social relations in colonial societies are structured by phenotype to define and represent differentiated social collectives in an institutionalized structure, the position of which reflects the discrepancy in access to instruments of power (Miles 1989: 75).
2. See, inter alia, Cox (1948), Banton (1955), Rex (1970), Bonacich (1972), Castles and Kosack (1973).
3. In this regard, see the chronology of relevant events presented in Rex and Tomlinson (1979: 39–47).
4. "Split labor market" in the original.
5. See the proposal by Wolpe (1986: 111).
6. The creation of the legal schemes that replaced slavery, transforming the "freed" into hired workers, was rooted in the perception that wealth could only be created in liberal economies through the plantation economy and that the only strong motive for investment would be cheap labor. These schemes emerged at the end of the nineteenth century, whereby indigenous populations were forced to pay taxes on wages and correctional labor was introduced. See Newitt (1997: 341).
7. The importance of the urban context for the process of ensuring the hegemony of the monetary economy is reinforced by the coexistence of parallel conflicting models outside the immediate area of influence of cities, in interior regions. Everything points to these regions being less "vulnerable" to coercive schemes to garner labor for agricultural complexes as well as the mining industry. See, for example, Vail and White (1980).
8. Even Catholic missionaries, who in nearby settings appeared to be an element opposing differentiated treatment of populations, largely represented the official policies of colonial authorities in Mozambique. See, for example, Cross (1987: 550–69).
9. The cultivation of cotton and the successive failures to establish a solid colonial cotton industry, until the program created during the Estado Novo period, makes for an interesting case study to observe the relationship between industry and capitalism, coercive production and control mechanisms used for labor. Among others, see Pitcher (1991) and Isaacman (1992).
10. Statistics for 1969 indicate approximately two hundred thousand maids (Brasão 2016: 139).
11. *A Batalha*, May 20–21, 1921.
12. *A Batalha*, August 18–19, 1921.
13. See, inter alia, Santos (1993), Reis (1994), and Viegas and da Costa (1998).
14. In the mid-1980s, France, Germany, Belgium, Luxembourg, and Holland agreed, in Schengen, Luxembourg, on a set of principles to harmonize external border controls and the free circulation of individuals. Other countries joined this agreement over the years.
15. See Anderson (2000) and Wall and Nunes (2010).
16. See, for example, Suleman and Suleman (2011).
17. See the ILO program "Decent Work for Domestic Workers" and the reports that have been published with the results of the programs and the campaign to ratify Convention 189 (http://www.ilo.org/ilc/ILCSessions/100thSession/on-the-agenda/dec ent-work-for-domestic-workers/lang--en/index.htm).
18. In this regard, see the results of the recently concluded Dinâmia-CET project, funded by FCT, Reference: PTDC/JUR/65622/2006.

19 Although the latest update of the specific system regulating domestic service contracts, by means of Decree-Law no. 235/92 of October 24, 1992, drew closer to the general normative framework, legislators continued to feel the need to highlight the singular nature of the sector, as has been mentioned in the introduction to the law: "The circumstance of domestic work being provided to families and hence generating professional relations with an accentuated personal nature, which require a permanent environment of trust requires, apart from considering its specific economic nature, that the regulatory system continue to have certain special features."
20 Respectively, 49.5 percent and 31.7 percent, likewise based on the 2001 census, without including the data from the 2011 census. There are few indications that this distribution would have changed significantly.
21 See Anderson's (2010) report on the construction of a "political community" based on mobilizing Filipina domestic workers in London, as well as the initiatives developed by the Associação Comunidária to pressure the Portuguese government to ratify ILO Convention 189 (http://www.comunidaria.org).

References

Anderson, B. (2000). *Doing the Dirty Work? The Global Politics of Domestic Labour*. London: Zed.
Anderson, B. (2007). "A Very Private Business: Exploring the Demand for Migrant Domestic Workers." *European Journal of Women's Studies*, 14(3): 247–64.
Anderson, B. (2010). "Mobilizing Migrants, Making Citizens: Migrant Domestic Workers as Political Agents." *Ethnic and Racial Studies*, 33(1): 60–74.
Baganha, M. I., J. Ferrão, and J. M. Malheiros (2002). *Os Movimentos Migratórios Externos e a sua Incidência no Mercado de Trabalho em Portugal*. Lisbon: Observatório do Emprego e Formação Profissional.
Banton, M. (1955). *The Coloured Quarter: Negro Immigrants in an English City*. London: Cape.
Bonacich, E. (1972). "A Theory of Ethnic Antagonism: The Split Labor Market." *American Sociological Review*, 37(5): 547–59.
Bonacich, E. (1999). "Class Approaches to Ethnicity and Race." *Critical Sociology*, 25(2/3): 166–94.
Bourdieu, P. (1994). *O Poder Simbólico*. Lisbon: Difel.
Brasão, I. (2010). "Serviço doméstico em Portugal: lugares de origem, êxodo e itinerários urbanos (anos quarenta a sessenta)." In N. Domingos and V. Pereira (eds.), *O Estado Novo em Questão*, 81–110. Lisbon: Edições 70.
Brasão, I. (2016). *O Tempo das Criadas: A Condição Servil em Portugal (1940–1970)*. Lisbon: Tinta da China.
Carneiro, R. (ed.) (2006). *A Mobilidade Ocupacional do Trabalhador Imigrante em Portugal*. Lisbon: DGEEP/MTSS.
Carvalho, A. de (1958). *As Criadas de Servir e o Serviço Doméstico: Estudos e Subsídios para a sua Regulamentação*. Lisbon: Private edition.
Castles, S., and G. Kosack (1973). *Immigrant Workers and Class Structure in Western Europe*. London: Oxford University Press.
Catarino, C., and L. Oso (2000). "La inmigración femenina en Madrid y Lisboa: hacia una etnización del servicio doméstico y de las empresas de limpieza." *Papers*, 60: 183–207.

Cox, O. C. (1948). *Race Caste and Class*. New York: Monthly Review.
Cross, M. (1987). "The Political Economy of Colonial Education: Mozambique, 1930–1975." *Comparative Education Review*, 31(4): 550–69.
Domingos, N., and E. Peralta (2013). *Cidade e império: dinâmicas coloniais e reconfigurações pós-coloniais*. Lisbon: Edições 70.
Dworkin, D. (2007). *Class Struggles*. Edinburgh: Pearson Education.
Eastman, C. M. (1994). "Service, Slavery ('utumwa') and Swahili Social Reality." *Afrikanistische Arbeitspapiere: Schriftenreihe des Kölner Instituts für Afrikanistik*, 37: 87–107.
Freudenthal, A. F. (2001). "Angola." In A. H. de Oliveira Marques (ed.), *O Império Africano 1890-1930 (Nova História da Expansão Portuguesa*, vol. XI). Lisbon: Editorial Estampa.
Geertz, C. (1963). "The Integrative Revolution: Primordial Sentiments and Civil Politics in the New States." In C. Geertz (ed.), *Old Societies and New States*, 105–57. Glencoe: Free Press.
Guibentif, P. (1991). "A opinião pública face aos estrangeiros." In M. C. Esteves (org.), *Portugal, País de Imigração*, 63–74. Lisbon: I.E.D.
Guibentif, P. (2011). *Rights Perceived and Practiced 2nd Part Results of the Surveys Carried Out in Brazil, India, Mozambique and the United Kingdom, as Part of the Project "Domestic Work and Domestic Workers Interdisciplinary and Comparative Perspectives."* Lisbon: WP Dinâmia/CET-IUL.
Isaacman, A. (1992). "Coercion, Paternalism and the Labour Process: The Mozambican Cotton Regime 1938-1961." *Journal of Southern African Studies*, 18(3): 487–526.
Leal, J. (2006). "O Império Escondido: camponeses, construção da nação e império na antropologia portuguesa." In M. R. Sanches (org.), *Portugal não é um País Pequeno. Contar o Império na Pós-colonialidade*, 63–79. Lisbon: Cotovia.
Macedo, M. (2012). "Império de Cacau: ciência agrícola e regimes de trabalho em S. Tomé no início do séc. XX." In M. Jerónimo (org.), *O Império Colonial em Questão (Sécs. XIX-XX). Poderes, Saberes e Instituições*, 289–316. Lisbon: Edições 70.
Machado, F. L., and A. F. da Costa (1998). "Processos de uma modernidade inacabada." In J. M. L. Viegas and A. F. da Costa (orgs.), *Portugal, que Modernidade?*, 17–44. Oeiras: Celta.
Meersschaert, L. (1986). "Alguns contributos para o estudo da identidade das empregadas domésticas em Portugal." *Análise Social*, XXII(92–93): 633–42.
Miles, R. (1989). *Racism*. London: Routledge.
Nare, L. (2011). "The Moral Economy of Domestic and Care Labour: Migrant Workers in Naples, Italy." *Sociology*, 45(3): 396–412.
Newitt, M. (1997). *História de Moçambique*. Mem Martins: Europa-América.
Pariser, R. (2015). "Masculinity and Organized Resistance in Domestic Service in Colonial Dar es Salaam, 1919–1961." *International Labor and Working-Class History*, 88(Fall): 109–29.
Peixoto, J. (2008). "Imigração e mercado de trabalho em Portugal: investigação e tendências recentes." *Revista Migrações*, 2: 19–46.
Penvenne, J. (1995). *African Workers and Colonial Racism: Mozambican Strategies and Struggles in Lourenço Marques, 1877–1962*. London: James Currey.
Pereira, S., and J. Vasconcelos (2007). *Relatório de Combate ao Tráfico de Seres Humanos e Trabalho Forçado—Estudo de casos e respostas de Portugal*. Lisbon: ILO.

Pitcher, M. A. (1991). "Sowing the Seeds of Failure: Early Portuguese Cotton Cultivation in Angola and Mozambique, 1820–1926." *Journal of Southern African Studies*, 17(1): 43–70.

Reis, A. (coord.) (1994). *Portugal—20 anos de Democracia*. Lisbon: Círculo de Leitores.

Rex, J. (1970). *Race Relations in Sociological Theory*. London: Routledge and Kegan Paul.

Rex, J., and S. Tomlinson (1979). *Colonial Immigrants in a British City: A Class Analysis*. London: Routledge and Kegan Paul.

Santos, B. de S. (1985). "Estado e Sociedade na Semiperiferia do Sistema Mundial: o Caso Português." *Análise Social*, 87/88/89: 869–901.

Santos, B. de S. (org.) (1993). *Portugal: Um Retrato Singular*. Porto: Edições Afrontamento.

Suleman, F., and A. Suleman (2011). *The Outsourcing of Household Tasks and Labour Contract in Domestic Work*, WP 2011/14. Lisbon: Dinâmia Working Papers.

Vail, L., and L. White (1980). *Capitalism and Colonialism in Mozambique: A Study of the Quelimane District*. Minnesota: University of Minnesota Press.

Veblen, T. (1899). *The Theory of the Leisure Class: An Economic Study of Institutions*. New York: Macmillan.

Viegas, J. M. L., and A. F. da Costa (orgs.) (1998). *Portugal, que Modernidade?* Oeiras: Celta.

Wall, K., and C. Nunes (2010). "Immigration, Welfare and Care in Portugal: Mapping the New Plurality of Female Migration Trajectories." *Social Policy and Society*, 9(3): 397–408.

Wolpe, H. (1986). "Class Concepts, Class Struggle and Racism." In J. Rex and D. Mason (eds.), *Theories of Race and Ethnic Relations*, 110–30. Cambridge: Cambridge University Press.

Zamparoni, V. (1999). "Género e Trabalho Doméstico numa Sociedade Colonial: Lourenço Marques, Moçambique, c. 1900–1940." *Afro-Ásia*, 23: 145–72.

Chapter 8

BRAZILIAN MIGRATION IN LISBON: PLACE, WORK, AND COLONIAL REPRESENTATIONS

Simone Frangella

In 2012, during an investigation on Brazilian immigrants in Lisbon, one of my interviewees Lúcia took me on a visit to Arroios, the neighborhood where she lived and which she claimed was also a central reference for "many other Brazilians, with everything at hand and close to everything—commerce, services, transport." She proposed to take me on a walk to get to know the neighborhood and see the "Brazilian things" that could be found there. This invitation, which I gladly accepted, seemed ideal to me, as I had already noted a substantial presence of Brazilians in the Arroios area, enjoying a significant visibility in one of the most central areas of Lisbon. I was interested in understanding what this neighborhood had to offer to become a reference point for immigrants who made their living from unskilled and low-paid jobs.

During our walk together on a Saturday morning, Lúcia showed me the places she went to, pointing out the traces of Brazil that we came across: food and clothing stores, butchers, cafeterias selling cheese bread, agencies for remitting money abroad, coffee shops where Brazilians usually met. But she also showed me non-Brazilian places in the neighborhood that she usually went to, including the Arroios market, the restaurant where she bought chicken, a supermarket, and other small businesses. Although she worked out of the area—she was a domestic cleaner paid daily in homes in different parts of Lisbon—Lúcia showed me how she managed to enjoy local life fairly well by accessing the goods and services offered there. She also assured me that "every Brazilian who arrives in Lisbon, comes here to Arroios, to look for a place to stay, to know where there is a job . . . There is even that funny song by Caipira da Zoropa, where he says: 'I'm going to meet a guy from Arroio' . . . Everyone stops in Arroios!"[1] It was not the first time that I heard this reference to Arroios as a resourceful place when it came to providing help and housing networks for Brazilians. The large contingent of Brazilian immigrants in Lisbon is spread over several areas, creating other central foci around the city, such as Costa da Caparica, localities along the Sintra line (Cacém, Rio de Mouro), Cascais, Alcabideche, or Odivelas (Ataíde and Dias 2012).[2] But Arroios still seems to work, above all, as a point of concentration and circulation of information for migrants as well as a residential area where people work.

This chapter is the result of ethnographic research,[3] inspired initially by the walk with Lúcia and unfolded in systematic empirical observations in Arroios, as well as a brief analysis of the area's history and its setting in the urban context of Lisbon. I had the following questions: What is the meaning of the neighborhood as part of the experience of these migrants? What kind of relationship do they establish with the other residents of the place? How is the sociability of the oldest inhabitants in light of the constant presence of non-Portuguese? What is the weight of the old colonial relations and their representations in the experience of Brazilians in the area? How have these migrant communities in Arroios resisted the increasing gentrification that this area has gone through in the past decade?

As a result of this investigation, I found a relationship of mutual constitution between the production of a place by Brazilian immigrants and the historical, social, economic, and urban processes of Arroios,[4] at a time prior to the urban rehabilitation processes that intensified dramatically in Lisbon from 2015 on.[5] Therefore, I paid attention to the dynamics of the emergence of Brazilian immigration and the way it is spatialized, as though reading concurrently the history of the place to see the conditions of production of this migrant experience. The interweaving between these two dimensions is the guiding thread that I intend to develop here.

Arroios became, for Brazilians, a piece of their domain,[6] a way of feeling relatively "at home." The place was constituted as a territory recognized by immigrants, concentrating a set of signs and places that nurture, reinforce, and resignify a repertoire of symbols associated with "Brazilianness." Brazilianness is understood here as a national ideal constructed over historical processes[7] and often repositioned in the context of migration. Instead of being part of the disordered (and often ignored by the state) processes of occupation of the territory that marked a certain continuity with a "colonial ghost" (Ascensão 2011),[8] the experience of Brazilians in this neighborhood indicates another way of reactivating colonial references. The continuous redefinition of the legacies of colonial relations—where links of descent, culture, and shared language stand out—as well as the long history of Portuguese emigration to Brazil—through which many images and interactions involving the Portuguese emerged (Feldman-Bianco 2002)—explain the ambivalent relationship between Portuguese and Brazilians, a relationship that becomes apparent in the space of Arroios through work and social life.

The neighborhood has become a privileged place to observe these frictional and ambiguous relations. The arrival of Brazilian immigrants was quite visible and has since characterized a particular sociability in that space, underlined by experiences of estrangement and exchange regarding other local actors. The condition of foreigner enunciates, to a certain extent, the limits of the possibilities of interaction in space. However, such limits prevent neither the establishment of good neighborly relations—based on exchanges of care and favors—nor the incorporation of migrant labor to supply the demand of the inhabitants who live there.

In the past decade the neighborhood I describe here has suffered some significant changes. In 2013, the parish of S. Jorge de Arroios[9] merged with the parishes of Anjos and Pena, and it was named parish of Arroios, producing an enlargement of urban references and migrant populations.[10] Thus, the parish of Arroios became a different territorial and social unit. Then, after 2015, the whole area was immersed in a gentrification project, raising rents and forcing a segment of labor immigrants to live elsewhere (Mendes 2017). Recently, there has been significant investment in real estate markets, more tourist development, the access to rent was tightened, and other Brazilian migrants' profiles, with higher economic standing, arrived. Today's Arroios is one of the main hubs of an advertised multicultural Lisbon, imagined by political and economic projects (see Oliveira and Cardão in this volume; and Carmo and Estevens 2017).

This chapter considers the construction of Arroios as a place of migratory strategies before these changes, exploring this particular ethnographic moment in this particular context. Therefore, focused on "the old Arroios," this chapter first explores a Brazilian migratory experience and its interaction with place-making in the city of Lisbon. The peculiar situation of the neighborhood by then—a place of little urbanistic or image investment and a platform for foreign circulation and mobility and for access to the labor market—fitted the conditions of this specific immigration. Second, and more importantly, this ethnographic moment reveals the communication between place, work, and colonial representations. Hence, my aim is to address the complexities of concrete experiences involving the constitution of places in contexts of migration, referring particularly to postcolonial tensions.

The aforementioned urban transformation of the past ten years has made Arroios less accessible for Brazilian migrants, above all regarding housing possibilities. And yet, the area has remained a strong point of reference and circulation for Brazilian migrants, their activities, and consumption products.

The Place of Arroios in the Urban Scenery

My interest in Arroios stems from the fact that, despite being a relatively large parish and connecting areas of great circulation and commercial and residential importance in the center of Lisbon, it was not visible in the discourses produced about Lisbon neighborhoods. Like its adjoining neighborhoods at the time, Penha de França and Anjos, with similar socioeconomic profiles and housing conditions, it is part of the central zone of Lisbon, far from the process of suburbanization the city went through during the twentieth century (Salgueiro 1977; Baptista 1999). However, at the same time, it was not a strong object of concern and interest to public and private institutions regarding urban planning issues in the capital. By the time of the fieldwork, it was also absent from advertising language and tourist materials.[11]

Also, Arroios was not identified as an urban or sociological object of study. It was never associated with the historical and urban neighborhoods usually deemed "typical" of Lisbon (Mendes 2012), defined by historical landmarks, strongly territorialized social units and intense collective living among its residents (Cordeiro and Costa 1999: 59), and neighborhood political associations. Attributes such as "typical," "historical," "popular," and "multicultural," which have been appropriated, recreated, and projected in narratives about Lisbon, raising the patrimonial value of these neighborhoods (61),[12] are not projected onto Arroios as a thematic unit that the neighborhood can capitalize on.[13] The area has built heritage of historical value, although it remains abandoned and in poor condition,[14] which was not singled out as distinguishing the area. They are only portraits of an "episode" of the city, recognized in some historical literature dispersed among aged buildings, without being objects of real estate or media interest. Therefore, unlike the "characteristic" Lisbon neighborhoods, Arroios was not the target of significant urban interventions for investment in its tourist potential or real estate value (Bastos 2004; Menezes 2009) for decades, and change has only been brought recently by Lisbon's intensified process of urban revitalization.

The area has characteristics resulting from historical processes, which helps to interpret the conditions that allowed the arrival of these immigrant populations. Since it is a space of central circulation and transit connecting with the rest of the city and creating mobile territorialities with gradual housing precariousness, the area stood out and contributed to the great migratory influx. The neighborhood became, from the point of view of its economic, residential, and social value, a somewhat residual space, although not totally precarious. It was historically constituted, since the thirteenth century, as a passage and frontier zone. Much later, in the twentieth century, it went through a process of increasing urbanization. Some working-class estates were built, marked by strong neighborhood ties and poor structural conditions (Rodrigues and Gomes 1996). In another part of the neighborhood, more noble, private investment, combined with municipal initiative, resulted in new constructions of a more bourgeois type, besides a whole set of gardens and tree-lined squares and statues (Póvoas and Vaz 1992; Reis 1997). We could say that the neighborhood's housing landscape continues to reveal this "mismatch" between the types of houses on either side of Avenida Almirante Reis,[15] although their appropriation is currently much more diverse.

Urban transformation immersed Arroios in an urban network that rapidly densified. With the expansion of the metropolitan area from the 1950s and 1960s onward, younger people spread into the suburbs and the older population remained in this housing stock until the mid-1990s, benefitting from low rental charges facilitated by the freezing of rents.[16] As the housing was considered aged and suffering from lack of renovation, it gradually emptied.[17] Precarious housing conditions, the population exodus, and the rent law itself were the conditioning factors that paved the way for both the arrival of immigrants and the offer of rented rooms and apartments to university students. Therefore, the area saw its population resized. By the end of 1990s, foreigners began to rent many of the emptied houses and the circulation of goods and services was increased by immigrants. The neighborhood started to congregate a range of residential experiences: a middle class with more resources, older people supported by the old rental conditions, students, and transient migrants. This, in turn, generated a variety of ways of being and created possible housing possibilities for the newcomers.

Immigrants from Eastern Europe and Brazil came after the first flow to Portugal of immigrants from the former African colonies and accessed, within the fragile structure of the immigration-oriented labor market, some of the more advantageous positions (Padilla 2006: 25). But people from Bangladesh, China, and Senegal, among other nationalities, have also lived and worked in the neighborhood. Arroios has functioned as a gateway for migrants—like the neighboring areas of Anjos, Pena, and Mouraria—and staying there is, to start with, a temporary investment.

The Neighborhood Experienced by Brazilians

The Brazilian social landscape in the Arroios neighborhood was built throughout a continuous migratory flow that increased significantly from the middle of 2000.[18] For Brazilians, Arroios has stood out as a stopping point and as somewhere to spend some time in, a place for residence, work, and for other social and cultural practices (Mayol 1997). Indeed, Brazilian migrants contributed considerably to the landscape and social reconfiguration of Arroios.

A decade earlier, religious practices introduced from Brazil were very visible in the area and played a pioneering role in this process. Most important was the arrival at Arroios of the Igreja Universal do Reino de Deus (Universal Church of the Kingdom of God; IURD), which bought the premises of the Cinema Império (Cinema empire) in 1992.[19] Despite great initial resistance,[20] the church produced an interactive dynamic between Portuguese, Brazilians, and immigrants from the former African colonies. In the following decade, other neo-Pentecostal churches of Brazilian origin set themselves up in Arroios, such as the Igreja Mundial do Poder de Deus (World Church of the Power of God; a great rival of the IURD), Semear a Vida (Sow Life), and the Assembleia de Deus (Assembly of God). There are also evangelical churches of non-Brazilian origin that Brazilian immigrants attend. Besides the built-up presence, these neo-Pentecostal churches interact with the neighborhood, distributing religious pamphlets and trying to appeal to possible believers.

In addition to the occupations associated with Brazilians in Portugal—civil construction, hotels/restaurants, and third sector employees (Peixoto and Figueiredo 2007)—occupations related to "care" were prominent in the Arroios neighborhood. These occupations, in the field of aesthetics in hairdressing salons, in caring for the elderly, and the cleaning sector, intensified over time.[21] Many Brazilians are also owners of, or employed in, computer services, tools, or graphics businesses, and many also work in shopping centers.[22] Although some do not have a professional activity in the neighborhood, for others, work and housing coexisted in the same place. Some parts of the neighborhood gained great prominence, for use or circulation, and because of the way they were instituted as a symbolic reference or imagined place for Brazilians. These areas have also been central for the other inhabitants of the neighborhood.

Brazilian food stores are a fundamental point of reference. Easily located and with evident national symbolism, they sell goods from the different Brazilian states from which immigrants come. There has been a continuous closing and opening of businesses, with slight changes of place, although within the same circle in the neighborhood. This dynamic suggests hurried investments are being made in a market that fluctuates according to the improving or worsening of economic conditions (after all, Brazilian products are more expensive), influenced by the precarious situation of consumers. Going to a Brazilian store implies a particular visual and sensory incursion. In their appearance and structure, they produce a plunge into an amalgamated and generalized "idea" of Brazil, either by their customers or by the promotional discourse that surrounds these establishments.[23] In addition to these stores, immigrants regularly use other services in the neighborhood such as supermarkets, butchers, popular household goods stores, Chinese stores, pharmacies, and so on.

Regarding gastronomic and entertainment places, the bars and taverns that serve Brazilian food were and still are very popular with immigrants and nonimmigrants alike, but become a meeting point for Brazilians. There are many Portuguese proprietors who supply this Brazilian food market in Arroios, along with entertainment and other goods and services. Entertainment venues are the preferred means of signaling Brazilians' presence in the public space of the neighborhood. The night scene involved bars and clubs aimed at or attracting Brazilians, or bars that provided Sunday afternoons with beer offers and space to play samba.

The practices of the neighborhood life presuppose an engagement that is repeated daily and result in sensory and cognitive production, creating familiarity among migrants, but also imply frictions and connections with the other inhabitants. But the circumscribed experiences of the neighborhood also tend to exceed its limits, indicating that socio-spatial interactions have permeable and elastic borders. Or, seen in another way, from the point of view of their inhabitants' social recognition, neighborhoods do not have stable territorial borders (Cordeiro and Costa 1999), they are not an a priori reality (Frúgoli Jr. 2013). However, thinking of Arroios as a neighborhood was useful as a research unit, insofar as it allowed circumscribing the relationships that are woven between immigration and the practice of space.

Identity Negotiations and Historical Representations

Although Arroios has served as a temporary reference for most of these people, it was not only a place of passage; for some, it was in fact a residence that made up a good part of their transnational journey. For others, it was a place where they created and used resources to situate themselves economically and socially. This implies daily interactions with the Portuguese and other foreigners, characterized by both familiarity and suspicion (Padilla 2006) and by the difficulty in stepping out of the low-skill labor structure. These difficulties coexist in contrast to the ease in consuming and living in an area of easy access to other places in the city and the opportunities that exist there. This panorama is relatively recent in the history of the neighborhood.

The memories of Selma, who has lived in Arroios practically since she arrived in Portugal in 2000, help us understand these transformations. She arrived in the neighborhood a month after landing in Lisbon, started working in a nursing home for over a year, and then went to work as a cleaning lady for a company. When she left, she rented three apartments, two in Intendente and one in Arroios, and organized them as residences or boarding houses. With few exceptions, the boarding houses basically received Brazilian newcomers in Lisbon, who were informed of these spaces by compatriots right at the airport, in a "word-of-mouth" dynamic. These lodgings were always full, with people ending up staying much longer than expected, making this accommodation their residence for their first years in Portugal. These houses were self-managed in terms of cleaning and organization and served as a meeting point for other Brazilians.

At the time of Selma's arrival, there were no commercial establishments selling Brazilian products. The only place that Selma remembered as connected to Brazilians in Arroios was a brothel, which, according to her, reinforced the "initial [prejudiced] idea that the Portuguese had of Brazilian women."[24] From 2003 onward, stores began to appear, slowly, along with the intensification of the migratory flow. "Africans," and even "Russians," gradually appeared in the neighborhood. Indian and Chinese restaurant owners also joined in. When running the boarding houses became too demanding, Selma closed the spaces and resumed her work caring for the elderly in private homes right there in the area. With her life stabilized, and now legalized[25]—she lives with her Brazilian husband in a rented apartment, comfortable, renovated, with an elevator, and located in a very pleasant street—Selma felt like a "Portuguese" and has established good relationships with her Portuguese neighbors. Although her daily sociability networks are maintained through activities with Brazilians who live nearby and belong to her church—located, by the way, outside the neighborhood—she also relates daily with non-Brazilians.

Selma's testimony encapsulates the complex adjustments these migrants had to make to the host society. Her journey shows how their expectations, their relationships, and their choices are intimately related to the neighborhood's characteristic openness. The echoes of a frontier space and a space of passage that are projected in the neighborhood now seem repositioned by the experience of a place as a workplace, as well as a space for conviviality. This, however, is crossed by clashes between the migrants who arrive there and those who belong to the society of the destination country.

As part of the process of updating and manipulating national identity images in transnational migration, Brazilians tend to reinforce elements of "Brazilianness," defining themselves as good-natured, warm, happy, belonging to a singular, authentic, and exotic national unit. However, particularly in Portugal, where they never go unnoticed and are continuously the target of media attention, stereotypes and experiences are intertwined in a confusing dialogue between the two countries, forming a dynamic texture of discrimination, estrangement, and proximity, in which migrants must constantly reposition themselves. Many images elaborated in this daily life are common-sense constructions that are fed, in general, by a relatively recent past, formed since Brazil's independence and throughout the twentieth century by complex processes of identity friction, and involving long-term relationships, both economic and in the migratory dynamics (Rowland 2002).

Allusions to the colonial period, where the genesis of some of these representations lie, are almost always caricatural and mythical, producing images like that of the "bad colonizer" (Portuguese) and of the "uncivilized" (Brazilians). Other stereotypes are the outcomes of an old double process: clichés, such as the Portuguese "dumb," the Brazilian "rascal," and the Brazilian "prostitute" feed a long circulation of representations (Rowland 2002), encompassing, on the one hand, the Portuguese presence in Brazil at the end of the nineteenth century and at the beginning of the twentieth century, through immigration;[26] on the other hand, multiple representations about Brazilians started to circulate in Portugal,[27] from those based on the lusotropical discourse (such as the hypersexualized Brazilian women) to those fed by Portuguese relatives returning from Brazil or by the Portuguese media (Gomes 2013).

The projection of stereotypes about Brazilian residents (positive or negative) in Portugal is part of a symbolic arsenal triggered by the Portuguese when a conflict arises, in disagreements at work, when dealing with bureaucratic institutions, or even in trivial situations, such as, for example, in the relationship between waiter and customer in a restaurant. With migrants being in a position of vulnerability vis-à-vis work, housing, and the state, such discursive resources can have the effect of reinforcing existing asymmetries and restricting the prospects of the migration project. They may be of a rhetorical order and cause attrition in interactions, or they may eventually influence the positions that these immigrants will occupy in the labor market and their daily experiences.

In the context of this labor immigration, there are forms of discrimination faced by Brazilians on a regular basis, from the legalization procedure to mistreatment suffered in the workplace, particularly from employers; to difficulties in renting a house; and sometimes to open hostility on the street.[28] Migrants react to these limitations by means of several resources. The first is to create their own stereotypes about the Portuguese, inverting the linguistic prejudice, for example, and mocking some terms spoken by the Portuguese, reiterating their semi-peripheral position in Europe, or their apparent apathetic behavior. The second involves reinforcing the attributes considered positive and authentic about Brazil and that can be capitalized for their own interests. Another reaction is through a process of *blending in* (Padilla et al. 2010: 10): modifying the accent, the public behavior, the dress, to attract less attention. Although these strategies hardly alter the possibilities of wider labor mobility, they have become a resource for confronting everyday discrimination and relocation in front of the social actors that question them.

Housing conditions were by then also quite representative of the relationship of estrangement and continuous negotiation of these immigrants with the Portuguese and among the Brazilians themselves. Selma is one of the few people interviewed who lived in an apartment in good condition. Most of the people interviewed live or had lived in rented rooms or residentials; others in very small or "old" houses or apartments, that is, houses with inadequate structural conditions. This was the case of the small apartment of Aline, neighboring the old Arroios Hospital, whose wooden window frames were cracked, cooling the rooms, and the air circulation conditions poor. Or the case of Lúcia, who was paying 400 euros a month for a tiny one-room apartment in the more "ennobled" area of Arroios where she lived with her husband and a daughter.

But the biggest challenge was really the access to housing. Selma said that although she personally had no problems renting the apartments, the task is not usually easy. Many Brazilians have great difficulty in even visiting the apartments found in the advertisements, facing resistance as soon as they talk on the phone with the landlords. A good number of the people I have investigated have obtained a contract themselves; few, however, have had it through the formal real estate mechanisms. Many of these contracts are made directly with the landlords and the circulation through them indicates a certain informality in these transactions. According to Selma, "The Portuguese have resistance to renting because they think that Brazilians fill the house too much," referring to the habit of Brazilian migrants of subletting apartments to decrease expenses and of receiving visits for an indefinite period. The stereotypical images of Brazilians as "troublemakers" and the Brazilian "prostitute" also weigh significantly in the process of settling in the city.

However, and despite all this, contracts or agreements were regularly signed since landlords needed tenants. In 2012, with an increasing exodus of the Portuguese population to the suburbs, the precarious property situation, and the growing presence of these immigrants, there were few possibilities left for landlords in the neighborhood. For tenants, on the other hand, poor housing was balanced by easy access to services and transportation and by the supply of entertainment venues, a recurring opinion of the neighborhood's Brazilian inhabitants. Currently, the housing market reality has changed this picture completely and made such "adjustments" impossible.

The experience of Brazilians in Arroios was also significantly marked by work relations, a central experience of "practicing the neighborhood" (De Certeau et al. 1994). The adjustment of Brazilians to the labor market in the jobs previously described was linked to the stereotypes and essentialized images with which this population is associated. This set of representations configures the so-called joy market (Machado 2006: 233), or "sympathy market,"[29] a domain of relationships where the image of the friendly and cheerful Brazilian is capitalized, especially in public service jobs. Thus, in most of the Brazilians' work activities, contact with people who frequent the neighborhood is assiduous and, in general, tends to reinforce stereotyped classifications between customers and employees. This essentialization becomes more painful when the immigrant has not been regularized since this facilitates exploitation by the employer.[30]

However, Brazilian migrants end up using these representations to their own advantage, and they reaffirm them in their workplace. They reinforce the same reified skills in the universe of "care" and public service, placing themselves in relation to the Portuguese, who are perceived as their "sad counterpoint" (Machado 2006: 233). Other attributes associated with Brazilians such as dedication to work and skill in cleaning—which are often self-constructed—contribute to success in this labor market, although to a lesser degree. In the field of aesthetic activities, women workers benefit from representations associated with a model of beauty and a lifestyle attributed to Brazilian women (Padilla et al. 2010), guided by the idea of sensuality and sexuality and by an allusion to "advanced Brazilian technologies in the area."[31] On many occasions, these aesthetic representations symbolically mediate the interactions with Portuguese clients and colleagues.

Although negotiations around mutual social representations help in maintaining a labor niche for Brazilians, they do not prevent the social and economic precariousness of these occupations. These services are usually based on irregular or temporary contracts, with high labor turnover. In the case of "care," for example, few are the elderly or their family members who can afford to pay for private services, which often makes them resort to the informal market (Wall and Nunes 2010). At the same time, the affective relationships that are built up between Brazilian caregivers or domestic workers and their employers are often mediated by socioeconomic exploitative relationships, either by extending the work hours, disrespecting the limits of the activities, or not paying the agreed amount. In other words, although this type of work has brought about a new way of repositioning relations between Brazilians and Portuguese, it is difficult to minimize the effect of the relationship between the labor market and immigration in maintaining an immovable position for these migrants (see Dias 2012; and Dias in this volume).

However, work activities create interactions that mitigate hierarchical and subordinate relationships in everyday encounters in the neighborhood. Caregiver tasks and domestic services are the activities that best express the complex intersection of these feelings and interactions. Linguistic and cultural proximities are among the factors that most justify the increasing acceptance of Brazilian women for these services (Wall and Nunes 2010). Although there is a certain gap between the cultural affinities alluded to and the actual possibility of sharing them, connections are created between these worlds, facilitated, I suggest, by the influence of Brazilian soap operas[32]—and the consequent "sensation" of getting to know the other through them—and by the settling of the Brazilian presence in the Portuguese capital, as well as the association with the "sympathy" market. These are jobs that generate interaction circuits between former residents of the neighborhood, their families, and these migrants; and the area, in turn, ends up being a space of multiple experiences for them. Alessandra, for example, established a relationship of deep affection with two Portuguese ladies who she took care of and who influenced her in the choice of a professional investment.

Finally, regarding sociability in the neighborhood, Brazilian immigrants who live in Arroios also frequent the Portuguese stores, pastry stores, and cafes, as well as spaces of other nationalities, such as Chinese restaurants. And they create their "street sociability" on weekends. Brazil is perceived by the Portuguese residents, by the parties in bars and the barbecues in the apartments, by the noises from the neo-Pentecostal churches and the discos. This perception, audible and visual, is confronted in this discourse with the apparent silence of the intimacy of the Portuguese in Arroios, with a more timid presence in the public spaces and squares (Bastos 2004). It brings up representations about the Brazilians, activated in different ways. For the Brazilians, it is an affirmation of their "joyful, festive identity" occupying their temporary place. For the Portuguese and other inhabitants, it is a mixture of appreciation of and annoyance with the "noisy and naughty" Brazilians.

These images often go hand in hand with the stereotypes Brazilians make of Portuguese and function as an initial reciprocal construction, which may or may not be challenged and attenuated (Silva and Schiltz 2007). Thus, Mafalda's son described to me with displeasure the World Cup festivities marked by Brazilian flags on several residential buildings, as well as the clatter of horns and shouting, which testified to the large—and not at all discreet—presence of Brazilians in this area. Ana, another Portuguese resident, told me about a small festival of Santo António,[33] organized by Portuguese and Brazilians in one of the streets of the neighborhood, with a decoration marked by the unfurling of flags from both countries placed side by side. During the organization, Ana was able to follow several negotiations, such as the one that sought to establish a "national" parity regarding the music to be played and the type of food. Her description reinforced the image of a realm of relations where stereotypes are always challenged by the concrete social interactions promoted by the Brazilian migratory presence.

Put another way, there is a hostility in the neighborhood, at times subliminal, at others overt, that refers to a representation of Brazilian immigration as an invasion and a threat. To this representation, the Brazilians respond with a jocular representation about the failure of the ex-colonizer, or their eternal "melancholic spirit." This latent animosity can have consequences for the life of Brazilian immigrants, even blocking their future investment plans and access to the labor market. At best, it can only result in daily constraints caused by feelings of mistrust. All this indicates, however, that if it is true that the reinforcement of stereotypes ends up maintaining a relationship of subordination (Machado 2006), this is fundamentally reproduced by the very structure of immigrant labor (Dias 2012).

Living in the neighborhood constantly related the experience of these immigrants with other Brazilians scattered around the city, through meetings in bars, church attendance, work sharing. There is no territorial and symbolic confinement here under any circumstances. In Arroios, Brazilian immigrants sought an access to the city itself, a step toward the realization of long-term migratory projects, such as buying a house or a successful return to Brazil. However, the contrast between this projection and the uncertainty in which these immigrants lived, whether in relation to the present or the future, makes the neighborhood a place of social investment as fluid as their own trajectories. Together with her husband Lúcia managed to buy a house in Lisbon, on the south bank of the Tagus river; Aline moved out to stay with the family in another neighborhood. Selma, like a few participants in my fieldwork, remained in Arroios, having negotiated her rent. In the past few years, being immersed in a larger area seriously affected by gentrification processes, the "old Arroios" shelters far fewer Brazilian migrants. Either because the high price of housing is leading migrants to move further within the city or because of recent situations that have prompted Brazilians to go back home, such as the last big economic crisis and the Covid-19 pandemic, Arroios has become significantly less seen as a place for Brazilian migrants to live. Nevertheless, it is still a reference for Brazilians as a place of information, of work experiences, and of social, religious, and intercultural sociability.

Final Considerations

If we think of the neighborhood as a "place of passage through the other, untouchable because distant, yet passable and recognized for its relative stability" (Mayol 1997: 45), we conclude that the experience of Brazilians in Arroios crosses two crucial elements. On the one hand, the neighborhood is temporarily a place of resources and of possibilities of survival and of a mobility that allows these immigrants to "win the city." On the other hand, it is also the space where, to ensure access to these resources, they need to face the roughness of the social conviviality in the city.

In this context, some of the clashes that emerge from these relations result from the labor migrant condition itself, with its economic and social vulnerabilities. But another part of these conflicts is anchored in the continuous identity and political and social repositioning that affect Brazilians in Portugal. In the immigration experience of former colonized people to European cities, it is possible to perceive a "cognitive dissonance,"[34] either for the city's population, which had the empire as a comprehensive and abstract imaginary, or for the immigrants, whose perception of the host country is a long way from that related to their first expectation of familiarity. In the Brazilian case, such experience is always tinged by a mutual familiarity, ambiguous and unbalanced in both Brazilian and Portuguese societies, transiting media images, political connotations, and kinship relations. All this guided by a continuous Atlantic movement that goes far beyond the colonial discourses and images, although these representations are a recurrent power resource in the asymmetrical relationship involving the migratory context.

Because of its relative invisibility, mixed configuration, dispersed history, and abandonment, Arroios looked like one of the urban fragments whose discursiveness is diluted in the many movements that pervade the city. But it was precisely this diffuse framework that has produced particular conditions for the emergence of a migrant experience marked by different levels of daily interaction between the local and the foreign populations. In the mosaic of Lisbon's urban formations, where several contrasting temporalities and ideological projections are expressed (Schwarz 1999), this adjustment results from filling forgotten spaces with a migrant traffic subtly incorporated in recent decades.

The recent Portuguese emigration to Brazil,[35] concurrent with Brazilian immigration, renews the "sharing" of colonial images. Thus, the past functions as a field of disputes, which has actually been happening since the end of the colonial period, passing through several other historical moments where mutual stereotypes have been condensing (Alencastro 1988; Rowland 2002; Machado 2006). In Arroios, the disillusionment felt upon arriving in Portugal regarding the welcome and the daily struggle to gain access to work and against the reproduction of prejudice coexist with the possibilities these migrants find in the neighborhood, calm (nonviolent) and precarious (which makes it more economically available), promoting their possibilities of geographical and social circulation. It is always an unstable movement but a significant one in the Brazilian experience. In this framework, colonial representations, very much a part of the European rhetoric on the immigration issue (L'Estoile 2008), are certainly present. However, these representations seem challenged by the urban practices of Brazilian immigrants, creating new possibilities and historical readings of the city itself (Schwarz 1999: 271).

Notes

This work was funded by national funds through FCT—Foundation for Science and Technology, IP, under the contract program established in Article 23(4)(5)(6) DL no. 57/2016 of August 29, amended by Law no. 57/2017 of July 19.

1 Music created and performed by a migrant in 2011; see http://www.youtube.com/watch?v=FvtdJQL9WxE (accessed October 1, 2021).
2 According to the 2011 Immigration, Border and Asylum Report, there were 111,445 Brazilian residents that year, equaling 25.5 percent of the foreign population. These numbers account for the resident population, not including people in non-regularized situations. After a decrease in the following years, the number rose again, with 183,993 Brazilian residents registered in 2020, equaling 27.8 percent of the foreigners (Ataíde and Dias 2011; Estrela 2021).
3 The research was conducted between 2011 and 2012 and, in addition to participant observation in the neighborhood, I conducted interviews with Brazilian immigrants and Portuguese living in the area.
4 I take "place" as a singular geography, marked by social experiences that redefine forms of socialization and the creation of a "proper" place for immigrants in transnational dynamics. Regarding the constitution of places in the process of international immigration—a flow marked by a neoliberal globalization that is projected into cities—the geographies of power and the repositioning of identity constitute dynamic vectors that cut across the very meanings given to place.
5 In the past decade, an intense process of a tourism gentrification has taken place in Lisbon, and it was around 2015 that the gentrification took over the region under discussion (Mendes 2017).
6 I use the notion of neighborhood as a scale in urban inscriptions of circulation, where dimensions of the most unknown (the city codes) and the most intimate (home) have a dynamic of continuity, allowing the user to feel recognized in this public space around his home (Mayol 1997).
7 This project was ongoing, a political effort that reinforces the idea of cultural and racial hybridity, forging an apparently unified national identity that is in constant cultural, economic, and political negotiation. In migratory transits this oneness, while being

reinforced when contrasted with the society of destination, is called into question by regional and cultural diversity that relocates their experiences (Frangella 2011).
8   That can be understood here as "hidden weights and legacies of colonialism in the process of informal urbanization in a postcolonial context" (Ascensão 2011: 128), which reveals itself very present in Lisbon urbanization.
9   Arroios is the popular name of the former parish of São Jorge de Arroios.
10 The administrative divisions of Lisbon underwent changes at the end of November 2012, but the changes were officially fulfilled at the end of 2013, after municipal elections. It should be considered, however, that the limits to which I am referring are those prior to this date. According to official data from 2011, the parish of São Jorge de Arroios had an area of 1.13 square kilometers and 18,405 inhabitants (data from Junta de Freguesia de São Jorge de Arroios, http://pt.wikipedia.org/wiki/S%C3%A3o_Jorge_de_Arroios; last accessed October 1, 2021).
11 Once the area was merged with other parishes, the whole territory became a new frontier for the real estate market and the touristic gentrification. https://ocorvo.pt/mouraria-intendente-e-anjos-estao-a-revelar-se-uma-nova-fronteira-de-interesse-para-o-capital-imobiliario-em-lisboa/.
12 Neighborhoods such as Mouraria and Bairro Alto are also subject to this type of analysis. To explore more about these two neighborhoods, see Bastos (2004), Mapril (2010), and Frúgoli (2013).
13 This usually characterizes historic or popular neighborhoods in this literature (Cordeiro and Costa 1999).
14 As it is the case of the Hospital de Arroios and the Portugália Beer Factory.
15 Avenida Almirante Reis is one of the main avenues of Lisbon, coming from the region of Martim Moniz until Francisco de Sá Carneiro Square, crossing many central neighborhoods and paving the way to the airport.
16 The rent freeze was a measure that lasted from 1945 to 1985, when there was a change in the law, allowing for a correction of the rents. The conservation status of the buildings suffered the direct effect of the freeze measure, since it made it impossible for the owners to carry out the appropriate works (Quental e Melo 2009: 17).
17 From 1960 to 1981, there was a 30 percent decrease in population (Velasco 1996: 8).
18 Systematic and significant flows of Brazilian migrants have been arriving since the 1990s, but it was in 2001 that the wave of poorly qualified labor migrants started arriving (Padilla 2006).
19 http://cinemaaoscopos.blogspot.pt/2010/08/imperio-1952-1983.html (accessed September 30, 2021).
20 The conflicts concerning the IURD gained visibility between 1994 and 1995 when the church started disputing noble spaces in the cities of Lisbon and Porto. For more on the subject, see Dias (2006) and Mafra (2002).
21 The work of Wall and Nunes (2010) indicated a significant growth in the recruitment of Brazilian women for the task of caregivers.
22 I am referring here to the Saldanha Residence and Atrium Saldanha shopping centers located nearby.
23 As an example, here is the text of Mercado Brasil Tropical (that began in 2007) on its original website:

> Mercado Brasil Tropical is a company that travels through smells and flavors bringing Brazil here to Portugal. The stores, composed of shelves full of Brazilian delicacies, make anyone who enters, have "Water in the Mouth." The wide range

of Brazilian products, among them: industrialized, natural, and self-made, exude intense, exotic, delicate and, mainly, authentic flavors. The mission of Brasil Tropical Market is to maintain the well-being of each countryman and more, is to arouse the interest of Europeans for the authentic flavor of each product, always providing the highest quality and the best price. (http://mercadobrasilt ropical.com/)

For more, see https://www.facebook.com/mercadobrasiltropical/.
24 Images remarking stereotypes of Brazilian women are very present in migration contexts, usually associated with prostitution or sexual practices. Although appropriated differently according to different receiving countries, these stereotypes are always present.
25 It is worth saying that Brazilians benefited greatly from the legalization permits that were issued from 2000 onward, and particularly with the agreement signed between Brazilian president Lula da Silva and Portuguese prime minister Durão Barroso in 2003 (Padilla 2006: 20).
26 Throughout the nineteenth century, there were anti-Portuguese demonstrations directed against the Portuguese merchants who lived in Brazil and had a dominant position in the market of foodstuffs and popular housing. The Portuguese immigration that followed this period into urban and industrial Brazilian society implies more nuanced relations of interaction between Brazilians and Portuguese, without eliminating the reproduction of stereotypes about the Portuguese (Rowland 2002).
27 The "borrowing" of the ideology of lusotropicalism here was essential for reinforcing some of the representations about Brazilians, particularly about Brazilian women (Machado 2006; Padilla et al. 2010).
28 When it comes to Brazilian women, the effect of discriminations is even more serious. Their fame insinuates itself in everyday speech, fed by incessant images present in the Portuguese media, namely in soap operas. We can find the genesis of this stereotype in the lusotropical discourse that reified the phenotype of the *mulata* or a mixed-race woman. Brazilian women are sometimes seen as "prostitutes" and sometimes as "sensual," and, many times, they are subjected to intense sexual harassment, suspicion, and hostility.
29 Padilla et al complements Machado's analysis by noting that public service workers and caregivers of the elderly are not only required to be cheerful or good-natured but also to be able to establish empathy with the public via a relationship of affection and care (see Padilla et al. 2010: 9).
30 Two other factors contribute to the "success" in these areas. The first is that these migrants speak Portuguese and are thus quickly co-opted for work. The second factor, more disguised but still present, is linked to racial issues of skin color. In the present research, cases and narratives indicate that a Portuguese employer is more unlikely to select women or men from African countries to work with the public. And even Black Brazilian women experience this constraint.
31 I am referring here to the various references by Portuguese beauticians and clients to the supposed superiority of techniques and aesthetic devices related to body hair removal, or even to the innovative styles or aesthetic creativity of beauticians in Brazil.
32 Brazilian soap operas became a national product sold in many countries in Europe, Latin America, the United States, Asia, and Africa. The first soap opera commercialized abroad was *Gabriela* (1975), broadcasted in Portugal.

33 The Festival of Santo Antonio, which takes place on June 13, is one of the main street festivals in Lisbon, characterized by multiple celebrations in different areas and streets.
34 A term Schwarz (1999) used to describe the difficulties of articulating the immigration experience that former colonized people had in European cities.
35 Due the recession in Portugal (2008–16), Portuguese emigration worldwide increased, and was particularly intense in Brazil, especially between 2011 and 2014 (Rosales and Machado 2019).

References

Alencastro, L. F. (1988). "Escravos e Proletários." *Novos ESTUDOS Cebrap*, 21: 30–57.
Ascensão, E. (2011). "The Postcolonial Slum: A Geography of Informal Settlement in Quinta da Serra, Lisbon, 1970s–2010." PhD diss., King's College, University of London.
Ataíde, J., and P. Dias (eds.) (2012). *Relatório de Imigração, Fronteiras e Asilo—2011*. Lisbon: Serviço de Estrangeiros e Fronteiras.
Baptista, L. V. (1999). *Cidade e habitação social—O Estado Novo e o programa das casas económicas em Lisboa*. Oeiras: Celta Editora.
Bastos, C. (2004). "Lisboa, Século XXI: uma pós-metrópole nos trânsitos mundiais." In J. M. Pais and L. M Blass (eds.), *Tribos urbanas: produção artística e identidades*, 181–210. São Paulo: Annablume/CAPES.
Carmo, A., and A. Estevens (2017). "Urban Citizenship(s) in Lisbon: Examining the Case of Mouraria." *Citizenship Studies* 21(4): 409–24.
Cordeiro, G. Í., and A. F. da Costa (1999). "Bairros; contexto e intersecção." In G. Velho (eds.), *Antropologia urbana: cultura e sociedade no Brasil e em Portugal*, 58–79. Rio de Janeiro: Jorge Zahar.
De Certeau, M. (1994). *A Invenção do Cotidiano I*. Petrópolis: Vozes.
De L'Estoile, B. (2008). "The Past As It Lives Now: An Anthropology of Colonial Legacies." *Social Anthropology*, 16(3): 267–79.
Dias, G. M. (2006). "Expansão e Choque: a IURD em Portugal." In I. R. Machado (ed.), *Um mar de Identidades: A imigração brasileira em Portugal*. pp. 299–323. São Carlos: EDUSFSCAR.
Dias, N. (2012). "'Construir as cidades para os outros': imigração e trabalho no Portugal contemporâneo." In B. P. Dias and N. Dias (eds.), *Imigração e Racismo em Portugal—O lugar do outro*, 29–71. Lisbon: Edições 70.
Estrela, J. (eds.) (2021). *Relatório de Imigração, Fronteiras e Asilo—2020*. Lisbon: Serviço de Estrangeiros e Fronteiras.
Feldman-Bianco, B. (2002). "Entre a 'fortaleza' da Europa e os laços afetivos da irmandade luso-brasileira: um drama familiar em um só ato." In C. Bastos, M. V. de Almeida, and B. Feldman-Bianco (eds.), *Trânsitos Coloniais: diálogos críticos luso-brasileiros*, 385–416. Lisbon: ICS.
Frangella, S. (2011). "'Brazilianness' in London: National Goods and Images in Transnational Mobility." In S. Simai and D. Hook (eds.), *Brazilian Subjectivity Today: Migration, Identity and Xenophobia*, 149–70. Villa Maria: Eduvim.
Frúgoli Jr., H. (2013). "Relações entre múltiplas redes no Bairro Alto (Lisboa)." *Revista Brasileira de Ciências Sociais*, 28(82): 17–30.
Gomes, M. S. (2013). "O imaginário social da Mulher Brasileira em Portugal: uma análise da construção de saberes, das relações de poder e dos modos de subjetivação." PhD diss., ISCTE-IUL, Lisbon.

Machado, I. (2006). "Estereótipos e encarceramento simbólico no cotidiano de imigrantes brasileiros no Porto." In I. R. Machado (ed.), *Um mar de Identidades—a imigração brasileira em Portugal*, 229–50. São Carlos: Edufscar/Fapesp.

Mafra, C. (2002). *Na posse da palavra—Religião, Conversão e Liberdade Pessoal em dois Contextos Nacionais*. Lisbon: ICS.

Mapril, J. (2010). "Banglapara: imigração, negócios e (in) formalidades em Lisboa." *Etnográfica*, 14(2): 243–63.

Mayol, P. (1997). "Morar," In M. de Certeau, L. Giard, and P. Mayol (eds.), *A invenção do cotidiano: 2—Morar, cozinhar*, 37–45. Vozes: Petrópolis.

Mendes, L. (2017). "Gentrificação turística em Lisboa: neoliberalismo, financeirização e urbanismo austeritário em tempos de pós-crise capitalista 2008–2009." *Cadernos Metrópole*, 19(39): 479–512.

Mendes, M. M. (2012). "Bairro da Mouraria, território de diversidade: entre a tradição e o cosmopolitismo." *Sociologia*, thematic number: Imigração, Diversidade e Convivência Cultural: 15–41.

Menezes, M. (2009). "A praça do martim moniz: etnografando lógicas socioculturais de inscrição da praça no mapa social de Lisboa." *Horizontes Antropológicos*, 32: 301–3.

Padilla, B. (2006). "Integração dos Imigrantes Brasileiros recém-chegados na sociedade portuguesa: problemas e possibilidades." In I. R. Machado (eds.), *Um mar de Identidades—a imigração brasileira em Portugal*, 19–43. São Carlos: Edufscar/Fapesp.

Padilla, B., M. Selister, and G. Fernandes (2010). "Ser brasileira em Portugal: migração, género e colonialidade." *Proceedings of the 1º Seminário de Estudos sobre a Imigração Brasileira na Europa*, 113–21. Barcelona: Universitat de Barcelona.

Peixoto, J., and A. Figueiredo (2007). "Imigrantes brasileiros e mercado de trabalho em Portugal." In J. M. Malheiros (ed.), *Imigração Brasileira em Portugal*, 87–112. Lisbon: ACIDI.

Póvoas, M. H. G., and L. Vaz (1992). *História do património escultórico em Arroios*. Lisbon: Junta da Freguesia de S. Jorge de Arroios.

Quental e Melo, I. (2009). "O Mercado de Arrendamento: Principais Oportunidades e Fragilidades face ao Mercado de Habitação Própria." MA diss., Instituto Superior Técnico, Lisbon.

Reis, J. A. (1997). *As meninas de Arroios—uma leitura arbórea de Arroios*. Lisbon: Junta da Freguesia de São Jorge de Arroios.

Rodrigues, A., and J. S. Gomes (1996). "Pátios e Vilas da Freguesia de S. Jorge de Arroios: práticas de intervenção e a reabilitação urbana." *Olisipo, Lisboa em discussão*, ii série, 3: 117–19.

Rosales, M. V., and V. P. Machado (2019). "Contemporary Portuguese Migration Experiences in Brazil Old Routes, New Trends." In C. Pereira and J. Azevedo (eds.), *New and Old Routes of Portuguese Emigration*, 193–207. Cham, Switzerland: Springer Open.

Rowland, R. (2002). "A Cultura brasileira e os portugueses." In C. Bastos, M. V. de Almeida, and B. Feldman-Bianco (eds.), *Trânsitos Coloniais: diálogos críticos luso-brasileiros*, 373–84. Lisbon: ICS.

Salgueiro, T. B. (1977). "Bairros Clandestinos na Periferia de Lisboa." *Finisterra*, 12(23): 28–55.

Schwarz, B. (1999). "Afterword—Postcolonial Times: The Visible and the Invisible in Imperial Cities." In F. Driver and D. Gilbert (eds.), *Imperial Cities*, 268–72. Manchester: Manchester University Press.

Silva, S. S. B., and A. Schiltz (2007). "A relação entre os imigrantes brasileiros e portugueses—a construção de imagens recíprocas." In J. M. Malheiros (ed.), *Imigração Brasileira em Portugal*, 155–70. Lisbon: ACIDI.

Velasco, E. M. (1996). *Mercado de Arroios*. Lisbon: Câmara Municipal de Arroios.

Wall, K., and C. Nunes (2010). "Immigration, Welfare and Care in Portugal: Mapping the New Plurality of Female Migration Trajectories." *Social Policy and Society*, 9(3): 397–408.

Part III

POPULAR CULTURE AND EVERYDAY COLONIAL LEGACIES

Chapter 9

DIASPORA IDENTITIES, COSMOPOLITANISM, AND THE PROMISE OF CITIZENSHIP: LUSOPHONY THROUGH THE MUSIC OF AFRICAN DIASPORAS

Rui Cidra

From the second half of the 1990s, the terms "Lusophony" and "Lusophone," until then almost exclusively used by linguists in allusion to the community of Portuguese speakers, became widely used to denote a set of cultural affinities between Portugal and the states that were once its colonial territories, especially affinities intrinsic in the sharing of the Portuguese language. The notions of "Lusophony" and a "Lusophone community" were the discursive support legitimizing the strengthening of economic and political relations, especially those of cooperation and consultation between the postcolonial Portuguese-speaking states. This reframing was institutionally materialized with the creation of the multilateral organization of the Community of Portuguese Speaking Countries (Comunidade dos Países de Língua Portuguesa; CPLP 1996) but also the media channels RDP (1996) and RTP Africa (1998). Expo 98 (1998), a high-profile international event organized around the theme of the oceans and commemorating the 500th anniversary of the beginning of Portugal's maritime expansion, also tested through its discourse and programming the dissemination of ideas of Lusophony.

In the field of popular music, the term indicated a category of cultural production handled within cultural policy and the music industry. It mostly comprised musicians from the Portuguese-Speaking African Countries (PALOP), their diasporas, Brazil, and occasionally from Portugal, as well as record publishers, networks for music mediation and circulation, and especially festivals and cultural events.

Although music and dance, along with literature, are mobilized as the clearest expressions of Lusophony, it is problematic to speak up for the "common thread of Portugality" (Fikes 2009: 48) contained in the concept in relation to many of the musical and expressive practices from the PALOP and Brazil, whether considering their histories of formation or their musical, choreographic, and, in many cases, linguistic materials. Similarly, it is not clear to what extent the category expresses understandings about coexistence and intercultural dialogue held by the musicians and audiences/communities that lie within it. Discourses and aesthetics of music, specifically, seem to point to very diverse conceptions about colonial and postcolonial histories of relationship between the Portuguese and the peoples they colonized in the past.

The present chapter aims to look into how musicians from Africa or descendants from African diasporas in Portugal dwell in the category of "Lusophony." It seeks to interpret aesthetics and discourses of musical and expressive practice in relation to ideas of "Lusophony" and "Lusophone music" by assessing how they account for continuities regarding official discourses or signal identity formations and historicities that could potentially enclose new wordings for thinking about postcolonial relations between African communities, their descendants, and the Portuguese white population. The chapter goes on to inquire whether popular culture, especially popular music, might suggest ways of narrating the relationship between Portugal and its former colonial territories that are alternatives to or transformative of official narratives inspired by tropicalism or Lusophony and may be close to a postcolonial episteme.

The voices of the musicians are critical for an understanding of Lusophony disconnected from institutional policies and discourses, since it is the musicians and the expressive traditions that they perform that embody the ideas proposed by this discourse. Meanwhile, musicians are simultaneously social actors with their own positionings regarding nationality, diaspora, ethnicity, gender, sexuality, social class, "race," and age, and amplified voices of the civil societies within the national and diasporic communities to which they belong. In some cases, thinking of the musicians who bring life to the category and who live in Portugal, they have played a critical part in the postcolonial history of these nations and their diasporas, articulating emerging questionings and political and social sensibilities. I argue that musicians appropriate the concept according to distinctive colonial, postcolonial, and diasporic trajectories; and that these appropriations or interpretations gather more wide-ranging projects of identity, citizenship, and cosmopolitan ethics.

What Is Lusophony? Community, History, Language, and Geography

The term "Lusophony" summarizes a discourse politically created in the late twentieth century that deals with the relations between Portugal or the Portuguese and the nations or peoples linked to its colonial history. It is a discourse inasmuch as it denotes a way of talking about these relations, produces meaning about them, and shapes perceptions and social practices, that is, it has practical effects (Foucault [1969] 2004, 1971). As a concept, it conveys, at a first level, a community formed by people whose trajectories and life experiences are rooted in or move through geographic spaces where Portuguese is the official language as a result of a common colonial history. The Portuguese language, taken as an archive of history, culture, and memory, embodies and materializes, in the logic of the concept, a cultural intimacy among those who speak it. The way this community imagines itself is then rooted in a concrete historical and cultural experience condensed in the sharing of the Portuguese language.

The term not only denotes a common history and language but also underlines the colonial encounter involving Portuguese and other peoples as the historical context that formed or shaped cultural practices characterizing the experience of African and Brazilian communities in music, dance, literature (artistic expression overall), gastronomy, architectural heritage, and some knowledge traditions. The idea of a shared asset such as Lusophony also includes emotional sensibilities and temperaments, personality and character traits of individuals and groups, notions of intimacy and proximity, all understood as affective and sensible heritage that favors mutual understanding.

In the 1990s, a set of measures described by the Portuguese and Brazilian states, working in conjunction with other Portuguese-speaking states toward mutual political and economic rapprochement, contributed to the redefinition of the term. The most important of these measures was the formalization of the CPLP (1996), a multilateral organization aimed at political and diplomatic conciliation between its member states, especially their representation in international relations forums, cooperation in all fields of political action, and the promotion and diffusion of the Portuguese language (CPLP 2007). As an organization seeking the political, economic, and social development of Portuguese-speaking countries, the CPLP was the corollary of the moves made by a number of actors in Brazilian and Portuguese politics and diplomacy during the 1980s and 1990s, although discussion of the project started in the late colonial period (Ribeiro and Ferreira 2003; Maciel 2010). The idea of the Portuguese language as "a historical bond and a common heritage resulting from a centuries long coexistence" (CPLP 1996) between the peoples provided the discursive support for a new political and institutional community and came to be the main link for the concept of Lusophony in the following years.

Lusophony as a category is the product of a specific temporality, marked by the geopolitical realignment that followed the end of the Cold War and the growing interconnectedness and mobility characteristic of late modernity. At the geopolitical level, it accounts for the transition from a time characterized by anti-colonial and nationalist values underscored by the one-party regimes in the new African states, and Portugal's turn toward Europe, to a time dominated by the assumption of a need for political and economic alliance predicated on history, language, and cultural affinities, on dialogue with a global context distinguished by transnational political and economic processes and by economic neoliberalism. Furthermore, it represents the political assumption of the postcolonial interlinking between the nations in question, mainly materialized through the migratory movements whose destination was Portugal.

The idea of a common cultural link of Portugality in the African experience and of the peoples whose historical trajectories were guided by Portuguese colonialism claims, as does the lusotropical discourse, the relevance of Portuguese culture and ethos in the formation of other cultural worlds and subjectivities. It is at the point where this tropicalist-inspired narrative meets up with a trajectory of modernity that the contemporary idea of Lusophony is rooted.

Alongside the political and institutional framework represented by the CPLP, the idea of Lusophony was particularly formulated by the radio station RDP África and the television channel RTP Africa. Between the 1980s and 1990s, the mass media were seen by the Portuguese state as crucial vehicles to disseminate the Portuguese language and knowledge of Portuguese culture in African countries. This would foster economic cooperation in the universalist and civilizing political language still prevalent in the period as ways to "affirm the image and presence of Portugal in the world," "accentuate the universalist matrix and project the language and culture in the world," and "strengthen affective and economic ties" (Sousa 2006). This policy orientation began with the creation of the television channel RTP Internacional (1992), which gave rise to the RTP África project (1998) and to the radio station RDP África (1996). The coming together of a daily corpus of news, information, discussion, and music choice in their broadcasts, interconnecting and treating the social realities of Portugal and PALOP at one and the same time, constituted a powerful vehicle for materializing Lusophony as a community.

Category Uses in Expressive Culture: From Multiculturalism to Interculturality

In the field of popular music, "Lusophony" has designated the creation of a category of cultural production handled in the context of "cultural policy" and the "music industry," especially encompassing cultural events and artifacts involving musicians and "performers" mostly from PALOP countries, their diasporas, Brazil, and occasionally Portugal.[1] But it is in relation to the former that the category becomes a reality.

As in other areas of social life, and as pointed out at the time by figures like the Angolan writer Ondjaki, the category excluded Portugal and the Portuguese (Fikes 2009; Maciel 2010) and became a shortcut label for "African migrants," the PALOP, and Brazil. Portugal and the Portuguese are seen as producers of Lusophony, not its products, and thus the category, since it is predicated on the reproduction of power relations inherited from the colonial period, only exceptionally includes them. The occasional inclusion of Portuguese musicians occurs under specific conditions: in Portugal, especially in cultural policy events that narrativize the cultural proximity between African and Portuguese musical genres (e.g., concerts promoting the idea of an aesthetic proximity between the Cape Verdean musical genre morna and fado); and abroad, when within the scope of music industry events, an image of a multicultural contemporaneous Portugal and Lisbon is represented, or collaborations between Portuguese musicians and musicians from Brazil are initiated, a direction taken by the music industry that has been widely exploited. Sporadically claimed as a historical result of the colonial movements between Portugal, Africa, and Brazil, fado is the genre that best suits the demands of Lusophony. However, its entry in the category is entirely contingent upon and subject to specific agendas (Losa 2019).

Like other widely used terms, especially those conveyed by the music industry, it is an open, porous, and moldable category. Its meanings vary in the context of its renewed use, especially within the programming of cultural events, denoting either a geography or a set of properties or cultural attributes.

The term qualifies, first of all, a geography of actual cultural production that can be traced between the PALOP and Portugal, particularly the Lisbon Metropolitan Area as inhabited and experienced by the diasporic communities originated in these countries. In this sense, the ideas of "Lusophony" and "Lusophone music" are shortcuts for *all* music produced in Portuguese-speaking African countries or within their diasporas. This meaning took shape with the emergence of the concept in the second half of the 1990s, when the terms "Lusophony" and "Lusophone" became identifiers of music from PALOP countries in circuits of cultural commodification in Portugal and Europe, especially in the broader market of "world music." The formalization of Lusophony allowed the entry of the "Lusophone world" into the world music market in the period, and an interest in PALOP music by the international music industry at a time when the Cape Verdean singer Cesária Évora emerged as one of its leading figures. As with the term "world music," "Lusophone music" in this sense groups together a multiplicity of expressive practices with complex and autonomous colonial and postcolonial histories.

In relation to this geography, the terms also qualify different meanings around cultural difference in the Portuguese context. When the formalization of the discourse and policies of Lusophony was taking place in the second half of the 1990s, the concept of Lusophony constituted the common denominator of cultural events celebrating or decrying "cultural diversity," "tolerance," and "difference" that mobilized African musicians and performers living in Portugal, as well as young people descended from African diaspora communities. In this period, the association of music and dance with "Lusophony" conveyed the idea of a newly formed multicultural reality in Portuguese society and the recognition of the need to build a common life around this coexistence (Hall 2000; Kymlicka 1995).

More than multiculturalism, in the years after its emergence the category of Lusophony associated with music mainly denoted ideas of hybridity, cultural fusion, and mixture linked to the image of Lisbon as a multicultural city and setting for cultural encounters between Europe, the South Atlantic, the Indian Ocean, Africa, and Brazil. In recent years, ideas of "hybridity" and "mixture" have been increasingly subsumed under the concept of interculturality. As a concept structuring European Union policies regarding cultural diversity and migration into the European space since the 1990s, interculturality "connotes a desire for sociocultural connections among peoples of different ethnicities, as opposed to the mosaic-inspired designs under multiculturalism." The term thus harbors the idea of "social interaction among different cultural groups" as a key to both "recognition" and "socioeconomic and political equality" (Pardue 2015: 138) among different communities. At the same time, the term was disseminated through policies of "cultural diversity management" (Oliveira 2013) associated with the implementation of the "neoliberal model of city production" in Lisbon

(Estevens 2017). Within a cultural economy characteristic of the neoliberal order, the production of a city brand associated with cultural diversity and the coexistence of different diasporic communities in the urban space is considered capable of attracting economic resources and producing value through tourism and investment (Estevens 2017: 189–90). The view of "interculturality" as an index of cultural dynamism convertible into resources, competitiveness, and value was analyzed in particular in the context of municipal policies associated with the changes in the Mouraria neighborhood[2] (Oliveira 2013; Sanchez 2016; Estevens 2017). Although in its institutional uses the term indistinctly condenses ideas of multiculturalism and hybridity, the interculturality understood according to this commodification logic brought to the bundle of meanings of Lusophony the realities of the everyday cultural "encounter," "interaction," and "exchange" (Estevens 2017: 192–3) in the city. Again, it is not clear whether white Portuguese populations with more sedentary trajectories are also covered by the concept and shaped by these intercultural dialogues.

Diaspora Identities and Cosmopolitanism

The idea of Lusophony is interpreted by musicians based on distinct histories, social trajectories, and identity positionings. The term is roughly taken as a synonym for colonial and postcolonial relations between Africans and Portuguese, equally enshrined in the field of expressive culture and music. More than a nexus of Portugality, it denotes the co-constitution of cultural realities and subjectivities. The singer and composer Lura started by placing Lusophony in a particular chronotope and historicity:

> It is a concept that ended up naturally being implemented in our lives, in our daily lives, in keeping with our history, with reality, with what happened, with the movement of peoples, with colonization. So, Portuguese became firmly rooted in Cape Verde. Cape Verde is also firmly rooted in Portugal and there always ends up being these exchanges at all levels, and in this case in particular the music is always influenced by these encounters that happened. Encounters and disencounters—isn't it?—that have been happening.[3]

Lura sees Lusophony as deriving from the historical intertwining between Cape Verde and Portugal, either the one that resulted from the process of "creolization" that shaped the colonization of the archipelago of Cape Verde since the fifteenth century and shaped the Cape Verdean Creole cultural practices or the one predicated on the labor migrations of Cape Verdeans who, between the twentieth and twenty-first centuries, headed for the territory of metropolitan or postcolonial Portugal. This interconnection is especially documented in popular music, as she pointed out by referring to a morna song (a Cape Verdean vocal genre with instrumental accompaniment) by B. Leza (Francisco Xavier da Cruz) to illustrate her own diasporic understanding of Lusophony:

There's a song that I interpreted a little while ago, and that's *Bejo de Sôdade*. That's an example of a song that I think is hugely meaningful and it's written magnificently, to show these close ties between Portugal and Cape Verde . . . And it's going to happen, and has been happening for many years, this, this state of living here, of living here in Portugal but always missing Cape Verde, of living in Cape Verde, but needing to come to Portugal because these two countries are part of us. And I'm an example of this. I've lived in Cape Verde for four years now, but I've missed Lisbon. There it is, I will always be something of a foreigner, both in Lisbon and in Cape Verde. Here I am a black Cape Verdean from other origins. And in Cape Verde I wasn't born there. And so, I always end up being a foreigner in both places. There is this nostalgia, this gives us a certain nostalgia, on the one hand. But on the other hand, it gives us an immense richness, because in fact we have both sides, culturally speaking; and at the level of language and music it enriches us immensely.[4]

The kind of diasporic awareness she describes, a double identification or cultural belonging that is paradoxically experienced in keeping with the feeling of being foreign in both places, is key to her understanding of Lusophony. Lura was born in Lisbon in 1975 to Cape Verdean parents. Her background when young was linked to sports and dance in cultural associations, and she started her connection to popular music at the age of seventeen by participating as backing vocalist in a record of the São Tomense singer Juka. Her interest in interpreting the genres of Cape Verdean popular music, especially since the recording of the album *Di Korpu ku Alma* (2004),[5] was part of a broader rediscovery of her cultural and family background that led her to travel to her parents' homeland more often and to get to know the cultural reality of the islands and the Creole language in greater depth. In fact, Portuguese was the first language she learned, since her parents' priority was for her to adapt to schooling in Portugal without language barriers; Creole was the language spoken by her parents, the "language of the Cape Verdean home."[6] The interlinking between Cape Verde and Portugal suggested by Lusophony is understood in Lura's case from a sense of double cultural belonging as a Cape Verdean Portuguese woman or a Creole Portuguese woman, whatever the order or vocabulary—someone who was born and grew up in Portugal within a diaspora community with its forms of identification and co-ethnicity supported by collective memory, affectivity, and the feeling of sharing the same culture and language.

For Lura, more clearly than for the other interviewees, the term "Lusophony" is also a potentially emancipating political category in the terrain of cultural politics and in the scope of the struggles for public representation of African communities and their descendants in Portugal. The production of popular music at this level is key since it is the main domain of cultural production that in Portuguese society is associated with cultural difference—specifically with the idea of an "African culture." Lusophony for her is an "integrating" concept of "cultural enhancement." It contains a promise of future "equality" in terms of material resources and social and political conditions between Portuguese, the African communities, and their descendants in Portugal, even if doubt still persists as to the effectiveness of the struggles of cultural representation under its sign—particularly regarding the bidirectional or reciprocal character of the relationships it qualifies:

> Over time integration has been found to be hard. Let's say that Lusophony ends up integrating us in a good concept. In a way it takes us a little bit out of the ghetto. Let's say it is a positive step. It's a step that leads us to cover more of the world . . . This has been a struggle. It has been a struggle of valuing ourselves and giving something to ourselves, but that others don't recognize. But with the passage of time these values are being recognized. The cultural value, the value of words, the value of our union, of accepting ourselves as we are, the value of being accepted by those who to some extent made us Cape Verdeans, and by those who made our language, and they are the Portuguese, and that is the Lusophone world. So let us say that it's a union and an integration, a comprehensive acceptance. There is already a global opening here—global within our Lusophone world—which is valid, which is good, which is important, and we are going in that direction. Let's see where it takes us. I hope that it heads towards equality at a general level and towards admitting that we are a people, because we end up being a mixed people, the people of Lusophony. There is a mixture here that in fact has to be accepted, not only of the Portuguese who are still in Cape Verde and have created a family there, left their hearts there, and has spread throughout Cape Verde, but also of the Africans who came to Portugal and created populations here in Portugal as well, and that somehow or other we do not know how far they are African or not, or Portuguese, or that they see themselves as such. I think that admitting this is the first step to freedom and happiness.[7]

In contrast to Lura, whose connection to Lusophony came about because she was a Portuguese who was socialized within a social formation of diaspora and relies on the very narrative of hybridity of Cape Verdean Creole, the identification of the musician António Costa Neto with the concept derives from a professional migration experience in the field of music from Mozambique, interpreted through a set of cosmopolitan values. His understanding of Lusophony is also predicated on a colonial and postcolonial history of the relationship between Africans and Portuguese, especially as it took shape in the multicultural environment of Lisbon, evident in his own biography and family history:

> I think history doesn't let us escape. We don't choose the history we have. Fortunately, it is a history that we can be proud of . . . In the case of those of us who came to live in Portugal, where a large diaspora was created, a special territory was also born, one without borders, a territory that is not physical, of the peoples of this Lusophony, where all these cultures merge. We end up resembling, or even being, a people, a unique people. Humans insist on creating boundaries . . . and we are often blind when it comes to identifying those territories—like the one I just mentioned—that do not . . . have physical boundaries. Because we

live together. I'll give you an example. My wife is Cape Verdean, my daughter is
Portuguese, and I am Mozambican. So where are we from?[8]

Costa arrived in Portugal in 1989, as part of a tour by the group Ghorwane. Before that, in the years after the country gained independence, he participated in various groups in the city of Maputo. He decided to stay in Lisbon and became a professional musician in a circuit of dance halls and concerts dedicated to popular music from the PALOP countries, with occasional tours outside the country, especially in Europe and Africa. He was a member of the musical groups of some of the main interpreters of Lusophone African music, such as the Angolans Bonga and Waldemar Bastos and the Cape Verdeans Paulino Vieira, Bana, Tito Paris, Cesária Évora, and Maria Alice (1989–2000), especially as a bass player. In addition to being a backing musician, he has also written songs in the Ronga language of the Maputo region that include rhythmic and melodic materials inspired by various Mozambican expressive cultures.

The fact that he is a Mozambican musician involved in the creation of popular music associated with other national and diasporic communities of Lusophone Africa in Lisbon makes him an important interlocutor for a reflection on issues of interculturality and "cultural mixture" implicit in the official discourses of Lusophony. As he told me, since the late 1980s, he has engaged in a practical and regular dialogue with the expressive traditions of the different PALOP nations:

> In fact, this experience of having lived with artists and musicians from different countries has enriched me immensely. First it enriched me musically because I got to know the musical genres more than just technically, but it also helps a lot to understand the various philosophies of life in different cultures, different peoples, etc., at the level of Lusophony. At least at the level of the Portuguese-speaking African countries, I mean, I feel at home everywhere. I arrive in Cape Verde as a Cape Verdean. I even have episodes of being really confused [*Laughs*].[9]

Although based on a diasporic positioning, Costa's identification with Lusophony is mainly supported by cosmopolitan values and practices. Costa projects to the Lusophone space the structuring principle of cosmopolitanism, according to which all human beings have moral duties to each other beyond their immediate community spheres (defined by region, nation, diaspora, ethnicity, etc.) (Brown and Held 2010). While, in the ethical orientation of cosmopolitanism, the engagement with the other is predicated on a shared humanity, in the kind of "Lusophone cosmopolitanism" that Costa advocates, this humanity is mediated by a common history. These values have also linked his practice as a musician to projects related to multicultural education and anti-racism, human and children's rights, and the fight against poverty, among other issues.

These values also underlie a practical cosmopolitan orientation, that of engaging with cultural and musical difference through his living in the city of Lisbon and his circulations in the transnational field of commodified music between the Lusophone and world music markets.[10] Like the other musicians discussed in this text, Costa does not fit the conventional profile of an African labor migrant living in Portugal. He is, rather, a professional migrant in the field of popular music production, with relative cultural capital, with a physical mobility conferred by his professional activity that allows him to occasionally move around the different territories of the Lusophone space according to travel arrangements that contrast with the mobility strategies of migrant workers from the PALOP countries. It is from this experience and the values that accompany it that he feels like "a citizen of the Lusophone world" who is "at ease"[11] in any of the Lusophone territories. Along with ideas of cosmopolitanism, multiculturalism, and interculturality, Costa Neto sees Lusophony as offering the possibility of a critique of colonial history—a "civic pedagogy," in his words, seeking a better understanding between the communities spanned by Lusophony in the postcolonial present:

> [At the center of Lusophony] is a common history that unfortunately has been little valued, especially with regard to civic education, because I think it is very important to feel that this history does exist . . . I think that it's quite brutal that so much has been forgotten in such a short time. We need to start talking about things in a clear and straightforward way. In the case of Portugal [this history] is largely forgotten because of ghosts that we are afraid to mess around with: the ghost of colonialism . . . the ghost of the slave trade . . . and also the racial issue in the case of Africa . . . But the only way of overcoming these ghosts is by talking about things! . . . We are so close, but we've put this ghost between us and it creates this false distance that doesn't even exist . . . Lusophony is us; Lusophony is our shared history.[12]

In brief, this vision of Lusophony describes a political category that must be occupied, whose performance must be negotiated and transformed by those it relates to, starting by questioning the institutions that represent it, notably the CPLP.

If the trajectories of Lura and Costa Neto occurred in dialogue with the cultural and political dynamics of a postcolonial time, the expressive practice of the Angolan musician Bonga (b. Porto Quipiri, Angola, 1942) followed the changes that marked the transition from the late colonial period to the present day. Bonga experienced both temporalities in a politically committed way, the first as an opponent of Portuguese colonialism, the second as a critic of the one-party MPLA regime led by José Eduardo dos Santos, but also of the relations between Portuguese and Africans in postcolonial Portugal. It is in accordance with this doubly critical condition of exile and diaspora that he evaluates Lusophony from Portugal. For him, Lusophony is the institutional translation of a common history and "interlinking"[13] between Africans and Portuguese—"it would make complete sense, gained from the years that the people have been together. And neither me nor my friend were to blame for this meeting."[14] Ideally, it would communicate the "coexistence" and "the salutary exchange" between people "who connect through language and culture."[15] But as he sees it, the existence of an ideal Lusophony is merely rhetorical and has no correspondence at the level of social relations:

> People have to practice through the other a relationship of harmony, of friendship and exchange. That's something that actually doesn't exist! . . . This experience doesn't exist. We don't go to anybody's house. It is easier for me to have someone come here that is known to me, or that wants to take care of something, I don't know what, than it is for us [with emphasis] to go to the house of a Portuguese.[16]

In his view, Lusophony is a promising but unfulfilled project, given the lack of "hospitality" shown by the Portuguese, a powerful metaphor to interpret the relations of distance and boundaries in everyday life between Africans and Portuguese living in postcolonial Portugal. In his view, this lack of hospitality is matched by the ineffectiveness of Lusophone policies to promote and appreciate a shared cultural heritage, where expressive culture is at its core.

Bonga grew up in the *musseque*s (shantytowns) of colonial Luanda, where he came into daily contact with various manifestations of expressive culture, especially those associated with the Ambundu ethnic group, historically settled in northeastern Angola and areas bordering Luanda and speaking Kimbundu. His link with percussion instruments started during his childhood, notably when he played the dikanza (an idiophone whose sound is produced by scraping, similar to a reco-reco) to accompany his father, a button accordion player in the tradition of massemba (a music and dance genre from the Luanda region, also known as rebita). During his youth, he was a percussionist in groups such as Kissueia, Os Ilundos, and Kimbandas do Ritmo. Reacting to the assimilationist policy of the colonial state, which rhetorically valued the adoption by Angolans of behaviors and values identified with Portugal (and with the idea of Europe) to the detriment of African culture and languages, these groups were part of the movement to valorize Ambundu-Kimbundu cultural and linguistic practices as a way to voice anti-colonial resistance and trigger nationalist feelings—a political and cultural awareness inaugurated during the 1950s by Liceu Vieira Dias and the group Ngola Ritmos (Moorman 2008).

Besides music, his performances as an athlete earned him an invitation to train in the metropole (1966) representing Sport Lisboa e Benfica and the national team, a route shared by athletes from other African colonial territories. Along with his activity as a sprinter, he became a percussionist for Angolan musicians performing in Portugal. His growing involvement in the anti-colonial struggle and the likelihood of being arrested by the political police led him to take refuge in Rotterdam (1972), a city with a significant community of Cape Verdean migrant workers linked to port and maritime work, but also a meeting point for political activists from different Portuguese colonial territories in Africa. Under the artistic and politically clandestine name Bonga or Bonga Kuenda, he recorded the LP *Angola 72*, accompanied by Cape Verdean Humbertona and Angolan Mário Rui Silva, both guitarists.[17] The album was a collection of Bonga's compositions with anti-colonial and nationalistic messages sung with a strong emotional charge in the Kimbundu language. The acoustic sound of the guitars, percussion, and wind instruments, the husky timbre and expressiveness of his vocal interpretation, established the aesthetic principles of his repertoire recorded in the period, especially distinct in *Angola 74* (1974) and *Raízes: Canções e Poemas de Angola, Brasil e Cabo Verde* (1975; *Roots: Songs and Poems from Angola, Brazil and Cape Verde*).[18] This latter record, which resulted from a collaboration between Bonga, the Brazilian musician Sebastião da Rocha Perazzo ("Tião," who became his main musical partner during the 1970s), and the Guinean Conakry saxophonist Jo Maka, seems especially important for assessing contrapuntally the musician's relationship with what would later be conceived as Lusophony.

By presenting the expressive practices of Angola (semba, rebita, and kilapanda), Cape Verde (morna and coladeira) and Brazil (samba, chorinho, baião, and coco) in continuity and in dialogue, emphasizing their cultural and stylistic proximity, the record elects the Black Atlantic and, in particular, the institution of slavery as implemented throughout Portugal's colonial empire as the historical event that shaped the Black diasporic cultures, specifically those of Cape Verde and Brazil, and the cultural affinities between those peoples and the people of Angola. The record project bases these cultural links not according to a mythical and heroic history of Portuguese expansion but according to a "diasporic intimacy" (Boym 1998) arising from a history of violence, subordination, but also resistance. Bonga focused more on the transatlantic links between Angola and Brazil in one of his most popular songs, the semba "Mulemba Xangola."[19] In his words, *Raízes* gives an account of one

> history of reunited peoples! And there are people who are afraid of the reunited peoples because when they meet up they've got something to say about everything, and about everything, including, [with emphasis] of course, going through the smacks they took on the hand, the whippings they took, the specific foods that they have and that they would like to continue to eat . . . isn't that right? Of the people who come and visit us and respect us. Ah, that's what *Raizes* is! *Raizes*, that's it.[20]

Recorded at the time African states were gaining their independence under the banner of cultural nationalism and anti-colonial values, *Raízes* communicates the possibility of the formerly colonized establishing alliances predicated on criticism of the former colonizer, on its decentralization, on the deprivation of its power of representation in history. In this respect, his proposal is based on values that are contrary to those that have been organized around the concept of Lusophony since the 1990s, not least because it seeks to reposition history by valuing the cultural practices of the colonized peoples in an alliance that is independent of that of the colonizers.

In line with these values, for Bonga there is currently a gap between the discourse and the practice of Lusophony, especially if we look at the relationships between Africans and Portuguese in Portuguese society.

In Bonga's view, Lusophony could be socially productive if it were a platform that ensured an egalitarian cultural representation stemming from a postcolonial critique of persistent colonial legacies. But instead, he sees Lusophony as a tropicalist-inspired narrative that reinstalls Portugal at the center of history and confers a nexus of Portugality on the cultural practices of the Portuguese-speaking world, in a detached way. Despite the years spent in Portugal, he does not feel like a Portuguese or Lusophone citizen. Additionally, his critical view of the Angolan political elites throughout the years have shaped him as an Angolan in exile and diaspora.

Concluding Notes

In the 1980s and 1990s, the concept of Lusophony was gradually disseminated through a set of policies involving Portuguese-speaking states, especially Portugal and Brazil, and widely circulated events, practices, and cultural objects that together contributed to its gradual entextualization. In Portugal, Lusophony was the translation of a historical moment in the country: the assumption of the increasingly multicultural nature of Portuguese society triggered by the substantial increase of postcolonial migrations to Portuguese territory, especially from Portuguese-speaking African countries and Brazil.

Lusophony not only communicated the actual idea of cultural difference but it also provided the framework from which to think about the relationship with difference in Portuguese society. Initially, and in continuity with the colonial period, it established a hierarchical relationship between Portugal and the former colonized nations by postulating the transcendent and universalistic character of Portuguese culture and language in the formation of other cultural worlds. It emphasized the cultural proximity of the Other relative to an imagination of Portuguese culture in order to assert the importance of the Portuguese historical and civilizing mission. In recent years, the ideas of hybridity and interculturality have sought to revise these asymmetries contained in the notion leaning toward the idea of a past and present of interconnection and mutual establishment. However, it is not clear whether the vernacular cosmopolitan exchanges associated with Lusophony focus as much on the cultural practices of migrants from Africa, Asia, or South America living in the city of Lisbon as on those of Portuguese citizens. The unique operation of the concept, its reduction of cultural difference to an outcome of Portuguese imperial history, and as the racialized disadvantage and exclusion that mark the experience of migrant populations in Portugal prevent Lusophony from acquiring full meaning for the populations it embraces, establishing itself as a community that truly represents them.

In the field of popular music, the discourse of Lusophony has generated a category that covers all the musical practices produced by musicians from Brazil, Portuguese-speaking African countries, and their diasporas in Portugal. Popular music was the main context for the reiteration of Lusophony as a concept. The main genres of music and dance from Portuguese-speaking countries, their contemporary circulation within the international music industry, as well as collaborations between musicians, especially those linked to the image of the multiculturalism of the city of Lisbon and the sociabilities of migrants in Portugal, figured metonymically for the common history that the concept institutionally denoted. Put into circulation by cultural policy institutions and music industry agents, the idea of Lusophony and its connection to popular music was materialized through cultural events such as festivals and thematic concerts, and occasional collaborations between African, Brazilian, and Portuguese musicians performing in shows or recordings.

The musicians whose perceptions of Lusophony are discussed in the text interpret the concept from individual trajectories and differentiated diasporic identities, either between themselves or in relation to other profiles of migrants or diaspora populations. In Portugal, they developed an activity as professional musicians, dialoguing with the traditions of their territories of origin according to cultural and material resources provided by the diaspora experience. Based in Lisbon, the main center of production and commodification of PALOP music, they disseminated their expressive practice through networks connecting diaspora centers and music markets in Europe and the African countries. Their access to the means of popular music mediation and their artistic creativity made them, from the perspective of national and diasporic audiences, recognized representatives of national cultures. In some cases, too, they were seen as important voices of the civil societies of those nations, commenting through the themes, characters, and places addressed in their songs, the common past, present, and future.

Although a place of origin is important for their public representation and artistic practice, these musicians no longer subjectively belong to just one "home." Their relationship with countries of origin is mediated by the diaspora in Portugal, where cultural practices and meanings associated with communities of origin coexist with, and are reinterpreted in light of, a life experience in the Portuguese territory; where practical and imagined relationships with the nation and the diaspora compete with the experience of life in Portuguese society and with the discourses that in Portugal shape the relationship with the difference, namely Lusophony. Their experience of diaspora, on the other hand, contrasts with that of African migrant workers since it is experienced from the status of a professional musician, someone who enjoys spatial mobility transnationally, even if only temporarily, when carrying out their work. Since they are in contact with Portuguese, European and African audiences, musicians are not confined to work contexts and community and kinship networks defined by national and diasporic belonging, as is characteristically the case with labor migrants. Taken together, these traces of experience contribute to acceptance, albeit critical, of the category, which necessarily involves the recognition of a connection to Portugal and a shared history that is mobilized in identity narratives. Their life trajectories carry the traces of various histories and cultural practices, and the term "Lusophony" makes it possible to synthesize or name them. In most of the examples discussed, this acceptance of Lusophony is rooted in a diasporic awareness that is "open," "complex," and harbors the possibility of belonging to "several homes," as some literature on diasporas has pointed out in past decades (Hall 2017).

When Lura, for example, comments on the "enrichment" that comes from this possibility of inhabiting two places (even if experienced from a permanent condition of being foreign), two cultural frameworks, or two languages, she is following the well-known idea of Homi K. Bhabha (1994) when he alludes to the act of "speaking from the destabilizing place between languages," negotiating and translating through their differences (Hall 2017: 173), a process that feeds her artistic creativity. From his family history, his professional experience, and his cosmopolitan values, Costa Neto is also affirming that he belongs to different homes, rooted in the cultural histories and practices that are interwoven along his journey. Bonga's path, meanwhile, marked by the anti-colonial struggle and opposition to the one-party regime in Angola, is close to a more traditional and "closed" configuration of diaspora, built from an "excluding border" between an "inside" and an "outside" (Hall 1999) and sustained on a relationship of loyalty, lived at a distance, in relation to a territory of origin that, in his case, is experienced in keeping with a sentiment of political exile.

The musicians start from musical and expressive practice to shed light on the multiple cultural histories encompassed by the category and to aim at perhaps formulating new political values governing the shared life of their multiple communities. The concept then holds the promise of articulating "non-normative forms of citizenship" (Lazar 2013). Lura believes these relate to the possibility of Lusophony promoting the "appreciation" and "recognition" of identities and cultural practices through the dialogic relationship with the significant Other—what Charles Taylor (1994) called the "politics of recognition." Lusophony thus responds to the dual call of multiculturalism in the search for social equality and justice, and simultaneously for the recognition of cultural difference. Costa Neto sees Lusophony ideally as the institutional guarantor of a postnational citizenship in the defense of human rights, democracy, freedom of expression, equality, and justice in Portuguese-speaking countries. These values should be supported by a "pedagogy" that includes a debate around colonial histories involving citizens of Portuguese-speaking countries, and a critique of persistent colonial legacies.

But it is above all through performative and expressive modes, more or less subject to reflexivity, that musicians expand the notion of Lusophony. In this direction, the category offers the chance to formulate geographies of imagination and alliance that comprise, and sometimes transcend, Portuguese-speaking countries, relativizing the centrality of Portugal and reviving routes of cultural circulation rooted in colonial and postcolonial histories. These "geographies of expressivity" (Losa 2019) that accommodate musical and expressive modes of relating to the Other, but also testimonies about the Other and about oneself (ibid.), allude to complex histories of cultural transformation that link African expressive cultures to Brazil and the Caribbean.

These complex stories of cultural appropriation, imagination, and identification more closely convey the soundscapes and cultural histories based on which the musicians register their creative processes and question the unity of cultural materials and processes of cultural interaction, clustered under the term "Lusophony." By emphasizing the irreducibility of cultural practice to institutionally formed notions of cultural and linguistic community predicated on a history expressed in imperial terms, they claim that the relationships between African communities and the Portuguese population could be formulated in an egalitarian way from the experiences and voices of all communities included within the category. Only an egalitarian orientation of this kind can show whether the term "Lusophony" will preserve its meaning in the future or whether another concept denoting a common colonial and postcolonial history and interculturality will take its place.

Notes

1. For histories of Lusophony in the realm of popular music that emphasize the contribution of musicians, cultural events, and institutions, see Cidra (2010) and Vanspauwen (2010).
2. Mouraria is one of the historic quarters of the city of Lisbon, currently part of the parish of Santa Maria Maior. Inhabited by the poor lower classes of the city and by immigrant populations of various origins, especially China, India, and Bangladesh, among others, and with a very degraded housing stock, Mouraria has recently undergone redevelopment works and has become a tourist hotspot of Lisbon.
3. Lura (Maria de Lurdes Assunção Pina), interview with Rui Cidra, Algés, September 19, 2018.
4. Lura, interview.
5. Lura, *Di Korpu ku Alma* (Paris, Lusafrica, 2004).
6. Lura, interview.
7. Lura, interview.
8. António Costa Neto, interview with Rui Cidra, Lisbon, December 12, 2017.
9. António Costa Neto, interview.
10. I draw here on a common distinction in the literature of cosmopolitanism between "philosophical" or "normative" cosmopolitanism and "actually existing cosmopolitanism," the latter pointing to an increasingly cosmopolitan reality close to the comprehensive category of globalization or, more concretely, to the idea of "cosmopolitanization" as proposed by Ulrich Beck. I find the first understanding of cosmopolitanism particularly well-stated in Appiah (2006) and in Brown and Held (2010). The second understanding is reflected in Beck (2000, 2006).
11. António Costa Neto, interview.
12. António Costa Neto, interview.
13. Bonga (José Adelino Barceló de Carvalho), interview with Rui Cidra, Alfornelos, February 1, 2018.
14. Bonga, interview.
15. Bonga, interview.
16. Bonga, interview.
17. Bonga, *Angola 72* (Rotterdam, Morabeza Records, 1972).
18. Bonga, *Angola 74* (Rotterdam: Morabeza Records, 1974); Bonga, *Raízes: Canções e Poemas de Angola, Brasil e Cabo Verde* (*Roots: Songs and Poems from Angola, Brazil and Cape Verde*) (Rotterdam: Morabeza Records, 1975).

19 AAVV, *Onda Sonora: Red Hot + Lisbon* (New York: Red Hot Records, 1998).
20 Bonga, interview.

References

Appiah, K. A. (2006). *Cosmopolitanism: Ethics in a World of Strangers*. New York: W.W. Norton.
Beck, U. (2000). "The Cosmopolitan Perspective: Sociology of the Second Age of Modernity." *British Journal of Sociology*, 51(1): 79–105.
Beck, U. (2006). *Cosmopolitan Vision*. Malden: Polity.
Bhabha, H. K. (1994). *The Location of Culture*. London: Routledge.
Boym, S. (1998). "On Diasporic Intimacy: Ilya Kabakov's Installations and Immigrant Homes." *Critical Inquiry*, 24(2): 498–524.
Brown, G. W., and D. Held (2010). "Editor's Introduction." In G. W. Brown and D. Held (eds.), *The Cosmopolitanism Reader*, 1–14. Cambridge: Polity.
Cidra, R. (2010). "Migração, Música e." In S. Castelo-Branco (ed.), *Enciclopédia da Música em Portugal no Século XX L-P*, 773–93. Lisbon: Círculo de Leitores.
CPLP (1996). "Declaração Constitutiva da Comunidade dos Países de Língua Portuguesa." https://www.cplp.org/Files/Filer/Documentos%20Essenciais/DeclaraoConstitutivaCPLP.pdf.
CPLP (2007). "Estatutos da Comunidade dos Países de Língua Portuguesa." https://www.cplp.org/Files/Filer/Documentos%20Essenciais/Estatutos_CPLP_REVLIS07.pdf.
Estevens, A. (2017). *A Cidade Neoliberal: Conflito e Arte em Lisboa e em Barcelona*. Lisbon: Outro Modo/Deriva Editores/Le Monde Diplomatique.
Fikes, K. (2009). *Managing African Portugal: The Citizen-Migrant Distinction*. Durham, NC: Duke University Press.
Foucault, M. ([1969] 2004). *The Archeology of Knowledge*. London: Routledge.
Foucault, M. (1971). "Orders of Discourse." *Social Science Information*, 10(2): 7–30.
Hall, S. (1999). "Thinking the Diaspora: Home-Thoughts from Abroad." *Small Axe*, 6: 1–18.
Hall, S. (2000). "The Multicultural Question." In B. Hesse (ed.), *Un/settled Multiculturalisms: Diasporas, Entanglements, Trans-Ruptions*, 209–41. Londres: Zed.
Hall, S. (2017). *The Fateful Triangle: Race, Ethnicity and Nation*. Cambridge, MA: Harvard University Press.
Kymlicka, W. (1995). *Multicultural Citizenship: A Liberal Theory of Minority Rights*. Oxford: Clarendon.
Lazar, S. (2013). "Introduction." In *The Anthropology of Citizenship*, 1–22. Oxford: Willey Blackwell.
Losa, L. (2019). " 'Ser Fadista é maior que ser Cantor': Intersubjectividade, Voz e o Ethos da Memória." PhD diss., Faculty of Social Sciences and Humanities, New University of Lisbon.
Maciel, C. (2010). "A Construção da Comunidade Lusófona a partir do Antigo Centro. Micro-comunidades e Práticas da Lusofonia." PhD diss., Faculty of Social Sciences and Humanities, New University of Lisbon.
Moorman, M. (2008). *Intonations: A Social History of Music and Nation in Luanda, Angola, from 1945 to Recent Times*. Athens: Ohio University Press.
Oliveira, N. (2013). "Lisboa redescobre-se: A governança da diversidade cultural na cidade pós-colonial. A scenescape da Mouraria." In N. Domingos and E. Peralta (eds.),

Cidade e Império: Dinâmicas Coloniais e Reconfigurações Pós-coloniais, 557–602. Lisboa: Edições 70.

Pardue, D. (2015). *Cape Verde Let's Go: Creole Rappers and Citizenship in Portugal*. Urbana: University of Illinois Press.

Ribeiro, M. C., and A. P. Ferreira (2003). "Apresentação." In M. C. Ribeiro and A. P. Ferreira (eds.), *Fantasmas e Fantasias Imperiais no Imaginário Português Contemporâneo*, 9–28. Porto: Campo das Letras.

Sanchez, I. (2016). "'Ai, Mouraria!' Music, Tourism and Urban Renewal in a Historic Lisbon Neighborhood." *MUSICultures*, 43(2): 66–88.

Sousa, H. (2006). "A mobilização do conceito de lusofonia: o caso dos canais internacionais da RTP." In M. L. Martins, H. Sousa, and R. Cabecinhas (eds.), *Comunicação e Lusofonia: para uma Abordagem Crítica da Cultura e dos Media*, 165–82. Porto: Campo das Letras.

Taylor, C. (1994). "The Politics of Recognition," in A. Gutmann (ed.), *Multiculturalism*, 25–73. Princeton, NJ: Princeton University Press.

Vanspauwen, B. (2010). "The (R)evolution of Lusophone Musics in the City of Lisbon." MA diss., Faculty of Social Sciences and Humanities, New University of Lisbon.

Chapter 10

COLONIAL REVIVALISM AND THE BESTSELLING PUBLISHING

João Pedro George

The history of the fifteen years prior to the fall of Portuguese colonial rule (1960–75) has recently become the topic of a revivalist trend in the production of commercially successful and widely popular literary works. Most of the books that can be framed within this revivalist surge have become bestsellers. All the books researched in this chapter were produced by major publishing houses within a Portuguese context of editorial and bookseller concentration.[1] Twelve were published by labels belonging to the Leya Group, and the rest were distributed by Esfera dos Livros (two), Grupo Planeta (one), and Gradiva (one).

In the present economic environment, decision-making powers on what is or is not published have passed from the hands of the editors to the editorial boards, where managers and those responsible for marketing have increasing authority. An identical process is currently underway in terms of retail and distribution, involving companies such as the French group FNAC, and Sonae, one of Portugal's biggest commercial groups, whose businesses include the sale of books in hypermarkets and large commercial stores. In such large editorial conglomerates, where market theory is uniformly and aggressively applied to the mediation and dissemination of culture, the commercial, accounting, and sales departments tend to interfere in editorial decisions.

In generalist-oriented publishers obsessed with financial results and the constant pressure to generate larger and more immediate profits, the search for books depends strictly on commercial and entertainment purposes (Schiffrin 2000). To reach wider audiences, the strategy followed by the commercial departments of these publishers is to expand the spectrum of new market territories, that is, those that in each situation, and in the short term, promise to be the most profitable. The encirclement created by the expectations of profit is expressed in the increase in the number of books published each year and in the number of books that replicate each other, driven by a previously drawn script whose ideas, views, and themes are uniformly indistinct and based on historical stereotypes, so that they can be shared by the maximum number of readers (Schiffrin 2000).

This strategy also involved the active selection by and commissioning from famous figures or celebrities, attracted by offers to flag their names. For example, a report in the newspaper *Diário de Notícias* (December 22, 2008) revealed that "the means by which the two editors [from Oficina do Livro] followed novelist Miguel Sousa Tavares' creative process, from beginning to end, is a little unusual in Portuguese editorial activity." Similarly, months earlier (February 24, 2008), interviewed by the newspaper *Correio da Manhã*, the journalist and novelist Júlio Magalhães revealed: "I never asked any publisher to write books. I am invited to write . . . A year ago, I was invited to write a romanticized work about Africa in a journalistic style, taking a historical fact as my starting point."

These two authors are among the individuals with enormous media exposure, especially journalists, who have become the main vehicles of the current wave of Portuguese colonial revivalism.[2] In Portugal, this new editorial trend, which reproduces a whole tradition of colonial literature (Meyers 1973; Said 1994; Quayson 2015), dates back to the pre- and postrevolutionary period of the 1970s and 1980s (George 2021). The two waves share common themes that are clearly identifiable as the mythification of African landscape and its wilderness, the almost absence of colonized peoples, and the pleasant and comfortable life of Portuguese settlers in the colonial capitals of Angola (Luanda) and Mozambique (Lourenço Marques). The pace of development there was faster, hard work was rewarded with economic and social upward mobility, and life was more informal, relaxed, and carefree. However, unlike the postrevolutionary wave, the current revivalism is led by large commercial publishers. They helped to multiply and disseminate a set of colonial representations that have always circulated among some groups, particularly of the so-called returnees (*retornados*) (Pires 1999, 2003), but which had never received such wide circulation.

Bestsellers on Portuguese Colonialism

In recent years, almost four decades after the Carnation Revolution (1974) and the definitive dissolution of Portugal's imperial domain (1975), publishers have strongly promoted the publication of books set in or dealing with the Portuguese colonial presence in Africa. Most of these works have been published in the past two decades and can be framed within what we could call the memory of the colonial period. These popular books are a subgenre—undoubtedly one with specific characteristics—within literature with a wide dissemination. In fact, all of them were published in Portugal during a period when popular history, used both in fiction and nonfiction, became very fashionable. While popular books of this kind have always existed in Portugal (Marinho 1999, 2005), since the beginning of the twenty-first century, historical novels have gained an increased impetus and become a significant publishing phenomenon (Tavares 2006),[3] promoted by publishers such as A Esfera dos Livros, established in Portugal since 2006 (Cunha 2020). Sofia Monteiro, the chief editor of A Esfera dos Livros in 2014, would claim at the time that in Portugal, history "was an area that had been very little explored.

History was not seen as a product for the public."[4] In order to follow this strategy, A Esfera dos Livros commissioned a series of books from authors, many of whom were public figures such as journalists and professional historians (Cunha 2020).

All the sixteen books analyzed here—ten novels and six pieces of investigative journalism (see the list of titles at the end of the chapter)—were authored by prominent journalists. Their plots are set in Angola (eight), Mozambique (three), Guinea-Bissau (one), and São Tomé e Príncipe (one), as well as three others whose settings cross several different colonial contexts. The success of these books—twelve of the sixteen books considered have had two or more editions—relied heavily on their author's public recognition, some of whom have become widely known for their production of works in the fiction genre.

Indeed, some of the novels in question, for instance, those by journalists Miguel Sousa Tavares, José Rodrigues dos Santos, and Júlio Magalhães, are currently in their thirty-eighth, twenty-fourth, and twentieth editions, respectively. Over the past few decades, Tavares has become one of the best-known journalists, writers, and television commentators in Portugal; Santos is a journalist from the public television broadcaster (RTP), where he has for several years now been a news anchor of the evening prime-time television news; Magalhães also made his career as a news anchor in the public television sector, later moving to a major private television channel (TVI), where he became chief news editor. He currently hosts a radio show in the new digital media channel *Observador*.

This category of books is intrinsically related to the diffusion circuits of general media channels. These three authors have virtually become household names (and faces) of Portuguese television. They are also often portrayed in chronicles of society magazines, featuring either the release of new books or their social life and presence at weddings, parties, and other events. Some of these books were even adapted for television with great success, such as Tavares's *Ecuador*.[5] This media exposure, which is enhanced by the strategies devised by aggressive sales teams and an extremely efficient network of contacts with newspapers, magazines, and television channels, is a catalyst for books on a national or even international scale.

The power of persuasion and the popular acceptability of these books also rely on the fact that their content is centered on a specific period, which is the Portuguese presence in African territories before the collapse of the empire. The end of an empire with nearly five hundred years of existence in Portugal was undoubtedly one of the most important events of the Portuguese twentieth century. Understandably, it still echoes deeply in the memory of many people who experienced it and who are still alive, people who lived in Africa and their relatives who never left Portugal, but also those who lived there and fought there, in the colonial wars.

For the returnees, many of whom were poorly received or viewed with suspicion in metropolitan Portugal after their repatriation in 1975, these books give cultural substance and social legitimacy to their life experiences in the colonies, together with a sense of comfort, familiarity, and even a personal recognition, which we might equate with a sense of empowerment. They are, in other words, the unmistakable demonstration that this past was not insignificant (Lubkemann 2003;

Peralta et al. 2017; Peralta 2019). By giving social importance to the biographical material of many readers, this recognition, that many still consider themselves creditors, is an important reason to buy and consume these books.

This phenomenon is further enhanced by the autobiographical character of some stories. Such is the case of *Os Retornados: Um Amor Nunca se Esquece* (Returnees: love is unforgettable; 2008), a novel by Júlio Magalhães, which addresses his own experience of repatriation. Tiago Rebelo too, author of *O Último Ano em Luanda* (The last year in Luanda; 2009), left the capital of Angola with his parents and brother on July 14, 1975 (when he was eleven years old). José Robrigues dos Santos's novel—*O Anjo Branco* (The white angel; 2010)—was equally inspired by his father's African experiences as a doctor commissioned in Tete (northern Mozambique) by the colonial administration, where he lived with his wife and children. Even though most of these novels cannot be considered strictly autobiographical memories, their privileged position in relation to persons who experienced or were very close to the events, and the very idea of first-hand material and testimonies, have certainly imbued these works with a value of trustworthiness; memories acquire verisimilitude or plausibility by being signed by authors who "were there" (Genette 1990).

Such attributes provide key knowledge to readers, trigger their expectations, and are an asset that can be capitalized on through marketing. The promotion of a book, in a medium characterized by the cult or devotion of exceptional figures—as all cultural creators, in some way, continue to be seen—becomes easier if a connection is established between the plot and the author's life trajectory (Green 2004).

Para-textual Speech

Para-textual elements are advertising vehicles whose main objective is to promote sales. The book covers, back covers, book flaps, prefaces, footnotes, photographs, and illustrations give a global image of books, guide their reception, and create reading expectations; they also suggest or propose interpretations, explain and justify the authors' purposes, and provide clues about the plot and the topics covered. In short, they sell a book as socially relevant, explain to readers why they should read that book—and how it should be read—and try to persuade them of the merits of authors and their works (Genette 1997; Buchanan 2010).

All the books addressed in this chapter can be interpreted as attempts to persuade and cajole anyone who was ever in touch with this experience of Africa, seeking to convey the illusion that their own narratives make them more able than others to penetrate the interiority of the characters (or at least to feel closer to the content). According to the back cover of *África Eterna: Testemunhos de um tempo que não se esquece* (Eternal Africa: testimonials of a time you won't forget; 2012), this book speaks directly to the reader: "Who knows, this may also be your history."[6] Similarly, *Deixei o Meu Coração em África* (I left my heart in Africa; 2005) is sold with a small round sticker on the cover with the teaser "For those who still love Africa." Yet another example, when it originally appeared, *Lourenço Marques* (2002), had a strap around the book that announced the book as a work "For those who were happy in Africa."

Either on the flaps or on the back covers, these books sell the imagination of happiness and the good life in the former colonies. On the back cover of *Angola, Terra Prometida: A vida que os portugueses deixaram* (Angola, promised land: the life that the Portuguese left; 2009), the publisher promotes the idea of a period of "golden years," the "best years in the life of many Portuguese who, in Angola, found a warm and generous land." This fact is confirmed by the reference to the "tranquil view of Luanda bay," the "hot sea baths," the "smell of the land," the "lobsters," the "ripe fruit," the "cold beer," and so on. *Luanda como ela era 1960–1975* (Luanda as it was 1960–75; 2016) is publicized as a book about the "happy memories of those who lived there," and in *Os Retornados* the author writes about his "homeland, where he lived the best years of his life."

These para-textual elements also emphasize the liberal lifestyles associated with the economic development of the colonies during the Portuguese dictatorship. The back cover of Garcia's book *Luanda como ela era*, set in Angola, refers to "the euphoria of economic growth" and the "freedom of customs"—significantly, the title itself includes the expression "promised land." Modern colonial Luanda is also represented as an "irresistible city" (*Luanda como ela era*), as the "the jewel of the Portuguese empire" (*Os Retornados*), or "the jewel capital of the crown of the Portuguese empire" (*O Último Ano em Luanda*).

The mirror effect in these books demands a claim to reality that provides evidence of colonial life "as it was" (Garcia's title). Accordingly, the blurbs on back covers and flaps refer to "portraits," as in these examples: "For many the novel that best portrays the society of Portuguese Africa and the Colonial War" (*Deixei o meu coração em África*); "*Equador* is a brilliant portrait of Portuguese society in the last days of the Monarchy"; *O Último Ano em Luanda* "draws a portrait of the capital's mundane evenings and the harsh and backward atmosphere of the colonies"; *Angola, terra prometida* "traces the portrait of these golden years"; and *Os Que Vieram de África: O drama da nova vida das famílias chegadas do Ultramar* (Those who came from Africa: the drama of the new life of families arriving from overseas; 2012) presents us with "the portrait of a small country grappling with a colossal task."

These books seek also to function as virtual "time machines"; for instance, *Lourenço Marques* is "a novel that revives the Mozambique from the seventies," and *Luanda como ela era* consists of a "trip to the past that will make you remember every corner, custom and taste of Luanda that still exists only in the happy memories of those who lived there."

The construction of this reality depends on an affective framework that awakens feelings and predisposes the readers' spirit to the outpouring of emotions: *Os Retornados* takes us on "a journey of emotions"; "it was there [Luanda] that our hearts beat faster" (*A Balada do Ultramar*—The ballad of overseas; 2009); *Angola, terra prometida* is "a book of memories, stories, and emotions. Of homesickness"; *Deixei o meu coração em África* tells us a "story written from the heart of those who lived in Africa and left it there forever"; *África Eterna* guarantees that "Africa remains in the heart of the Portuguese."

Although this Africa no longer exists, it is still present in the memories of those who lived it. In this context, remembering "is a balm that helps to heal many wounds" (*A Balada do Ultramar*). Taken as emotional shelters or refuges, from which people derive emotional comfort, these fictional narratives use the universally consumable motif of the romantic love story, which is a common dimension in all types of bestsellers (Illouz 1997, 1998; Hochschild 2012; Brooks 2019). The back cover of *Lourenço Marques* mentions how the capital of Mozambique—the "city of acacias, the pearl of the Indian Ocean"—was the city where the protagonist fell in love for the first time, so that "27 years after leaving Mozambique, he returns to look for the woman he loved"; *Deixei o meu coração em África* is defined as a story of "love in times of war"; *Retornados* describes, among other things, the love between the narrator and a flight attendant (Joana) who worked on one of the planes that, during the Air Bridge, brought returnees to Portugal; *O Último Ano em Luanda* tells the adventures of a couple in love who, having separated because of the civil war in Angola, "fight to survive" in the midst of chaos, horror, and insecurity.

The comfortable colonial lifestyle takes on a more conflicted political dimension in the face of an irreversible decolonization process. It is only at that moment that notions of justice and injustice, responsibility and irresponsibility, guilt and excuse are mobilized by the returnees to explain the meaning of what happened to them: "the anguish of those who lost everything and had to start a new life" (cover flap of *A Balada do Ultramar*); the inevitability of having to drop everything and escape, through an "air and sea bridge that marks the greatest exodus in the history of this people" (back cover of *O Último Ano em Luanda*). All this is followed by the hardships of a precipitate and undesired arrival in Portugal, "the uncertain future in a society they did not know, hostile to their presence," in which "they went hungry and cold, faced unemployment and lived huddled in degraded houses or rooms" (cover flap of *Os que vieram de África*), "an arrival in Lisbon with the only patrimony that was saved and contact with a society so different that it looked with suspicion at these new people" (back cover of *África Eterna*).

Colonial Iconography

The images reproduced in many of these books, especially those of a journalistic or documentary nature, are crucial para-textual elements. For the readers who lived in the colonies, or for the returnees who remain attached to these images, tangible things like photographs or books become material aids that reduce the distance from the past, confirming and reframing historical and autobiographical experiences.

While photographs are effective as indexes of reality that confer objectivity and lend verisimilitude to subjective experience and memory, selected by the publishers they not only narrate the past but also speak of the present. Additionally, the authority of the photographs chosen is inseparable from the authority (in the sense of authorship) of those who took them. These are photographs that fix and shape the gaze of white colonists on the way the colonial world was organized; it is their perspective that these images fix or shape (Blanchard et al. 2018). Through these images, we are led to look back upon that past through the same lens or through the same gaze as the white colonists of the time, so that their lifestyle, what they had and enjoyed, the pleasures and leisure, the places of partying, sport, and friendly interaction can be remembered and relived. Faced with these photographs, readers who have been in Africa can find themselves in them and establish relationships between the scenarios therein reproduced and their own biography. For those who do lack that lived experience, such an identification can be made indirectly through the more complex contextualization of a postcolonial national history, as it continues to be generally taught in schools (Araújo and Maeso 2011; Viana 2011). Hence, it is not only the returnees' lifestyle that becomes the object of desire and fascination, it is the colonial past itself that comes to be observed with an aesthetic interest (Vicente 2014).

The fascination or appeal that these documents elicit, however, cannot serve to hide the fact that we are dealing with images that establish a double segregation. On the one hand, by massively reproducing the scenarios where white leisure activities took place, these images reinforce the illusion that among the colonists there were no hierarchies or social inequalities. Put more crudely, in these images you never see the poor, as if the white poor did not exist, some of whom lived in the suburbs of Luanda and Lourenço Marques among the Black African population (Ferreira 1955; Curto 2020). Paradigmatic of this is the image on the book cover of *Lourenço Marques*: a photograph of several white settlers (fourteen adults, three of whom are women, and two children, dating from 1925) on the terrace of the famous and luxurious Hotel Polana, erected as a symbol of the Portuguese presence in Mozambique. But the contrasts between the lives of whites and Blacks are never exposed; the wide world of Blacks that surrounded white settlers is completely absent.

By exclusively representing the colonists' microcosm, from which Blacks are invariably excluded, these photographs can be analyzed from a double point of view. First, as the involuntary recreation of the true characteristics of a colonial world that discriminated against Black people, and as the maintenance and reaffirmation, today, of the values of a colonial culture that segregated Blacks. Second, by isolating details of the colonists' lives—detaching them from the wider setting that comprised the colonial environment—they can be seen as further obscuring the past, as mystification rather than clarification, as the extension of an idealized colonial world, false and without historical depth, which reproduces the exclusion of Blacks and segregates them from their own past. As subsidiaries of colonial power, these narratives continue, therefore, to serve the vision of white settlers, in whose history Blacks are almost never situated, forcing us to establish relations of continuity with the present and posing, for example, the question of knowing to whom the meaning of that past belongs.

Colonial Representations and the Bestseller Formula

Almost all the works under analysis fix their gaze on the social experience of white settlers and spread a selective memory of the colonial period, where Blacks and their conditions of life are practically absent (with the consequent implication of hiding the political and institutional dimension on which the exercise of power in the colonies was based). But what representation do these books convey of the African colonial context, in the light of editorial codes that seek to approach an imaginary reader created in the marketing departments of publishers, through the adaptation of the plot, the characters, the context of the action, and the tone of the language to the conditions or characteristics of a bestseller?

To engage with this imaginary reader, the theme of love, explored in all types of bestsellers (Illouz 1997, 1998; Hochschild 2012), is the usual strategy. *Lourenço Marques, Retornados, Equador*, and *O Último Ano em Luanda*, for instance, are based on the premise of love as an obstinate goal (but which takes on a more rampant, and consequently more metaphorical, dimension in Africa). This includes the use of recurring issues such as obstacles to the union of lovers or marital crises. With their plot taking place in the period immediately before the independence and the massive flight of the returnees, this love is born, strengthened, or put to the test in a highly dramatic context, whose ingredients are despair, fear of dying, helplessness, emotional exhaustion, anguish. Hence the titles with the words "drama" or "SOS," or expressions like "the last year in Luanda" or the "life that the Portuguese left," placing these stories under the sign of fatality and tension and inviting the reader to establish an emotional engagement with the fate of the characters.

The fact that the relationships between the characters develop in an environment that is as grandiose as it is rife with dangers—fitting into the aesthetic category of the sublime (Mothersill 1997)—also expands the potential for romantic adventures. Thus, romantic stories that take place in environments of frustration, where love is hailed as the force that helps characters to overcome adversity, are another classic bestseller scheme. After all, love is a universal feeling so powerful that it can change the course of human actions, relationships, and events.

The romantic heroes of these novels are always Caucasian and beautiful, courteous, jovial, and sensitive; they are never paunchy, bald, or socially incompetent—especially with the opposite sex. In *A Jóia de África* (Jewel of Africa; 2003), Joana is the "most beautiful woman in Africa," she has "the lion's wild blond hair, the ivory-white skin, the blue, green and gray eyes like the colors of the Indian Ocean, and the cheeks of the sunset that spreads over the savannah" (Arouca 2003: 17). Significantly, intimate relationships between men (invariably white) and women (whether white or Black) tend to replicate the hunter-prey dichotomy: "But later, after leaving Matilde's room that night and the hotel the following morning, he [Luís Bernardo] had, as always, only the pride of a satisfied hunter" (Sousa Tavares 2008: 59).

Still following the bestseller's formula (Hall 2012; Archer and Jockers 2016; Bessard-Banquy et al. 2021), the fiction books analyzed here are sexualized narratives, fertile in erotic passages or even purely explicit sex scenes that reinforce the masculinity of the characters, including the narrator. To keep the readers' interest, the "complexities" of the heart and the carnal enjoyments tend to override their ideological anxieties and the pressing social and political issues of colonial reality.

Historical Narration

In these plots, members of the native populations never feature in leading roles but can appear either as healers or sorcerers, with visions that are beyond rational explanations (e.g., *A Jóia de África* and *Lourenço Marques*), or as submissive and naive servants (*Equador* and *O Anjo Branco*). The locals can also awaken the wild instincts or the carnal passions of the white settlers, as in *A Jóia de África* when the author describes the effects that the presence of Biti, daughter of the *régulo* (chief), has upon Miguel: "Miguel, with the most primitive impulses running through his body, like a wild animal as it senses that the prey [a Black woman] is within reach" (Arouca 2003: 110).

Self-recognition and reorganization of personal events experienced in the past are narrative patterns that help to explain the cognitive dissonance between the highly idealized account of colonists' personal and family memories and the systematic exclusion of references and information relating to atrocities, misery, executions, sexual abuse, and humiliation of the colonized; these practices were consistent with the colonial experience and a trait of the lifestyle and social position of many white Portuguese people.

While they ignore the misery of the local indigenous populations during the period of Portuguese domination, these books commonly describe and emphasize the current misery found in those same African territories after independence, through desolate portraits of worn-out streets, lack of drinking water, rationing, deserted old gardens, garbage bins, street kids sniffing glue, piercing their arms with syringes or just drinking beer, the world of prisons (Viegas 2002: 193; Rebelo 2009: 445; Magalhães 2008: 131). To preserve the sense of comfort and prevent any ideological confliction in the readers, the ideas expressed by the characters or triggered by the situations and events avoid confronting the social, political, religious, and cultural conventions.

It is not surprising, therefore, that the narratives are conventional and cautious, aiming first to satisfy and confirm their readers' expectations, for whom books are mainly a source of entertainment and reading is a leisure activity, but who also seek them as a source of information, as means to learn about this period of the country's history through more accessible cultural products. The very elementary and Manichean recourse to history is limited to the external and superficial observation of events. This is achieved through its insertion into the narrative, either through the psychological construction of the characters or by using typical journalistic reports of a historical nature that do not contradict aesthetic requirements and the need for evasion.

To meet the tastes of their readers, the revivalist discourse conveyed in these novels takes the form of a scenic spectacle that relies on the associative component of memory through which a "utopia of the past" or "retrotopia" (Bauman 2017) is staged; this is an idealized past to which readers travel recreationally, in order to satisfy their need for exoticism and information from distant regions, perceived as fascinating, fantastic, exciting, strange, and fearful (Huggan 2001; Nederveen Pieterse 1992).

Lost Paradise and Romanticism

These dramas unfold in a natural context—the African landscape—described as a special or wonderful world, which mixes real and fantastic elements. As places of phantasmic projection, they are built and reconstructed to respond, on the imaginary plane—as in a postcard or hologram—to the ubiquitous theme of the "lost tropical paradise." Such representation is achieved through the use of expressions such as "the simple pleasures of a tropical paradise" (Garcia 2016: 28), "an African Eden" (Borges 2020: 42), "the garden of delights referred to in the Bible," and "our piece of paradise" (Acácio 2009: 41, 70), or "we are together, you and me, in this paradise" (Rebelo 2009: 26).

Images of a mythical Africa, of a nature yet to be domesticated, of an Arcadian existence in a world still in gestation, evoking paradise, and the fertility of planet Earth's beginnings, become the landscape and setting where the colonists can enjoy an original representation of nature. In *Equador*, for example, Angolans who were forcibly displaced to work in the fields of São Tomé and Príncipe "wept for their other Africa, for open plains, for grass dried in the sun, for animals running free, for the bush where lions stalk zebras and leopards silently pursue antelope, for rivers navigated in frail canoes between sleeping alligators and hippopotami, for nights in the savannah, listening to cries from the jungle" (Sousa Tavares 2008: 122). This mystique of the African natural beauty, of savannas extending as far as the eye can see, of landscapes that add up to wonders adjust to the touristification and commodification of memory (Nattrass 2021).

The romanticism of African nature is notoriously associated with hunting activities, evident in the photographs of settlers posing beside dead animals. Sensory images further enhance this type of representation: "the noises of the evening," "the afternoon light," "the red earth," "the smell of guava and mango," "the smell of the night," "the hot and humid smell," "the suffocating heat and humidity," or, as the cover of *África Eterna* says, "even today, several decades after decolonization, countless thousands of people remember the sunset in the bay of Luanda, the weekends spent on the island of Mozambique, the odyssey of crossing the savannah for days to visit friends."

Such imagery reproduces the emotional and pantheistic bond between the Portuguese and those lands: "we never truly managed to free ourselves from Africa," "Africa remains in the hearts of the Portuguese," the Portuguese "left their souls in Africa," they have "the blood of Africa running through [their] veins," "Africa remains alive and endures in the hearts of the Portuguese," and "they bring Angola to the soul."

The adventure of wildlife acquires all its relevance in contrast to the hard-working Europeans on farms, in the tea, coffee, and tobacco plantations, in the diamond mines, and so on. The bush and the black villages are a counterpoint to the colonial power and authority responsible for carrying out major works and modern urban development, which delimited the known, protected, and predictable world of roads and wide avenues, colonial architecture in modern buildings (some of them lined with seaside roads), in fortresses, in military clubs, in "an enviable school network," in "a modern and advanced health system" that "made Angola an attractive country with a future that could place it close to the great world powers."

But what stands out most starkly in these evocations of the colonial past are descriptions of leisure and places of entertainment, fun, sport, and sociability. The confused evocation of the settlers' leisure facilities—endless pages densely filled with redundant and stressful listings, which seek to reproduce the disordered rhythm of memories—is obligatory in these exercises of revivalism. To instill in the reader the idea of duration, the feeling of something that endures through time or becomes unforgettable and incomparable, these books obsessively repeat certain terms, words, or expressions associated with a dense psychological time: "a scenario that he could not forget," that "he will never forget," that "he could never forget," "this world has not ended, this world has never ended," "would come back to that image several times throughout his life" (Viegas 2002: 88, 29, 51).

In contrast with this idealized past, the moment of the return, after April 25, 1974, is characterized by misfortune, despair, sadness, and the struggle for a better life on the European continent: "for many, living no longer made sense," "a broken heart," "a heart full of nothing," in the heart "there was not even room for a glimmer of hope," "misfortune touched everyone," the need to "cut the umbilical cord with Africa once and for all."

Such stylistic resources, triggered to awaken a world whose laws of perception many readers feel as "truer," still tend to naturalize the idea of the exceptionalism of the Portuguese colonies in relation to the metropolis (Cahen and Matos 2018). On the one hand, by implicitly creating the feeling that capitalism was more dynamic in the colonies, with fragrant esplanades, crowded restaurants (where a drink such as Coke, banned in the metropolis, was freely sold), commercial establishments, more dynamic companies, and industries, and so on. On the other hand, through explicit descriptions of informal, joyous, relaxed, and carefree lifestyles; where, for instance, youths enjoyed a more liberal education and parents were not so strict in matters of coexistence between the two sexes, where boys and girls could go together to the beach, to the movies, and to parties at each other's houses; where dating was less controlled; where women could wear low necklines and miniskirts; and where men did not always have to wear a suit and tie to work.

The World in Reverse

Most of these texts convey the false impression that there were no class differences between white settlers—"bosses and employees could sit side by side for a whiskey and soda, a gin and tonic or a beer at Baleizão (known, above all, for ice cream)"—but also, in a way, between whites and Blacks: "If, on land, whites lived on paved streets and blacks in *musseques* (suburbs of Luanda), on the beach they were all the same" (Garcia 2016: 31).

The image of a daily life that was both peaceful and pleasure-friendly, without conflicts, oppositions, or resistance, is awkward in a context of a colonial war that lasted thirteen years across three military scenarios simultaneously (Angola, Mozambique, and Guinea-Bissau) and involved about one million Portuguese soldiers. Despite being mentioned in these books—and even assuming a central role in *Deixei o Meu Coração em África* and in *O Anjo Branco*—the war never seems to jeopardize the joyful memories. Ultimately, once the decolonization processes were under way, the history of the "good ones" (the white developmentalist settlers and the abstractly loyal and obedient Blacks) is replaced by the history of the "bad ones" (Blacks in general, treacherous, and violent, and the white politicians and military officers that were responsible for decolonization). It is only from this moment onward that colonized Africans finally gain actual subjectivity.

Most importantly, this colonial revivalism, based on the equivocal description of homogeneously white societies, recreates and reproduces the marginalization of the colonized. The fleeting appearances of Blacks and some situations of racial discrimination are far from conveying an image, even approximate, of a social context marked by injustice and segregation, to which most of the non-Europeans living in those regions were subjected. Apparently, the lifestyle enjoyed by colonists prevented them from seeing the suburbs they had to cross to reach the beaches. Mentioned only vaguely and tangentially, the neighborhoods in the suburbs of Luanda (*Musseques*) and Lourenço Marques (*Caniços*)—lacking basic infrastructure and sanitary conditions, subject to arbitrary, degradation, and violent attacks either by the colonial authorities or by some colonists, in search of women to fornicate freely—do not seem to deserve even a modicum of attention from these authors.

Nevertheless, the world described above, closed upon itself, did have a reverse; a world of easements and extreme needs, systematically erased from the colonial imagination displayed in these books. The human range of Blacks and the oppressive circle to which they were subjected are deliberately ignored, not least because it might compromise publishers' commercial expectations and rationales.

This compartmentalization of the white environment, where Blacks do not circulate (despite the widespread knowledge that many settler families had Black servants, many of whom took care of their white children) is not neutral; it results from a conscious editorial option as well as a choice of the authors themselves. They choose not to consider the foundations of the Portuguese colonial project, the regimes of intensive colonial exploitation, which depended on the economic value of forced Black labor on farms, plantations, and mines or the daily work of servants (which responded to the commercial and domestic interests of city settlers) and the violence and the brutality involved.

Moreover, in these books, the Portuguese are never described as an occupying power, whose presence was achieved through forceful expropriation and often violent domination that destroyed hunters and indigenous shepherds, that operated violent physical and social relocations of native villages (Curto et al. 2016), and that dramatically and forcibly reduced the rights of those individuals. An occupying power that imposed legal codes, regulations, and the payment of taxes, which resulted, for example, in huge restrictions on the agricultural development of Black producers.

Thus, these books help to perpetuate the historical invisibility of the colonized by selling a distorted image of that historical situation, reediting a certain ideological view of the past, thereby contributing to encapsulate the rhetoric of Portuguese civilizational exemplarity.

Conclusion

The editorial codes inscribed in the books analyzed here seek to accommodate the codes of a projected or imaginary reader devised by the marketing departments of publishers, notably by adapting the plot, characters, context of action, and language tone to the conditions or characteristics of the bestseller. Evidently, the first and sole objective of this approach or editorial strategy is to produce highly profitable books. This implies a narrative plan whose criteria are inevitably found outside what we might call the realm of authorial creativity, thus highlighting the interplay between cultural production and economic rationality in the book sector.

Therefore, Portuguese colonialism has been the object of instrumentalization by highly professionalized business structures—publishing conglomerates—through a mixture of emotional intensity, partial and simplified historical information, and glorification of a collectively significant national past (Volvic and Andrejevic 2016). To make them even more profitable, they are signed by famous journalists with a particular popular appeal. Many of the elements present in these bestselling books reproduced a whole tradition of Portuguese colonial literature and are variations on old themes, that is, they emerged as an intensification of Portuguese literary traditions of its colonial past. This past, in the form of the ambiguous term "colonial," has been part of a continuous present in Portugal throughout the past half century.

Portuguese colonial revival in bestselling literature is much more than a new phenomenon; it is a social, political, and commercial manifestation of an ongoing relationship between past and present. An initial phase defined by a postrevolutionary returnee literature (until the second half of the 1970s), mostly of an autobiographical nature and published by less professionalized publishing houses (George 2021), gave way to a literature of historical dissemination, less autobiographical, authored by mediatic individuals—many of them journalists— and produced for the market by highly professionalized commercial publishers.

Today, this revivalism has an evident economic dimension. The success of these books is closely bound to a set of factors that are independent of the colonial theme, namely the formulas of popular literature that have given birth to numerous bestsellers. These formulas combine love, sex, beautiful women, white protagonists (the chief target audience for these books) in search of happiness, exoticism, the mystique and evasive role of African nature, and the lost tropical paradise and weave them into simplistic dichotomous schemes (good versus evil), conservative worldviews, and avoidance of confronting political conventions (e.g., in the suppression of the grim or darker realities of colonial life). These are works aimed at fulfilling an individual need to revisit aspects of lost youth, a desire to remember some episodes of that golden age. A desire, we should note, that is not specific to colonial life stories. On the contrary, it is a common need, and it refers to the objective and subjective importance of finding a common thread capable of unifying, giving meaning, and socially legitimizing the selective and fragmentary memories of the past, whether or not they include colonial experiences.

These books materialized at the height of the novel and essay of historical dissemination, at a time when the idealization or reconstruction of a supposed integrity and authenticity of the past, as well as the "appeals to lost heritages," have acquired more and more commodity value and are sold as a consumer good (MacCannell 1992). But they also emerged at a time when interest in the Portuguese colonial past has expanded in the spheres of academic and scientific research, in the realm of political debates and struggles, and in the public space generally—a phenomenon that partly explains the success of these books. What remains to be demonstrated is whether such an interest is a cause or a consequence of the current movement that we are witnessing in Portugal of public denouncement of and political struggle against structural racism. As I have tried to show, what we do know is that the power to articulate revivalist feelings through cultural products remains clearly in the hands of the market—in this case, the large editorial groups (Werry 2005; Miller 2006; Thompson 2010)—and some dominant groups (e.g., entrepreneurs, publishers, renowned journalists) in the public sphere.

Notes

1 Defined by the purchase of companies and the formation of large groups, examples of which are Porto Editora and Leya.
2 The concept of "revivalism" relates here to how different cultural productions from the past are updated, to give them a present veneer and use.
3 However, fiction based on historical colonial facts had existed since at least the beginning of the 1980s. For example, in 1984, the novel *José do Telhado em África*, by Eduardo Noronha, was published and had four editions.
4 "Quando a história vira romance" (2014), *Notícias Magazine*, November 27. https://www.noticiasmagazine.pt/2014/quando-a-historia-vira-romance/historias/9255/ (accessed August 24, 2021).
5 *Ecuador* premiered in Portugal in December 2008. It was also later screened Brazil in October 2011. Between December 2008 and July 2009, millions of spectators watched the thirty episodes of the series, which was broadcast every Sunday in TVI's prime-time slot and became the biggest and most expensive Portuguese television production ever.

6   Apart from *Ecuador*, already translated into English, all book titles, flaps, back covers, and excerpts have been translated by the author of this chapter from the original Portuguese editions.

References

List of Books Analyzed

1. AA.VV. (2012). *África Eterna: Testemunhos de um tempo que não se esquece*. Lisbon: Oficina do Livro.
2. Acácio, M. (2009). *A Balada do Ultramar*. Lisbon: Oficina do Livro.
3. Adamapoulos, S. (2012). *Voltar: Memória do colonialismo e da descolonização*. Lisbon: Planeta.
4. Arouca, M. (2003). *A Jóia de África*. Lisbon: Texto Editora.
5. Arouca, M. (2005). *Deixei o Meu Coração em África*. Lisbon: Oficina do Livro.
6. Borges, D. (2020). *Amor Eterno*. Lisbon: Oficina do Livro.
7. Fonseca, A. S. (2009). *Angola, terra prometida: A vida que os portugueses deixaram*. Lisbon: A Esfera dos Livros.
8. Garcia, R. (2011). *SOS Angola: Os Dias da Ponte Aérea*. Lisbon: Oficina do Livro.
9. Garcia, R. (2012). *Os Que Vieram de África: O drama da nova vida das famílias chegadas do Ultramar*. Lisbon: Oficina do Livro.
10. Garcia, R. (2016). *Luanda como ela era 1960–1975*. Lisbon: Oficina do Livro.
11. Magalhães, J. (2008). *Retornados: Um Amor Nunca se Esquece*. Lisbon: A Esfera dos Livros.
12. Rebelo, T. (2006). *O Tempo dos Amores Perfeitos*. Lisbon: Asa.
13. Rebelo, T. (2009). *O Último Ano em Luanda*. Lisbon: Oficina do Livro.
14. Santos, J. R. dos (2010). *O Anjo Branco*. Lisbon: Gradiva.
15. Sousa Tavares, M. (2008). *Equator*. London: Bloomsbury (Original ed.: *Equador* [2003], Lisbon: Oficina do Livro).
16. Viegas, F. J. (2002). *Lourenço Marques*. Lisbon: Asa.

Araújo, M., and S. Maeso (2011). "A institucionalização do silêncio: a escravatura nos manuais de história portugueses." *Ensino Superior (Revista SNESup)*, 39: 32–9.
Archer, J., and M. L. Jockers (2016). *The Bestseller Code: Anatomy of the Blockbuster*. New York: St. Martin's.
Bauman, Z. (2017). *Retrotopia*. Cambridge: Polity.
Bessard-Banquy, O., S. Ducas, and A. Gefen (eds.) (2021). *Best-sellers: L'industrie du succès*. Paris: Armand Colin.
Blanchard, P., N. Bancel, G. Boëtsch, D. Thomas, and C. Taraud (eds.) (2018). *Sexe, race & colonies: La domination des corps du XVe siècle à nos jours*. Paris: La Découverte.
Brooks, A. (2019). *Love and Intimacy in Contemporary Society: Love in an International Context*. Abingdon, Oxon: Routledge.
Buchanan, I. (2010). *A Dictionary of Critical Theory*. Oxford: Oxford University Press.
Cahen, M., and P. F. de Matos (2018). "New Perspectives on Luso-tropicalism." *Lusophone Studies Association Meeting*, Aracaju, Brazil. *Portuguese Studies Review*, XXVI(1). doi: 9771057151007. ffhalshs-02472799f.

Cunha, S. S. (2020). "Editora A Esfera dos Livros fecha escritório em Portugal." *Visão*, January 15.
Curto, D. R. (2020). *O Colonialismo português em África: de Livingstone a Luandino*. Lisbon: Edições 70.
Curto, D. R., B. P. da Cruz, and T. Furtado (2016). *Práticas coloniais em tempo de revoltas—Angola circa 1961*. Porto: Edições Afrontamento.
Ferreira, V. (1955). *Estudos Ultramarinos, Vol. IV—Colonização e diversos*. Lisbon: Agência Geral do Ultramar.
Genette, G. (1990). "Fictional Narrative, Factual Narrative." *Poetics Today*, 11(4): 755–74.
Genette, G. (1997). *Paratexts: Thresholds of Interpretation*. Cambridge: Cambridge University Press, 1997 (French original ed., 1987).
George, J. P. (2021). "Retornadiana: The Writing of the Retornados and the Memorialisation of the Return in Postcolonial Portugal." In E. Peralta (ed.), *The Retornados from the Portuguese Colonies in Africa: Memory, Narrative, and History*, 193-222. London: Routledge.
Green, M. C. (2004). "Transportation into Narrative Worlds: The Role of Prior Knowledge and Perceived." *Discourse Processes*, 38(2): 247–66.
Hall, J. W. (2012). *Hit Lit: Cracking the Code of the Twentieth Century's Biggest Bestsellers Paperback*. London: Random House.
Hochschild, A. R. (2012). *The Outsourced Self: Intimate Life in Market Times*. New York: Metropolitan Books.
Huggan, G. (2001). *The Postcolonial Exotic: Marketing the Margins*. London: Routledge.
Illouz, E. (1997). *Consuming the Romantic Utopia*. Berkeley: University of California Press.
Illouz, E. (1998). "The Lost Innocence of Love: Romance as a Postmodern Condition." In M. Featherstone (ed.), *Theory, Culture & Society*, 15(3–4): 161–86.
Lubkemann, S. C. (2003). "Race, Class and Kin in the Negotiation of 'Internal Strangerhood' among Portuguese Retornados, 1975-2000." In A. L. Smith (ed.), *Europe's Invisible Migrants*, 75–93. Amsterdam: Amsterdam University Press.
MacCannell, D. (1992). *Empty Meeting Grounds: The Tourist Papers*. London: Routledge.
Marinho, M. de F. (1999). *O Romance Histórico em Portugal*. Porto: Campo das Letras.
Marinho, M. de F. (2005). *Um Poço sem Fundo—Novas Reflexões sobre Literatura e História*. Porto: Campo das Letras.
Meyers, J. (1973). *Fiction & the Colonial Experience*. Totowa, NJ: Rowman and Littlefield.
Miller, L. J. (2006). *Reluctant Capitalists: Bookselling and the Culture of Consumption*. Chicago: University of Chicago Press.
Mothersill, M. (1997). "Sublim." In D. Cooper (ed.), *A Companion to Aesthetics*, 407–12. London: Blackwell.
Nattrass, N. (2021). "Conservation and the Commodification of Wildlife in the Anthropocene: A Southern African History." *South African Historical Journal*, doi:10.1 080/02582473.2021.1909117.
Nederveen Pieterse, J. (1992). *White on Black: Images of Africa and Blacks in Western Popular Culture*. New Haven, CT: Yale University Press.
Noronha, E. de (1984). *José do Telhado em África*. Porto: Domingos Barreira.
Peralta, E. (2019). "A integração dos 'retornados na sociedade portuguesa: identidade, desidentificação e ocultação." *Análise Social*, 2(231): 310–37.
Peralta, E., B. Góis, and J. Oliveira (eds.) (2017). *Retornar: Traços de Memória do Fim do Império*. Lisbon: Edições 70.
Pires, R. P. (1999). "O regresso das colónias." In F. Bethencourt and K. Chaudhuri (eds.), *História da Expansão Portuguesa*, vol. 5, 182–96. Lisbon: Círculo de Leitores.

Pires, R. P. (2003). *Migrações e Integração: Teoria e Aplicações à Sociedade Portuguesa*. Oeiras: Celta.
Quayson, A. (ed.) (2015). *The Cambridge Companion to the Postcolonial Novel*. Cambridge: Cambridge University Press.
Said, E. W. (1994). *Culture and Imperialism*. New York: Knopf.
Schiffrin, A. (2000). *The Business of Books: How International Conglomerates Took Over Publishing and Changed the Way We Read*. London: Verso.
Tavares, A. (2006). "Aprendemos História a ler romances." *Público* (supplement *Ípsilon*), September 30.
Thompson, J. B. (2010). *Merchants of Culture: The Publishing Business in the Twenty-First Century*. Cambridge: Polity.
Viana, C. (2011). "Manuais de História ainda contam o mundo à moda do Estado Novo." *Público*, March 27.
Vicente, F. (ed.) (2014). *O Império da visão: fotografia no contexto colonial (1860–1960)*. Lisbon: Edições 70.
Volvic, Z., and M. Andrejevic (eds.) (2016). *Commercial Nationalism: Selling the Nation and Nationalizing the Sell*. London: Palgrave Macmillan.
Werry, M. L. (2005). "Cultural Revivals." In M. C. Horowitz (ed.), *New Dictionary of the History of Ideas*, 2317–19. New York: Scribner's.

Chapter 11

EMBRACING POSTCOLONIAL DIVERSITY? MUSIC SELECTION AND AFFECTIVE FORMATION IN TAP AIR PORTUGAL'S IN-FLIGHT ENTERTAINMENT SYSTEM

Bart Paul Vanspauwen and Iñigo Sánchez-Fuarros

Contextualization

Despite its short history, air transport has become a major player in an increasingly mobile, hyper-globalized, and interconnected world. Since the 1930s, and until the appearance of the first private airlines, the contours of modern aviation were shaped by the policies of nation-states. In fact, for most of the post–Second World War period, the airline industry remained the preserve of state-owned airlines that actively instrumentalized promoting the power, prestige, and hegemony of each country beyond its national borders.

From their outset, modern aircraft carried not only people and cargo but also cultural content. Technological advances and the popularization of in-flight entertainment systems have accelerated this process, making aircraft interiors a "stress-free" place for cultural consumption. However, any social and cultural history of aviation, exploring the active role of national airlines in producing and circulating ideas, imagery, traits, and cultural artifacts linked to national identity, is still in the making.

The Portuguese flag carrier Transportes Aéreos Portugueses (TAP, later called TAP Portugal and nowadays TAP Air Portugal), founded in Lisbon in 1945 on the orders of Humberto Delgado, then director of the Civil Aeronautical Secretariat, was proposed as a public service company to serve as a link between the metropolis and the Portuguese communities, initially scattered throughout the empire and later throughout the world. Since the 1946 inauguration of the "Imperial Air Line" between Lisbon, Luanda (in the then Portuguese colony of Angola), and Lourenço Marques, the former designation of the city of Maputo (in the then Portuguese colony of Mozambique) through to today, TAP managed to maintain strong bonds of identification with Portuguese populations, both at home and abroad, by readapting its promotional discourse according to the social, political, and cultural impulse of each era. A "product of the empire," a "national symbol," or the "image of the Portuguese people" are just a few of the popularly used names that would suggest TAP did in fact play a central role in constructing and disseminating a hegemonic Portuguese cultural identity, serving as a national cultural ambassador on many occasions. In 2019, TAP transported 17 million passengers, had 4 million clients in its loyalty program, and counted on 2.1 million followers across different social networks. The company closed 2019 with services to 94 destination airports and around 137,000 flights per year, expanding its presence in Africa and North America and leading the market to Brazil. It has also recently modernized its long-haul fleet, now with an average age of 3.9 years against the 15 years recorded in 2018.[1]

As a European country that maintains strong relations with its former colonies, Portugal has long been sensitive to international recognition of its cultural identity practices.[2] In this sense, the political notion of Lusophony has become increasingly verbalized to designate the shared histories and cultures between Portuguese-speaking communities around the world. Recent studies frame Lusophony more as a movement of return to the expressive cultures and memories of the former colonial territories of Portugal than as a mere linguistic, economic, or political field. Therefore, it seems fruitful to explore Lusophony as a fluid postmodern concept that transcends postcolonial contexts as well as the authority of the nation-states themselves. In fact, various studies (Castelo 1998; Sanches 2006; Almeida 2008; Marques 2012; Domingos and Peralta 2013; Sousa 2015) have pointed out how Portuguese society is not yet permeable to "non-Western" influences as it did not develop critical readings of these expressions or strategies able to promote integration. Intercultural relationships are built upon the dynamic flow between cultures and alterity. As such, they allow for investigating how socially induced notions of political correctness—racial tolerance and multiculturalism—can actually be applied as tools to accommodate notions of difference (Ponzanesi and Blaagaard 2011).

Taking the airplane as a chronotope, a moving element that represents a political and cultural unity and connects fixed but geographically dispersed spaces and scapes in fluid, imaginary ways, this project situates itself at the crossroads between corporate branding and cultural governance by a national airline (and one of the few remaining) controlled by a former colonial power in contemporary Europe. Competition between airlines causes former imperial legacies to be negotiated and reinterpreted for national and commercial purposes, revealing the workings of cultural strategies as a form of covert politics. In turn, expressive culture is one of the cultural forms actively mobilized by airlines to promote and construct certain ideas of national identity.

This chapter aims to explore how the Portuguese national airline TAP represented and/or negotiated Portugal's relations with other Portuguese-speaking countries through the mediation of expressive cultural practices such as music, on the one hand, and corporate branding and publicity strategies, on the other. Given that TAP connects Portugal daily with other Portuguese-speaking destinations, such as Brazil, Angola, Cape Verde, Guinea-Bissau, Mozambique, and Sao Tome and Principe, we are particularly interested in exploring how the discursive categories deployed within the in-flight entertainment system operate as sociopolitical instruments to circulate representations of being (and feeling) "Portuguese," on the one hand, and a broader sense of "Lusophone" belonging, on the other.

Framing our work conceptually within the theories of flow and mobility, this chapter is inserted into postcolonial studies of the Lusophone world with a particular focus on transnational identity narratives and social memories. We particularly strive to better understand the "Lusophone" cultural perspective employed by TAP. While we quantitatively analyze the categorization of music as a tool for managing the company's corporate identity, we also reflect on the individual sound experiences that emerge through the on-board customizable playlists. On a broader level, TAP's advertising and publicity materials—across their visual, sonic, and discursive dimensions—are also subject to analysis in the light of eventual transitions or ambiguities between the colonial and postcolonial. Ultimately, our goals include understanding processes of music selection, taste formation, and brand management as TAP seeks to leverage existing cultural affinities to inform and construct loyalty in its overall Portuguese-speaking passenger community.

Cultural categories can be applied as sociopolitical instruments and thus represent/conceal power interests. As such, we here seek to lay bare the transnational identity narratives (present) and the social memories (past) of this flagship airline. We are particularly interested in how corporate branding strategies feed into the cultural categories for marketing in the air and on the ground. Our working hypothesis is that many of TAP's marketing phrases, images, and sounds are instrumentalized to discursively construct fluid cultural images.

This project is unprecedented in a number of ways. First, mobility studies have only recently turned their research attentions to national airliners (Staniland 2003; Cwerner et al. 2009; Adey 2010), mobility (Bull 2006; Gopinath and Stanyek 2013), and on-board entertainment (Govil 2004; Wilkie 2012). Second, heritage studies have only marginally approached the history of airlines from a postcolonial viewpoint (Coller et al. 2016; Paludi 2017; Kivijärvi et al. 2019). Third, the general interest of brands—as identity symbols that have tangible relations to cultural symbolism—to anthropology has only recently been established (Manning 2010; Matsanuga 2016). Fourth and last, the existing research on TAP focuses on its historic and visual aspects but does not seem to sufficiently problematize postcolonial relationships (Gentil-Homem 2014; Figueiredo 2016).

For this purpose, the prism of the music field allows an understanding of the role played by the governance of auditory meanings in the formation of social and political orders. Based on an ethnomusicological approach, we intend to perceive the narratives of modern Western empires as constructions in which audibility involves musical interactions that reflect concrete social and cultural negotiations, particularly, but not exclusively, over the traumas of colonialism. In the case of TAP and Portugal, the country it was founded to represent, there is an urgent need to ascertain more about this specific "colonial complex"—from lusotropicalism to the interspaces and inter-identities of the postcolonial period (Arenas 2005; Feldman-Bianco 2007; Freixo 2009; Peralta 2011).

How has TAP played with its political and affective economies and dependencies from a Lusophone and global perspective?[3] How has it commodified the Lusophone space and made it economically profitable through popular cultural representations—which are in fact ideological framings/stagings of tradition/ history? Which visual, sonic, and discursive elements get deployed to evoke hospitality? We hope our research may help in revealing whether and how TAP has conveyed national projections, cultural policies, and ideas about ethnicity and difference in their representations of the expressive cultures of the transnational Lusophone world (Born and Hesmondhalgh 2000; Radano and Olaniyan 2016).

From Portugality to Lusophony in Three Musical Mo(ve)ments

Music is an active ingredient of the air travel experience. Musical sounds welcome passengers as they board the aircraft and bid them farewell on the plane arriving at its destination. Especially during long-haul flights, passengers can personalize their listening experience through the selection made available to them via the different music and video channels. Music references also frequently crop up in the in-flight magazines whether in the form of articles, album reviews, or featured interviews with local and international musicians and bands. Furthermore, beyond the confined space of the airplane cabin, music is also part of airline marketing campaigns, providing yet another facet to their corporate image. In the case of national carriers such as TAP, the connections between the experience of flying, music, and the circulation of certain ideals and images of national and cultural identity are particularly strong.

In the 1970s, for example, it was common for passengers traveling in TAP's business class—the reputed Navigator Class—to receive an LP as a gift at the end of the flight. One of these albums—produced by the company itself—was entitled *Take a Musical Tour through Portugal* and contained a selection of different Portuguese musical traditions, from fado to fishermen songs from the Algarve to recordings of the musical repertoires of Portugal's northern regions. A map of Portugal printed inside the album further substantiates this idea of musical travel. This example is interesting because the music in some way reinforced a broader narrative about what it was like to be "Portuguese" in a historical period when the idea of Portugal was constructed according to popular traditions and customs and images of Portugal as a rural and sunny country of simple and welcoming people. This also connects to a broader array of contemporary music albums that links tourism to the discovery of local traditions by the contemporary jet set (Elliot 2020), including, for instance, Frank Sinatra's *Come Fly with Me* (1958), Bing Crosby's *Holiday in Europe* (1962), Tony Bennett's *If I Ruled the World: Songs for the Jet Set* (1965), and—decades later—Shegundo Galarza's *Holiday in Portugal* (1990).

A second historical period refers to TAP's forty-fifth anniversary commemorations in the early 1990s. Within the context of these celebrations, the company commissioned a musical piece from the acclaimed Portuguese guitar virtuoso Carlos Paredes.[4] The theme, appropriately titled *Asas sobre o Mundo* (*Wings over the World*), was used as boarding and disembarking music

Figure 11.1 Album covers of the disks distributed on TAP flights. On the left, Carlos Paredes's *Asas sobre o Mundo* (1989); on the right, a compilation of Portuguese folkloric music titled *Take a Musical Tour of Portugal* (c. 1974–9). *Source*: TAP Museum.

and would eventually become the airline's signature music. Differing from our first example, the Portugueseness that Paredes's composition evokes refers to a more comprehensive idea ("I wanted to associate your birthday with the universal appeal and musical excellence of this composer," text extracted from the album inlay; cf. Figure 11.1) and exudes a kind of colonial nostalgia that aligns with the symbolism of the caravel and its voyages of discovery associations the company had deployed as part of its corporate image since the early 1960s.

A third and final moment refers to the song "De Braços Abertos" ("With Arms Wide Open"), launched in 2011 as part of a viral marketing campaign that signaled the sonic renewal of TAP's image and name (Figure 11.2). This song, which would become the company's new anthem, features three well-known artists from the Lusophone music scene: Paulo Flores, from Angola; Portuguese (with Mozambican roots) fado singer Mariza; and Brazilian singer Roberta Sá. This rebranding of the company implied a redefinition of the very notion of Portugality on which TAP's corporate image had been built, explicitly embracing the notion of Lusophony as part of a strategy emerging halfway between the commercialization of culture and the promotion of a fluid notion of Portuguese identity, which in practice translated into a renewed interest in representing cultural connections between Portugal and other locations in the Portuguese-speaking world. Based on different musical influences (semba, fado, and Brazilian popular music) and a shared cultural and linguistic past, "With Arms Wide Open" represents cultural collaboration as a central component of this new identity. The lyrics, on the other hand, reposition the common trope of hospitality as a distinctive feature of being "Portuguese" within a global perspective.

These three examples reflect how, at different times in its corporate history, TAP turned to music to spread differing ideas about what it means to "be Portuguese." This trend may also be observed and analyzed in the music selection provided via

Figure 11.2 Video stills from the official music video of "De Braços Abertos." https://www.youtube.com/watch?v=S1vfiu9qJj0 (accessed June 25, 2021).

the in-flight entertainment system available on long-haul flights as we shall now detail.

The Musical Experience On-Board TAP Airplanes

Recent work in the field of mobility studies proposes thinking of this concept not only as physical bodies moving from one place to another but also as a social and cultural resource requiring analysis as a corporate experience and practice, as "a way of being in the world" (Cresswell 2006). In the global and digital age, in which people, ideas, images, objects, and capital travel across borders with unprecedented ease, considering the implications of these forms of mobility in our experience of time and space, in our dwelling practices, and within the very concept of citizenship represents an urgent task. As discussed in the previous section, music provides one of the cultural forms actively mobilized by airlines to both promote and build certain ideas of national identity.

The first signs of the presence of music on TAP in-flight entertainment systems date back to the second half of the 1970s with the arrival of the first airplanes equipped with personal audio systems—the Boeing 747 and the Boeing 707. These systems enabled seated passengers to access various music channels through headphones. In the beginning of on-board music, the selection was the responsibility of a small group of employees with musical interests who made their work in the company (as flight attendants, technical specialists, etc.) compatible with the musical curatorship of the audio channels. This was the case of the music journalist and jazz critic José Duarte, who started work in the company's ramp services but was also responsible for the musical content of the audio channels for several years. In an interview with the authors, Duarte himself reported how he often took advantage of the international flights the company offered its workers to attend concerts and buy books and records that were otherwise forbidden in Portugal at that time. This opportunity to get to know the world was in fact one reason that impelled Duarte—and many of his generation of colleagues with whom we had the opportunity to speak within this research context—to work at TAP. The process of programming the audio channels started out with the selection of the albums and songs to include on each channel, often made in accordance with criteria based on personal taste. For example, José Duarte is proud to have included in his playlist themes and musicians from the orbit of protest songs and intervention music that were censored in Portugal at that time as a way of making Portuguese music known to his fellow countrymen. Similarly, he took advantage of his position as a TAP music programmer to publicize his great passion, jazz. The almost artisanal production of the playlists in this early phase was completed by the recording of the musical selection on audio tape in TAP's own sound studios, thus enabling the subsequent reproduction on the aircraft's audio systems.

From the 1980s onward, TAP began distributing a brochure detailing the in-flight music and cinema service to passengers on its Boeing 747s and Boeing 707s. This brochure included two films and six audio channels: classical music, youth music, music from Portugal, jazz, miscellaneous and movie themes. This division of audio channels by musical categories remained virtually unchanged until the mid-1990s when the incorporation of new aircraft as well as technological advances in on-board entertainment systems allowed for the distribution of the music across twelve audio channels. It was also at this time that the production of the audio channels was outsourced to an independent production company. Subsequently, TAP signed a contract with Rádio e Televisão de Portugal (RTP), Portugal's state-owned radio and television company, by virtue of which the latter would provide audio and video content for all of the company's medium and long flights from 2011 onward. For example, from 2015 onward, when we are able to work with the concrete data sheets made available to us by TAP, the company offered twelve radio channels on its long-haul flights—including Portugal, Fado, Bossa and Jazz, Africa, Brazil, and World— and a collection of albums called CDteca with more than five hundred titles, all divided into musical categories (with considerable attention to the connections between Portugal and the rest of the Portuguese-speaking world). In addition, passengers could personalize their trip by creating personal playlists from the albums included in the latter.

The main purpose of this chapter extends beyond providing detailed and systematic analysis of the musical depth and scope broadcast on TAP's airplanes (audio channels and CD collection), which would undoubtedly enrich our analysis of the company's strategies around conveying particular ideas about Portuguese cultural identity in constant dialogue with its own corporate identity. However, our partial interpretation of material made available by TAP in 2015 suggests some tentative conclusions. For example, the "Canal Portugal" (Channel Portugal) category formerly contained a lot of fado, which led to the creation a separate fado channel in 2011, the year this genre received UNESCO recognition.[5] Some discursive allusions to Portugal were made through song titles, for example, "O fado e a alma portuguesa" ("Fado and the Portuguese soul") (featuring Portuguese fadistas such as Camané, Mariza, Ana Moura, Carminho, and Ricardo Ribeiro). A second tendency for "Canal Portugal" was the frequent appearance of protest song singers, linked to the April 1974 Carnation Revolution in Portugal (which also interconnects with the former African colonies that, except from Guinea-Bissau in 1974, declared independence in 1975). Third, the category "Canal Portugal" occasionally included Lusophone (non-Portuguese) musicians who have been historically significant to Portugal (such as the Angolan Duo Ouro Negro—defined as "Lusophone world music") or who have featured in multicultural Portuguese collaborations. Finally, the "Canal Portugal" label also presented established Portuguese pop singers such as Rui Veloso, Jorge Palma, Paulo Gonzo, Pedro Abrunhosa, and others, most of whom have also made high-profile collaborations with Lusophone musicians from Africa and Brazil.

Lusophone connections also emerge in some of the other musical channels or categories within this research framework. For example, at the time of our analysis, "Channel Africa" contained links with more or less established musicians of Lusophone African countries that reside in Lisbon or have connections there (these countries include Angola, Cape Verde, Guinea-Bissau, and Mozambique, as well as the United Kingdom, Cuba, and the Netherlands). In turn, curiously, other channels, such as "Canal Portugal Jovem" ("Portugal Youth Channel") and "Channel Kids," broadcast content featuring multicultural, so-called alternative bands residing in Lisbon but also with their origins in other Lusophone countries and with hip-hop as the prevailing genre. Third, "Channel World Music" included Brazilian next to Cape Verdean and Portuguese musicians. This channel thus played musicians of whom the majority have since become household names not only nationally but also internationally as regards the so-called Lusophone music scene ("música lusófona"). Finally, two separate channels, "Channel Brasil"[6] and "Channel Bossa Nova," dedicated themselves to Brazilian musical genres and their performers, albeit not exclusively. For example, the bossa nova category included Portuguese musicians as well as collaborations with musicians from other Lusophone latitudes. On the whole, musical collaborations are recurrent across all the categories discussed above. Their numerous and intentional selection seems to prescribe or at least affirm the notion of a "musical Lusophony," thus proposing a shared sense of belonging and connectedness between Lusophone musicians across nations, languages, and genres.

The Promotion of Lusophone Interstitiality as a Marketing Strategy for Postcolonial Reconciliation

For approximately fifteen years, TAP's official discourse and image as applied in launching marketing campaigns have increasingly displayed sonic, visual, and discursive elements that promote, or at the least evoke, a new, modern, and mixed image of an Atlantic-oriented Portugal, which tries to stand out economically and touristically as one of the most southerly European Union member states. In this respect, we have selected five key moments that exemplify this "Lusophone" ambition: (1) the rebranding of TAP's logo in 2005, involving new paint schemes for the airplanes and updated outfits for cabin crews; (2) the launch of the in-flight magazine *UP* in 2007, with the slogan "Dare to dream higher"; (3) the launch of the CD *TOP Executive Collection*, setting the tone for Lusophony in TAP's corporate branding, in 2008; (4) the dissemination of the company hymn "*De Braços Abertos*" through YouTube and other social media from 2011 onward; and (5) the celebratory exhibition at the Lisbon Fashion and Design Museum (MUDE) on the occasion of TAP's seventieth anniversary in 2015. Here, we present our brief analysis of the discourses on record (retrieved from interviews, press releases, online internal communications, and general publicity and advertising campaigns).

The press leaflet accompanying the MUDE premiere exhibition on July 15, 2015, widely attended by TAP personnel and government representatives, and taking place in one of Lisbon's most emblematic streets and tourist hotspots (the Rua Augusta leading up to Terreiro do Paço), may serve as a good starting point: this refers to "the collective consciousness of TAP as a national symbol" and displays the "close relationship between TAP and the different ideological, political and economic contexts of Portugal," in particular the "historical discourse mainly revisiting the Discoveries and the Portuguese Diaspora, and extolling a seafaring people."[7] During our visit to the grand opening of this exhibition, we saw various visual examples of the latter. One publicity advert entitled "Big in experience" showed a colorful image with flowers and caravels, sea and countryside, and a trijet with the colors of TAP and read as follows: "This spirit of exploration is our Portuguese heritage . . . Our airmen follow in the tradition of our sailors of the time of the Discoveries when, almost anywhere you sailed, you found Magellan or Vasco da Gama had got there first. That get-there-first spirit still reaches across the centuries."[8]

In a second advertisement, a ship's captain is compared to an airplane captain, showing an image of Vasco da Gama with a TAP plane below, stating that "our Captains have been flying to and from Africa for 500 years" and "when you fly to Europe fly with the Discovers." In a third leaflet, evoking the arrival of the Boeing 747, a simplified, painted map showing both planes and caravels came accompanied by the following text: "In 1492, Portugal helped start group excursions across the Atlantic. On April 1st, 1972, our new 747 navigator jets will help you do the same." In a final publicity item, the following discourse read: "We fly to Brasil [sic] the way we fly home. We discovered Brasil 500 years ago. And we can help you to discover it today: we fly to four destinations in a country that speaks our language. No wonder TAP is the European airline that knows Brasil best." And it then describes sonic and visual sensations: "The creole charm, the exciting development, the exuberant music, lively tradition and delicious cuisine. Brasil is a country of warmth and beauty. In its scenery, its sea, its colour and the warm-hearted welcome of its people. Let us discover it for you."

However, the MUDE exposition also focused on the TAP corporate identity in the twenty-first century. One printed text from 2006 that drew our attention, written by Carlos Coelho, one of the great Portuguese references in the field of brand building and management in Portugal, referred to TAP as "national equity"[9] at the time of its rebranding: the "result of Portugal's historical past and its Empire that left roots all over the world," "TAP being one of its most modern and significant symbols of belonging," "to gather collective feelings through the projection of values; in the case of Portugal, values that exist for centuries, even if they remain dominant." According to Coelho, the "new TAP, with the national colours more open and vibrant, is the portrayal of a hot and sexy country, owner [sic] of an immense Atlantic territory." Furthermore, TAP's rebranding "meets in all respects the unshakable sense that the re-contextualization of the Portuguese symbols is a fundamental matter to the revitalization of our economy."

Echoes of Coelho's discourse also emerged in 2011 at the time of the launch of the company's anthem "De Braços Abertos" in TAP's online journal.[10] Besides redefining the company's values as "friendliness," "availability," "cooperation," "responsibility," "professionalism," "enthusiasm," "passion," and "dynamism," the document pinpoints three of TAP's "differentiating attributes": "FUSION: a natural, irreproducible and refreshing encounter of European, African and Brazilian influences," "SOMETHING CONTAGIOUS: a brand that is always able to spread smiles and convert discomfort into well-being," and "GATEKEEPER: the most authoritative figure in connecting Europe (Portugal), Africa and Brazil to the world" (our translation).

In the same edition, the then TAP vice president Luiz Mór explained its move toward more emotional communication. "What unites us is the Portuguese-speaking world. It is not just the language that gives us a unique identity. It is also the warmth of the welcome, the color and the joy, common to Portuguese, Brazilians and Africans," says Mór, adding that "the art of welcoming is in the DNA of TAP's staff" (our translation).

Also in the same edition, Pedro Pina, president of McCann Worldgroup Portugal, responsible for producing TAP's signature track "De Braços Abertos," describes the song as a "new positioning, with a strong emotional appeal, based on the characteristic features of Lusophony." As Pina explains, it is on the "routes serving Portuguese-speaking countries that the company finds its cultural affinity," and in "the Portuguese diaspora market—in Europe and the USA—that TAP encounters its most loyal passengers." In sum, he maintains that with TAP these passengers "feel at home and well-received, sharing not only our language, but our warmth and our embrace." According to Pina, music is a "platform par excellence through which the union of Lusophone cultures is made more explicit and perfect. We share not only the same language but also the rhythms that dialogue and echo throughout a common and unavoidable history" (our translation).

Actually, this idea of Lusophone interconnectedness is confirmed in TAP's own words for the sleeve notes of the *TOP Executive Collection* CD, released three years earlier, in which the airline was already proposing its own role as a fundamental instrument for connecting and uniting communities. The music selection effectively materializes TAP's marketing strategy by linking music to discourse. However, there is a semiotic ambiguity between the Portuguese text and its English translation curiously enough as regards the very identity definitions that are central to this chapter: *lusofonia* and *portugalidade*.[11] For example, the unknown author of the sleeve notes defines "Lusophony" as "a concept that integrates a wide variety of cultural identities and a number of countries that are united by the common link of the Portuguese language," comparing this to an "enormous, diversified and identifying patchwork (that) is made up by millions of people and different communities that stretch to the four corners of the world." Listing the Portuguese-speaking countries in a rather playful and alphabetical manner without making any reference to colonial rule, and curiously placing Portugal last,[12] the author then equates Lusophony to the Portuguese diaspora, which in our view is a separate migration system—that is, while some in the Lusophone world are effectively Portuguese emigrants or descendants, it would hardly be fair to state that the indigenous populations of Portugal's former colonial possessions also fall under this classification.[13] The Portuguese diaspora is nowadays only one part of the Lusophone world, but this still does not necessarily address the (post)colonial issue. This ambiguity between Lusophony and "being Portuguese"/*portugalidade* permeates the text. While on the one hand, the text situates TAP's purpose as precisely "to encourage cultural exchange, thus promoting the Portuguese-speaking language and culture" in a "stimulating and original blend of musical influences that enriches their common cultural heritage,"[14] on the other hand, it contradictorily states that the CD "highlights the best of being Portuguese—in music—in an anthology that presents some of the musical greats of Portugal," "thus confirming the continued commitment to Portugality." Curiously, the text mentions fado musicians as performers of Lusophone music,[15] hinting at cross-cultural musical fusions between genres, stereotypes, and nations, while listing migrant/resident Lusophone performers as secondary to Portugal's domestic circuit: "some of these Portuguese-speaking artists perform with other greats

Figure 11.3 "Can you hear the fado?" *Source*: TAP's official Instagram account @tapairportugal, August 10, 2019 (accessed June 25, 2021).

of the international scene, primarily, Dulce Pontes with Waldemar Bastos from Angola, Anabela in duet with Paulo de Carvalho and Rui Veloso singing a duet with Afro-singer Nancy Vieira."

Nowadays, TAP actively assumes itself as a privileged window into Portuguese culture, exemplified by a recent social media picture of a decorated plane window, unifying the sonic and visual facets of this tradition: "Can you hear the fado and see the beautiful traditional tile designs? You're arriving in Lisbon!" (Figure 11.3).

In addition, a number of recent onboard performances have stressed TAP's function as cultural ambassador on behalf of fado and of musical performers with more modern facets or origins in other Portuguese-speaking countries within an overall perspective of interconnection. One early example was the fado performance by *fadista* Cuca Roseta on a TAP plane en route to Brazil during the 2014 Football World Cup in support of the Portuguese national team. A second example came with TAP's celebration of Cape Verdean mornas when this musical genre was declared UNESCO Intangible Cultural Heritage,[16] featuring inflight performances by Cremilda Medina[17] and guitarist Armando Tito (who was in Cesária Évora's band). Third and fourth examples involve concerts by female singer Kataleya (born in Rio de Janeiro but raised in Switzerland) on the occasion of carnival in 2019 and by Cape Verdean rapper Djodje (Figure 11.4).

The visual-textual evocations of Lusophone music and culture similar to those referenced above also crop up in randomly chosen TAP advertising and

Figure 11.4 Video stills from different onboard promotional performances by Lusophone artists. From top to bottom, and left to right: Kataleya, Djodje, Cuca Roseta, and Cremilda Medina with Armando Tito. https://www.youtube.com/watch?v=tQSO_X3Psxs; https://www.youtube.com/watch?v=2cTrmnHhHcU; https://www.youtube.com/watch?v=OFtGRiXWTYM; https://www.youtube.com/watch?v=DU9cCFHJYz8 (all accessed June 25, 2021).

publicity. For example, wordplays such as "Relax with the beat of lukewarm waves," "Nobody knows Cape Verde like us," or "We fly to Brasil [sic] the way we fly home"[18] add to a sense of mixed belonging across the visual, sonic, and discursive facets.

Concluding Remarks

In this chapter, we adopted sonic experience as the primary lens for developing diachronic readings of processes of sociocultural identity representation by the Portuguese national airline TAP. In a postcolonial and neoliberal context, competition between global airlines causes old imperial and national legacies to be negotiated and reinterpreted for commercial purposes. Fortifying Portugal's intermediate role in the Portuguese-speaking world thus becomes not only a fundamental strategic issue (Lopes 2011) but also a factor of economic relevance (Pereira 2011), making TAP for many, "more than a company, a "national equity'" (Coelho 2006), which in the interplay between spaces, mobility, and linguistic-cultural affects unites imagined communities with collective practices (cf. Adey 2010). Cultural categories in general and music labels in particular can serve to claim certain rights, respect, and recognition while also susceptible to realignment by the people defining and deploying them. Even though the airplane represents one of the last social network-free places without stress and (in most cases) still without total access to wi-fi, TAP influences its passengers with cultural content that is anything but neutral.

How has TAP's music offering evolved over time and how has technology nurtured this evolution? From our analysis of the visual, sonic, and discursive outputs of this Portuguese airline—from amateurism to business, at the crossroads of markets, cultures, and nations—various examples of hegemony and controversy in the social representations of history emerge. Should we take into account the way in which TAP's sociocultural identity was built up discursively, we may observe a progressive widening of the scope of the notion of "being Portuguese," from a restricted idea of Portugality (*portugalidade*)—a notion interrelating with the imposition of Portuguese nationalism on the former colonies, to a more broadly encompassing concept of Lusophony (*Lusofonia*), a geopolitical and politically planned notion linked to the euphemism of language to denote interconnectedness in the postcolonial Lusophone world. This change, we would argue, has been paramount not only to redefining TAP's current market value as a global player in an increasingly competitive industry but also for the Portuguese themselves in transnationally rethinking their cultural and historical heritage. In fact, this very idea may be sourced from the sleeve notes of the *TOP Executive Collection* CD where the company itself adopts the role of a fundamental tool for connecting and joining affective Portuguese-speaking communities. The motto "With Arms Wide Open" would thus promote TAP as a synonym for Portuguese culture, nation, and values—patent in the metaphoric *abraço* (embrace) that semantically appears in a number of events, eventually evoking proximity, connection, friendship, or consideration, rendering the Lusophone postcolonial or Portuguese diasporic dimension (together with its ethnic or race components) rather implicitly.

As detailed above, in the words of Pedro Pina, TAP's recontextualization of Portuguese symbols, values, and sentiments mainly serve to revitalize the country's economy and make it attractive within the global mercantile system. However, to what extent have TAP's semantic recodifications contributed to the decolonization of minds, culture, and society at large? In congruence with other recent research findings about the (post-)colonial performance and prescriptive rhetoric of transnational state airlines such as Pan America Airways and British Airways, research into the "various networked processes through which particular organizational narratives are told [may help] us to uncover the relational aspects in the performance of history" (Kivijärvi et al. 2019: n.p.). In the same sense, Coller et al. argue that a "focus on the various human and non-human relationships that constitute an archive can help the researcher to identify the hidden influences on the production of history that can otherwise serve to enroll him or her," thus turning corporate history into a "powerful way of communicating or challenging its culture and identity" (2016: 1). Still furthermore, in the words of Paludi, the "understanding of multi-nationals in the creation of postcoloniality" through "decolonial lenses acknowledges their role in perpetuating colonial/imperial legacies, and cultural imperialism today" (2017: 249).

Our analysis of the transnational cultural flows and encounters in TAP's marketing efforts—as well as the interpretation of evocations of hospitality through visual, sonic, and discursive channels—may offer new perspectives on how cultural governance and brand marketing work to articulate identities that either conform with or depart from the received narratives of Portuguese national culture. In line with Castellano (2018: 1), we position TAP as a kind of narrator-curator that deals with both the legacies and predicaments of colonialism in the postcolonial present. Our analysis posits that seemingly peaceful representations of cultural practices may reveal concealed tensions, creating in-between places where old imperial tendencies and neoliberal ideals converge. TAP's cultural output still tends to reflect old imperial sentiments as its discursive, sonic, and visual dimensions are intimately intertwined with historical power structures. While on a macro level, TAP is clearly in the process of negotiating the myth and grandeur of the discoveries to "mirror a democratic and multicultural present-day Portugal" (2018: 2) and various narrative elements "reveal evidence of postcolonial thinking," they "do not facilitate an uncovering of the voices" of those who were "neglected, silenced, or misrepresented" in the former colonies (Paludi 2017: 242). Indeed, from TAP's diachronic marketing efforts emerges a sense of mixed and even inverted belonging—they fly to Brazil or Cape Verde just like they fly home, feeling as if some "owner of an immense Atlantic territory" (in Carlos Coelho's words), and apply their "big experience" to help others "discover" local cultures all the while avoiding any explanations about the colonial past, the ensuing return movements, or even the Lusophone populations with their origins in the former colonies who have chosen Portugal as their new home. This may be perceived as a subjective construction or a distortion of history, especially regarding ideas of lusotropicalism—Portuguese exceptionalism under imperial rule—which never gets mentioned.

However, an emotional understanding of Lusophony, as cited above in the words of Luiz Mór, may still open the way for effective trauma training regarding silenced postcolonial taboos. Universal values such as cooperation, language bonds, cultural affinities, and overall human warmth and respect (metaphorically represented in the *abraço*—the embrace—"with arms wide open") may be intended to overcome cruel memories forged by colonialism in not-so-distant times: forgiving the past and embracing the future, often used by TAP in marketing efforts for the Rio de Janeiro destination.

Through its 2011 company anthem, TAP Air Portugal actively positioned itself as a prescriptive Lusophone interface that mediates colonial scars and postcolonial stereotypes and identifies with existing cultural affinities to affectively reach out to its transnational customer community. Thus, the Portuguese flag carrier conveys new meanings to the complexity of European and Lusophone belonging, on the one hand, and stimulates the discovery of both "the other" and the degree of tolerance of our proper selves, on the other. In keeping with Paludi, finally, we hope that our research may eventually reframe the way we envision diversity management today, challenging postcolonial binaries with lived understandings of *mestizaje* and hybridity (2017: 249).

Notes

Our special thanks go out to both current and former TAP employees who generously devoted part of their time to answering our questions and, in particular, to the employees of the TAP Museum. This work has been supported by the Portuguese Fundação para a Ciência e a Tecnologia (FCT) within the framework of the research project "Sounds of Tourism" (PTDC/ART-PER/32417/2017). It also received support of a RyC grant (RYC2018-026083-I) funded by MCIN/AEI/10.13039/501100011033.

1 Taken from then CEO Antonoaldo Neves's monthly editorial in the in-flight magazine *UP*, January 1, 2020.
2 This relationship is shaped not only by the colonial legacies that persist today but also because of the significant presence of populations from Portugal's former colonies in the country itself, especially in the Lisbon Metropolitan Area.
3 An idea inspired by Jocelyne Guilbault's oral presentation at NOVA University of Lisbon on December 6, 2018.
4 Carlos Paredes (1925–2004) was a Portuguese composer and guitar player. He was one of the main people responsible for the dissemination and popularity of the Portuguese guitar and is considered to be one of the unique symbols of Portuguese culture.
5 The decision to declare fado an Intangible Cultural Heritage of Humanity was taken on November 27, 2011, at the meeting of the VI Intergovernmental Committee of the United Nations Educational, Scientific and Cultural Organization, held in Nusa Dua, on the Indonesian island of Bali. The initiative of the nomination was launched by the Lisbon City Hall in 2004, and the application was presented in June 2010 by the City of Lisbon and the Fado Museum.
6 Differently from the other channels that were produced by RTP, "Canal Brasil" was sent in independently by Brazilian record company Biscoito Fino, and for this reason, it is excluded from our analysis here.
7 *Source*: https://www.mude.pt/exposicoes/tap-portugal-a-imagem-de-um-povo-identidade-e-design-da-companhia-aerea-nacional-19452015_66.html.
8 Ferdinand Magellan (*Fernão de Magalhães*) (1480–1521) was a Portuguese explorer who led the Spanish expedition during which the passage between the Atlantic and Pacific Oceans was crossed. Vasco da Gama (c.1460s–1524), was a Portuguese navigator and the first European to reach India by sea.
9 *Source*: https://www.ivity-corp.com/pdfs/7tap%20national%20equity.pdf. The English translation we discuss here was displayed at the MUDE exhibition.
10 *Source*: Jornal TAP 85 ("Especial Novo Posicionamento"), February 2011, https://jornal.tap.pt/Jornal/jornalTAP_85_especial.pdf (accessed June 25, 2021).
11 All texts were extracted from the sleeve notes.
12 "Lusophony is a concept that integrates a vast set of cultural identities covering several countries, whose common feature and unified link is the Portuguese language. The spectrum goes from Angola to Brazil, from Cape Verde to Guinea-Bissau, from Macau to Mozambique, from São Tomé and Príncipe to East Timor, without forgetting, of course, Portugal."
13 "This entails an enormous, vast and diverse identity patchwork composed of millions of people and diverse communities spread across the four corners of the world, the so-called diaspora."
14 "This collection reflects a stimulating and original crossover of musical influences from Portuguese-speaking countries, a musical proposal that only enriches the

common heritage of Portuguese-speaking peoples. As an added value, the fact that some of these Lusophony artists cross their musical culture with other big names on the international scene."
15 "In this musical anthology, one can hear keynote names in Lusophone music, such as Amália Rodrigues, Carlos Paredes, Madredeus, Carlos do Carmo, Mariza, Dulce Pontes, Cristina Branco, Ana Moura, Bonga, Waldemar Bastos, Paulo Flores, Manecas Costa or Os Tubarões."
16 The decision to declare Cape Verdean mornas an Intangible Cultural Heritage of Humanity was taken on December 11, 2019, at the fourteenth annual meeting of UNESCO's Intergovernmental Committee for the Safeguarding of the Intangible Cultural Heritage held in Bogotá, Colombia. The State of Cape Verde, through the Ministry of Culture and Creative Industries, submitted to UNESCO, in March 2018, the application process of morna as Intangible Cultural Heritage of Humanity.
17 On the occasion, TAP also surprised passengers with two hundred CD books that included a compilation of mornas and texts detailing the genre's history.
18 Batuque both refers to the act of drumming and the music genre; morna both connotes the temperature of water and the music genre.

References

Adey, P. (2010). *Aereal Life: Spaces, Mobilities, Affects*. London: Wiley-Blackwell.
Almeida M. V. (2008). "Portugal's Colonial Complex: From Colonial Lusotropicalism to Postcolonial Lusophony." Paper presented at the Queen's Postcolonial Research Forum, Queen's University, Belfast, April 28.
Arenas, F. (2005). *(Post)colonialism, Globalization, and Lusofonia or the "Time-Space" of the Portuguese-Speaking World*. Berkeley: Institute of European Studies.
Born, G., and D. Hesmondhalgh (eds.) (2000). *Western Music and Its Others: Difference, Representation, and Appropriation in Music*. Berkeley: University of California Press.
Bull, M. (2006). "Investigating the Culture of Mobile Listening: From Walkman to iPod." In K. O'Hara and B. Brown (eds.), *Consuming Music Together: Social and Collaborative Aspects of Music Consumption Technologies*, 131–49. Dordrecht: Springer.
Castellano, C. G. (2018). "Curating and Cultural Difference in the Iberian Context: From Difference to Self-Reflexivity (and Back Again)." *Journal of Iberian and Latin American Research*, 24(2): 103–22.
Castelo, C. (1998). *"O modo português de estar no mundo": O luso-tropicalismo e a ideologia colonial portuguesa (1933–1961)*. Porto: Edições Afrontamento.
Coelho, C. (2006). "TAP, mais que uma empresa, uma 'national equity.'" *Atlântico: Revista mensal de ideias e debates*, 2(18): 60–1.
Coller, K., J. H. Mills, and A. J. Mills (2016). "The British Airways Heritage Collection: An Ethnographic 'History.'" *Business History*, 58(4): 547–70.
Cresswell, T. (2006). *On the Move: Mobility in the Modern Western World*. London: Routledge.
Cwerner, S., S. Kesselring, and J. Urry (eds.) (2009). *Aeromobilities*. London: Routledge.
Domingos, N., and E. Peralta (eds.) (2013). *A cidade e o colonial. Dinâmicas coloniais e reconfigurações pós-coloniais*. Lisbon: Edições 70.
Elliot, R. (2020). "Revisiting Old Haunts in a Time of Lockdown: Holiday Records, Virtuality and the Nostalgia Gap." Paper presented at the international conference

Urban Nostalgia: The Musical City in the 19th and 20th Centuries. Centre de recherches sur les arts et le langage—CRAL, Paris, July 5–7.

Feldman-Bianco, B. (2007). "Empire, Postcoloniality and Diasporas." *Hispanic Research Journal*, 8(3): 279–90.

Figueiredo, S. (2016). *Design de cartazes da TAP (1945–2016).* PhD diss., Aveiro, UAveiro.

Freixo, A. (2009). *Minha pátria é a língua portuguesa: a construção da idéia de lusofonia em Portugal.* Rio de Janeiro: Apicuri.

Gentil-Homem, P. (2014). *Sobre as nuvens: Design para a companhia aérea de Portugal (1945–1979).* PhD diss., ULisboa, Lisbon.

Gopinath, S., and J. Stanyek (eds.) (2013). *The Oxford Handbook of Mobile Music Studies,* vol. 1. Oxford: Oxford University Press.

Govil, N. (2004). "Something Spatial in the Air: In-Flight Entertainment and the Topographies of Modern Air Travel." In N. Couldry and A. McCarthy (eds.), *Mediaspace: Place, Scale and Culture in a Media Age,* 223–52. London: Routledge.

Kivijärvi, M., A. J. Mills, and J. H. Mills (2019). "Performing Pan American Airways through Coloniality: An ANTi-History Approach to Narratives and Business History." *Management and Organizational History,* 14(1): 33–54.

Lopes, E. R. (ed.) (2011). *A lusofonia—uma questão estratégica fundamental.* Lisbon: SaeR/Jornal Sol.

Manning, P. (2010). "The Semiotics of Brand." *Annual Review of Anthropology,* 39: 33–49.

Marques, M. M. (2012). "Post-Colonial Portugal: Between Scylla and Charybdis." In U. Bosma, J. Lucassen, and G. Oostindie (org.), *Postcolonial Migrations and Identity Politics: Europe, Russia, Japan and the United States in Comparison,* 127–53. London: Berghahn.

Matsanuga, L. (2016). "The Corporate Brand: Toward an Anthropology of Branding." In H. Nakamaki, K. Hioki, I. Mitsui, and Y. Takeuchi, *Enterprise as an Instrument of Civilization: An Anthropological Approach to Business Administration,* 227–43. Tokyo: Springer.

Paludi, M. (2017). *Representation of Latin America in Pan American Airways: Decolonial Feminism on a Multi-national.* PhD diss., Halifax, Saint Mary's University.

Peralta, E. (2011). "Fictions of a Creole Nation: (Re)presenting Portugal's Imperial Past." In H. Bonavita (ed.), *Negotiating Identities: Constructed Selves and Others,* 193–217. Amsterdam: Rodopi.

Pereira, S. M. J. (2011). *A dimensão cultural da Lusofonia como factor de relevância económica.* Lisbon: U Católica Portuguesa.

Ponzanesi, S., and B. B. Blaagaard (eds.) (2011). *Deconstructing Europe: Postcolonial Perspectives.* London: Routledge.

Radano, R., and T. Olaniyan (eds.) (2016). *Audible Empire: Music, Global Politics, Critique.* Durham, NC: Duke University Press.

Sanches, M. R. 2006. "Where is the post-colonial? In-betweenness, identity and 'Lusophonia' in trans/national contexts." In F. Heidemann and de Toro, A. (ed.), *New hybridities: societies and cultures in transition,* 115–45. Hildesheim and New York: Georg Olms.

Sousa, V. (2015). *Da 'portugalidade' à 'lusofonia.'* PhD diss., UMinho, Braga.

Staniland, M. (2003). *Government Birds: Air Transport and the State in Western Europe.* Oxford: Rowman and Littlefield.

TAP Portugal (2011). Jornal TAP 85 ("Especial Novo Posicionamento"). February. https://jornal.tap.pt/Jornal/jornalTAP_85_especial.pdf (accessed June 25, 2021).

UP Magazine (2020). January. https://www.flytap.com/en-us/on-board/up-magazine?accordionid=7326722c-d0a0-42df-88b6-56d6750a5625 (accessed June 25, 2021).

Wilkie, F. (2012). "'Choreographies of Nationhood': Performing Aviation as Spectacle." *PUBLIC*, 23(45): 201–11.

Online Videos

TAP Air Portugal (2011). "Mariza, Paulo Flores e Roberta Sá—De Braços Abertos." YouTube, February 25. https://www.youtube.com/watch?v=S1vfiu9qJj0 (accessed June 25, 2021).

TAP Air Portugal (2014). "Cuca Roseta faz surpresa a bordo de um voo da TAP em apoio à Seleção." YouTube, June 22. https://www.youtube.com/watch?v=OFtGRiXWTYM (accessed June 25, 2021).

TAP Air Portugal (2018). "Concerto de morna a bordo da TAP." YouTube, September 3. https://www.youtube.com/watch?v=DU9cCFHJYz8 (accessed June 25, 2021).

TAP Air Portugal (2019). "TAP celebrou o Carnaval com Kataleya." YouTube, March 7. www.youtube.com/watch?v=tQSO_X3Psxs (accessed June 25, 2021).

TAP Air Portugal (2019). "Djodje surpreendeu passageiros da TAP com um concerto abordo." YouTube, April 8. https://www.youtube.com/watch?v=2cTrmnHhHcU (accessed June 25, 2021).

CDs

Bennett, T. (1965). *If I Ruled the World: Songs for the Jet Set*. Colombia.

Crosby, B. (1962). *Holiday in Europe*. Radio Recorders.

Galarza, S. (1990). *Holiday in Portugal*. Monitor.

Paredes, C. (1989). *Asas sobre o Mundo*. Universal Music.

Sinatra, F. (1958). *Come Fly with Me*. Capitol.

TAP Portugal (2008). *TOP Executive Collection*. EMI Music Portugal.

TAP. The Airline of Portugal (c. 1974–9). *Take a Musical Tour of Portugal*. Estúdio.

Chapter 12

NEW LISBON: MUSICAL HYBRIDISMS AND THE
REINVENTION OF A POSTCOLONIAL CITY

Marcos Cardão

The city of Lisbon has been the scene of profound changes that have affected the urban fabric and the symbolic and cultural worlds of the city. One of the distinctive features of this transformation is the growing cosmopolitization associated with the creation of a new city identity, developed largely by institutional forms of governance. These are embodied in the promotion of brand images that stylize cultural diversity, in strategic programs that focus on the touristification of certain areas of the city, and in the upgrading of the urban fabric through the evocation of Lisbon's history.[1] The redefinition of the city's identity is not exhausted in institutional programs and strategies; forms close to an everyday or alternative cosmopolitanism have also emerged, resulting from the encounters, and social and cultural practices that are a feature of the city (Oliveira 2020). Some of them occur in the field of popular music, with the emergence of new practices, languages, and musical repertoires that characterize the global postcolonial condition in which Lisbon is seeking to involve itself.

Music mobilizes a network of discourses and narratives and is one of the ways of performing identities, establishing differences, and imagining local specificities. The emergence of new performers and subcategories associated with dance music or electronic music, in close dialogue with various genres of "African music" (Cidra 2010), such as afro-house, *zouk*, *kuduru*, *funaná*, *batuque*, *tarraxo*, and *kizomba*, has contributed to the sonic and expressive redefinition of Lisbon. Although the emergence of musical hybridisms is not exclusive to Lisbon (Canclini 2005), indeed, it is something of a global trend and a way of territorializing musical genres,[2] and several discursive practices have emerged, spread by various agents who seek to manage and capitalize the emerging musical genres, giving them specific identities. Lisbon would then host an unusual "meeting of cultures," an identity topic with a huge historical ballast that was reappropriated to reimagine the city.

It was in this context that Lusophony acquired the role of explanatory category and gained symbolic efficacy in an attempt to reflect the uniqueness of the cultural encounters taking place in Lisbon (Barre and Vanspauwen

2013). It is a category that was not only promoted and used locally but also conveyed by international agents to explain Lisbon's originality, particularly by large multinational companies such as Red Bull, a brand of energy drinks that created a global platform within the so-called creative industries to promote urban lifestyles and musical creativity, particularly in the area of dance and electronic music.

The concept of Lusophony emerged in the mid-1990s in the wake of a process of redefining an identity triggered by European integration, and it will have served as a compensatory mechanism of imperial imaginary in the postcolonial period (Margarido 2000; Lourenço 2004; Sanches 2006). Lusophony had an institutional framework with the creation of the Community of Portuguese Language Countries (CPLP), founded on July 17, 1996, and a media extension with the emergence of radio station RDP Africa, created in 1996, and the television channel RTP Africa, created in 1998. As with similar concepts, such as Anglophony or Francophony, Lusophony would come to support the idea of a Lusophone community, seen as the result of a historical and cultural experience shared by Portugal and the former colonial territories, which adopted Portuguese as the official language after gaining independence. The Portuguese language would thus function as a repository of common history, culture, and memories, also incorporating an idealized notion of cultural familiarity.

Like Lusophony, which is an example of how identity construction processes seek to legitimize a representation of the past, musical classification practices play a part in constructing their objects, characterizing them by identification or differentiation, that is, they create realities, produce effects, and impose an interpretation (Hacking 1999). Accepting that the process of construction of national identities is an international phenomenon that is defined by relationship and complementarity, no matter how much national histories may suggest otherwise, this chapter sets out to analyze the practices of musical mediation used by various agents. It looks at the role they had in redefining the image of Lisbon, as a cosmopolitan and plural city, from a cultural point of view. It also intends to ascertain how the mediation practices, in particular those exercised by Red Bull, engaged with the locally produced discourses, largely in acknowledgment of a rhetoric of "meeting of cultures." Instead of creating false oppositions between the local and the global, or between the national and the international, it has chosen to underline how these categories interact with one another, complement each other, and are in permanent dialogue.

The chapter is divided into two sections: the first seeks to identify some musicians, producers, and performers who contributed to promoting the city of Lisbon as a new global creative center. This section is entitled "Nova Lisboa," the title of a song by the musician Dino d'Santiago, which has become a kind of anthem/manifesto celebrating the city, marked by the emergence of new artists, expressive practices, and musical hybridisms. Dino d'Santiago and Kalaf Epalanga, musician and writer, are examples of two Black artists who have gained media visibility in recent years and have helped to redefine the image of Lisbon as a postcolonial city, open to new themes and protagonists.

The second section will analyze the role played by Red Bull in the mediation of new musical trends, referring to some initiatives that the company has undertaken in Lisbon. The aim is to see how the mediation of Red Bull has internationalized and is possibly contributing to foster the career of some artists, while producing effects on how the city is imagined, in particular by reinforcing the idea of Lisbon as a global, modern, and cosmopolitan city. At the same time, it tries to appreciate how the appearance of new protagonists and musical hybridisms have put the city of Lisbon in tune with the overall postcolonial condition and opened a space to question postcoloniality. Understood in different ways, and not always harmoniously, the postcolonial condition has favored the emergence of musical hybridisms. These were partly converted into items of tourist marketing and identity consumption, fitting to some extent into the institutional strategies for managing the city, even if they did not prevent flagging the gaps and discontinuities with the colonial past, giving rise to social practices close to what Paul Gilroy (2004) calls "postcolonial conviviality."

"Nova Lisboa"

Nowadays called Huambo, during the colonial period "Nova Lisboa" was the name of a city in Angola, built to symbolize imperial modernity.[3] But the name "New Lisbon" is today mostly associated with a song title by Dino d'Santiago, a Portuguese musician and songwriter who was born in Quarteira (Algarve) of Cape Verdean parents, and who first became known for taking part in *Operação Triunfo*. This was a television program shown on RTP (Rádio Televisão Portuguesa) between 2003 and 2011 in which contestants were selected to stay at a music academy and then take part in a weekly show put on by the program's production team.

After his time on the contest, Dino d'Santiago pursued his musical career in the area of soul, R&B, and hip-hop. His first solo album, entitled *Eva* (Lusafrica, 2013), was marked by Cape Verdean culture and expressive practices, including songs such as "DJonsinho Cabral," originally recorded by the group Os Tubarões.[4] Dino d'Santiago would later develop forms of musical hybridism, appropriating current information and communication technologies and emerging sounds, especially after the release of the album *Mundu Nôbu* (Sony, 2018), which would give the musician media visibility. The album was praised by specialized critics and won the "Best Album and Critics' Prize." The musician received the distinction of "Best Solo Artist" in the first edition of the Play Awards (2019) and also won in the category of "Best International Rhythm" at the Cabo Verde Music Awards. The album led to the internationalization of his career, and Dino d'Santiago became a prominent figure in specialized publications such as the *Rolling Stone* magazine (Leight 2019), even collaborating on Madonna's album *Madame X* (Warner Music, 2019).

"Mundu Nôbu" is mainly sung in Cape Verde Creole. It is characterized by the fusion of various musical styles and languages and features the participation of various guest producers, including Branko & Pedro, from Enchufada, an independent record label founded in 2006 by João Branko Barbosa and Kalaf Ângelo, who would later change their name to Kalaf Epalanga (https://enchufada.bandcamp.com/). The two were members of Buraka Som Sistema, a group that pioneered the fusion of electronic music with African musical genres, particularly *kuduro* (Moorman 2014; Barre 2019).

Alongside Príncipe Discos, perhaps the label that has given greater international visibility to the afro-house genres produced in the outskirts of Lisbon,[5] Enchufada is another independent label seeking to rejuvenate global electronic music and, as stated on its official page, bring "the sounds of the diaspora and rhythms of the global south to the forefront" (Barry 2013; Keeling 2014).

If mentioning the "sounds of diaspora" reflects the importance of transnational traffic and connections, the reference to the "rhythms of the global south" seems to communicate with a concept that in recent years has been worked on in the academic field, particularly in the area of postcolonial and decolonial studies, part of them committed to alternative projects of social and political transformation. Sociologist Boaventura Sousa Santos has developed several projects in this field, working on concepts such as "Epistemologies of the South" (Menezes 2008: 5–10) in order to broaden the discussion on epistemological diversity in the social sciences and humanities, question the hierarchical relations that exist between the North and the South, and develop a process for appreciating the practices and knowledge of the so-called Global South. The concept of "Epistemologies of the South" has prompted several debates (Santos 2003), notably in the field of what has been called "decolonial theory,"[6] and has continued the academic work of rescuing traditions that have been marginalized, discredited, or forgotten by the Western canon and by thinking rooted in ethnocentricity.

While the mention of the "sounds of the diaspora and rhythms of the global south" tends to place the Enchufada label in tune with the global postcolonial condition, thus embracing the possibilities of dialogue between diverse musical genres and expressive practices, the valorization of Lisbon's specificities suggests a link between the celebration of global diversity and a locally sourced narrative. Indeed, Enchufada intends to be a creative platform to promote and celebrate the city of Lisbon "as one of the epicenters of global electronics and a cultural link."[7] This programmatic line makes the label one of the promoters of redefining Lisbon's identity, participating in an apparently invisible but effective way in changing the city.

Mundu Nôbu has the collaboration of several producers, who contribute to the stylistic diversity of the album. There are songs that approach musical genres such as kizomba (Sedano 2020: 91–109), in "Nôs Crença," or funaná, in "Nôs Funaná" or "Fidjo de Poilon," a music and dance genre historically associated with Santiago Island, the largest island of the Cape Verde archipelago. Funaná is also used in the official merchandise of Dino d'Santiago, who in video clips and promotional photographs wears printed t-shirts that read: "Funaná is the new Punk," "Funaná is the Funk," or "Funaná is the new Grime." After the release of the album *Kriola* (Sony Music, 2020), which came with a press release that referred to the "creolization of the world,"[8] Dino d'Santiago started wearing t-shirts that read "Lisboa Kriola."

The musicians and producers Seiji and Kalaf Epalanga, relevant names in the field of global dance music, were the producers of the song "Nova Lisboa," which gained the status of anthem/manifesto of the album *Mundu Nôbu*. In an album sung mostly in Creole, the song "Nova Lisboa" is interpreted in Portuguese, with a small excerpt in Creole that functions as the motto of the song, in which it refers that they are not here to sell "saudade," or nostalgia, nor the idea of "morabeza."

The lyrics were written by Kalaf Epalanga (Valle 2018: 31–47), who was also the executive producer of the album *Mundu Nôbu*. They suggest a desire to displace a historical representation of the Cape Verdean diaspora (Cidra 2021), mainly associated with *saudade* (a word which describes a simultaneous feeling of loss, lack, distance) and *morabeza* (a word in Cape Verdean Creole which means friendliness), and to present contemporary forms of musical hybridism by placing musical genres of Cape Verdean origin, such as *batuque* and *funaná*, at the center of global electronic music. Besides displacing a historical representation of Cape Verdeanness, associated with the histories, identities, and cultural practices of the Cape Verde islands, there is also the desire to present a new generation of Black musicians, producers, and performers who have recently ceased to be a "silent presence" in the city, as used to happen in the past, to become an integral part of Lisbon, redesigned as a Creole city.[9]

The song "Nova Lisboa" celebrates the role of Lisbon as a producer of cultural encounters and musical hybridisms, dialoguing on the one hand with an identity narrative with historical ballast but not exhausting itself in it.[10] The celebration of the city also took place through promotional interviews, in which Dino d'Santiago highlighted the unique nature of Lisbon as a place that favored the mixing of sounds and cultures (Belanciano 2017). The idea of Lisbon as an acculturated,[11] or even Creole, city (Glissant 1996) unfolds in the allusion to new ways of feeling the city—as suggested in the verse "come and feel, feel, feel this new Lisbon"— initiating an extra-discursive representation that encompassed the senses, the affections, and emotions (Leight 2020).

The sensory dimension was supported by the presence in the public space of a new generation of Black musicians and performers, such as Kalaf Epalanga. Even though he is not a new figure on the Portuguese artistic scene,[12] Kalaf Epalanga gained more media visibility when he started his activity as a writer, first with the chronicles published in the *Público* newspaper, starting in 2008, and edited in the book *Estórias de Amor para Meninos de Cor* (Caminho 2011). Kalaf Epalanga again published a book of chronicles, entitled *O Angolano que Comprou Lisboa* (Caminho 2014), and then his first novel, entitled *Também os Brancos Sabe Dançar: um romance musical* (Caminho 2018), a work of autofiction that covers a portrait of Benguela, the city where Kalaf was born, and of contemporary Lisbon, whose population comes from various backgrounds. The novel's starting point is Kalaf's arrest by Norwegian immigration police while traveling by bus with an expired Angolan passport.[13]

Both in the novel and in the books of chronicles, Kalaf Epalanga refers to the cultural exchanges and cultural hybridisms that occur in the city of Lisbon, valuing the city's ability to embrace cultural diversity. But he does not fail to mention cases of racial discrimination (Mendonça 2018), a subject that was practically invisible in the Portuguese public space, but which has been gaining visibility in recent years with the emergence of Afro-descendant and anti-racist movements in Portugal (Henriques 2017).

From musician, promoter of forms of musical hybridism, to writer with media visibility, Kalaf Epalanga became one of the first Black artists to occupy the position of public intellectual and, in part, to represent the desires and anxieties of the Afro-descendant community in Portugal. Several of his public interventions brought the themes of identity, race, gender, and ecology out into the open (Ribeiro 2015). Taking advantage of the media visibility that the literary medium provides, particularly through literary festivals such as the International Literary Festival of Paraty, Kalaf also developed a critical discourse on Lusophony, lamenting that Lusophony is still "in the hands of politicians, it is not in the hands of the people, of the producers of culture, of those who make culture" (Ré 2019).

Mostly institutional in nature, Lusophony and the narrative of affinities of feeling and culture have given rise to various criticisms and distinct forms of appropriation. At the same time as it serves for Portuguese identity consumption, Lusophony and the rhetoric of the "meeting of cultures" has been appropriated and transformed by quite a few musicians, performers, and cultural agents, sometimes in a creative way, with the translation unfolding in subversion and destabilization (Cidra 2021). These creative transformations do not prevent other cultural agents, especially international ones like Red Bull, from appropriating Lusophony as a way to characterize the "Lisbon difference" in the world electronic music market.

The Distribution of the Possible

Red Bull became a milestone in the contemporary music industry,[14] notably from the late 1990s, when the Red Bull Music Academy (RBMA) was founded. It emerged in a particular historical context, marked by the dawn of the digital era and the appearance of the first streaming platforms (MySpace, YouTube, and later Spotify, Soundcloud, and Bandcamp). The emergence of streaming platforms forced the music industry to modify and reinvent its business models.

RBMA started as a support platform for emerging artists to become an influential brand in the global electronic music field. The RBMA website has served as a platform for publishing music online and has offered producers, DJs, and other music industry figures the chance to work for free at various recording studios. RBMA has also created a radio station, produced podcasts, edited films, published the *Daily Note* newspaper, which brought together a team of writers, designers, and artists from different cities, and organized festivals, talks, workshops, and conferences in over sixty countries.[15]

All these media highlight the role that the RBMA ascribes to the production of knowledge, not only with the intention of representing or knowing, but producing effects in the field that it seeks to describe and interpret. By creating categories and participating in the construction of new objects, the RBMA helped to determine modes of visibility and perception. The attempt to assign meaning and impose an interpretation on different contemporary musical expressions is part of the strategy of a consulting firm called Yadastar (Budzinski 2015), responsible for turning Red Bull into a global institution committed to promoting creativity in urban music.

The brand management operated by Yadastar imposed a strategy and sought to guide all aspects of its execution. The aim was to turn Red Bull into one of the most respected brands in the music industry, with recognized cultural capital, highlighting it as a large multinational company that could help develop new musical practices and expressions. Several multinational companies have abandoned traditional marketing methods since the 1990s, based essentially on the production of brands and logos, and turned to creating stories and narratives that engage the public, making them appropriate and becoming an integral part of their lives (Salmon 2017; Taylor 2012).

The way Red Bull is associated with the music industry, providing resources and tools for a number of artists to develop new musical expressions and boost the careers of emerging musicians, allows us to reexamine the relationship between companies whose objective is to legitimize the brand and fix identities, and the artists associated with alternative musical styles, whose modes of production are mostly "artisanal" and collaborative. In effect, the ethos of independence, summed up in the expression "do it yourself," and associated with dance music through codes and conventions, particularly in the question of authorship, with artists opting for a certain dilution of identity by signing their records with pseudonyms, contributed toward the creation of a marginal, or alternative, culture to the so-called mainstream (Collin 2018). At the same time, the celebration of the hedonism of the dance floor in connection with questions of "race," gender, and sexuality (Lawrence 2004), reconfigured through juvenile practices and sociabilities, gave rise to new relationships between music and politics.

Discussions on popular culture usually operate through opposing pairs regarded as stable and permanent, which lie between the pure autonomy of cultural artifacts and total encapsulation. The mediation practices created by RBMA contribute to shuffling these pairs of opposites, so that possible contaminations can be contemplated and new questions raised: What are the risks of delegating the control of music production to large multinational companies? While facilitating the production, recording, and dissemination of genres considered marginal, do the mediation practices of the RBMA end up by draining off differences, cataloguing them in a prescriptive and conventional manner, either through the assignment of fixed identities or through the reuse of national narratives (Gillett 2019)?

The production of the documentary *Lusofonia, a (R)evolução* (2006) was the first initiative undertaken by Red Bull in the Portuguese music scene (Alge 2015). The documentary had RTP as an institutional partner, which broadcasted the documentary several times on its channels. The RBMA also established protocols with the Camões Institute, a public institute created in 1992 to promote Portuguese language and culture abroad, and with the CPLP (Community of Portuguese Speaking Countries) to disseminate and promote the documentary in Portuguese-speaking countries.

The documentary portrays Lusophony as an eminently Portuguese characteristic, the result of five centuries of history and a "unique cultural root."[16] These characteristics, considered "unique," would contribute to the fusion of musical elements from Portuguese-speaking countries and integrate them into emerging genres of urban music. These would come to be seen as specific musical products of Lusophony, which gained the status of a singular identity and a distinctive mark in the global context. Mobilizing categories such as miscegenation, conviviality, crossing, and fusion of cultures, the documentary established a dialogue with the official representations of Portuguese identity, in which Lusophony assumed a dominant role, trivializing a contributary representation of the historical memory of the Portuguese empire.

In a process described without ambiguities or contradictions, Lusophony would be responsible for triggering immediate forms of dialogue and intercommunication, without apparent misunderstandings, only made possible thanks to the existence of strong cultural ties and a common history. By amalgamating and mythifying five centuries of history, reducing them to the narrative of the meeting of cultures, the documentary erased the effects of colonialism in the present and helped to promote a sanitized image of Lisbon as a postcolonial city without cracks or antagonisms. In effect, the category "postcolonial" seemed to indicate a form of merely historical or chronological periodization, that is, the period following colonization, which appeared portrayed without the unequal power relations produced by colonialism (Seth 2018: 45–75). As a simple chronological marker, the "postcolonial" did not encompass a critical assessment of the history of colonialism, nor did it deconstruct its effects in the present. This means that the uncritical appropriation of the concept of Lusophony made by the RBMA was limited to reproducing an identity narrative of local scope, deliberately partial, to reuse it in the global market, without questioning the "durability" of colonialism or the dividing lines of postcolonial society.

The remaining RBMA initiatives in the country were already held in a context in which Lisbon was abandoning its semi-peripheral nature to come closer to and, especially in terms of tourism, "compete" with other cities around the world. In this climate, culture, especially the practices and sociabilities associated with music, came to mean not only an object of consumption but also an opportunity to advertise the city.

It was from about 2015 onward that electronic music began to figure as one of the distinctive brands of Lisbon, which began to welcome emerging musical genres as a form of urban branding and tourism marketing, indicators of a way of governing the city in terms of major international events, namely, dance music festivals. In 2014, the first edition of Lisb/on Jardim Sonoro was held, a festival that each year brings together the most celebrated names in international dance music. The festival's institutional partner is Lisbon City Hall, and it is sponsored by Tourism of Lisbon. The first edition of the Lisboa Dance Festival was then held in 2016, an annual festival, which included conferences and performances by various international artists. From 2019, the festival would be renamed Id No Limits Contemporary Sounds. In 2017, the first edition of the Lisboa Electrónica festival appeared, an initiative that also encompassed live performances, conferences, and workshops with different professionals in the area, including musicians, agents, and promoters. From 2018, the festival started to host the lectures and conferences curated by RBMA. In 2018, the Nova Batida festival was held for the first time. In addition to electronic music, it offered the chance to experience several different activities and lifestyles, including surf lessons, beach parties, and yoga sessions in its program.

Even before Lisbon became an international stage for electronic music events, RBMA had already organized the first Boiler Room in the city in 2013. An event that became one of RBMA's brand images, which consisted of organizing a party in a secret location in a city, considered global, to be broadcast in live streaming to the rest of the world, later becoming available to be viewed in the Boiler Room archive (https://boilerroom.tv). In 2016, RBMA once again held another event in Lisbon, called Cultural Clash, another initiative with great international media coverage, which had already passed through cities such as London, New York, or Toronto. The first Boiler Room held in Lisbon featured the performance of Buraka Som Sistema, perhaps the biggest symbol of new musical trends that emerged in Lisbon in recent years. Buraka Som Sistema had already curated an event organized by RBMA in 2015, which aimed to document the different musical expressions of Lisbon, giving an account of the "influences that inspired and shaped their distinctive sound," as stated in the event's synopsis.[17] In the event's announcement, the RBMA was again using the Lusophony category to describe the singularity and originality of the Portuguese phenomenon:

> Portuguese and Portuguese-speaking (or to use the correct—and brilliant—term, "Lusophone") music has crept into international consciousness through all kinds of diverse and fascinating routes. The nation has a cultural identity which thrives on constant and close relationship with the former colonies in Africa including Mozambique and Angola, plus the utterly unique mid-Atlantic Cape Verde Islands, but also has a constant trans-Atlantic to-and-fro with the musical powerhouse that is Brazil.[18]

Like what had happened with the film *Lusofonia, the (R)evolution*, Lusophony was again the concept chosen to describe the presumed cultural affinities between Portugal and the states that had previously been colonial territories. In this specific case, the imagination of diversity on a global level did not dispense with the use of local narratives, which were reused to singularize the country's current specificities.

Although its use persisted in some mediation practices, Lusophony would become an explanatory category more scrutinized and subject to criticism. In recent years, various agents, including journalists and promoters, have tried to find new designations to characterize emerging musical trends, contributing in the same way to redefine Lisbon's identity as a postcolonial city. *Batida de Lisboa* (Lisbon beat) was one of the terms used to describe and singularize the new musical expressions, even being used as the title of a documentary about the new musical expressions in the city.[19] The designation intended to characterize the new musical hybridisms that occurred in the city, recognizable in musical genres such as *kuduru*, *tarraxo*, or afro-house. The name was later taken up by international publications that also sought to signal the originality of the sounds produced in Lisbon (Beta 2014).

Música afro-portuguesa (Afro-Portuguese music) was another expression used to try to characterize emerging musical trends and ascribe specific characteristics to them. Coined by journalist Vítor Belanciano, the term highlighted the fact that the new musical trends were mostly produced by Afro-descendants.[20] In addition to distancing itself from the concept of Lusophony, the expression "Afro-Portuguese music" sought to signal the role of the Black diaspora, also known as *afroeuropeia* (Afro-European) (Pitts 2019), in the creation of new musical styles and languages.

According to Paul Gilroy, music and its rituals make it possible "to create a model where identity can be understood as something different from a fixed essence" (1993: 102). Although the label "Afro-Portuguese music" reflected the vitality of the Portuguese artistic field, stressing the role of Afro-descendants in its diversification, it did not fail to nationalize musical expressions that had been characterized by the movement, fluidity, and crossover of a diasporic culture. This meant that the possibility of shifting the identity axis and escaping the fixity of national identity, more prescriptive than plastic or flexible, was undermined.

Based on international exchanges and connections and dynamic processes of hybridity, itinerancy, and mixing, emerging musical trends are perhaps less Lisbon-based than some mediation practices would like to suggest or indicate. Although mediation practices have real effects and are central to reimagining the city, Lisbon's specificity is neither unequivocal nor linear. In fact, the reinvention of Lisbon as a postcolonial city and an aggregating pole of musical hybridisms is partly the result of methodological nationalism, which continues to use the category of "nation" to explain local specificities, not forgetting the relevance of "banal nationalism" (Billig 1991) and the recreation of "neocolonial" concepts, such as Lusophony (Cahen 2013: 297–315), which support this narrative.

If the transnational dynamics, intensified by the global circulation of music through streaming platforms and accessible software such as Fruity Loops (FL Studio), contributed to put the centrality attributed to the city of Lisbon into context, the fact that the musical landscape of the city is being redesigned from its periphery—a considerable number of the musicians responsible for the introduction of new musical genres comes from neighborhoods such as Bairro da Quinta do Mocho (Sacavém), Cova da Moura (Buraca), Rio de Mouro (Sintra), and so on—allows us to call on other histories and, in particular, shift them from the rhetoric of exchanges, interaction, and peaceful cohabitation imagined from the city center. Instead of attributing a unique and almost always positive and conciliatory sense to the postcolonial condition, these other histories gather processes of social marginalization and spatial segregation, histories marked by makeshift housing, socially discredited and underpaid jobs, estrangement from institutions, and forms of political participation.

The other geography of the city of Lisbon, composed mostly of social housing estates or unlicensed buildings, also embraces distinct forms of sociability that are not exhausted in major international events, music festivals, forms of tourist marketing, or essentialist narratives of national and local identity. There are several artists who would like to detach themselves from normative discourses about the city of Lisbon, that is to say, artists linked to anti-racist movements, such as the rapper Chullage, stage name of Nuno Santos, resident in Arrentela (Seixal) and activist of Plataforma Gueto, an anti-imperialist and anti-racist Black movement,[21] who recently criticized the linear way of commodifying the musical genres emerging in the suburbs of the city of Lisbon:

> Lisbon sells itself as the capital of Angolan music, of Cape Verdean music, albeit with electronic nuances, and that music is in Lisbon, obviously. When we talk about afro-house, we talk about Marfox and various artists who have changed the sonic texture of Lisbon. But they've been changing it for 20 years and they do it in the peripheries. I wouldn't see a problem with that if you really embraced that African Lisbon. What you can't do is embrace the sonic texture of African Lisbon and not embrace the social skin of African Lisbon, the men and women of color who live here. You can't make them invisible and, once the African body is clinging to the music and the vibration to exist, hold onto that and, in the act of commodifying it, whiten it and say this is the music of Lisbon. (Lopes 2020)

The representations of a Creole and mixed-race Lisbon, a stage for encounters and interactions, emerged at a time when the issue of racism became more visible in the media, which contributed to questioning linear narratives and forms of mediation and discussion of the initiatives to represent the city as a place that welcomes diversity and enhances musical hybridism. The same city that invested discursively in the idea of meeting and cultural diversity, whether institutionally or through forms of mediation introduced by various agents, was also characterized by forms of social marginalization, spatial and labor segregation, reinforced by ethno-racial markers, which exposed the effects of structural discrimination.

The term "postcolonial conviviality" is intended to describe the processes of cohabitation and interaction that have made multiculturalism a common feature of social life in postcolonial cities (Gilroy 2004: xii). Contrary to the melancholy of discourses lamenting the loss of imperial hegemony and looking for things to compensate for it, and distinct from forms of governance of cultural diversity, postcolonial conviviality presupposes ways of living with difference in urban settings. Built from practices, encounters, and forms of negotiation, "postcolonial conviviality" is hardly exhausted in univocal discourses, representations, and practices.

Defining a community according to a homogeneous identity brand, endowed with similar and identifiable characteristics, be it Lusophony or the rhetoric of cultural encounters, excludes other forms of identification, expropriates singularities, and erases differences. The attempt to redefine the identity of Lisbon through institutional programs and strategies, cosmopolitan electronic music festivals, or mediation practices manufactured by multinational companies, or introduced by other agents, neither exhausts the narratives nor covers the processes, encounters, and sociabilities that gave rise to the new musical hybridisms. In the specific case of afro-house, the genre was already circulating in the peripheral areas of the city and on streaming platforms before entering the established commercial circuit and being covered by legitimating discourses. Instead of a history of diversity and cultural encounters, there would be several histories that, although not unrepresentable, operated a displacement of the dominant modes of mediation and classification.

Conclusion

Music, its practices and sociabilities, has been mobilized discursively by various agents, including musicians, promoters, publishers, journalists, academics, companies, and so on. None of them have a privileged look on the phenomenon, nor do they possess a relationship of exteriority that only allows them to describe, know, and interpret it. In this sense, writing about music, classifying musical genres, or developing mediation practices that seek to attribute specific characteristics is not simply an "occupation" that is applied to a preexisting object; it is, rather, a cognitive enterprise that conceives and constructs its object (Seth 2004: 85–101). Recognizing that describing and interpreting is also regulating does not preclude questioning the ways of naming, classifying, or mediating a given event or reality.

This chapter has tried to show, or at least indicate, different ways of describing the emergence of new artists and forms of musical hybridism in the city of Lisbon. Various musicians and producers have tried to harmonize the emerging musical genres with the global postcolonial condition, valuing the transnational dialogues and the possibilities of transforming Lisbon's sonorities. They were also converted into a tourism marketing item and a way to specify Lisbon's distinctiveness as a stage of encounters in the postcolonial context, seen more from a chronological than a social or political point of view. Although postcolonial histories encompass forms of hybridity and mixture, conjugation and adaptation, exchange and interaction, they still signal the gaps in the contact zones. That is, they presuppose a critical evaluation of colonialism, the identification of its duration, and the deconstruction of its effects today.

Part of the postcolonial stories told about Lisbon highlighted the continuities, the affective ballast of a common history, instead of the metamorphoses, discontinuities, and ruptures. The identity references that enliven the imagination of a common history, of which postcolonial Lisbon would be a consequence, tend not to embrace the different ways of combining community and national narratives, giving primacy to the latter. The attempt to create a "Creole Lisbon," in the context of shared practices and sociabilities that are part of life in the outskirts of the city, suggests the redrafting of narratives of identity content, where the valorization of exchanges and interactions does not dismiss the questioning of the continuities of the colonial period, particularly in the representations that refer to the alleged Portuguese exceptionalism. Instead of being an arena for musical hybridisms endowed with unique characteristics, "Nova Lisboa" can perhaps be a place to train empathy, question privileges, and rehearse less scanty forms of postcolonial conviviality.

Notes

1 The city's application for UNESCO World Heritage status "Historic Lisbon, Global City" emphasizes the uniqueness of the urban landscape, alluding to the crossroads of cultures promoted by the Portuguese, "testimony to a millennial history of exchange of cultures, peoples and religions." https://www.am-lisboa.pt/451600/1/,000512/index.htm (accessed September 11, 2021).

2 In recent decades, vernacular forms of electronic music have emerged in several cities previously considered peripheral in the music industry. For example, in Dar es Salaam, Tanzania's largest city, Singeli has emerged, a music genre inspired by dance music styles, particularly subgenres such as Techno Hardcore and Gabber. Singeli has become one of the most popular music genres in East Africa, especially among the young population. In Kampala, Uganda's capital, the Nyege Nyege Tapes label was founded by Derek Debru (Belgium) and Arlen Dilsizian (Greek) and includes musicians from Tanzania, Kenya, and Uganda. In Durban, South Africa, a similar process is taking place with the emergence of Gqom, a genre also characterized by the crossing of musical genres associated with dance music. Other examples would be Electro Chabbi, created in Cairo, or Kuduro, which emerged in the outskirts of Luanda. Various forms of musical hybridity are also present in several South American cities. For example, the emergence in Rio de Janeiro of Baile Funk, or Funk Carioca, in the early 1990s, or Reggaeton, which emerged in Panama and Puerto Rico and has become a musical genre on a global scale.

3 The city of Huambo was created by decree in 1912, during the term in office of High Commissioner Norton de Matos. In 1921, the city was elevated to the status of a *sede de município* (equivalent to U.S. county seat), and in 1928, the year in which Salazar was appointed to head the Ministry of Finance, the draft was approved that changed the name of the city to Nova Lisboa. This name was only abolished in 1975, after the independence of Angola. The creation of a new city on the central plateau of Angola resulted from the convergence of European settlement plans with the layout of the Benguela Railway line, expressing the ambitions of imperial modernity, which included building a new administrative, commercial, and industrial center in Angola. The idea of modernity was associated with a specific location, the West, and exported to areas considered peripheral, particularly those under European colonial rule. Modernity was taken as a kind of corrective to solve the "colonial backwardness" and converted into a standard ideal, which made it incompatible with inequality and the paradigms of colonial governmentality (Chakrabarty 2000: 42–6).

4 Os Tubarões was a Cape Verdean band active from 1969 to 1994. It was one of the most representative groups of Cape Verdean music in the transition period toward independence and democracy.

5 The first record issued by Príncipe Discos, originally released in 2006, was entitled *Dj'S Do Guetto*, a pioneering compilation that included emerging afro-house artists, including Dj Marfox, Dj Nervoso, Dj Fofuxo, and others. See https://principedis

cos.wordpress.com/2013/02/10/pr001-va-djs-do-guetto-vol-1/ (accessed September 1, 2021).

6 The so-called decolonial practices have emerged from various parts of the globe, especially South America, where projects and strategies to decolonize knowledge and language have been developed. For the decolonial movement, decolonization is not only territorial, nor does it end with political independence, or national sovereignty; instead, it is a process that has a lasting impact that can be seen in the renewal of categories, knowledges, and knowledge (Mignolo 2011).

7 The annual celebrations of the Enchufada label began in 2017, following the compilation edition of the Enchufada Na Zona and the premiere of the show with the same name on NTS Radio (online radio station started in 2011, quite important in the field of electronic music). The last Enchufada Na Zona festival took place during the Covid-19 Pandemic and was renamed Enchufada na Zona ON AIR and converted into seven hours of streaming from the Lisbon nightclub Lux Frágil. It was in this context that João "Branko" Barbosa stated, "At a time when live music is going through a process of transformation, it makes more sense than ever to continue celebrating Lisbon as one of the epicentres of global electronica and a cultural link. That's exactly what we intend to do with the compilation and with Enchufada Na Zona ON AIR" (ReB Team 2021). In addition, João "Branko" Barbosa, accompanied by director João Pedro Moreira, created the documentary series "Club Atlas" in partnership with RTP. In the series, João "Branko" Barbosa travels through some of the most interesting cities from the point of view of new musical languages, including Lisbon, Lima, Montreal, Bombay, Arca, São Paulo, and Cidade da Praia.

8 In one of the promotional interviews for the album *Kriola* (Sony Music, 2020), Dino d'Santiago refers to the work of Ananya Kabir, who has been developing research on transnational processes of creolization (Brito 2020; Kabir 2019).

9 In his pioneering study, José Ramos Tinhorão mentions the silent presence of the Black population in Portugal over time, specifically referring to the contribution of the Black population to the appearance of the *fado-canção* in Lisbon: from this intimacy between whites and Blacks in the popular areas of Lisbon would result historical evidence that shows that the relations between the two ethnic groups were much deeper and more constant than has been imagined (Tinhorão 2019; Varela and Pereira 2020: 1–36).

10 The topic of the "meeting of cultures" came back into the media spotlight with the controversy over the possible construction of the museum of the Discoveries, or of the discoveries, in Lisbon, a designation that tended to crystallize a partial truth about a historical period. Supporters of the construction of the museum again evoked the exceptionalism of Portuguese colonization, seen as less violent, favorable to miscegenation and the meeting of cultures (See V/a 2018; Malhado 2018).
   Note that the expression "meeting of cultures" was also used in the context of the creation of the National Commission for the Commemoration of the Portuguese Discoveries (CNCDP), whose purpose was to prepare, coordinate, and organize the commemoration of the 500th anniversary of the Discoveries. Through a multifaceted program, CNCDP initiated a commemorative cycle, active between 1986 and 2002, which contributed to the renewal of the representations of the Portuguese Discoveries, particularly through the celebration of Portugal's role in opening up to the world, promoter of dialogue between cultures and catalyzer of multiculturalism (Cardão 2019: 17–47).

11 Dino d'Santiago stated that

> Lisbon is a good example of an acculturated, Creole city, which mixes and knows how to live with differences. And it is completely different from other capitals, such as Paris, London, New York. Cities that have various cultures in them, yes, but you can clearly feel that everything is very separate and segregated. And here in Lisbon, no. The big difference between Lisbon and the other capitals is that in our capital you experience acculturation and in the others you experience [various] cultures. (Mendonça 2019)

12   Kalaf Epalanga was one of the pioneers of the Drum and Bass movement in Portugal, a subgenre of dance music. As part of the Cooltrain Crew collective, he was involved in various musical projects, recorded two "Spoken Word" records, with 1 Uik Project and Type, a performance genre associated with hip-hop, at the time practically nonexistent in Portugal. In 2003, together with João "Branko" Barbosa, he founded the Enchufada label and was also a founding member of the Buraka Som Sistema. See https://www.publico.pt/autor/kalaf-angelo (accessed September 2, 2021).
13   The more celebratory side of the musical hybridisms that occur in the city of Lisbon tends to hide the processes of inequality, particularly in the field of rights, since some artists are not covered by the nationality law, which allows them to move freely within the Schengen area, and depends on the granting of a residence permit to stay in the European territory. This is the case of Kalaf Epalanga and conductor Andro Carvalho, who, when they were part of the group Buraka Som Sistema, were detained several times in Portugal for not having a residence permit (Belanciano 2020: 82).
14   Red Bull is an energy drink created in the mid-1980s, which became world-renowned for having developed a unique marketing strategy. The association of Red Bull with various events, both cultural and sporting, has given the brand visibility, distinguishing it in the field of functional drinks. https://www.redbull.com/pt-pt/energydrink/empresa (accessed September 4, 2021).
15   In the twenty years since then, RBMA lectures and conferences have included artists from various continents. The official RBMA website mentions the artists, musicians, and venues where the lectures have taken place, concluding that "RBMA lecturers represent an unparalleled source of musical knowledge and universal inspiration across genre and generation." https://www.redbullmusicacademy.com (accessed September 4, 2021).
16   The synopsis is available at https://www.rtp.pt/programa/tv/p22088 (accessed September 5, 2021). The documentary is available at: http://www.redbullmusicacademy.com/video-archive/documentaries/3 (accessed September 5, 2021).
17   The event, called "Lisbon: Red Bull Music Academy Takeover," took place on January 21, 2015 and, according to the synopsis, the aim was for "Red Bull Music Academy & Boiler Room [to] present an artist-curated event that tells the stories of Lisbon's most innovative artists, exploring the people, spaces and influences that have inspired and shaped their distinct sound." https://www.redbull.com/sg-en/events/red-bull-music-academy-takeover-boiler-room-lisboa (accessed September 7, 2021).
18   https://boilerroom.tv/lisbon-is-our-fifth-member-buraka-som-sistema-on-the-city-they-love-and-its-music/ (accessed September 7, 2021).
19   The documentary "Batida de Lisboa" (2019), by Vasco Viana and Rita Maia, covers a route through the suburban areas of Lisbon to portray the new musical trends. See also Estevens, in this volume.
20   Recently, several Black artists have emerged to reclaim the historical role of Black culture in the creation of different genres of electronic music (Wheeler 2020). On the

role of Black culture in the creation of different genres of electronic music, see Eshun (1998).
21 See https://plataformagueto.wordpress.com (accessed September 8, 2021). See also Raposo et al. (2021: 269–91).

References

Alge, B. (2015). "Lusofonia, a (R)Evolução: Discourses of Atlantic Roots and Routes in Luso World Music." *Norient: Network for Local and Global Sounds and Media Culture*, March 6. https://norient.com/academic/alge2013/ (accessed December 10, 2021).

Barre, J. (2019). "Sampling Lisbon: Kuduro and the Lusophone Imagination." *Journal of Popular Music Studies*, 31(1): 109–30.

Barre, J., and B. Vanspauwen (2013). "A Musical 'Lusofonia'? Music Scenes and the Imagination of Lisbon." *The World of Music*, New Series, 2(2): 119–46.

Barry, R. (2013). "This Is Our Grime: DJ Marfox, DJ Nigga Fox, Principe Records and the Sound of the Lisbon Ghettos." *FACT Magazine*, November 18. https://www.factmag.com/2013/10/18/this-is-our-grime-dj-marfox-dj-nigga-fox-principe-records-and-the-sound-of-the-lisbon-ghettos/ (accessed December 18, 2021).

Belanciano, V. (2017). "Dino d'Santiago e também do Algarve, do Porto e da nova Lisboa." *Público-Ípsilon*, October 12. https://www.publico.pt/2018/10/12/culturaipsilon/entrevista/dino-d-santiago-e-tambem-do-algarve-do-porto-e-da-nova-lisboa-1846731 (accessed December 18, 2021).

Belanciano, V. (2020). *Não Dá Para Ficar Parado—Música afro-portuguesa, celebração, conflito e esperança*. Porto: Edições Afrontamento.

Beta, A. (2014). "Lisbon's Batida Revolution." *Pitchfork*. https://pitchfork.com/features/electric-fling/9490-lisbons-batida-revolution/ (accessed December 18, 2021).

Billig, M. (1991). *Banal Nationalism*. London: Sage.

Brito, V. (2020). "(Entrevista) Dino D'Santiago." https://www.rimasebatidas.pt/dino-dsantiago-a-unica-forma-de-nao-fecharmos-fronteiras-e-assumirmos-a-criouliza cao-como-algo-positivo/ (accessed December 1, 2021).

Budzinski, N. (2015). "Eternal Pish." *Wire*, January. https://www.thewire.co.uk/about/contributors/nathan-budzinski/nathan-budzinski_eternal-pish (accessed December 18, 2021).

Cahen, M. (2013). "Portugal Is in the Sky: Conceptual Considerations on Communities, Lusitanity, and Lusophony." In M. Cahen and E. Morier-Genoud (eds.), *Imperial Migrations Colonial: Communities and Diaspora in the Portuguese World*, 297–315. Basingstoke: Palgrave Macmillan.

Canclini, N. (2005). *Hybrid Cultures: Strategies for Entering and Leaving Modernity*. London: University of Minnesota Press.

Cardão, M. (2019). "A grande aventura: Televisão, nacionalismo e as comemorações dos Descobrimentos portugueses." *Práticas da História, Journal on Theory, Historiography and Uses of the Past*, 8: 17–47.

Chakrabarty, D. (2000). *Provincializing Europe: Postcolonial Thought and Historical Difference*. Princeton, NJ: Princeton University Press.

Cidra, R. (2010). "Migração, Música e." In S. Castelo-Branco (ed.), *Enciclopédia da Música em Portugal no Século XX, L-P*, 773–93. Lisbon: Temas e Debates/Círculo de Leitores.

Cidra, R. (2021). *Funaná, raça e masculinidade: Uma trajetória colonial e pós-colonial*. Lisbon: Outro Modo.
Collin, M. (2018). *Rave On: Global Adventures in Electronic Dance Music*. Chicago: University of Chicago Press.
Epalanga, K. (2011). *Estórias de Amor para Meninos de Cor*. Lisbon: Caminho.
Eshun, K. (1998). *More Brilliant Than the Sun: Adventures in Sonic Fiction*. California: Quartet.
Gillet, R. (2019). "Not Quite Postcolonial Paris: Imperial Voices, a Kiwi Café, and Black Panther." *American Historical Review*, 124(3): 996–1001.
Gilroy, P. (1993). *The Black Atlantic: Modernity and Double Consciousness*. London: Verso.
Gilroy, P. (2004). *After Empire: Melancholia or Convivial Culture?* Oxfordshire: Routledge.
Glissant, E. (1996). *Introduction à une poétique du divers*. Paris : Gallimard.
Hacking, I. (1999). *The Social Construction of What*. Cambridge, MA: Harvard University Press.
Henriques, J. G. (2017). "As várias faces do activismo negro em Portugal." *Público*, September 16. https://www.publico.pt/2017/09/16/sociedade/noticia/as-varias-faces-do-activismo-negro-1785487 (accessed December 18, 2021).
Kabir, A. J. (2019). "Decolonizing Time through Dance with Kwenda Lima: Cabo Verde, Creolization, and Affiliative Afromodernity." *Journal of African Cultural Studies*, 31(3): 318–33.
Keeling, R. (2014). "The Ghetto Sound of Lisbon." *Resident Advisory*, March 10. https://ra.co/features/2021 (accessed September 18, 2021).
Lawrence, T. (2004). *A History of American Dance Music Culture, 1970–1979*. Durham, NC: Duke University Press.
Leight, E. (2019). "Dino d'Santiago Is Bringing Funaná to the World." *Rolling Stone*, January 17. https://www.rollingstone.com/music/music-features/dino-dsantiago-mundu-nobo-como-seria-video-779901/ (accessed September 18, 2021).
Leight, E. (2020). "'The Lusophone Sound Is Coming': Inside Dino D'Santiago's Intricate Fusions." *Rolling Stone*, April 3. https://www.rollingstone.com/music/music-latin/dino-dsantiago-kriola-album-974357/ (accessed September 18, 2021).
Lopes, M. (2020). "Esta transformação vai trazer uma mudança de pele." *Público Ípsilon*, June 26. https://www.publico.pt/2020/06/26/culturaipsilon/entrevista/chullage-transformacao-vai-trazer-mudanca-pele-1921895 (accessed October 18, 2021).
Malhado, A. (2018). "Museu das Descobertas ou da Expansão? Nome abre guerra entre historiadores." *Sábado*, May 15. https://www.sabado.pt/portugal/detalhe/museu-das-descobertas-ou-da-expansao-nome-abre-guerra-entre-historiadores (accessed September 18, 2021).
Margarido, A. (2000). *A Lusofonia e os Lusófonos: Novos Mitos Portugueses*. Lisbon: Edições Universitárias Lusófona.
Mendonça, B. (2018). "O racismo em Portugal continua absolutamente presente, mas está mais sofisticado." *Expresso*, February 16. https://expresso.pt/podcasts/a-beleza-das-pequenas-coisas/2018-02-16-Kalaf-O-racismo-em-Portugal-continua-absolutamente-presente-mas-esta-mais-sofisticado (accessed September 18, 2021).
Mendonça, B. (2019). "Lisboa é uma cidade crioula, aculturada, que se mistura e sabe conviver com as diferenças." *Expresso*, November 29. https://expresso.pt/podcasts/a-beleza-das-pequenas-coisas/2019-11-29-Dino-DSantiago-Lisboa-e-uma-cidade-

crioula-aculturada-que-se-mistura-e-sabe-conviver-com-as-diferencas (accessed September 22, 2021).

Menezes, M. P. (2008). "Epistemologias do Sul." *Revista Crítica de Ciências Sociais*, 80(March): 5–10.

Mignolo, W. (2011). *The Darker Side of Western Modernity Global Futures Decolonial Options*. Durham, NC: Duke University Press.

Moorman, M. (2014). "Anatomy of Kuduro: Articulating the Angolan Body Politic after the War." *African Studies Review*, 57(3): 21–40.

Oliveira, N. (2020). *Diversidade(s): Paradigmas, modelos e governança*. Lisbon: Editora Mundos Sociais.

Pitts, J. (2019). *Afropean: Notes from Black Europe*. London: Allen Lane.

Raposo, O. V., P. Simões, and R. J. Campos (2021). "Nos e fidju la di gueto, nos e fidju di imigranti, fidju di Kabu Verdi: estética, antirracismo e engajamentos no rap crioulo em Portugal." *Sociedade e Estado*, 36(1): 269–91.

Ré, C. (2019). "Kalaf Epalanga: A Lusofonia ainda está nas mãos dos políticos, não está nas mãos das pessoas." *Público-Ípsilon*, July 20. https://www.publico.pt/2019/07/20/culturaipsilon/noticia/kalaf-epalanga-nao-ha-troca-horizontal-cultura-produzida-lusofonia-1880639 (accessed September 18, 2021).

ReB Team (2020). "De Lisboa para o Mundo." July 7. https://www.rimasebatidas.pt/o-segundo-volume-da-enchufada-na-zona-sai-esta-semana/ (accessed September 18, 2021).

Ribeiro, A. M. (2015). "Kalaf Epalanga. O grande agitador." *Público-Ípsilon*, May 24. https://www.publico.pt/2015/05/24/culturaipsilon/noticia/o-gramde-agitador-1696225 (accessed September 21, 2021).

Câmara Municipal de Lisboa (2016). Apresentação para candidatura à UNESCO "Lisboa histórica cidade global." https://www.am-lisboa.pt/451600/1/,000512/index.htm (accessed September 11, 2021).

Salmon, C. (2017). *Storytelling: Bewitching the Modern Mind*. London: Verso.

Sanches, M. R. (2006). *"Portugal não é um país pequeno": contar o "império" na pós-colonialidade*. Lisbon: Livros Cotovia.

Santos, B. S. (2003). *Conhecimento prudente para um futuro decente: "Um discurso sobre as ciências" revisitado*. Porto: Afrontamento.

Sedano, L. J. (2020). "Kizomba beyond Angolan-ness and Lusofonia: The Transnational Dance Floor." *Atlantic Studies*, 17(1): 91–109.

Seth, S. (2004). "Reason or Reasoning? Clio or Shiva." *Social Text*, 78: 85–101.

Seth, S. (2018). "Pós-colonialismo e a história do nacionalismo anticolonial." *Práticas da História*, 7: 45–75.

Taylor, T. (2012). *The Sounds of Capitalism: Advertising, Music, and the Conquest of Culture*. Chicago: University of Chicago Press.

Tinhorão, J. R. (2019). *Os Negros em Portugal: Uma presença silenciosa*. Lisbon: Caminho.

V/a (2018). "A controvérsia sobre um Museu que ainda não existe. Descobertas ou Expansão?" *Expresso*, April 12. https://expresso.pt/cultura/2018-04-12-A-controversia-sobre-um-Museu-que-ainda-nao-existe.-Descobertas-ou-Expansao- (accessed September 18, 2021).

Valle, P. (2018). "The Endless Deterritorialization: Imagining Contemporary Portugal Through the Chronicles by Kalaf Epalanga." *Via Atlântica*, 34: 31–47.

Varela, P., and J. A. Pereira (2020). "As origens do movimento negro em Portugal (1911–1933): uma geração pan-africanista e antirracistageração pan-africanista e antirracista." *Revista de História*, 179: 1–36.

Wheeler, D. (2020). "Barcelona, a Musical Olympus? Live Concerts, Club Cultures, Television and City Branding." *Journal of Spanish Cultural Studies*, 21(1): 79–96.

Filmography

Soares da Silva, A., J. Xavier, and M. M. Matos (2006). *Lusofonia, a (R)Evolução*. Red Bull Music Academy.
Viana, V., and R. Maia (2019). *Batida de Lisboa*.

AFTERWORD: OUTLINE OF A RESEARCH APPROACH TO COLONIAL LEGACIES

Nuno Domingos and Elsa Peralta

The choice of three thematic groups into which the chapters of this book are inserted, and from which we sought to analyze the legacies of the Portuguese colonial empire, does not exhaust an inventory of themes and problems related to this object of study, which is likely to be organized in different clippings and combinations. However, in their thematic, theoretical, and methodological diversity, these chapters respond to assumptions that establish a relationship between the research work of the various authors and that allow, above all, the formulation of a common basis for questioning the production of Portuguese colonial legacies, the functions they perform, and their everyday uses. We would like to briefly state these assumptions, which represent ideas common to the organizers, and to a large extent to the authors, although we know that each of them will be closer to our positions on some issues than others.

A first assumption that presided over the organization of this volume relates to the political and civic urgency of discussing what the Portuguese colonial empire was in Portugal, in the former colonies, and more broadly throughout a global public space interested in understanding colonial experiences and using comparison as a form of historical inquiry. This urgency is now shared by people from different fields and occupations who seek to challenge dominant accounts of what the Portuguese imperial experience was. These accounts are still influenced by a nationalism that mobilizes colonial images to claim historical exceptionality, seen as the result of a specific ethical, moral, or cultural condition. This struggle has institutional dimensions, at first academic and political, but it also takes place within a whole array of spheres of activity, with emphasis on those led by the state, which has greater responsibility for and wider impact on the processes of public narration of national history.

The interrogation of the memory of empire is all the more urgent because it interferes with contemporary processes of citizenship. Old colonial myths, converted into (more or less) disguised forms of racism, remain in the institutions through the reproduction and naturalization of representations of the "other" and through practical systems of discrimination. These are interconnected and overlap with other processes of institutionalization of inequalities, notably those resulting from an economic system that produces highly stratified societies, those that operate to maintain asymmetric gender relations, or those that unequally distribute school and academic competences, which are further reflected in a labor market divided along class lines.

Thus, as far as its first key assumption, this book must be read as part of a broad struggle for the pluralization of national memory, a process that must fundamentally be accompanied by the recognition of those whose colonial pasts remain hidden or subjugated. We have thus been driven by a sense of justice and recognition, which should not be confused with using research to make historical trials. Moreover, this work tries to strengthen the transformative role of the public space, contributing to a debate about the obstacles to the creation of a democratic society in workplaces, in relations with the state, in the right to housing, in the functioning of social and legal protection mechanisms, in labor relations, in environmental justice. The way we seek to participate in this struggle indicates a second assumption that unites us in this collective work.

In the chapters in this volume, the practice of research is taken as the medium of participation in these struggles and debates. It is a confined medium, operating fundamentally in delimited institutional worlds, but it is one that we believe can operate as a means of public participation. Despite its constraints, we think that the better we investigate and argue, the more tools we provide for the development of an informed and critical public space. This certainly does not mean an unlimited belief in the virtues of science, which we know is fallible, often normative, and certainly permeable to values, starting from this case, since it is our declared desire to critically turn colonial legacies into an element of public discussion. Preferably, the interpretations presented here will be discussed, corrected, improved, and even refuted. And yet they will convey research findings and analytical frameworks that will productively feed a debate that, most of the time, lacks information to better substantiate it.

The early state of research on colonial and postcolonial contexts makes the interpretations of the Portuguese situation open to prescriptive analytical models that are highly dependent on the struggles in the political field. This type of analytical strategy included lusotropicalism and its imperialist political uses, past and present, which is the most obvious example of a preconceived and undisputed model of explanation that is projected over a social and cultural space that is represented as a "Lusophone space." In the same vein, critical perspectives on colonization and its aftermath, which are based on the obvious evidence of enduring racial discrimination and institutional violence in Portuguese society, end up being reduced to a terrain of difference and struggle almost entirely dependent on racial categories. Being a tool for political action—a fair political tool if we consider how the Portuguese political field after the 1974 revolution neglected the importance of the racial question, even by the parties on the left— this representation is reductive. Imported from other contexts, its rhetoric and conceptual apparatus creates generalization, homogenization, and omission, a problem that becomes more obvious in analyses of the general framework of domination and power relations in Portugal.

The rejection of Portuguese colonial exceptionalism, which was a creation of the Estado Novo propaganda that permeated institutions and national common sense, is the first step in placing the Portuguese case in a comparative perspective. The Portuguese empire, like other colonial empires, was an agent of territorial occupation, military expansion, state coercion in the form of legal and social discrimination, institutionalized racism, and radical economic exploitation based on the use of various forms of labor organization, which, generically, we may place in the wake of other authors, under the epithet of "slavery by another name."[1] This use of comparison is in itself enough to question the Portuguese public space, making it more plural and permeable to debates that should be common to modern democracies.

This certainly does not mean that the Portuguese colonial context and its postcolonial extensions did not have important specificities. We have highlighted some of them in the Introduction to this book. First, the importance of empire in the mythical and representational construction of Portuguese nationalism. In a country that, unlike the metropolises of other European empires, was not a pioneer of industrial modernity and modern scientific and artistic genius, the construction of national is mostly substantiated in the historical duration of empire itself. And despite the fundamental rupture brought by the revolution of April 25, 1974, imperial pride did not disappear, but its narrative style was updated. We also highlight the importance of the Estado Novo in the process of building national pride. Unlike most other colonial empires that began, albeit in a limited way, a public debate about their imperial sovereignty after the Second World War and continued it, to varying extents, after decolonization, in Portugal the prolongation of the dictatorial experience crushed public space and information channels almost completely until the mid-1970s. The colonial war (1961–74) increased the strength of propaganda, and the fall of the regime, dictated by social dissatisfaction—particularly by discontent among the military with the prolongation of the armed conflict—ended up limiting a collective debate about the colonial experience. Although the newly founded democratic public space has steadily created the formal conditions for the establishment of a more plural debate, this opportunity has been successively postponed by new appropriations and rhetorical uses of the imperial past. It has only been relatively recently, and largely as a result of a knock-on effect of the growth of global anti-racism, that criticism of Portugal's colonial legacies has taken shape in public space.

Finally, we have pointed out the importance of Portugal's structural fragility compared with the examples of other empires, ruled by economic and military powers. Much has been written about this intermediate position of Portugal and its empire. In fact, this position is often invoked to define the particularities of Portugal's circumstances, once again exhibiting fractures in the political field. On the one hand, this national backwardness explained why particularly violent and coercive forms of exploitation continued until the last days of Portuguese colonial rule, particularly in the context of the exploitation of African labor, but also of organized state violence. This reality is supported by new research, which even calls into question the supposed Portuguese reformism of the late-colonial period, historically linked to a set of political and legal changes that marked the end of the *indigenato* system (Curto, Cruz, and Furtado 2016; Cruz 2022). However, this same specific place of the Portuguese empire was also evoked to explain how successive national governments, in very different political scenarios, managed to maintain imperial sovereignty by playing skillfully on various diplomatic chessboards (Meneses and Oliveira 2011; Jerónimo 2012; Oliveira 2017). Regarding this pride in the agility of national diplomacy, it has been pointed out that this diplomatic position actually made Portugal and its empire—an empire among empires—an agent of foreign interests, a space for sourcing cheap labor and raw materials, a place where foreign companies had more freedom to exercise a robust and often unscrupulous economic activity outside the law (Isaacman and Isaacman 1983; Allina 2012; Cleveland 2017; Direito 2020).

But perhaps the most ambiguous and hardest to interpret point to be drawn from this intermediate position relates to the relationship between colonizers and colonized in the imperial space. From which models can this relationship be conceived? Gilberto Freyre's lusotropicalist program proposed to solve the question by producing a culturalist fiction: the supposed miscegenation character of the Portuguese-founded Creole societies, a new cultural block that functioned as an integrated social system. This theory has been contested in various ways, but to a great extent by accounts based on consistent research into the violence and exploitation, including where sex and gender were involved, that surrounded the imperial expansion and which produced mixed-race offspring in the colonial context. The colonial terrains' "truth" revealed a perversity that far exceeded what was regulated by the edifice of this discretionary system based on deeply discriminatory imperial legal and administrative codes. Portuguese colonial institutions and elites managed racism, violence, and discrimination, and their mental schemes reproduced the logic of a radically unequal society.

But as pointed out by some authors, the fragile position of the empire itself offered opportunities to a set of other agents to develop their strategies on the margins of this officialdom or along the paths that the empire left open (Pina-Cabral 2010; Havik and Newitt 2015; Hespanha 2019). We speak of poor settlers, traders, adventurers, lowly civil servants, missionaries, and their descendants. Benefiting from the power provided by imperial citizenship, and all the resources that this guaranteed them, these individuals established relations with the local populations that in most cases were very unequal and where coercion and violence went hand in hand. However, this resulted in the creation of new frameworks of relationship, which cannot be understood from studies of state norms and policies or from observing the worlds where the political, economic, and religious elites circulated. Indeed, the structural position occupied by Portugal and its empire in global configurations, world economies or world systems, created realities—*Lusotopias*, to use the name of a well-known journal—which deserve to be investigated as ambiguous, difficult to capture, contradictory, and susceptible to slight political and ideological appropriations. These frames of relationship cannot be understood without considering the structural place occupied by the

Portuguese empire, and without investigating the worlds it helped create, largely as a result of notorious economic underdevelopment and established state incapacity.

The description of this reality can easily fit in with lusotropical narratives, however. Accordingly, weakness was actually the most important characteristic of Portuguese imperialism, and it manifested itself in fragile institutions and decadent elites. This view, however, disempowers the centers of power, absolving the authorities that represented the nation and the empire. This ends up working as a mechanism of national absolution and functions as another line of recreation of Portuguese imperial historicity. To prevent these appropriations, it is essential to enable research on these social worlds created by the empire, the relationships and mobilities that constituted them, and the individuals who played a leading role in them; their "autonomy" must be protected from the great political narratives that seek to stamp a character on the Portuguese imperial experience.

Therefore, it is fundamental to deepen investigations that reconstitute the logic of the Portuguese imperial space and delve into the complexities of its postcolonial space, which must be seen as places of both distance and social proximity, and within whose framework specific struggles occur. These investigations into the relations between colonizers and colonized, and into the relations between local populations and those from outside, specifically the racialized ones whose lives were shaped by imperial transits and colonial displacements, are also crucial to create a comparative project with other empires and postcolonial societies and therefore as a means to investigate colonial legacies. This project must be able to identify the structural factors that operate in processes of exclusion and discrimination, which must not be disentangled from the institution of racialized models of citizenship governance that work in favor of an international division of labor intrinsic to (post)imperial capitalism (Cooper 2014). The organization and functioning of empire depended heavily on this social and economic differentiation, and in democratic Portugal, too, several dynamics of discrimination, some of them institutionalized, reveal how race is an operative category in numerous everyday circumstances.

As such, this research program should also be able to perceive how the logic of racial categorization was and still is crossed by other processes of differentiation. This will make power relations more composite, by pondering together, under certain circumstances, the several factors that define modes of economic, housing, educational, and cultural socialization and belonging, a frame of analysis that questions black and white representations of the world. If this is revealing in the imperial landscape, it is more evident in contemporary Portugal, where whites and Blacks, possessors of capitals of distinction unequivocally dependent on the color of their skin, are presented as internally heterogeneous collectives. This implies that their distribution throughout the social space is subject to a complex logic of social differentiation, directly motivated by the economic, work, educational, and housing place in which they are located. Moreover, this complex distribution explains proximities and networks of solidarity based upon shared practical conditions and similar worldviews, which remain largely hidden either because they are poorly studied or because they are politically irrelevant, or even disturbing.

It is our contention that the study of colonial legacies should thus consider both the production of dominant discourses and practices and the web of complex relations created within (post)imperial structures. In this book, the chapters by Peralta, Domingos, Oliveira, Cardão, Cidra, George, and Sanchez and Vanspauwen show how in Portugal in the postcolonial period, struggles over the legacy of empire and the authority to narrate it continue to be observed, involving dominant symbolic producers—in academia, in the intellectual milieu, in the sphere of state institutions—and within the framework of mass communication mechanisms and popular culture. The texts by Ascensão, Estevens, Frangella, and Dias sought to examine how colonial relations were reproduced in the postcolonial context through family and economic networks, kinship and gender relations, labor exclusion, networks of solidarity, and leisure practices, matrimonial strategies, consumption desires, and mobility, in cultural productions and grassroots political resistance, or in the everyday uses of public services. We sought to interpret all these contemporary social frameworks "in relation," in a social place where colonial legacies are projected differently, and not as a given created by a prescriptive model of social relations, however well intentioned.

The importance of empire in the configuration of Portuguese nationalism and the long authoritarian dictatorship of the Estado Novo partially explain why it has been so difficult to insert the debate on the legacies of the colonial empire into Portugal's public space. This situation has recently been changing, thanks to the emergence of a more plural and dynamic civil society itself informed by, and connected with, the ongoing global debates about race and "immigration" in contemporary multicultural societies. Yet some of the theoretical generalizations offered, which often conflate historically situated (post)colonial histories, conditions, motivations, and lifeworlds, have also worked to put the study of colonial legacies as hostage to master interpretations over the legacies of colonial pasts. Taking the Portuguese example, the shortage of empirically grounded research about both the colonial and postcolonial landscapes has contributed a great deal to fuel political competition between existing grand narratives. Only through comparative analysis soundly based on the social, economic, and political contexts in which colonial legacies are embedded will it be possible to overcome this political and theoretical impasse. This book aims to be contribution in that direction.

Note

1 Used originally by Douglas A. Blackmon in *Slavery by Another Name: The Re-enslavement of Black Americans from the Civil War to World War II* (2008), it was adapted to the reality of the Portuguese colonialism in Mozambique by Éric Allina (2012) in *Slavery by Any Other Name: African Life under Company Rule in Colonial Mozambique*.

References

Allina, E. (2012). *Slavery by Any Other Name: African Life under Company Rule in Colonial Mozambique*. Charlottesville: University of Virginia Press.

Blackmon, D. A. (2008). *Slavery by Another Name: The Re-enslavement of Black Americans from the Civil War to World War II*. New York: Doubleday.

Cleveland, T. (2017). *Diamonds in the Rough: Corporate Paternalism and African Professionalism on the Mines of Colonial Angola*. Athens: Ohio University Press.

Cooper, F. (2014). *Africa in the World: Capitalism, Empire, Nation-State*. Cambridge, MA: Harvard University Press.

Cruz, B. P. da. (2022). "As origens institucionais da moderação da violência: regedorias e concentração em Angola (1914–1974)." PhD thesis in Globalization Studies, Faculdade de Ciências Sociais e Humanas da Universidade Nova de Lisboa.

Curto, D. R., B. P. da Cruz, and T. Furtado (2016). *Políticas Coloniais em Tempo de Revoltas—Angola circa 1961*. Porto: Afrontamento.

Direito, B. (2020). *Terra e Colonialismo em Moçambique*. Lisbon: Imprensa de Ciências Sociais.

Havik, P. J., and M. Newitt (eds.) (2015). *Creole Societies in the Portuguese Colonial Empire*. Cambridge: Cambridge Scholars.

Hespanha, A. (2019). *Filhos da Terra: Identidades mestiças nos confins da expansão portuguesa*. Lisbon: Tinta-da-China.

Isaacman, A., and B. Isaacman (1983). *Mozambique, from Colonialism to Revolution*. Colorado: Westview.

Jerónimo, M. B. (2012). *A Diplomacia do Império: Política e Religião na Partilha de África (1820–1890)*. Lisbon: Edições 70.

Meneses, F. R., and P. A. Oliveira (eds.) (2011). *Primeira República Portuguesa Diplomacia, Guerra e Império*. Lisbon: Edições 70.

Oliveira, P. A. (2017). "A arte do compromisso: José Calvet de Magalhães, um diplomata entre dois regimes." *Ler História*, 71: 103–26.

Pina-Cabral, J. (2010). "Lusotopy as Ecumene, Lusotopia como Ecumene." *Revista Brasileira de Ciências Sociais*, 25(74): 5–20.

CONTRIBUTORS

Eduardo Ascensão is a researcher at the Center for Geographical Studies and Laboratory TERRA, Institute of Geography and Spatial Planning, University of Lisbon. An anthropologist and urban geographer, his research is on urban informality, postcolonial urbanisms, infrastructure, and architecture. Eduardo has published in journals such as the *International Journal of Urban* and *Regional Research, City and Antipode* and in edited volumes such as the *Handbook of Gentrification Studies*. He is currently developing a multisited project on the models of slum intervention in Portuguese-speaking cities Bissau, Macau, Lisbon, and Rio de Janeiro.

Marcos Cardão holds a PhD in Modern and Contemporary History from the ISCTE—Instituto Universitário de Lisboa (2013). He is an integrated researcher at the Center for Comparative Studies (CEComp—FLUL), University of Lisbon, and is the author of "Fado Tropical. Luso-tropicalismo na cultura de massas (1960–1974)" (2020) and coauthor of "Gilberto Freyre: novas leituras, do outro lado do Atlântico" (2015).

Rui Cidra is a researcher at the Institute of Contemporary History (IHC)/Associate Laboratory for Research and Innovation in Heritage, Arts, Sustainability and Territory. His main research has focused on Cape Verdean music and the ways in which it was racialized across colonial and postcolonial historical conjunctures. He is the author of *Funaná, Raça e Masculinidade: uma Trajetória Colonial e Pós-colonial* (2021).

Benoît de L'Estoile is Research Professor (Directeur de recherche) at the National Center for Scientific Research (CNRS, CMH), in Paris. He has done extensive fieldwork in Brazil. He focuses in political anthropology, and has written among other on colonial governmentality, on museums of the Self and the Other, on colonial legacies. He is the author of *Le goût des Autres. De l'Exposition Coloniale aux Arts premiers* (2007), and co-edited *Empires, Nations and Natives. Anthropology and State-Making*, Duke University Press, 2005. He currently coordinates the French-Brazilian project Governing Uncertainty: Territories, Markets, Houses.

Nuno Dias is a research fellow at CICS.NOVA and a guest professor at NOVA University of Lisbon—School of Social Sciences and Humanities. His research focuses mainly on the relations between migration regimes, racialization processes, gender, and labor market segmentation. He has published recently on migration and categorization processes in colonial and postcolonial contexts and migrant care and domestic workers.

Nuno Domingos is a senior researcher at the Institute of Social Sciences of the University of Lisbon. He researches the history of Portuguese colonialism in the twentieth century, with special reference to the urban contexts in Mozambique. His focus on the study of cultural practices and consumptions includes studies on reading practices, the social and cultural policies of the Portuguese New State, and the configurations of modern sport. He is the author of *Football and Colonialism: Body and Popular Culture in Mozambique* (2017).

Ana Estevens is a geographer and researcher at Center of Geographical Studies and Associated Laboratory TERRA, Institute of Geography and Spatial Planning, University of Lisbon. She holds a PhD in Human Geography from the University of Lisbon. Her research has focused on the complexity of social relations in the contemporary city, with a particular focus on the connections between the arts, space production, and socio-territorial innovation but also on migration and housing.

Simone Frangella is a research fellow at the Institute for Social Sciences, University of Lisbon. Her research interests include urban space, corporeality, mobilities, migration, and connections between historicity and territoriality. She has published on homelessness and corporeality, family and mutual help in transnational movements, cultural production, urban territorialities through housing, and uses of the city in migration contexts. She co-coordinates the Portuguese Foundation for Science and Technology–(FCT)–funded project "Constellations of Memory: A Multidirectional Study of Postcolonial Migration and Remembering" (PTDC/SOC-ANT/4292/2021).

João Pedro George is a postdoctoral researcher in the Portuguese Institute of International Relations (IPRI), NOVA University of Lisbon. His research interests focus on the Portuguese literary field, the memory of late Portuguese colonialism, and historical journalistic investigation. He has published on sociology of culture and on biographical genre. His most recent book is *Annoying Camões: Survey on Portuguese Cultural Life* (2021).

Nuno Oliveira is a senior researcher at the Center for Research and Studies in Sociology, CIES (ISCTE-IUL) and an invited teacher of Sociological Theories in the School of Sociology and Public Policies (ISCTE-IUL) where he develops work on the local dynamics of integration of immigrants and urban policies, the meaning of intercultural models, and the political and theoretical transition from multiculturalism to interculturalism. He has published in various international and national journals, such as *Territory, Politics, Governance, Policy and Politics, Journal of Intercultural Communication, New Diversities, French Journal of*

Media Research, and *Sociologia Problemas e Práticas*. His most recent book is *Diversidade(s). Paradigmas, Modelos e Governança* (2020).

Elsa Peralta holds a PhD in anthropology and is a senior research fellow at the Center for Comparative Studies, Faculty of Arts and Humanities of the University of Lisbon. Her work is highly interdisciplinary and focuses on the intersection between private and public modes of recall of past events, in particular the colonial past. She coordinates the Portuguese Foundation for Science and Technology (FCT)–funded project "Constellations of Memory: A Multidirectional Study of Postcolonial Migration and Remembering" (PTDC/SOC-ANT/4292/2021). She recently edited the book *The Retornados from the Portuguese Colonies in Africa: Memory, Narrative and History* (2021).

Iñigo Sánchez-Fuarros is a Ramón y Cajal Postdoctoral Researcher at the Institute of Heritage Sciences (INCIPIT, CSIC), Santiago de Compostela, Spain. He holds a PhD in Anthropology from the University of Barcelona, and his research focuses on urban sound and music cultures. He is currently the Principal Investigator of two research projects: Sounds of Tourism (PTDC/ART-PER/32417/2017) and HabitPAT (PID2020-118696RB-I00).

Bart Paul Vanspauwen is an integrated researcher at the Institute of Ethnomusicology, Center for Studies in Music and Dance (INET—md), NOVA University Lisbon, where he obtained an MA and PhD in Ethnomusicology. He has a special interest in Afro-Portuguese and Luso-Brazilian cultural relations. His most recent project participation was in Sounds of Tourism (PTDC/ART-PER/32417/2017), with particular focus on TAP Air Portugal. Together with Iñigo Sánchez-Fuarros, he is currently guest-editing a special issue for the *American Anthropologist* World Series, entitled "Postcolonial Airliners as Cultural Mediators. Corporate Branding and Cultural Governance in Transnational Contexts."

INDEX

Abreu, A. 114
Abrunhosa, Pedro 206
Acácio, Manuel 190
Adey, P. 201, 211
Afonso Henriques (King of Portugal) 73
African communities 164, 169, 178
African national liberation
    movements 9, 85
Afro-descendant movements 11
Agualusa, José Eduardo 73
Aguiar, J. A. de 55
Alencastro, L. F. 155
Alexandre, V. 6, 12, 30, 47
Algarve 97, 136, 202, 221
Alge, B. 225
Allina, E. 13, 242
Almeida, J. C. 33–4
Almeida, Leopoldo de 36
Almeida, M. V. 63, 74, 200
Alves, A. R. 95
Alvor Treaty (Angola) 9
Ambundu (ethnic group) 173
Amin, A. 65
Anabela (Anabela Braz Pires) 210
Anderson, B. 134
Anderson, W. 8
André, I. 114
Andrejevic, M. 193
Anglo-Portuguese Alliance 6
Angola 6, 9, 12, 17, 32, 35–6, 47–9, 51,
    53–4, 73, 83, 89, 98, 107, 112, 118,
    166, 171–5, 177, 182–6, 190–2,
    199–200, 203, 206, 210, 221, 223,
    227, 229
Anissabeni, Elisa 51
anthropology 201
anti-racism 5, 171, 224, 229, 241
Antunes, M. J. L. 12
Arenas, F. 201
Araújo, M. 50, 187
archaeology 31–2, 40

Archer, J. 188
architecture 4, 14, 28, 36, 71
    colonial architecture 15, 191
    Estado Novo architecture 56
    exotic architectural styles 4
    international architectural styles 56
    Luso-African architecture 54
    Manueline (architectural style) 28, 30
    Moorish architecture 75
    Portuguese architecture 54
    modern 46, 56
    tropical architecture 54
Armstrong, G. 52
Arouca, Manuel 188–9
Ascensão, E. 13, 15, 83, 88, 92, 94, 97,
    100, 144
Assembleia da República Portuguesa 53
Assembleia de Deus (Assembly of
    God) 147
Associação Renovar a Mouraria 71–2
Ataíde, J. 143
Atlantic 154, 207–8, 213, 227
    Black 174
    South Atlantic 167
AUGI—Áreas Urbanas de Génese Ilegal
    (urban areas of illegal genesis) 92

B. Leza (Francisco Xavier da Cruz) 168
Bachmann, B. 96
Baganha, M. I. 136
Baily, J. 114
Balibrea, M. P. 38
Bana (Adriano Gonçalves) 171
Bandeirinha, J. A. 92
Bangladesh 11, 67, 75, 112, 147
Baptista, L. V. 145
Barbosa, C. 114
Barbosa, João Branko 222
Bastos, Waldemar 171, 210
Barre, J. 219, 222
Barry, R. 222

Bastos, C. 68, 146, 153
Batalha, L. 88
Bauman, Z. 190
Beja-Horta, A. P. 86
Belém's
  Cultural Center (CCB) 28, 38
  Palace 28, 31
  Pastéis 28
  Tower 28–9, 35, 37–8
Benfica, Sport Lisboa e 46, 49–52, 173
Benguela 223
Bennett, Tony 202
Belanciano, V. 223, 228
Berlin 76
Berlin Conference (1884–5) 6, 128
Beta, A. 228
Bethencourt, F. 6, 30, 50
Bessard-Banquy, O. 188
Bhabha, H. K. 177
Billig, M. 46, 228
Bissau 55, 84, 91
  bairros indígenas 84, 91
Blaagaard, B. B. 200
Black 11, 49–50, 56, 73, 84–5, 88, 92–5, 115–16, 119, 125, 128–33, 169, 173–4, 187–93, 220, 223–4, 228–9, 243
Black Atlantic 174
blackness 125
Blanchard, P. 187
Boeing 205, 208
Bonacich, E. 126–7
Bonga (José Adelino Barceló de Carvalho) 171–4, 177
Borges, David 190
Born, G. 202
Bourdieu, P. 52, 54, 117–18, 137
Boyer, M. C. 4, 34, 38
Boym, S. 174
Branco, J. F. 31
Brasão, I. 86, 132
Brazil 6, 12, 16, 33, 112, 135, 143–4, 147–54, 163, 165–7, 174–7, 200, 206, 208, 213, 227
Brazilian
  occupations 147–9, 151–2
  prejudices against women 149–52
  stereotypes about 150–3
  see also gastronomy, Brazilian; immigrants, Brazilians; music, Brazilian
Brazilianness 143–4, 147–9, 151, 153
British Airways 212
British Ultimatum 7, 30
Brooks, A. 186
Brown, G. W. 171
Bruheim, Flora 51
Brussels 85, 109
Buchanan, I. 184
Budzinski, N. 225
Buettner, E. 3
Bull, M. 201
Buraka Som Sistema 222, 227

Cabecinhas, R. 10
Cabral, Amílcar 109, 110, 116
Cachado, R. 13, 84, 99
Cahen, M. 191, 228
Camané (Carlos Moutinho dos Santos) 206
Camões Institute 225
Camões, Luiz Vaz de 30, 50
Camões Tercentenary 30, 31
Canavilhas, Gabriela 39
Canclini, N. 219
Caniço (Lourenço Marques slums) 84, 192
Cape Verde 16, 69, 83, 88–90, 99, 107–12, 116–20, 168–71, 174, 200, 206, 211, 213, 221–3 *see also* languages, Creole
Capelo, Hermenegildo 50
capitalism, capitalist 2, 14, 15, 63, 65, 75, 125–9, 131, 137, 191, 243
Cardão, M. 11, 13, 50, 114, 145
Cardina, M. 47, 109
Caribbean 177
Carminho (Maria do Carmo Andrade) 206
Carmo, A. 13, 145
Carmo, João Garizo do 54
Carneiro, R. 136
Carvalho, A. de 132
Carvalho, Alberto 119
Carvalho, Fernão Simões de 54
Carvalho, Mário de 116, 118
Carvalho, Paulo de 210
Castellano, C. G. 213
Castela, T. 91

Castelo, C. 8, 12, 200, 213
Castro, Augusto de 34
Catarino, C. 134
Catholicism 7, 51, 132
Catholic Church 48
Center for Studies in Ethnology 37
Chega (Portuguese political party) 11
China 29, 67, 111–12, 147
Chinese restaurants (in Lisbon) 149, 152 *see also* food
Christianity 6–8, 66–7
Chullage (Nuno Santos) 28, 37
Church of St. Francis Xavier of Goa 34
Cidra, R. 13, 108, 113–14, 219, 223–4
Cinema Império 147
citizenship 2–4, 9, 15, 18, 41, 76, 85, 95–7, 117, 164, 177, 205, 241–3
class, 2, 4, 10, 17, 73, 108, 118, 125, 132–3, 164, 240
   class homology, 16, 137
   consciousness 116
   and gender 16, 86, 88, 107, 112, 127–37, 143, 152
   middle classes 9, 65, 134, 146
   peasants 132
   and race 85–8, 92, 125–7, 131, 135, 137
   ruling classes 47
   upper classes, 77, 129
   working classes 12, 51, 88, 125, 146
Cleveland, T. 50, 242
CML-Câmara Municipal de Lisboa 68–71, 97
Coelho, C. 208, 211, 213
Coelho, J. N. 50
Cohen, M. 85
Cold War 9, 48, 165
Coller, K. 201
Collier, M. 114
Collin, M. 225
Colonial Act (*Acto Colonial*) 13
colonial society
   citizenship, 2–3, 8–9, 51, 85, 242
   inequality 11, 13, 57
   and racism 2, 11, 13, 115, 239, 242–3
   settlers, 12–13, 16–17, 41, 47, 49, 52, 56, 128, 131, 182, 187–92, 242
colonial studies 2, 137, 222
   academic fields 46, 53–5, 56, 222

   and anti-racism activism 5, 11, 194, 239, 241
   and Marxism, 126–7
   and political narratives 243
colonial wars (1961–75) 2, 8, 9, 12, 29, 41, 45, 47, 91, 107, 114, 183, 185, 192, 241 *see also* wars of liberation
Colonial Urbanization Office/Overseas Urbanization Office 55
Coluna, Mário 49
commemoration 1, 10, 27, 29, 31, 33, 36, 37, 163, 202
commodification 27, 37, 63, 65, 75, 134, 167, 168, 176, 190
commonwealth 3
Community of Portuguese Speaking Countries (CPLP)/Portuguese speaking world 12, 17, 48, 110, 163, 165, 166, 172, 175, 177, 200, 201, 203, 206, 209–12, 220, 225–7
Companhia de Jesus (The Jesuits) 74
Contador, A. 108, 114
Cooper, F. 2, 3, 8, 243
Cordeiro, G. Í. 146, 148
Cordeiro, Luciano 31
Cordoaria Nacional 39
Corkill, D. 33, 34
Correio da Manhã (newspaper) 192
cosmopolitanism 3, 37, 63, 74, 163, 168, 171, 172, 219
Costa, Λ. F. da 134, 146, 148
Costa, Vasco Vieira da 54
Covid-19 137, 154
Cox, O. C. 126
Cresswell, T. 204
Crosby, Bing 202
Crozat, D. 95
Cruz, B. P. 13, 55, 242
Cunha, L. 10
Cunha, S. S. 182, 183
Curto, D. R. 13, 50, 87, 100, 187, 193, 242
Cwerner, S. 201

Daily Note (newspaper) 224
Dar es Salaam 131
De Certeau, M. 151
decolonization 1–5, 8, 12, 14, 17, 37, 41, 47, 48, 85, 107, 114, 127, 186, 190,

192, 212, 241 *see also* Independence of African colonies
de Guchteneire, P. 64
De L'Estoile, B. 3, 4
Delgado, Humberto 199
demolitions (houses) 99, 113
Deplano, V. 3
Diário de Notícias (newspaper) 182
Dias, Jorge 37, 47
Dias, Nélia 39
Dias, Nuno 11, 152, 153
Dias, P. 143
diaspora 110, 117, 119, 120, 163, 164, 166, 167, 170, 172, 175–7, 207, 209, 222, 223, 228
digital media 16, 101, 116, 183, 224
Dikanza 173
Dili 89
diplomacy 2, 48, 165, 242
Direito, B. 242
Direção-Geral da Política de Justiça (Directorate-General for Justice Policy) 113
Discoveries Foundation 38
Djass Association 41
Djodje (rapper) 210, 211
domestic
  imperialism 12
  space 5, 134
  violence 113
  work 16, 86, 88, 107, 112, 127–37, 143, 152
Domingos, N. 4, 7, 11, 49, 55, 84, 100, 129, 200
Dos Santos, I. 12
Drew, J. 54
Du Bois, William 125
Duarte, José 205
Duo Ouro Negro 206
Dworkin, D. 125

Eastman, C. M. 131
East Timor 35, 89
Edensor, T. 46
Eldridge, C. 5
Elias, H. 30, 34
Elliot, R. 202
emigration, Portuguese emigration 12, 13, 107, 144, 154, 209

Emissora Nacional 51
Enchufada 221, 222
Enes, António 50
Epalanga, Kalaf 220, 222–4
Epistemologies of the South 222
Esfera dos Livros 181–3
Estado Novo (Portuguese regime) 7, 8, 10, 12, 33, 35, 37, 45, 47, 49, 54, 86, 130, 132, 241, 244
  censorship 52
  patriarchal society 51
  propaganda 7, 33, 35, 46, 47, 49, 50, 51, 53, 56
Estevens, A. 13, 69, 114, 145, 168
Estrada Militar 112
ethnographic fieldwork 68, 108, 145, 183
ethnology (Portuguese) 31, 32, 37
European Economic Community 9, 37, 48
European Union 108, 109, 167, 207
Eusébio (Eusébio da Silva Ferreira) 15, 46, 49, 51, 56
Évora, Cesária 167, 171, 210
exotic 4, 17, 28, 33, 51, 75–7, 149
  exoticism 115, 190, 194
Expo'98 World Exhibition 10, 94
expressive culture 168, 171, 173, 177, 200, 202

Feldman-Bianco, B. 144, 201
Fernandes, J. M. 53, 54
Ferrão, J. 136
Ferreira, A. P. 165
Ferreira, A. R. F. 55
Ferreira, Ondina 110
Ferreira, V. 187
Ferreira, V. M. 35
festivals (music) 163, 176, 224, 226, 229, 230
FFH—Fundo de Fomento à Habitação 92
Figueiredo, A. 147
Figueiredo, S. 201
financial crisis, Great Recession of 2008 12, 41, 53, 137, 154
Fikes, K. 84, 88, 163, 166
Flores, Paulo 17, 203
FNAC 181
Fonseca, M. L. 112
football 15, 45, 46, 49, 50–3, 56, 210
  1962 Football European Cup 50

1966 Football World Cup 50
2014 Football World Cup 210
Fortes, T. S. 119
Foucault, M. 99, 164
Fradique, T. 114
França, J. A. 33
France 5, 12
Francophonie 3
Frangella, S. 13
Freixo, A. 201
Freudenthal, A. F. 129
Frey, M. 54
Freyre, Gilberto 8, 47, 50, 74, 242
Frúgoli Jr., H. 148
Fruity Loops (FL Studio) 228
Furtado, T. 13, 242
Fusion Market (Lisbon's) 69, 71

Gabinete Lisboa Encruzilhada de Mundos 69
Galarza, S. 202
Garcia, Fernando 51
Garcia, Rita 185, 190, 192
Gaspar, J. 86
gastronomy (food) 144, 174
   Bangladeshi 75
   Brazilian 148, 153
   Chinese 68 *see also* Chinese restaurants
   Lusophone 2
   World 5
Geertz, C. 126
gender 2, 8, 11, 16, 86, 88, 110, 116, 126–8, 130, 132, 133, 136, 137, 149–52, 188–93, 224–5, 240, 242, 244
Genette, G. 126, 184
Gentil-Homem, P. 201
George, J. P. 182, 193
gentrification 15, 65, 67, 70, 71, 114, 144, 145, 153
Germany 12
Ghorwane 171
Gillet, R. 225
Gilroy, P. 72, 221, 228
Glick Schiller, N. 63
Glissant, E. 223
Global South 222
globalization 15, 45, 52, 63, 64, 74, 75, 111, 134

Goa 29, 34
   migrants 84
Gomes, M. S. 150
Gonçalves, I. 54
Gonzalez, P. A. 46
Gonzo, Paulo 206
Gopal, P. 7, 47
Gopinath, S. 201
Gomes, J. S. 165
Gouveia, H. C. 31, 32
Govil, N. 201
Gradiva 181
Graham, S. 99
Great Britain 6, 7
Green, M. C. 184
Grupo Planeta 181
Guerra, I. 91
Guibentif, P. 134, 136
Guillaume, M. 38
Guinea-Bissau 54, 84, 88, 91, 107, 112, 183, 192, 200, 206
Gulbenkian Planetarium 28

Hacking, I. 220
Hall, C. 3
Hall, J. W. 188
Hall, S. 167, 177
Hannigan, J. 65
Harrison, D. 37
Harvey, D. 65
Havik, P. J. 242
Heilmar, Hans-Peter (Lonha) 110, 111, 119
Held, D. 171
Heleno, Manuel 32
Henriques, I. C. 100
Henriques, J. G. 224
heritage 4, 11, 14, 27–8, 30, 35, 37–8, 41, 46, 53, 55–7, 70, 75, 117, 120, 146, 165, 173, 194, 201, 207, 209, 210, 212
heritagization 56
Hesmondhalgh, D. 202
Hespanha, A. 242
hybridity 17, 167, 168, 170, 175, 213, 228, 230
Higher Institute of Overseas Studies 36
Higher Institute of Social Sciences and Overseas Politics (ISCSPU) 36
Hindu 69, 84

hip-hop 115, 206, 221
Hitchcock, M. 37
Hochschild, A. R. 186, 188
Holston, J. 96
Hotel Polana 187
hotels 112, 133, 136, 147
housing 2, 13, 15, 16, 33, 55, 83, 85, 86, 91–3, 97–100, 107, 112, 143, 145–7, 150, 151, 154, 229, 240, 243
housing estates 85, 88, 89, 94, 95, 100
Huambo 221 *see also* Nova Lisboa
Huggan, G. 190
Humbertona (Humberto Bettencourt dos Santos) 173

identity
  corporate 201, 206, 208, 211–13
  ethnic 63, 75, 114
  Lisbon's 17, 70, 219, 221–3, 227, 229, 230
  multiplicity of 64, 67, 75, 114, 228, 229
  national 1, 3, 4, 16, 27, 125, 126, 149, 154, 168, 220
  politics 5, 41
  Portuguese national 7, 10, 27, 31, 32, 34, 36, 38, 40, 41, 47, 48, 107, 132, 176, 199, 200, 203, 205, 206, 208, 209, 212–13, 220, 224–8
  postcolonial 132, 137, 226, 230
  professional 132, 137, 226, 230
  social 68, 73, 114, 229
  transnational 201
  underclass 88
ideology (colonial)
  aesthetization 46, 53–7
  biography 15, 45, 46, 49–53, 55, 56, 109, 184, 186, 187
  civilizing mission 7, 175
  commodification 27, 37, 65, 75, 167, 190
  fields of activity 14, 47, 55, 56
  governance 11, 14, 17, 63–6, 76, 200, 213, 219, 229, 243
  imaginaries 11, 14, 17, 48
  marketing 74, 75, 181, 184, 193, 201, 207, 209, 213, 221, 225, 226, 229, 230
  mysticism 7, 33
  miscegenation 8, 73, 226, 242

narratives of transition, 15, 45, 46, 56
  see Portuguese exceptionalism (post-colonial)
Independence of African colonies 9, 35, 45, 49, 89, 89, 109, 110, 150, 171, 174, 188, 189, 206, 220, 225
Illouz, E. 186, 188
immigrant
  associations 95, 96
  ghettos 70
  integration 16, 70
  populations 64, 65, 68, 70, 75, 83, 92, 107, 113–15, 136, 144–6, 149, 155, 176
  rights 65, 95, 96, 244
  suburbs 13
  women 16, 134, 136, 137, 149
immigrant's descendants 11, 15, 16, 107, 111–14, 117
immigrants
  African 15, 67, 126, 149, 166, 172, 175, 176
  Algerian 85
  American 67, 175
  Angolan 112
  Bangladeshi 11, 112
  Brazilian 16, 73, 112, 143–55, 175,
  Cape Verdean 16, 69, 88, 107, 108, 111, 112, 116–18, 120, 168, 170, 173
  Chinese 67, 71, 72, 112, 147
  East European 67, 136, 147
  from PALOP countries 136, 166, 172, 175
  Goan 84
  Guinean 69, 112
  Hindu 69
  Indian 112
  Lusophone 11, 209
  Maghreb 85
  Nepalese 11, 112
  Pakistani 11, 112
  Romanian 112
  Russian 149
  Senegalese 11
  Southeast Asian 72, 73
  S. Tomense 69, 112
  Ukrainian 112
immigration
  Europe 4, 13, 155, 167

from African colonies 2, 5, 10, 11, 16, 83, 84, 88, 89, 100, 170, 173
  Lisbon 6, 7, 14, 15, 27, 28, 32, 33, 35, 39–41, 46, 50–1, 63, 64, 66–76, 83–6, 88, 112, 113, 116, 117, 131, 143–9, 151–5, 175, 176, 206, 207, 210, 219–21
  policies 96, 107, 112
  postcolonial 13, 15, 83, 85, 92, 125, 126, 134, 136, 137, 165, 175
  Portugal 11, 12, 66–70, 73, 75, 83, 86, 111–13, 118, 165, 176
  to South Africa 52
Imperial Air Line 199
India 30, 31, 34, 35, 50, 67, 68, 73, 111, 112, 149
Indian Ocean 167, 186, 188
Indigenato Statute 8, 242
Institute of Tropical Medicine 36
Instituto da Habitação e da Reabilitação Urbana (IHRU) 93
interracial 9, 10, 15, 47, 50
Isaacman, A. 13, 242
Isaacman, B. 242
Ivens, Roberto 50

Jacobs, J. M. 4, 76
Japan 111
Jensen, L. 12
Jerónimo, M. B. 8, 13, 242
Jerónimos, Monastery of the 28, 30–3, 35, 36–9
Jews (expulsion) 74
João, M. I. 32, 50
Jockers, M. L. 188
Jordi, J.-J. 4
Juka (Castro) 169

Kalter, C. 9
Karneval der Kulturen, Berlin's 75
Kataleya 210, 211
Kaya (rapper) 116
Keeling, R. 222
Keese, A. 13
Keil, R. 64
Keith, M. 63
Kimbandas do Ritmo 173
King, A. 4, 85, 86
Kissueia 173

Kivijärvi, M. 201, 212
Koenig, M. 64
Kusno, A. 86
Kymlicka, W. 167

Lafleur, J.-M. 114
Lammert, C. 4
Landry, C. 64
languages
  African 173
  Creole 16, 107–20, 168, 169, 170, 208, 221, 223, 229, 230, 242
  Kimbundu (Angola) 173
  Lusophone 207, 212, 213, 228
  Portuguese 39, 40, 107–11, 115, 117, 118, 120, 144, 163–6, 169, 170, 172, 175, 208, 209, 220, 225
  Ronga (Mozambique) 171
Laschi, G. 3
Lawrence, T. 225
Lazar, S. 177
LBC Soldjah (Flávio Almada) 115, 119
Leal, J. 39, 131, 132
Leal, S. 118
Leight, E. 221, 223
Léonard, Y. 7, 33
Leya Group 181
liberal democracies 10, 65
Lima, Isabel Pires de 38
Lima, M. 11
Lisb/on Jardim Sonoro (musical festival) 226
Lisboa Dance Festival 226
Lisboa Electrónica Festival 226
Lisboa Kriola 222 *see also* Lisbon, Creole
Lisbon
  African 229
  Arab, Moors 67, 68, 7374
  branding 63, 64, 69, 70, 72–4, 226
  vapital of empire 36
  Creole 108, 222, 223, 229, 230 *see also* Lisboa Kriola
  informal settlements 91, 93, 100, 107, 113, 115
  outskirts, periphery 11, 15, 16, 85, 86, 91, 222
  multicultural 145, 167, 170, 176, 223, 228, 229, 230

postcolonial 17, 115, 220, 221, 226–9
post-imperial 95, 97, 100
shantytowns 85
soundscape 17, 67, 120, 227–9
tourism 15, 27–9, 70, 71, 74–6, 145, 146, 168, 219, 221, 226, 229, 230
see also identity, Lisbon's 17, 70, 219, 221–3, 227, 229, 230
see also immigration, Lisbon
Lisbon Academy of Sciences 32
Lisbon City Council 34, 35, 40, 41, 68–9, 71–3, 226
Lisbon Geography Society 32
Lisbon Metropolitan Area/Área Metropolitana de Lisboa (LMA/AML) 83, 84, 93, 108, 112–16, 136, 167
Lisbon Metropolitan Area Locations
  Amadora 112, 115, 116, 118
  Alcabideche 143
  Almada 90
  Arrentela 113, 116, 229
  Buraca 95, 228
  Cacém 144
  Casal de Cambra 92
  Cascais 112, 143
  Costa da Caparica 143
  Cova da Moura 95, 112, 113, 115, 116, 228
  Damaia 112, 118
  Loures 86, 98, 112
  Miraflores 95
  Moita 113, 116
  Odivelas 143
  Oeiras 112
  Pedreira dos Húngaros 95, 113
  Prior Velho 95
  Quinta da Fonte 94
  Quinta da Holandesa 84
  Quinta da Vitória 84
  Quinta do Conde 91
  Quinta do Mocho 228
  Quinta da Serra 86, 88, 90–2, 94, 95, 98
  Vale da Amoreira 113, 116
Lisbon's neighborhoods/parishes
  Alto de Santa Catarina 112
  Anjos 145, 147
  Ajuda 91
  Arroios 16, 143–9, 151–5
  Belém 15, 27–31, 33, 35–9, 41
  Mouraria 63, 64, 66–71, 73–6, 147, 168
  Pena 145, 147
  Penha de França 145
  Restelo 28
  Santa Luzia 91
  São Jorge de Arroios (renamed Arroios) 145
  Socorro 68
Lisbon Tourism Association 74, 226
literature 10
  Cape Verdean 119
  colonial 182, 183
  Lusophone 163, 165
  popular 17, 182, 193
  returnee 193
Löfgren, O. 46
Logan, J. R. 65
London 85, 227
Lopes, E. R. 211
Lopes, G. 11
Lopes, M. 229
Lorcin, P. M. 4
Loreta (Nuno Mendonça) 116
Losa, L. 166, 177
Lourenço Marques (today's Maputo, Mozambique) 49, 51–3, 55, 84, 128, 182, 185–9, 192, 199
  Football Association 49
  segregated neighborhoods of 49, 51, 52, 84, 187, 192
  sporting of 51
Luanda 55, 84, 173, 182, 184–7, 190, 192, 199
Lura (Maria de Lurdes Assunção Pina) 168, 169, 170, 172, 177
Lusaka agreement (Mozambique) 9
Lusofonia, a (R)evolução 225, 227
Lusophone
  belonging 200–1, 213
  citizens 175
  community 17, 163, 220
  context 11
  "cosmopolitanism" 171
  countries 206
  cultures 209
  images, imaginary 48, 115
  perspective 201
  policies 173

populations 213
space 171, 172, 202, 207, 240
time 45
world 167, 170, 172, 201, 202, 209, 212
see also gastronomy, Lusophone; immigrants, Lusophone; languages, Lusophone; literature, Lusophone; music, Lusophone
Lusophony (*Lusofonia*) 17, 48, 163–78, 200, 203, 207, 209, 212, 213, 219, 220
lusotropicalism 8, 9, 14, 15, 63, 72, 74, 201, 213, 240

Macao or Macau 29, 34
  Chinese temple 34
MacCannell, D. 194
Macedo, M. 129
Machado, F. L. 118, 134
Machado, I. 151–3, 155
Maciel, C. 165, 166
MacKenzie, J. M. 3
Madonna 221
Maeso, S. R. 50, 187
Mafalala (Maputo's neighborhood) 49, 51
Magalhães, A. 54
Magalhães, Júlio 182, 183, 194, 189
Magnusson, W. 64
Maka, Jo 174
Malheiros, J. M. 13, 67, 108, 112, 136
Manning, P. 201
Manuel I (Portuguese King) 30, 74
Manueline (architectural style) 28, 30
Mapril, J. 11
Marcuse, H. 108
Marfox (DJ) 229
Margarido, A. 48, 220
Maria Alice (Rocha Silva) 171
Marinho, M. de F. 182
Mariza, (Mariza dos Reis Nunes) 17, 203, 206
Marques, M. M. 200
Martiniello, M. 114
Marxism, Marxian 125, 126
masculinity 127, 128, 189
mass media 14, 50, 166
Mata, I. 115
Matateu (Sebastião Lucas da Fonseca) 49
Matias, A. R. 117, 118
Matias, N. 91

Matos, P. F. de 50, 191
Matos, S. C. de 6, 47, 50
Matsanuga, L. 201
Mattoso, J. 74
Mayol, P. 147, 154
Medina, Cremilda 210, 211
Medina, Fernando 40
Meersschaert, L. 132
memorial 3, 10, 15, 27, 29, 30, 34, 41, 72
Memorial to Enslaved People 29
memory
  anti-colonial 109
  autobiographical, personal 149, 184–6, 194
  collective 4, 7, 34, 113, 169
  colonial, of colonialism 3, 4, 10, 12, 15, 27, 185, 186, 188, 191, 192, 200, 213
  "complex" 27, 29, 34
  counter 28, 29, 41
  European 2–4
  camily 189
  habitual 28
  imperial, of the empire 27, 31, 33, 35, 37, 38, 48, 72, 226, 239
  official 14–15, 41, 46
  popular 67, 69, 72, 74
  Portuguese national 1, 41, 45, 46, 164, 220, 240
  postcolonial 85
  private 12
  public 12, 15, 27, 28
Mendes, L. 145
Mendes, M. 112
Mendes, M. M. 68, 145
Mendonça, B. 224
Meneses, F. R. 242
Menezes, M. 67, 72, 146
Menezes, M. P. 222
Mestizaje, mestizo 17, 49, 51, 213
Meyers, J. 182
Mignolo, W. 12
Migrant Integration Policy Index (MIPEX) 107
migrant workers, labor migrants 9, 16, 126, 129, 131, 133–6, 143, 144, 147, 149, 150, 152–4, 168, 170, 172, 173, 176
migrations
  colonial 12, 13

forced 88
  internal 16, 83, 86, 131, 133
  transnational 16, 66, 149
Miles, M. 114
Milheiro, A. V. 54, 55
Miller, L. J. 194
Military officers 46, 102
Ministry of Justice, Portugal 113
Mitchell, T. 97
modernism 29, 33, 34, 45, 53–5
Molotoch, H. L. 65
Monteiro, C. A. 108
Monteiro, J. P. 8, 13
Monument to Overseas Combatants 29
Moorman, M. 173, 222
Mór, Luiz 208, 213
Morabeza 223
Mothersill, M. 188
Moura, Ana 206
Mouraria and Intendente Festival 70
Movement for Democracy (MpD, Cape Verde) 109
mozambique 6, 9, 12, 30, 35, 37, 45–54, 56, 83, 84, 128, 131, 133, 136, 170, 171, 182, 183, 184, 185–7, 190, 192, 199, 200, 203, 206, 227
MPLA-People's Movement for the Liberation of Angola (Angolan Party) 172, 177
multiculturalism 3, 10, 14, 166, 71, 74, 167, 168, 172, 176–7, 200, 229
multiracial 9, 10, 15, 47, 50
multiracialism 72
museums
  Colonial Agricultural Museum 33
  Colonial and Ethnographic Museum 32
  Colonial Museum 32, 37
  Quai Branly Museum 39
  MUDE (Design Museum) 207, 208
  Museu Mar da Língua Portuguesa 39
  Museu Nacional dos Coches 28, 40
  Museum of the Discoveries 39, 40
  Museum of Popular Art 29, 35, 39
  Museum of the Orient 29
  Museum World of Discoveries 39, 40
  National Museum of Archeology 28, 36, 39, 41
  National Museum of Ethnology 29, 37
  Navy Museum 28, 31, 35, 36, 39
  Overseas Museum/Ultramarine Museum 29, 35–7
  Portuguese Ethnological Museum (rebaptized as the National Museum of Archaeology and Ethnology in 1965) 32, 35, 36, 39
  TAP Museum 203
music, musicians
  African 16, 17, 114, 120, 164–7, 171, 176, 206, 219, 222
  Afro-Portuguese 227, 228
  Angolan 17, 172, 173
  Brazilian 153, 163, 165, 166, 174–6, 203, 206
  Cape Verdean 108, 116, 119, 120, 166, 168–70, 206, 221, 223, 229
  corporate 201, 202, 205, 206, 208, 209, 211
  Creole 108, 115, 116, 119, 120
  Lusophone 2, 164, 167, 168, 171, 174, 176–8, 203, 206, 207, 209, 210, 226–8
  Mozambican 170, 171
  PALOP's 163, 166, 167, 171, 175, 176
  popular 163, 164, 166, 168, 169, 172, 172, 175, 176, 203
  Portuguese 166, 176, 202, 205–7, 209, 221, 225, 226
  urban 225, 226, 228–30
  world 167, 172, 206
music industry 164, 166, 167, 171, 175, 176, 224, 225
music styles
  Afro-house 17, 219, 222, 228, 229, 230
  baião 174
  batuque 17, 219, 223
  bossa nova 206, 207
  chorinho 174
  classical 205
  coco 174
  coladeira 174
  dance 17, 219, 223, 225, 226
  electronic 219, 220, 222–4, 226, 227, 229
  fado 17, 66, 71, 74, 166, 202, 203, 206, 209, 210
  funaná 17, 219, 222, 223
  jazz 205, 206
  kilapanda 174
  kizomba 17, 219, 222

kuduro, kuduru 17, 219, 222, 228
morna 120, 166, 168, 174, 210
rap music 16, 108, 113–17, 120, 210, 229
R&B 221
rebita 173, 174
samba 148, 174
semba (Angola music style) 17, 173, 174, 203
soul 221
tarraxo 17, 219, 228
zouk 17, 219
musical hybridism 219–21, 223, 224, 228–31
muslims 67
Musseques, Luanda slums 84, 173, 192

Nare, L. 135
National Commission for the Commemoration of Portuguese Discoveries (CNCDP) 10
National Pantheon (Lisbon) 46, 49, 52, 53
nationalism 4, 6–7, 10, 47, 50, 117, 126, 174, 212, 228, 239, 241, 244
  Banal nationalism 228
Nattrass, N. 190
Nederveen Pieterse, J. 190
neoliberalism 165
Neo-Pentecostal churches 147, 153
Nepal 11, 67, 112
Neto, António Costa 170
Neves, J. 47
New York 108, 227
Newitt, M. 130, 242
Ngola Ritmos 173
nostalgia 74, 169
  colonial 2, 5, 203
  imperial 4
Notting Hill Carnival 75
Nova Lisboa, city (today's Huambo, Angola) 221
"Nova Lisboa" (song) 220, 221, 223
Nunes, C. 152
Nunes, J. A. 83

Observador (digital media channel) 183
Observatório das Migrações 112
Olaniyan, T. 202
Oliveira, P. A. 242

Oliveira, N. 11, 64, 65, 70, 76, 145, 167, 168, 219
Ondjaki 166
Orient Foundation 29
Ortigão, Ramalho 31
Os Lusíadas 30, 50
Oso, L. 134
Os Tubarões 221
Overseas Hospital 36

Pacheco, Duarte 35
Padilla, B. 70, 76, 147, 148, 150, 152
PAICV (African Party for the Independence of Cape Verde) 109, 110
PAIGC (African Party for the Independence of Guinea and Cape Verde) 109, 110
Pais, J. M. 10
PALOP/PSAC-Portuguese-Speaking African Countries 9, 84, 112, 136, 163, 165–7, 171, 172, 175, 176
Pakistan 11, 112
Paludi, M. 201, 212, 213
Palma, Jorge 206
Pan America Airways 212
Pan-Africanism 109
Panayi, P. 4
Panelli, R. 114
Paraty, International Literary Festival of 224
Pardue, D. 116, 167
Paredes, Carlos 202, 203
Paris, bidonvilles of 85
Pariser, R. 128, 131
Paulo, J. C. 50
Peixoto, J. 136, 147
Pélissier, R. 13
Peña, Maritza Rosabal 111
Penvenne, J. M. 13, 128, 129, 131
Peralta, E. 4, 12, 129, 184, 200, 201
Perazzo, Sebastião da Rocha (Tião) 174
Pereira, S. 107, 112, 135
Pereira, S. M. J. 211
Pereira, V. 12, 55
Pes, A. 3
Pieds-noirs 5
Pina, Pedro 209, 212
Pina-Cabral, J. 12, 242

Pink Map (or Rose-Coloured Map) 6
Pinto, A. C. 10, 47, 48
Pinto, P. R. 83
Pires, R. P. 182
Pitts, J. 228
Plataforma Gueto 229
Pontes, Dulce 210
Ponzanesi, S. 200
popular culture 2, 11, 16, 46, 49–53, 108, 114, 164, 225, 244
populist politics 126
Porto, city (Portugal) 31, 40, 83, 97, 131, 172
Portuguese colonial exceptionalism 1, 7, 8, 9, 11, 13, 15, 45, 46, 48, 50, 56, 88, 191, 213, 231, 241
Portuguese Constitution
  Revision of 1951 8
  of 1976 13, 87
Portuguese empire, colonialism 1, 6, 8–10, 14, 28, 30, 51, 73, 85, 90, 107, 128, 185, 226, 241, 243
  assimilation 2, 41, 51
  Creole societies, 168, 242
  forced labor 13, 41, 128
  geopolitical position, 5, 6, 8, 165, 242
  international division of labor 2, 243
  lifestyles 5, 186, 187, 189, 192
  plantations 88, 98, 129, 191, 192
  slavery 40, 41, 73, 74, 115, 128, 174, 241
  urban planning 46, 53–5, 84, 86, 91, 99, 100
  vulnerabilities 6, 11–13, 241–3
  white colonialists, 131, 187, 189, 191
Portuguese expansion 1–3, 8, 10, 28, 30–5, 38–40, 163, 174, 241, 242
Portuguese Nationality Law
  of 1959 9
  of 1975 9, 85
Portuguese Parliament 11, 52, 53
Portuguese World Exhibition (1940) 27, 29, 33–9
postcolonial city 17, 63–5, 75, 76, 85, 107, 120, 219, 220, 226–8
post-Fordist urban model 64
Póvoas, M. H. G. 146
Pozzi, G. 99
Praia, city (Cape Verde) 88

Pratt, M. L. 72
Prince Henry, The Navigator 29, 31, 36
Príncipe Discos 222
property 92, 151
  property speculation 15
Público (newspaper) 223

Quarteira (Algarve, Portugal) 221
Quayson, A. 182

Rabinow, P. 97
race 2, 4, 17, 75, 85, 88, 113, 125, 126, 128, 131, 137, 164, 173, 212, 224, 225, 229, 242–4
racial
  classifications, categories 1, 2, 11, 55, 88, 92–3, 125, 126, 128, 129, 229
  concepts, notions 4, 8, 127, 172
  discrimination 11, 13, 15, 113, 192, 223–4, 240, 243
  exclusion, segregation 88, 108, 137
  relations 8, 11, 14, 125, 129
  segregation 2, 49, 113, 125, 128, 131
  see also interracial; multiracial
racialism 49 *see also* multiracialism
racialization 2, 5, 7, 13, 94, 125, 126, 134, 135, 175, 243
racism 5, 11, 15, 41, 72, 93–5, 113, 116, 171, 194, 229, 239, 241, 242
racism and citizenship (exhibition) 41
Raco, M. 65
Radano, R. 202
Radice, M. 63
Rádio e Televisão de Portugal (RTP) 183, 203, 205, 221, 225
  RTP Africa 163, 166, 220
  RTP Internacional 166
Radiofusão Portuguesa, RDP Africa 163, 166, 220
Raposo, I. 92
Raposo, O. 95
Ré, C. 224
Rebelo, Tiago 184, 189, 190
Red Bull (company) 220, 221, 224, 225
  Red Bull Music Academy (RBMA) 18, 224, 225
refugees (colonial) 9, 12
rehousing 85, 92–6, 98, 113

Special Rehousing Program (*Plano Especial de Realojamento - PER*) 92, 93, 100
Reis, J. A. 146
republicans 7, 30, 47
    republican period (1910–26) 7, 47
resistance 16, 54, 72, 99, 100, 108, 111, 113–16, 119, 120, 129, 130, 173, 174, 192, 244
retornados (returnees) 2, 15, 182, 183, 186–8, 193 *see also* repatriated colonial settlers
Retrotopia 190
return (of settlers from African colonies) 12, 17, 41, 191
return: Traces of Memory (exhibition) 41
revivalism 181, 182, 190–3
Ribeiro, A. M. 224
Ribeiro, M. C. 165
Ribeiro, Ricardo 206
Rio de Janeiro 210
Rio de Mouro 143, 228
Rita-Ferreira, A. 52
Rodrigues, A. 165
Rodrigues, C. M. 83
Rodrigues, Francisco Castro 54
Rodrigues, I. N. 109
Rodrigues, W. 66
Rolling Stone (magazine) 221
Roma populations 92, 94, 115
Romania 112
Roque, R. 8
Rose, S. 3
Roseta, Cuca 210, 211
Rotterdam 173
Rothermund, D. 4
Rowland, R. 150, 155
Ruby, C. 114

Sá, Roberta 17, 203
Sacavém Parish Council 87, 228
Said, E. W. 182
Salazar, António Oliveira 7, 33
Salgueiro, T. B. 83, 86, 91, 145
Salmon, C. 225
Sanches, M. R. 200, 220
Sanchez, I. 168
Santiago, Dino d' 220–3
Santiago Island (Cape Verde) 89, 90, 222

Santos, Boaventura de Sousa 12, 134, 222
Santos, José Eduardo dos 172
Santos, José Rodrigues 183, 184
Santos, R. V. 8
São Tomé and Príncipe 83, 88, 107, 112, 183, 200
    plantations of 88, 98, 129, 190
Sarkowsky, K. 4
Sassen, S. 64
Saudade 223
Schengen 134
Schiffrin, A. 183
Schiltz, A. 153
Schuch, J. 63
Schwarz, B. 154, 155
Scott, J. C. 76, 99
Second World War 3, 7, 13, 33, 47, 199, 241
Sedano, L. J. 222
SEF – Serviço de Estrangeiros e Fronteiras (Foreigners and Borders Service) 112
Seixal 116, 229
Semear a Vida (Sow Life) 147
Senegal 11, 147
Serpa Pinto, Alexandre de 50
Serra, N. 83
Seth, S. 226, 230
settlers 56, 88
    colonial settlers 12, 13, 17, 49, 52, 56, 128, 131, 182, 187–92, 242
    Repatriated colonial settlers 5, 15–17, 41, 47 *see also* Retornados
Silva, Cristino da 36
Silva, C. N. 84, 91, 100
Silva, Mário Rui 173
Silva, S. S. B. 153
Silveira, J. 84, 91
Simões, S. 114, 117
Sinatra, Frank 202
Sintra 91, 112, 116, 143, 227
Slater, D. 13
slavery 40, 41, 115, 126, 128, 129, 174, 241
Smiers, J. 114
Soares, João 71
Sobral, J. M. 6, 8, 50
Social Democratic Party-PSD (Portuguese) 40
Socialist Party-PS (Portuguese) 39, 40
Sociedade de Geografia de Lisboa 32

Sonae 181
SOS Racismo, anti-racist association 72
Sousa, H. 166
Sousa, V. 200
Sousa Tavares, Miguel 182, 183, 188, 190
South Africa 49, 52
Spain 33
Staniland, M. 201
Stanyek, J. 201
Stepanik, H. 114
Stoler, A. L. 2
streaming platforms 224, 227, 228, 230
Switzerland 210

Tagus River 29, 36, 73, 153
TAP Air Portugal 17, 199–213
Taşan-Kok, T. 65
Tavares, A. 182
Taylor, C. 177
Taylor, T. 225
Teixeira, N. S. 10
Telmo, Cottinelli 33, 36
Terreiro do Paço 207
Thailand 28
Thompson, A. 3
Thompson, J. B. 194
Tito, Armando 210, 211
Tito Paris (Aristides) 171
Todos Festival 69, 70–2, 75
toponymy (Lisbon)
    Albuquerque, Afonso de Garden 28,
    Almirante Reis Avenue 66, 67, 71, 146
    Angola Street 35
    Bartolomeu Dias Street 31
    Bartolomeu Perestrelo Street 29
    Belém Tower Garden 28, 37
    Cabo Verde Street 35
    Damão Square 35
    Damião de Góis Street 29, 35
    Diu Square 29, 35
    Dom Manuel I Square 35
    Goa Square 29, 35
    Fernão Mendes Pinto Street 35
    India Avenue 35
    Ílha de Sao Tome e Príncipe Street 35
    Junqueira Street 36
    Macao Street 35
    Malaca Square 29
    Marginal Avenue 29
    Martim Moniz Square 67, 68, 70–2
    Mozambique Street 35
    Portas de Santo Antão Street 32
    Praça do Império (Empire Square)
        28, 33, 34
    Rua Augusta 207
    São Francisco Xavier Street 35
    square 31
    statue 31
    Timor Street 35
    Vasco da Gama Avenue 29
    Garden 28
    Zaire Street 35
Toronto 227
tourism, touristification 1, 4, 10, 14, 15,
    27–9, 35, 37, 38, 40, 46, 57, 66, 70, 71,
    74–7, 145, 146, 168, 190, 202, 207,
    219, 221, 226, 229, 230
Tower of Belém 28
Trindade, L. 50
Trás-os-Montes 86
tropical 54, 190, 194
    architecture 54
    gardens 54
Trovão, S. 84
Turino, T. 108, 114
TVI (Independent Television) 183

Ukraine 112
UNESCO 28, 37, 120, 206, 210
Universal Church of the Kingdom
    of God; IURD 147
urbanism 63
    informal urbanism 86, 100

Vala, F. 13
Vala, J. 11
Valente, A. 92
Valle, P. 223
Vanspauwen, B. 219
Varma, R. 4
Varnhagen, Francisco Adolfo 30
Vasco da Gama 28, 30, 31, 35, 50, 73,
    207, 208
Vasconcelos, J. 135
Vasconcelos, José Leite de 32, 39
Vaz, L. 146
Veblen, T. 128
Veloso, Rui 206, 210

Viana, C. 187
Vicente, F. 187
Viegas, Francisco José 189, 191
Vieira Dias, Liceu 173
Vieira, M. 100
Vieira, Nancy 210
Vieira, Paulino 171
Virdee, P. 4
Viseu 36
Volvic, Z. 193

Wall, K. 152
Wang, Q. 63
wars of liberation 91, 109 *see also* colonial wars
Weber, Weberian 125

Weeks, S. 88
Werry, M. L. 193
western
  empires 126, 201
  Europe 3, 12
  narratives 125, 134, 222
  nations 134
Williams, R. 49
Wilkie, F. 201
Wood, P. 64
World Church of the Power of God 147

Yadastar 225

Zamparoni, V. 128, 130

www.ingramcontent.com/pod-product-compliance
Lightning Source LLC
Chambersburg PA
CBHW071812300426
44116CB00009B/1282